16,000 Miles
to Mexico City

16,000 Miles to Mexico City

The 1970 London to Mexico World Cup Rally

ROBERT CONNOR

McFarland & Company, Inc., Publishers
Jefferson, North Carolina

ISBN (print) 978-1-4766-6967-0
ISBN (ebook) 978-1-4766-4578-0

Library of Congress and British Library
cataloguing data are available

Library of Congress Control Number 2022007837

Front cover: The Annabel's nightclub-sponsored Mercedes 280SE of Innes Ireland, Michael Taylor and Mark Birley, Italy (photograph courtesy of Andrew Lees)

Printed in the United States of America

McFarland & Company, Inc., Publishers
Box 611, Jefferson, North Carolina 28640
www.mcfarlandpub.com

In memory of Rob McAuley.
A nicer man you could
never hope to meet.

Acknowledgments

In addition to all the men and women who found the time, patience, and willingness to share their memories with me, I owe a particular debt of gratitude to Mike Bailey, Stan Clark, Guido Devreker, Ken Green, Rachel Harris-Gardiner, John Hemsley, Gabriel Hinojosa Rivero, Rob Howell, Teresa Jensen-Redgrave, Alexander Matveev, Simon Maxwell for his image enhancement skills, Anne McAuley, Campbell McAuley, Brian Millen, Ron Pellatt, the late Martin Proudlock for his cartographic artistry, Chris Rabbets, the late Tracie Riddell, Michael Ryman, David Scothorn, Pat Smith for affording me access to her meticulous archive, the late John Sprinzel, Patrick Vanson, Mike Wood, and especially Andrew Bradbury for his constant support and Ted Taylor for his passionate interest and boundless enthusiasm.

Table of Contents

***Between pages 146 and 147 are 20 color plates
containing 41 photographs***

Preface

This all started at the British Motor Heritage Museum at Gaydon in Warwickshire, England, in 2015. I had submitted the manuscript for my book about the 1968 London to Sydney Marathon to my publisher and had been invited to be interviewed as part of an event celebrating historic marathon rallies. I got talking to a couple of competitors from the 1968 event who had contributed to the book, as well as the owner of an expertly restored car that had competed in the 1970 London to Mexico World Cup Rally. The conversation went as follows:

"The manuscript is with the publisher."

"So, what are you waiting for? Now you need to write about the London Mexico!"

I must make a confession at this point. In 1970, as a six-year-old, I continued to be obsessed with cars and especially with the perhaps more mundane automobiles on the roads, the family sedans and wagons that transported their occupants to and from schools and shops, businesses and vacations, and so on. Not for me the sleek sports cars and coupés, the supercars like Ferrari or Lamborghini or Maserati. No, I was fascinated by the cars my friends' parents drove, or those that featured in some of my favorite TV shows, like *Randall and Hopkirk (Deceased)* and their white Vauxhall Victor FD, or the ubiquitous Ford Escorts, Zephyrs, and Zodiacs serving as fictitious police patrol cars in *Dickson of Dock Green*, *Z-Cars*, and *Softly, Softly Task Force*.

What I wasn't obsessed with was soccer, or, as the British call it, football. At elementary school in 1970, soccer was very much front and center on the sports curriculum, and every week, come rain or shine, boys—and only boys—were required to don shorts and t-shirts and get "down the field for games!" In other words, crowd onto the sidelines of a makeshift school soccer pitch, get picked for opposing teams by the assigned captain, and then, as the whistle blew, "kick off." Even as a child, I couldn't see the point, running up and down, trying to get the ball or defend the ball or kick the ball into the net or—worst of all—trying to stop the ball from getting past me into the net! My ambivalence towards the game has continued throughout my life, only occasionally being stirred during big international events like the European Championships or … the World Cup.

As I write this preface, the irony of researching and writing about a motorsports event that inexorably linked itself to "the" international soccer event of the year, or every fourth year, does not escape me, but looking back to the 1970 World Cup, held across Mexico and culminating in Mexico City's Aztec Stadium on June 21 of that year, I do recall the excitement of it all, the copious newspaper coverage, and the stars of the England squad. Names like Bobby Moore, Jackie and Bobby Charlton, "Nobby" Stiles, and Gordon Banks are somehow cemented into my consciousness, and I remember how excited I was when, each time my mother or father pulled into an Esso gas station to fill the tank of our trusty Morris Oxford VI, I had the opportunity to collect another of the commemorative silver coins that were offered for free if four gallons (4.8 U.S. gallons) of gasoline were purchased. Each coin was embossed with the face of a member of the England soccer team, underneath which their signature was rendered. There were 30 coins to collect and all could be slotted into a large presentation card labeled with the players' names. The 1970 World Cup Coin Collection really did capture my imagination, even if the sport itself left me decidedly underwhelmed, and I still remember feeling bitterly disappointed at my parents' inability to purchase more and more gasoline, or their decision to choose alternative brands of fuel. Suffice to say, I never did complete the collection!

Even as I was vainly attempting to obtain the very last coin to put into its slot, work was underway to hold a rally unlike any other. Though the 1968 London to Sydney Marathon was grueling and event-filled for many of the privately entered competitors and cars attempting it, many of the professional rally drivers and navigators who got to the Warwick Farm stadium in Sydney just before Christmas 1968 felt that the 10,000-mile slog from England to Australia had been perhaps a little less than challenging. As premier British rally driver Roger Clark commented, "I had more sleep between London and Bombay than I normally get in England."[1] Hence, by early 1969, thoughts had already turned towards organizing something much more difficult, more demanding, an event that would really separate the enthusiastic amateur from the skilled professional. This time, there would have to be more tortuous special stages, stages that would need to stretch for hundreds of miles where average speeds of 70 miles per hour or more would be expected across rocky, dusty terrain, if competitors were to avoid penalty points or even disqualification for lateness. There would also be the unique challenge of needing to drive at altitude, at elevations approaching 16,000 feet, and the probable need to use oxygen in order to traverse these heights, not to mention the modifications that an internal combustion engine would require in order to continue working at maximum efficiency, despite a substantially reduced oxygen supply. Alongside these challenges would be the unprecedented endurance of a nonstop event spanning 16,000 miles over 38 days across geography that would present sheer drops and precipices, two-plank bridges, winding mountain passes littered with fist-sized boulders, wayward trucks and buses, ox carts jostling with motorized traffic, vast unpopulated expanses, and not one but three water crossings—make good time or miss the boats!

The route would take professional and amateur competitors alike from England through eight countries in Western and Soviet-controlled Eastern Europe, including twice across France, before arriving in the city of Lisbon, capital of Portugal. Along the way, cars and crews would be presented with five special stages or *primes*, named after the test stages on the *Tour de France* cycle race. Each *prime* would follow sections of the main contemporary European rally events, and each would have a required completion time—failing to achieve these times would mean penalty points. From Lisbon, surviving cars would be loaded onboard a freight vessel and transported across the Atlantic Ocean to Rio de Janeiro, Brazil's capital city. Meanwhile, competitors would have the opportunity to rest and recharge before boarding a Rio-bound jetliner. On arrival, those who wanted could explore the many sights that Brazil's capital had to offer before being reunited with their vehicles. Then the really hard work would start as the route passed out of Brazil and then took in the varied and, for most competitors, completely alien landscapes of Uruguay, Argentina, Chile, Bolivia, Peru, Ecuador, Colombia, Panama, Costa Rica, Nicaragua, Honduras, El Salvador, Guatemala, and finally Mexico.

The competitive field would comprise 229 men and 12 women from more than 20 countries, and the event would see 96 cars set off from England in the hope of reaching Mexico City. Once again, among the teams of rally-hardened professionals that would wrangle their expertly and intricately prepared rally cars along the route, there would also be yet more enthusiastic and good-spirited amateurs and privateers, inspired by the extensive print and broadcast media coverage of the 1968 Marathon and its tales of extraordinary successes and heartbreaking failures. There would be even more bespoke and unusual vehicles competing than 18 months before, and despite the apparent attempts of rally organizers to prevent all but the toughest professionals from reaching Lisbon, let alone Mexico City, the event ultimately offered up more than a few surprises along the way.

Something that intrigued me were a few similarities between the 1968 London–Sydney Marathon and the rally from London to Mexico City in 1970. Twelve women competed in 1968 and 12 women competed in 1970. Of the total number of starters to Sydney, just under 75 percent got to Bombay and a ship crossing to Perth in Australia. Of the total number of starters to Mexico City, just under 75 percent got to Lisbon for a ship crossing to Rio de Janeiro. Would the same percentage that arrived at the Warwick Farm stadium in Sydney, Australia, in December 1968 also get to the Aztec Stadium in Mexico City in May 1970?

We shall see.

Once again, in addition to the many interviews I conducted, I have been able to draw from the extensive international press coverage that the World Cup Rally generated. Furthermore, an increasing number of publications have been produced by those who competed or played a part, whether published at the time or subsequently, and I have had the good fortune to draw from these as well as a number of films, professional and amateur, that were made during the rally.

Unless indicated, all quotations are from the transcriptions of interviews I undertook with competitors and those who played a part in the World Cup Rally. Any monetary values are as they were in 1970, as are most references to names of countries and places. Place names are mostly as they appeared in the rally roadbooks. Where possible, the sport being played at the 1970 Mexico World Cup is referred to as "soccer," although quotes may refer to "football," the term used in England.

In the end, I hold three people responsible for this book—Mike Bailey, John Hemsley, and David Scothorn.

I know where you live!

Introduction

There are a number of countries that have legally defined national sports. For example, the 1994 National Sports of Canada Act legally recognizes lacrosse and hockey as that country's *de jure* national sports. In Brazil it's *capoeira*, and the *de jure* sport in Mexico is the *charreada*. While many other countries haven't enshrined a sport within their statutes, certain activities are forever associated with different nations. Although some may disagree, when one thinks of the national sport of the United States, one thinks of baseball. Cricket probably embodies Englishness like no other sport, but in terms of popularity, it's soccer that sits at the heart of national identity. Usually called football by English fans and journalists alike, when it comes to newspaper and television sports coverage, soccer dominates. Each year, from August to the following May, soccer stadiums up and down the land throw up mighty roars as crowds of supporters pour into the terraces to cheer on their teams. Players of the game stand to earn huge sums of money as they establish themselves and become commodities, being traded and purchased by national and international teams. In 2017, the BBC reported that French soccer team Paris Saint-Germain had "signed Brazil forward Neymar [da Silva Santos Júnior] for a world record fee of 222m euros (£200m) from Barcelona."[1] In some countries, English football teams are almost as popular as they are on their home turf, and the list of players and former players who have gone on to become celebrities is long and growing, typified by none more so than David Beckham. The former Manchester United, Real Madrid, LA Galaxy, and England national team player is now considered a global brand, alongside his wife, former Spice Girl Victoria Beckham. Together they have either launched or been associated with a host of high-end products, including perfumes, cosmetics, clothing, and cars—Beckham even has his own namesake fragrance.

Soccer has long been at the heart of popular English culture and through the decades has witnessed both tragedy and triumph. On February 6, 1958, a passenger plane carrying the Manchester United soccer team home from a successful European Cup quarterfinals match crashed on takeoff from Munich airport in Germany, causing the loss of 21 lives. On April 15, 1989, 96 fans were crushed to death at the Hillsborough Stadium in Sheffield, England, during a national Football Association Cup semi-final. These disasters, and those who lost their lives, must never be forgotten in the history of both soccer and the nation itself, just as the triumph of 1966 never will be.

The 1966 *Fédération Internationale de Football Association* or FIFA World Cup got underway on July 11 and saw group, knockout, and final matches played in eight stadiums across England. The national teams of 16 countries qualified for the World Cup, including then-world champions Brazil, who had beaten Czechoslovakia to take the title in Chile in 1962. Twenty-eight matches were played, leaving the final four teams—the Soviet Union, Portugal, West Germany, and England—to face off in the semifinals. On July 25, West Germany secured their place in the final by beating the Soviet Union at the Goodison Park Stadium in Liverpool and, on the following day, England and Portugal faced off at London's Wembley Stadium. England won by two goals to one, with both English goals scored by Bobby Charlton. So it was that on July 30, 1966, before HRII Queen Elizabeth II, the English and West German national teams walked out onto the pitch at Wembley, led by captains Bobby Moore and Uwe Seeler. The whistle blew at 15:00, and the final of the 1966 FIFA World Cup began. Twelve minutes later, Helmut Haller scored to take West Germany one up. Six minutes after that, Geoff Hurst headed the ball into the net to equalize the match. At the 77th minute, Martin Peters found the goal in his sights to take England to a 2–1 lead. Twelve minutes after that, the West Germans fought back with a shot by Wolfgang Weber to tie the teams again. The tension in the stadium was at its height when the whistle blew and the match moved into extra time, to allow for the moments lost by stoppages during the 90 preceding minutes. A second goal by Hurst took England back into the lead, but not without controversy—the debate about whether Hurst's goal was legitimate continues to this day! Then, with just one more minute of play remaining, England captain Bobby Moore made a long pass to Hurst and, even as triumphant England supporters began to run onto the pitch in celebration, Hurst put the goal into the back of the net to cement England's victory as FIFA World Cup champions for the first time in history.

Three and a half years later, the euphoria that followed was probably on the mind of Australian event promoter and public relations professional Wylton Dickson. Dickson was managing PR for England's Football Association as they geared up to defend the World Cup title, and he had previously come up with the idea of having a mascot for the 1966 World Cup, "World Cup Willie." He was, as Evan Green described him, "an ideas man of extraordinary talent, with a record of successful, novel and occasionally bizarre promotions."[2] At a drinks party in London during the 1968–1969 Christmas and New Year festivities, Dickson struck up a conversation with Irish rally driver and recent runner-up in the 1968 London–Sydney Marathon, Paddy Hopkirk. Paddy's wife, Jenny, worked for Geers Gross, an advertising agency set up by Americans Bob Geers and Bob Gross, and it was at Gross's home that Hopkirk and Dickson met. As Hopkirk told it: "At this party I met this big Australian guy, Wylton Dickson, who told me he was the promoter for the football World Cup.... I said 'I've just been to your country on a rally' ... later in the evening he came over and said 'why don't we have a World Cup rally?' I thought to myself that he should go and have another drink."[3] However, a little checking up by Hopkirk revealed that Dickson was who he said he was, so they spoke again and, as a result, approaches to the British *Daily Mirror* newspaper and to the Royal Automobile Club were made. Why not start an international endurance rally at the place where England won the 1966 FIFA World Cup and have it end where the 1970 World Cup final would take place—the

Aztec Stadium in Mexico City? Why not try and get the rally to pass through as many of the countries that qualified for the 1966 World Cup as was practicable? Thus, the preposterous idea of a man who knew nothing of rallying or motorsports turned into the beginning of an event (although, according to *Daily Mirror* journalist Anthony Howard, "Dickson made his pitch, saw his idea deftly appropriated, and found himself confined to the shadows"[4]).

Ideas and promises of financial backing and major sponsorship were all very well, of course, but what would actually be needed, what work would need to be done, how many people would need to be mobilized, before the first car could roll off the ramp at Wembley Stadium and set off for the 16,000-mile-long, 16,000-foot-high adventure from London to Mexico? Certainly, the London–Sydney Marathon of the previous year had only been possible because a carefully selected committee of experienced and motorsports-savvy individuals had been brought together to plan and organize the route, international border crossings, recces, international PR and communications, rally rules and regulations, a sea crossing, marshaling and time control management, and more. People other than representatives from a national newspaper and someone whom Anthony Howard described as an "ad-man"[5] would need to step up again and take charge of what soon-to-be competitor Richard Hudson-Evans described as "this Grand Daddy of all."[6]

But who?

The idea was cast; now the real work would have to begin.

1

Getting Organized

The organizational success of the London–Sydney Marathon of 1968 was primarily due to the motorsports experience, determination, business acumen, and international connections of its planning and management committee. Former British saloon car champion Jack Sears had been invited to join the committee and plan the route and the associated logistics of border and sea crossings. Jack hadn't had any involvement in rallying for some time, so he recruited Tony Ambrose, 1965 European Rally Champion (with Rauno Aaltonen) and hugely experienced navigator, to the effort. Jack and Tony went on to drive the proposed route from London to Bombay, ensuring that arrangements would be in place for speedy border crossings during the actual event and making overtures to the various national automobile clubs within each country the route would traverse to elicit their support. From India they flew on to Australia to continue the mapping out and planning of the route from Perth to Sydney.

In 1969, according to Tony Ambrose, the committee that was convened to organize, manage, and control the World Cup Rally consisted "largely of Daily Mirror employees and a few names from the world of football. There were very few people with international motorsports experience."[1] Those that did have motorsports experience were Clerk of the Course Dean Delamont, Secretary of the Rally John Sprinzel, and Assistant Secretary John Brown. Delamont was the British Royal Automobile Club's competitions manager and had also served as committee member for the 1968 Marathon. Sprinzel had won the 1959 European Rally Championship with Stuart Turner, was an experienced circuit and rally driver, and had competed with Roy Fidler in the 1968 Marathon. Brown was an experienced club rally competitor and had invented the Targa timing system to improve accuracy when calculating competitor times on rallies. Other committee members included Wylton Dickson; the England national soccer team manager, Sir Alf Ramsey; Cesar Carman, president of the *Federación Interamericana de Touring y Automóvil Clubes*; and Marcus Chambers, former British Motor Corporation (BMC) competitions manager and, as Rootes Group competitions manager, the man responsible, together with Rootes Rally Manager Des O'Dell, for preparing the Hillman Hunter that took Andrew Cowan, Colin Malkin, and Brian Coyle to victory in the 1968 Marathon. The chairman of the organizing committee was H.W. "Tommy" Atkins, who was director of the *Daily Mirror*. Atkins was about to retire, and the rally was to be his last big endeavor.

The committee was meeting once a month but, according to John Sprinzel, the

Getting organized: (*left to right*) John Sprinzel, Tony Ambrose, and unidentified others, London 1970 (courtesy John Sprinzel).

non-motorsports membership felt the format he and Brown were applying to the rally was too difficult. Delamont recruited Tony Ambrose to bring them back in line, a tactic that failed because Ambrose was in agreement with their approach! Sprinzel and his wife, Pam, undertook the initial reconnaissance, or recce, from Monza in Italy to Lisbon in Portugal, following the route he and Brown had designed and, later, they recced the route from Yugoslavia to Monza. Sprinzel also surveyed the planned route from Rio to Mexico with John Brown, and the same partnership wrote the rally's regulations, which loosely followed the Liège-Rome-Liège principles. The Liège-Rome-Liège Rally, otherwise known as the *Marathon de la Route* or Road Marathon, was an extremely challenging annual rally event that, with changes to route and geographies, was held between 1931 and 1971. It was an arduous open road event run with extremely challenging time schedules, a factor that definitely emerged on the World Cup Rally, as we shall see!

The challenges posed were substantial and included a number of obvious and less obvious hurdles that needed to be crossed. Just as Jack Sears, Tommy Sopwith, and Ambrose had engaged with authorities from each country along the route of the 1968 Marathon, so this needed to happen for each country along the route between London and Mexico City. Less obvious was the fact that it had been announced that HRH Prince Michael of Kent had thrown his hat into the ring and declared that he would be competing in the rally. Prince Michael is cousin to HRH Queen Elizabeth II and, as of 2020, was 48th in line of succession to the British and Commonwealth throne. For the World Cup Rally, Prince Michael would take up his place in a team

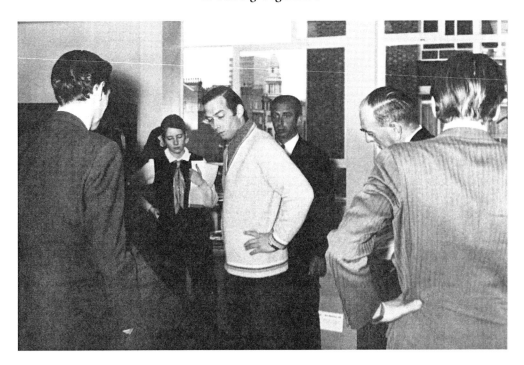

HRH Prince Michael of Kent (*center*) sports the latest British wool fashions (courtesy Gavin Thompson).

that would include British Army officer Captain Gavin Thompson, who had previously competed in the 1968 London–Sydney Marathon in a 4x4 Land Rover that, in order to comply with Marathon regulations, had had its drivetrain restricted to two-wheel drive! Prince Michael's entry therefore proffered the added complication of needing to add British and Commonwealth Royal protocols into the mix, which demanded an avoidance of commercially exploiting the House of Windsor, although no doubt British Wool were delighted to be a sponsor of the Royal Maxi. "They were great," Thompson recalled, "although we had to wear these uniforms that they made… We wore them on the day but after that, very much Dunlop, those racing overalls … they did the seats as well … the whole car was … done beautifully."

The *Daily Mirror* announced the 1970 London to Mexico World Cup Rally on June 6, 1969, with journalist Patrick Mennem declaring that "competitors will need a fast, rugged car, a crew to take on jungles, deserts and some of the highest mountains in the world. Measure up to this," he wrote, "and anyone can enter."[2] Once again, as with the 1968 London–Sydney Marathon, the rally was open to all comers, professional or amateur, as long as they had the price of entry. The announcement also reported that Sprinzel and Brown were busy mapping out the route in South America.

It wasn't long before expressions of interest and intent were being made. The first was reported on June 10, 1969, as the *Daily Mirror* announced that, via the manufacturer's British distribution company, four Moskvič sedans would be entered in the rally. The Soviet automobile manufacturer had previously entered four of its cars in the 1968 Marathon and had seen all of them make steady progress in reaching Sydney. Now, in a clever marketing ploy, UK distribution company general manager

from international soccer in 1969 but continued playing nationally until 1980. Having Greaves as a Ford Team member ticked all the right boxes; he was able to combine soccer and motorsports—what was at the heart of the World Cup Rally. Whether he could actually perform and deliver alongside highly skilled professional rally drivers would remain to be seen.

The British Leyland Motor Corporation (BLMC) Competitions Department avoided any such PR exercise, instead announcing a very British leading lineup to spearhead BLMC's attempt at World Cup Rally victory. Andrew Cowan was fresh from his victory at Sydney in 1968, but because the Rootes Group competitions team had been subsumed by parent company Chrysler, Cowan was invited to join and drive for BLMC on the rally. BLMC also had two experienced and gifted works drivers in Brian Culcheth and Paddy Hopkirk. Again, both had competed on the Marathon in 1968, and Hopkirk had taken the runner-up prize. Thus, during July 1969, BLMC presented Scotsman Cowan, Englishman Culcheth, and Northern Irishman Hopkirk to the press as representatives of their three premier entries. By the time the rally was ready to go, BLMC would add more teams in support of their assault.

In 1970, 21-year-old Mike Broad was one of the youngest people to get involved in the organization of the London to Mexico World Cup Rally. What began as a brief "gofer" role eventually saw Mike travelling and problem-solving from Rio de Janeiro all the way to Mexico, with quite a few adventures along the way.

2

The Adventures of Speedy

In 1969 and early 1970, Michael "Mike" Broad was working for his father's travel agency in Birmingham, England, by day and getting involved in local car club rallies by night. Not claiming to be especially good at it, he nevertheless aspired to the kinds of successes his local rally heroes John Bloxham and Richard Harper were experiencing. Therefore, he explained, "every time I got to the end of a night rally, I would try … to go and have a chat with them or go and have breakfast with them or something like that—they must have thought I was a real pain!"

Pain or not, Broad was all ears when, in October 1969, Bloxham and Harper began talking about how they wouldn't be doing any rallies in 1970 because they had decided to get involved in the London to Mexico World Cup Rally, Bloxham as a competitor and Harper, who could only take a week off work, as a marshal on the European section. The what? This was the first Mike had heard of the World Cup Rally and being a marshal sounded like a very interesting proposition, so he asked the pair how he might go about getting involved. One conversation between Harper and rally organizer John Sprinzel later and, in December, Mike received a call from one of the other organizers, former rally co-driver and Monte Carlo Rally winner Tony Ambrose. Could Mike get himself to the Royal Automobile Club HQ in London for a chat? Yes, he could!

"I don't know whether they knew I was a travel agent or what," Mike explained, "but I went down and they gave me an interview and then they gave me a map of South America with the projected route on it and asked me whether I could work out how many marshals we would need to do the event.… I panicked!" He also quickly realized this was a logistics exercise, a task to ensure the right people would be in the right place at the right time, so he asked for the ABC Air Worlds timetables, two large directories of all the scheduled flights in the world, sat down and worked it all out. Presenting the no doubt impressed organizers with the results, he returned to Birmingham.

Christmas 1969 came and went, and Mike heard nothing so, taking matters into his own hands, he called Ambrose, explaining that although he very much wanted to help organize the rally, he already had a job and didn't need another and, really, they needed him more than he needed them! They asked if he could start the following Monday. This, however, presented a new challenge—how to tell Mr. Broad senior that junior was going to quit his nice, secure job at the travel agency and go and join the (motorsports) circus? It didn't go well. "He wasn't happy," Mike remembered. "He

Peter Samuelson stated that the rally "will give us an unqualified opportunity to show the world that the Moskvich [*sic*] is ideally suited to overcome the toughest terrain."[3]

On June 30, the *Daily Mirror* announced details of how to get preliminary regulations and entry forms, and what the costs would be: the entry fee would be $1,480 for one car and two competitors. Any additional crewmembers over and above two would mean a further fee of $434 per person.

More details were announced on July 4, including confirmation that the fee would include all sea and river crossings and the assurance that any competitor failing to qualify at Lisbon would receive a proportionate refund. On top of the fee, all competitors were required to pay an undisclosed insurance premium. Official regulations would be available on September 1.

Statements of intent were now being made by the manufacturers' competitions departments. In a clever publicity coup, while still ruminating on its team's composition, Ford GB announced that England international soccer player Jimmy Greaves would take his place within the Ford team for the rally. Greaves began his senior soccer career in 1957, playing for Chelsea, and he went on to play for a number of other teams, including Football League Division One teams Tottenham Hotspur, a.k.a. "Spurs," and West Ham United, which he joined only a month before the World Cup Rally began. His international career included playing for the England team during their triumphant performance in the 1966 World Cup, although injury in a group match meant he was not able to play in the knockout rounds or the final. He retired

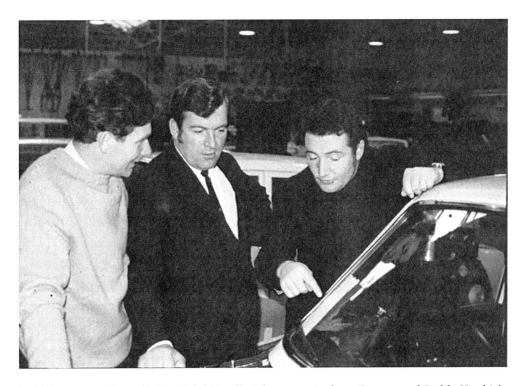

BLMC team members: (*left to right*) Neville Johnstone, Andrew Cowan, and Paddy Hopkirk, Abingdon, England, 1970 (courtesy Mike Wood).

was a very Victorian-type chap, was my dad. If you were still in the boulevard where we lived, I think the hole would still probably be in the ceiling! He was not happy and I was not allowed home for quite a long time."

Undaunted, off Mike went to start work as assistant to John Sprinzel and Tony Ambrose, moving into bed-and-breakfast accommodation shared with a friend who was also in London. On his first morning, so unfamiliar was Mike with the hustle and bustle of life in the country's capital that, waiting for a London Underground train, he let the first few go on, certain that the next would be less crowded. During rush hour! Furthermore, used to being at work ready to start at nine o'clock, he was puzzled that no one else was there; the organizing team rarely if ever rolled into the office before ten! However, he had secured a paid job as office junior working with the people who were organizing the London to Mexico World Cup Rally. He was in his element, even if his father's angry words echoed in his ears, not least because his contract was actually due to expire the day the rally started! Mike had other ideas, of course, and worked tirelessly to make himself indispensable. Each time he was given something to do, he would do it, say he'd done it, and then ask, "What's next?" In this fashion, he became known as "Speedy."

By the time Mike started work for Ambrose, Sprinzel, et al., the rally route was mostly agreed upon and thoughts had turned to how the two sections, in Europe and in South America, would need to be staffed. All of the controls, whether transport stages, passage controls, or start and finish points for the *primes*, would need marshals. These people would work with local car club representatives to physically set up a control station at the agreed location, whether in a town, city or the absolute middle of nowhere, and then literally marshal proceedings, i.e., await the arrival of each car, stamp and sign or initial competitors' roadbooks, and record arrival and/or departure times, depending on the type of control. Given that there would be more than 30 controls throughout Europe and more than 40 in South America, that meant a large number of people needed to have transport and accommodation arranged to ensure the right steward was in place, kitted out with the required materials and equipment, at the right time. Local rally headquarters would also need to be identified and secured at crucial points along the way.

As Mike explained, "Europe was brilliant and fairly easy but South America was another thing. There was a wonderful guy called Stan … from MAT Transport, who were our official travel agent, and he virtually worked with me for three months to get everything done." Between them, they were able to solve problems: When unable to arrange flights in Bolivia, they approached the Bolivian embassy to ask for use of one of the Bolivian Air Force's Dakotas. On discovering that Hertz was just opening a car rental concession at the Montevideo airport, they ensured all four cars being made available were booked for use by rally officials for the week.

Working with the rally organizing committee was a real eye-opener for 21-year-old Mike, who assumed everybody worked from nine until six each day. Not the rally committee folks at the RAC club! Two-hour lunches, starting the day at ten, weekly deliveries of assorted alcoholic beverages, stored in metal filing cabinets! Then there were the people. "Absolutely nobody knew me," Mike explained, "but I was going to meet everybody in the world of rally that I wanted to all in one place. …

British Leyland and Ford ... we'd have meetings with them every week or fortnight and it got to the point at the end, back-end of March, where Ambrose said, 'You'd better chair this meeting, Mike, because you know what's going on.' So, there I am with Stuart Turner and Peter Browning!"

Not surprising then that, by the beginning of March, Tony Ambrose realized Mike's assistance would be needed during the event itself. So, on April 19, 1970, while competitors were queuing up to be flagged away from London's Wembley Stadium, Mike was hot-footing it down to the port of Dover on England's south coast to help make sure all the cars got onto the channel ferry over to Boulogne in France. Mike accompanied cars and competitors on the boat, but once they had disembarked and started the long run east, he returned to London where, until May 4, he was to assist at the *Daily Mirror*. "They set up this results place in their foyer at the offices at High Holborn, with lots of girls and computers," he recalled. "Well, there was a computer on the wall, but the timings were phoned in by marshals etc. ...We'd got a rota of people and local motor club people helped us as well." On hand to help research any piece of information or answer any technical question the *Mirror* might have, Mike found himself alone among the banks of telephones during a tea break during a late shift one night. When a phone began to ring, Mike picked it up and provided the required information. The following evening, he returned for another shift and was buttonholed by a manager, who tersely advised him that he was *not* there to answer telephones and, should he do it again, the *Mirror* would have an industrial dispute on its hands, so strong was the union then. "I was not there to answer telephones," Mike recalled. "I'm not one of the union members, I was there to stand there and speak when spoken to!"

Not put off, Mike continued helping out at the newspaper offices, but after May 4 he flew to Rio de Janeiro to help set up the rally's headquarters in the capital city in readiness for the restart on May 8. From there, he travelled south to help Valerie Morley set up the Uruguay *prime* finish control at Salto. As Valerie Domleo, she was Rosemary Smith's co-driver when they won the Dutch Tulip Rally outright, a rare female victory in a mostly male sport. Mike was thrilled to meet Valerie, explaining to her that they had practically been neighbors for a while back in Sutton Coldfield in England.

His duties at Salto complete, Mike journeyed onwards to the Chilean capital, Santiago, to help official-in-charge John Brown and other organizers and marshals in attendance, including Donald and Erle Morley, Dean Delamont, Tony Ambrose, and John Sprinzel's wife Pamela. Santiago was to be an arrival control, *parc fermé* and then departure control over the 24-hour period of May 13 and May 14. There was also a rally HQ at the city's Carrera Sheraton Hotel, where any logistical or other organizational problems could be addressed. And logistical problems there most certainly were as Sprinzel and Co. received call after call advising of delays in getting marshals to their designated locations, severe snow blocking the rally route over the Andes, and even reports of earth tremors in Argentina!

After Santiago, the route was to take competitors northwards to Putaendo and the start of the 200-mile Chilean *prime*, which would finish at Sotaquí and then turn east and upwards, delivering surviving competitors into Argentina via the Paso de

Vintage transport in Uruguay: Mike Broad and Valerie Morley, May 1970 (courtesy Mike Broad).

Agua Negra or Agua Negra Pass, at an elevation of 15,600 feet. This was the section of the route that was blocked, causing a last-minute scramble to arrange a revised route. What about rerouting the Chilean *prime* so that its start remained the same but its finish would now be at Illapel, some 110 miles to the south of Sotaquí? Competitors could then be rerouted back down the Pan-American Highway via Los Vilos, La Ligua, and La Calara, before turning eastwards to the Argentinian frontier between Cancha Pelada in Chile and Las Cuevas in Argentina, via the Cumbre Tunnel.

Assorted marshals were either en route to other controls further along the route, fog-bound at airports, or struggling with broken-down rental cars, so Tony Ambrose gave Mike instructions: take a car from the hotel carpark, get to Illapel, and set up a control! "It was about a four-hour drive," Mike remembered. "It was literally 'go to Valparaiso and turn right and start climbing up the Andes,' at night, by yourself. Pretty scary! Then you get there at about three o'clock in the morning and you think, well, am I on the right road? …they had to shorten that *prime* to Illapel … they put an absolutely impossible time schedule on it but forgot to tell me!" It's a testimony to Mike's unbridled enthusiasm that he not only got to Illapel in the early hours of May 14, 1970, but that he also set up a working control, complete with banner, table, stopwatch and record book! The adventure wasn't quite over, however, as he had been advised that the fastest cars should arrive by a certain time. That time came. That time went. "I just had this picture in my head that there was something like 20 cars at a T-junction somewhere north of where I was, thinking well, there's supposed to be a control here!" he recalled. Suffice to say, it wasn't long before cars came barreling in and Mike was immediately busy stamping books and recording times!

Mike's next assignment was at the arrival control at La Paz airport in Bolivia, where the local authorities were extremely helpful, and then he was sent up to Desaguadero, at the border between Bolivia and Peru, where he was charged with ensuring a smooth frontier crossing. Previous reports had suggested the crossing could take up to three hours, which would seriously compromise the rally. Mike was accompanied by a British embassy official to assist with language barriers and, together with the judicious use of cartons of cigarettes, they were able to facilitate much expedited border formalities for the rally cars. "We managed to convince this customs boss that these cigarettes were only made for embassy staff and Her Majesty the Queen, and he wasn't going to get any more ever again," Mike explained. "'Do you want some?' A thousand cigarettes later, five cartons later, and off we went!"

From there he was sent to Cali in Colombia, via Lima in Peru—if competitors reached as far as Cali, they would be technically classified as "finishers" on the rally. Another of the travelling marshals, Jack Sears, had gone on ahead to Cali to meet with local government and motor club representatives to ensure that arrangements were in place so that competitors could arrive at Cali, place their cars in *parc fermé* for a rest stop, and then continue on to Buenaventura the following day, where cars would be loaded onto a ship bound for Panama. Jack Sears had been hugely instrumental in organizing the London–Sydney Marathon 18 months before, and was especially skilled in the art of diplomacy, having ensured that on the road from England to Australia, country after country had willingly suspended border crossing bureaucracy to ensure that that endurance rally's momentum had been uninterrupted. Now, Mike was scheduled to assist with arrangements in Colombia, together with fellow marshal and London–Sydney Marathon veteran Jim Gavin. "If you ever had to go to South America in the seventies," Mike exclaimed, "the person that you want is Jim Gavin!"

Jim and Mike took a nonstop flight from Lima, but a problem with the landing gear hydraulics forced the aircraft to land at Quito in Ecuador, which in turn led to an increasing delay. Eventually, as Mike recalled, "Jim literally charged straight into their office … and said, 'What the hell is going on? We've got to get out of here, so either you tell us you're not going and we'll go and charter a flight or we're going now!'" They were then witness to an exchange of almost comedic proportions as pilot, co-pilot, and airline HQ were all on shortwave radios, testing instruments onboard the plane to see what worked and what didn't. "As we overheard all this," Mike remembered, "we were then not allowed out of that office, in case we spoke to any of the other passengers on the aircraft! Literally, it was a wing and a prayer. Then they decided they'd go for it and there were five people that knew this hydraulic system was not really working properly."

Keeping tight-lipped, Jim and Mike made it to Cali and joined Jack Sears for discussions with local representatives, including senior military officers, but, to Jack's consternation, Jim began insisting on assurances that the promises of organizational endeavor were to be backed up by actions, which were not as forthcoming as Jim would have liked. Mike overheard one of the senior military officials telling Jim that everyone in Buenaventura was waiting for them and all was arranged. "Jim said something like, 'Well, can I have the name of the captain or sergeant or even private that you have been talking to?'" Mike recalled. "'I do not need to tell you that, it is all arranged.' Jim literally said, 'Well, in that case, Mike, we're going down there in the morning.' Jack went nuts with Jim in the end. After the meeting he took Jim aside and said, 'Don't you ever do that again. You undermined my authority in that room.'"

Notwithstanding bruised pride, it turned out Jim had been right to call out the senior officials in Cali as, when he and Mike made it to the Colombian port, they caught the local shipping offices completely off guard. Then, to make matters worse, financial arrangements had been made only to ship cars still in competition, yet a number of other teams, now disqualified but still on the road, also arrived at Buenaventura, all determined to seek passage, claiming this was the only way they could get out of South America! "Nobody had got any money to pay!" Mike recalled. "I've got correspondence … from the *Daily Mirror* afterwards saying they'd just had a bill from the shipping company for five extra [cars]. Where have you put the money? Well, you weren't there, it was impossible!" Eventually, the ship found space for all cars still competing, plus the disqualified vehicles and a number of civilian cars.

Mike was indeed relieved to depart onboard the ship as his experience of Buenaventura has been less than comfortable. A driver had brought him and Jim from Cali and dropped them at the hotel, strongly advising them to stay put while he set up a meeting with port officials and the shipping company. He would then return and collect Mike and Jim. However, as Mike explained, "Jim, being Jim, said, 'No, no, we'll walk on down to the port, it's only a mile or so, I want to see what Buenaventura is all about.'" Thus, having checked in, off the intrepid pair went but had only gone about 600 yards when a police car stopped, picked them up, and returned them to the hotel! "We couldn't understand what was going on and they took us back to the hotel and the bloke at the hotel said, 'Don't go out of the room,'" Mike recalled. "It was bandit-land in those days, Buenaventura, and if they saw you with a nice shirt and they wanted that shirt, they'd just … get the shirt. They wouldn't ask for it!"

Both Jim and Mike joined competitors aboard the ship, enjoying the chance to kick back and relax before, as planned, Mike would then fly back to England. However, at Panama, he was now instructed by Tony Ambrose to get himself to Mexico City as there were still a few more tasks requiring his attention, one of which was to drive out to the airport to collect 1968 International Formula One Champion Graham Hill because the *Daily Mirror* had got him in to do the prize-giving. "He was on his way to Indianapolis … for the Indy 500," Mike explained. "Anyway, I got the distinct impression that … when he saw that it was me, just me, a 21-year-old, knackered, completely 'out of it' fella, and I didn't even have a driver, it was just me. He was not impressed at all!"

At last, having formally completed the rally in Fortín de las Flores, the victor of the 1970 London to Mexico Word Cup Rally led a procession of surviving cars and competitors into Mexico City and to the Aztec Stadium. Mike was thrilled to be given a seat in the lead escort vehicle, which in turn became the follow-up vehicle as rally cars overtook them. "I've never seen so many motorcycle outriders in my life," Mike recalled. "There must have been 15 or 20 Mexican police outriders and we started on the outskirts of Mexico City … every single traffic light was on green, we went through at about 60 or 70 miles an hour through the center of Mexico City! My worry was the boys at the back, their cars were almost not capable of keeping up…. The cars were knackered, they were knackered, and these policemen thought these are rally cars, these boys can race, come on, let's go! Jesus, and they were on big Harleys, you know?"

The 1970 London to Mexico World Cup Rally proved to be a life-changing experience for Mike, not least because, during the few remaining days in Mexico City before he flew home, he got to know Ford works team duo Tony Fall and his co-driver, former England soccer player Jimmy Greaves. Fall and Greaves had taken a very respectable sixth place at Fortín de las Flores and, three or four years later, Fall would remember Mike and invite him to take the co-driver's seat on a number of international rallies.

Mike finally returned to England and was eventually welcomed back into the family fold and travel agency by his father. He also worked to ensure his face remained familiar at rally events, which in turn led to the opportunity to begin co-driving regularly, a career that saw him compete on the international rally circuit for 20 years. He also seized the chance to co-drive in the 1977 London–Sydney Marathon, with none other than 1968 Marathon winner Andrew Cowan.

That, however, is a whole other story!

3

Where Are We Going?

On July 6, 1969, John Sprinzel and his wife, Pamela, set off to survey and notate the proposed European route from Yugoslavia to Monza, which would include two special stages or *primes*. Tony Ambrose was in charge of surveying the remainder of the proposed route to Lisbon. The rally was planned for April and May, so this recon was a little on the late side; ideally Sprinzel wanted recces and rally stages to occur in the same season (12 months apart) so that weather patterns could be understood and any associated challenges, e.g., snow or strong potential for rain, factored into instructions, especially across South America.

The European route would take cars from London down to Dover, across to Boulogne in northwest France, and then through West Germany, Austria, Hungary, and Yugoslavia. Cars would then pass into Bulgaria, back into Yugoslavia, and then on to Italy, back into France, across the border to Spain and finally Portugal.

As a result of their surveys, the team agreed that from London to Titograd in Yugoslavia there were to be passage controls at Saarbrücken and Munich in West Germany; Austria's capital city of Vienna; Budapest, capital of Hungary; and Yugoslavia's capital city, Belgrade. The purpose of each passage control was to ensure that competitors were following the prescribed route and were doing so within the time allowances. There would be a time control at Sofia in Bulgaria whereby competitors arriving early would be given a scheduled time and would not be allowed to depart for Titograd until that time. Titograd would mark the beginning of the rally's first special stage, the Montenegro *prime*, which would take competitors to Kotor on the Adriatic Sea. From Kotor, competitors would travel northwest up the coast to Glamoč and the start of the second special stage, the Serbian *prime*, which would run from Glamoč to Bosanska Krupa, via a passage control at Sanski Most. From Bosanska Krupa, the route would take the cars out of Yugoslavia and into Italy, destination Milan and the *Autodromo Nazionale di Monza*, the historic racetrack at Monza, where there would be a time control and official *parc fermé*. In motorsports, *parc fermé* is the closed area established to prevent unauthorized access to vehicles during an event.

From Monza, the route would head south to Genoa and then west to Ville San Pietro and the start of special stage number three, the San Remo *prime*, which took competitors south to Camporosso. From there, cars would travel over the border to France and head for Menton before heading north and then up to the passage control in the Col de Turini pass in the Alps. From there, competitors would drive to a

Road repairs on the Serbian *prime*, Yugoslavia, April 1970 (courtesy Mike Wood).

The San Remo *prime*, Italy, April 1970 (courtesy Mike Wood).

tiny settlement, Les Quatre Chemins, literally "the four paths," a junction between the French D2 and D5 roads and a winding minor road up into the mountains, from where the fourth stage, the Alpine *prime*, would see cars speed to a passage control at Sigale and another at Entrevaux, before completing the *prime* at Rouaine. After Rouaine, a long transport stage would take the field out of France, via passage controls at Moustiers St. Marie, Chalet Reynard, Sauvas, Rodez, Tournon-d'Agenais, and L'Isle-de-Noé and then over the border from Somport into Spain where the route ran southwest to the Portuguese border at Vilar Formosa and on to the town of Arganil and the last passage control before the final European special stage, the Portuguese *prime*, that would run from Arganil to Pampilhosa. After that, it would be a southward run down to Lisbon and the final time control before South America.

Four thousand five hundred miles in total, to be completed in five days.

Many of the professional competitors would be familiar with the European *primes* as they followed sections of a number of established European rally competitions—the historic Liège-Sofia-Liège, the Monte Carlo, the Alpine or *Coupe des Alpes*¸ the San Remo and the Portuguese TAP or *Rally de Portugal*. Others who would be familiar were the team of travelling marshals that Sprinzel and Co. had invited to participate and staff the time and passage controls across Europe and South America. Among them were highly experienced rally drivers in their own right. Valerie Domleo won the Ladies Cup on the 1960 RAC Rally and the 1961 Monte Carlo Rally. Her husband, Donald Morley, twice won the Alpine Rally, or *Coupe des Alpes*, in 1961 and 1962, with his twin brother Erle. They too took up the role of controllers, as did Jim Gavin, veteran of the London–Sydney Marathon and driver of one of the first Ford Escorts to be prepared, albeit privately, for a stage rally—we shall see how far the Escort had come in the 18 months thereafter! Having helped him recce part of the European route, Sprinzel's wife, Pamela, also joined the band of travelling controllers. These and others would be the familiar faces presented to the professional competitors as they raced to get their roadbooks stamped along the route.

Five or six weeks before the European route was surveyed and agreed, John Sprinzel and John Brown—accompanied by *Daily Mirror* journalist James Wilson—flew out to Rio de Janeiro to recce their proposed route for the rally from Brazil on the South Atlantic Ocean to Mexico on the Pacific. A multitude of challenges faced them. Having slavishly pored over maps back in London, they now had to follow the route they had sketched out, to ensure that it was both physically achievable and that there were no obstacles that might require a re-route. As Sprinzel mischievously wrote in the official regulations, the route "is a very straightforward one … with over sixteen thousand miles of motoring we hardly needed to introduce obstacles."[1]

The team would also have to wrestle with a series of logistics, including investigating the requirements for obtaining *carnet*—the international customs and temporary export-import documentation required to allow competing cars to enter and leave each country as they moved south, then west, then north. There would also be two water crossings to organize, first across the River Plate from Montevideo in Uruguay to Buenos Aires in Argentina, and later between Buenaventura in Colombia and Cristóbal in Panama, necessary because the Darién Gap, that remote, roadless stretch of jungle between Colombia and Panama, was impassable. In fact, it wouldn't be until two years later that, as part of an expeditionary party attempting to complete a 17,000-mile journey along the Pan-American Highway, from Alaska to Cape Horn, soon-to-be World Cup Rally competitor and British Army officer Captain Gavin Thompson would achieve the impossible and actually traverse the Gap in two Range Rovers. Although GM had "driven" three Chevrolet Corvairs through the Gap in 1961 in order to produce an extraordinarily ambitious promotional film for their innovative rear-engine automobile, the key difference with the Range Rover expedition is that while the Chevys were basically carried, dragged, and pushed through the wilderness—only two Corvairs actually emerged on the other side—the 1973 expedition achieved the crossing under the vehicles' own power. In fact, as Gavin Thompson explained, on their return to England *Motor* magazine tested one of the expedition cars at speed against a new Range Rover. "They said, 'Gavin's car—there's only about one second in it, 0-60… but we did notice a slight damp smell!'"

Another challenge that Sprinzel and Brown had to overcome or endure was waiting: waiting at embassies and government ministries, waiting at Ford factories in order to negotiate the borrowing of transportation for their odyssey across South America—no mean feat, given some of the terrain and altitudes they planned to travel—and waiting upon local and national car clubs, with the express purpose of recruiting their members into the drive to resource and support the passage and time controls along the way, even if the extraordinary distances proposed between controls meant that fewer personnel might be needed per country than the European section. Applying a "belt-and-braces approach, Sprinzel ensured that his travelling stewards would be on hand to manage any over-enthusiastic behavior among any inexperienced local club support!

"From the Pampas to High Andes: from the civilization of Ipanema Beach and Rio's skyscrapers to the wild hinterlands of Bolivia and Peru: along the trails of Incas and Aztecs; in mountain snows or tropical jungle."[2] This was how John Sprinzel described the 11,500-mile journey that would lie ahead of competitors who were brave enough, skilled enough, and lucky enough to get to Rio de Janeiro. Sprinzel and Brown had mapped the route southwest from Rio to Ventania via São Paulo and included a passage control at Piedade. At Ventania, the first South American special stage, the Parana *prime*, would take competitors south to Bateias along dirt roads. After receiving their first taste of the speed and endurance challenges a South American *prime* might offer, crews would head south to Ituporanga and the start of the Rio Grande *prime*, which would run the 240 miles to Canela, approximately 70 miles north of Porto Alegre, and would require careful concentration over countless narrow wooden bridges.

The next stretch would take the cars west towards the border crossing at Santana do Livramento and over into Uruguay where the route would head south to Tacuarembó and the start of the Uruguay *prime*, a rough stage, which would arrive at Salto to the north and west. From there, a transport stage would lead competitors south to a passage control at Santiago Vazquez and then on to the *parc fermé* at Montevideo. At this stage, cars would have been travelling for 40 hours nonstop and would have covered 2,000 miles—Sprinzel and Brown therefore graciously allowed an overnight rest stop!

The following day, cars and crews would board a ferry to take them across the River Plate to Argentina and its capital Buenos Aires, from where the next stage, the Pampas *prime*, would commence at Saladillo and take cars southwest to Espartillar. This stage promised either dust or thick mud, depending on weather conditions. Once completed, the route progressed down to San Antonio Oeste on the San Matías Gulf, which marked the start of the next stage, the Trans-Argentine *prime*, the third longest stage at 310 miles of rough, punishing roads across Patagonia to Bariloche and then onward to the southern end of the Andes mountain range, the southern-most point of the rally. Cars would climb up to the Puyehue Pass at 4,000 feet, cross the border into Chile, and then head north on the fast, Pan-American Highway to a time control at Santiago, *parc fermé*, and another overnight rest.

The following day, cars would depart *parc fermé* and make for the departure control at Huechuraba before heading north to Putaendo and the start of the Chilean *prime*, which would take competitors north to a passage control at Chincolco and a second at Illapel before finishing at Sotaquí. After Sotaquí, the route would head east to the frontier with Argentina, again crossing the Andes mountain range but this time via the Agua Negra Pass at an elevation of almost 16,000 feet!

Having survived this ordeal, crews would then descend to Rodeo and the beginning of the second longest *prime*, the Gran Premio. At 510 miles, this stage would be especially grueling as it would mean competitors driving to an elevation of 15,000 feet while also having to contend with a mix of straight sections, hairpin bends, and sheer drops, finishing at La Viña in the north.

Intentionally, Sprinzel and Brown gave no allowance for a rest stop here and

Summit of the Agua Negra Pass, Chile, 1970 (courtesy Mike Wood).

instead routed competitors northward to the Bolivian border at Villazón and the start of the Bolivian Coffee *prime*, another long, mountainous stretch, this time at a mere 11,000 feet, which would end at Potosí before heading onward to La Paz, Bolivia's capital city and the highest administrative capital in the world at almost 12,000 feet. A time control here would mean that competitors making good time would have the chance for some rest before setting off again, this time towards the Peruvian border at Desaguadero and onwards to Cusco at just over 11,000 feet and the entrance to the longest stage of the event, the 560-mile Route of the Incas *prime*, which included a section of track carved out of the cliff, with a 300-foot drop below. Ending at Huancayo to the northwest, the route would again cross the Andes range via the Ticlio Pass, which would mark the highest point of the event at 15,870 feet. From Huancayo, competitors would descend to rather more oxygen-rich Lima, a time control, *parc fermé* and a night stop.

Only three *primes* would remain.

After Lima, the route would take remaining competitors north along the coast to the Ecuadorian frontier at La Tina and then to Macará and the start of the Ecuador *prime* that would run north and east to Cuenca. After Cuenca, teams would head for Cali in Colombia, crossing the border at Ipiales. At Cali, competitors would find a time control and *parc fermé*. They would also be classified as finishers here, even though there would still be almost 3,000 miles to go. From Cali, a neutralized section to the port of Buenaventura would then see competitors and cars board a ship for the two-day passage to Cristóbal in Panama, followed by another neutralized section to the departure control at Panama City and the restart of the final stretch of the rally. Neutralized sections carried no risk of additional penalty points. Drivers simply had to get to the endpoint.

From Panama City, the route would again follow the Pan-American Highway, over the border into Costa Rica and to Paso Canoas for the beginning of the penultimate stage, the Costa Rica Coffee *prime*, which would pass through coffee plantations and finish at Cartago. From there, the route would continue northeast, across the border into Nicaragua at Peñas Blancas and then via Managua and Esteli to the frontier with Honduras at El Espino. Through Honduras to the border and over into El Salvador, then to the Guatemalan border at Candelaria de la Frontera, via San Miguel and San Salvador. Finally, via Guatemala City, cars would pass into the last country on the route, Mexico, still with 1,300 miles to go and one last stage, the Aztec *prime*, running from Oaxaca northward to Tuxtepec. After that, all that would be left would be the drive to Fortín de las Flores and the last time control, followed by a neutralized section to the Mexico City limits and finally into the Aztec Stadium to obtain the very last control stamp and signature in competitors' roadbooks.

Qualifying as a finisher at Cali, however, would not necessarily mean all challenges were over, as 1968 London–Sydney Marathon veteran Major John Hemsley and his freshman co-driver, Sergeant Walter "Wally" Easton, were to discover.

4

Shocks and Surprises
(Part One)

Having established a successful profile during the 10,000-mile 1968 endurance rally between London, England and Sydney, Australia, the British Army Motoring Association (BAMA), and specifically BAMA member Major John Hemsley, was extremely keen to capitalize on performance by proposing a considerably larger-scale effort for the much-vaunted London to Mexico World Cup Rally. John had competed on the road from London to Sydney and had achieved an overall position of 37th out of 56 finishers, despite persistent suspension problems that plagued both his Rover 2000 and that of fellow BAMA competitor Major Michael "Mike" Bailey.

As soon as the London Mexico event was confirmed during the first half of 1969, John led an assault on Army authorities "to see whether it would be possible this time to run a full team with proper Army support together with all the advantages and resultant publicity that this would entail." Discouragingly, initial reaction was tepid with personnel representing the Army's recruitment and publicity arms dismissing the potential benefits such an international motorsports event might have in promoting the Army as a desirable career, especially as the projected overall cost of running a team of three cars with support crews was calculated at approximately $37,000. The cost-benefit analysis just didn't stack up!

However, John was not without the talent for persuasion. He was "highly instrumental," Mike Bailey explained, "in obtaining the support of General Sir Antony Read, the Quartermaster General and Colonel of the Light Division, who intervened on behalf of BAMA to find sufficient financial support which allowed us to make the initial entry for the three cars and enough backing to enable us to start the planning for the event." Mike also got to work and struck upon the idea of arranging "a practical demonstration of rally cars at the Military Vehicles Experimental Establishment Alpine Test track in Bagshot [in the English county of Surrey]." With this in mind, he made contact with the Establishment and was granted access to the track on an agreeable date. Members of the Army Board were duly invited to attend, strap themselves into assorted vehicles, and be hurtled around the multi-terrain track. Referred to as the "Generals' Gyrations," senior military personnel were also invited to witness the kinds of pressures and challenges a team might have in maintaining a car on an endurance rally against the clock. The outcome was favorable and so, with further support from Major-General Claxton, the Transport Officer in Chief, and Colonels King and Low of the Army School of Transport, the Army Central Fund finally

Major Freddie Preston (*beneath hood facing camera*) and Major Mike Bailey (*beneath hood in front*) keep busy during the "Generals' Gyrations," Bagshot, England, 1970 (courtesy Mike Bailey).

surrendered and agreed to meet the cost of entry into the rally for three teams plus cost of gasoline. Additional backing, however, would need to be secured from other, non-public sources, and that would crucially include the procurement of three cars!

BAMA members made overtures to the various British motor manufacturers for obvious reasons but were somewhat surprisingly met with ambivalence, although it should probably be stressed that, of the main automobile producers in the UK in 1970, British Leyland and Ford were already immersed in developing their own attack on the London to Mexico Rally and the Rootes Group was slowly but inexorably being swallowed by the USA's Chrysler Corporation, which wasn't especially interested in rally as a motor sport.

What to do? As Mike explained, John "and Major Ted Moorat came up trumps. Both had been associated with the Peugeot Company in the past. The company was keen to participate in the World Cup but was undecided which of their current models would be the most suitable—the 504, 404, or 204. To help them to decide on the most suitable vehicle, the Company entered one of each type of car in the 1969 RAC International Rally." Thus, with a BAMA team driving each of these models, Peugeot awaited the outcome of the event, which resulted in the 504 performing the best. Peugeot then communicated with its British dealership network, inviting proactive participation and, as a consequence, the Hampshire-based company Kerridges stepped forward to prepare and pay for three Peugeot 504s for the BAMA team, in partnership with the south of England's Peugeot distributor. Then, cementing this Anglo-French undertaking, Mike approached the *Paris Match* magazine and secured an additional $4,800 of financial sponsorship and the BAMA effort was secured. The fact that this was a less than British affair was not lost on the British government, however. Mike recalled: "Questions were asked in the House of Commons when Anthony Wedgwood-Benn, the Minister of Technology, asked the then Defence Secretary, Denis Healey, 'Why is it that the British Army would be driving foreign cars, why were they not driving British cars?', to which Denis Healey replied that '…the British Army would have been delighted to have been able to drive British cars only … no British company was prepared to provide them.'"

The cars and backing secured, all that was left was for the three teams to be finalized. As with all BAMA rallying involvement, each team would be two-up, a driver and co-driver/navigator. Having performed admirably during the London–Sydney Marathon, not least in the face of adversity in Afghanistan and the Australian Outback, Mike would again co-drive for Major Freddie Preston. John's usual co-driver, Warrant Officer Frank Webber, was on a tour of Cyprus, so he drafted in Sergeant Wally Easton, who had skillfully prepared the Hemsley/Webber BLMC 1800 for the previous rally season. Making up the third team would be Warrant Officer John Rhodes and Staff Sergeant Joe Minto. A fourth 504 was also entered by the British Royal Fusiliers Regiment, independent of the BAMA/*Paris Match* team.

Testing times for a BAMA Peugeot 504, Bagshot: Warrant Officer John Rhodes (*driving*) and Staff Sergeant Joe Minto, 1970 (courtesy Mike Bailey).

The time that was left before the rally began was a scramble of activity, from ensuring the cars were thoroughly prepared to confirming that foreign currency, passports, international travel documentation, servicing locations, and sites for replacement tires were all in place. John recalled: "The result was that each one of us found ourselves working until half past three or later every morning for the few weeks preceding the event; and indeed, most of us had more sleep once the Rally started than we had managed to achieve immediately prior to the start!"

The three cars were delivered to Kerridges from Peugeot France with strengthened suspension and additional fuel tanks, together with oil pan guards, gasoline tank shields, and additional spot- and auxiliary driving lamps. Even so, the three rally-hardened teams further specified another 120 modifications to ensure readiness for the 16,000-mile drive, all of which were undertaken by both Kerridges mechanics and by the teams themselves. John recalled that the overtime bill for one week's worth of the mechanics' time amounted to $430!

As the rally would take competitors to elevations of 16,000 feet, one of the additional preparations was the inclusion of portable oxygen bottles within the list of items each car would need to carry. Furthermore, arrangements were made for the six men to attend the RAF School of Medicine at the Royal Aircraft Establishment at Farnborough in Hampshire. There, under close supervision, they would be placed in the faculty's decompression chamber. "Each one of us was issued with an oxygen mask connected to a central oxygen supply, a clipboard, and pencil," Mike explained. "We would take it in turns to remove our oxygen mask and respond to simple arithmetical questions, which the squadron leader would ask us to work out and write down." The men were then decompressed to match an elevation of 40,000 feet, told to remove their masks and write down the answers to the math questions. After a few seconds, their ability to write anything meaningful disappeared, at which point they were instructed to replace their masks and were recompressed to normal levels. They were also strongly advised that, when they found themselves driving at altitude, they should use the oxygen supplies and closely monitor each other's performance. Mike acknowledges that "this training proved to be of considerable value during the South American part of the rally."

Finally, on April 18, all three 504s were present and correct at London's Wembley Stadium for scrutineering and passed the preparedness and acceptability assessment with flying colors, although not without a few issues for the Hemsley/Easton car. John recalled: "My wife, who has a slightly more practical eye on these occasions, asked if there was really meant to be all that oil underneath the car. There wasn't—the car was jacked up and the bonnet [hood] lifted to reveal a broken brake pipe." Three hours of frenetic activity ensued before all was as it should be, although John felt rather less than comforted, given the long road ahead!

April 19, 1970, dawned bright and clear in London, and so it was that the three BAMA Peugeots took their places. John and Wally had been drawn No. 6, with the Rhodes/Minto car at No. 8. Mike and Freddie had a longer wait, having been allotted No. 72 in the draw, but finally, at 11:12, after the pair had endured the assorted entertainments offered up to the 25,000-strong crowd in the stadium, England soccer team manager Sir Alf Ramsey flagged the Preston/Bailey car away. For six British

Decompressing the BAMA team, Farnborough, England, 1970: (*left to right*) **Sergeant Wally Easton, unknown, unknown, Major John Hemsley, Major Mike Bailey, Major Freddie Preston (courtesy Mike Bailey).**

Army Motoring Association officers, propelled by a little Gallic flair, the adventure had begun.

All three cars performed exceptionally well on the long transport stage from London through France, Germany, Austria, Hungary, Yugoslavia and into, then back out of Bulgaria, John noting that the 504 was more than capable of cruising quite happily at 100-plus miles per hour on the fast German autobahns. This was of course during the Cold War period, so the crossing from Austria into Hungary represented driving behind the Iron Curtain, the boundary imposed by the Soviet Union to separate itself and its satellite countries from "the West." Once again, as he had felt during the London–Sydney Marathon 18 months before, serving British Army officer Mike Bailey reflected that, in driving into Eastern Europe, "one felt as though we were being photographed and checked out by the 'apparatchiks' in case we might be members of MI6 or CIA! The word *paranoia* comes to mind!" Despite the perhaps alarming visibility of Hungarian military personnel, and who knows who else, cars were welcomed by huge crowds of fascinated spectators as they moved onwards, and all three cars reached the time control at the Balkan Hotel in Bulgaria's capital, Sofia, without incident.

Now the rally would commence!

Heavy snow had fallen on the best-laid plans of Mr. Sprinzel and his co-organizers, which meant that the first special stage, or *prime*, had to be re-routed and shortened at extremely short notice. Thus, departing from Sofia, cars retraced their track for a short while before turning off and making for the revised start control at Titograd in Yugoslavia. Again, the three Peugeots performed well as they drove northwest, then west, then south, but this was about to change for at least one of the cars into the second speed test of the rally.

The first *prime,* the Montenegro, although revised, was still a fast, twisting, rough stage that took cars up and through the Lovćen national park, which—an added hazard—remained open to regular traffic. There were "cars and lorries completely oblivious to our presence until the last minute when either they went off the road or you did!" Mike recalled. The latter part of the section led cars down through a dizzying sequence of hairpin bends overlooking the Adriatic Sea with perilous drops and only the occasional low parapet wall to prevent oblivion! This was poor Wally Easton's first real experience of what John described as "fresh air corners," the car getting a wee bit too close to the edge for his liking! Nevertheless, John and Wally lost just eight minutes on this section, as did Mike and Freddie, compared to Rhodes and Minto, who reached the finish control at Kotor 24 minutes down.

After a transport stage along the Adriatic coast, the next *prime,* the Serbian, promised winding country lanes and forest tracks, 120 miles from Glamoč to Bosanska Krupa, including a passage control at Sanski Most, designed to make sure all were on the right track. Mike explained that this section was undertaken at night and that the directions to which they had access were vague to say the least. Leaving one village in the dark, they suddenly found themselves confronted with a body of water. Had they gone wrong? The map suggested not, and a line of telephone poles that skirted the road only emphasized the point, as they continued in a line out into the water! Unable to cross, Mike and Freddie determined to navigate their way along whatever detour they could calculate. They made it to Bosanska Krupa but lost 63 minutes in the process. The going was harder still for John and Joe, who lost 147 minutes by the time they found the finish control while the Hemsley/Easton Peugeot demonstrated the beginnings of a problem that would come to plague them for the remainder of their rally: the car's rear shock absorbers failed, which in turn led to damage to the differential. A check of the back axle revealed that the diff casing had breached, losing all its oil in the process. Topping up, they made it to Bosanska Krupa with 64 penalty points, changed the shocks, and proceeded onwards to the rest stop, service stop, and scheduled *parc fermé* at Monza in Italy. All the while John mulled over why the shocks had failed in the first place.

Thoroughly rested after Monza, the BAMA teams headed on to the start of the third European *prime,* the San Remo, which would run a fast 65 miles from Ville San Pietro to Camporosso in Italy, with drivers needing to negotiate dust, gravel, hairpins, and spectacular, albeit potentially distracting views! Mike and Freddie applied the principle of "steady-as-you-go," determined to keep everything together and thus enhance their chance of a Mexico finish. Thus, although 23 cars arrived at the finish control without penalty, No. 72 was 17 minutes down as they checked in at Camporosso, two minutes faster than John and Wally and four quicker than John and Joe.

From Italy, the rally headed into France and the fourth *prime,* the Alpine, which followed part of the international *Coupe des Alpes* rally route from what was little more than a rural French road junction, Les Quatre Chemins or "the four roads," to

The San Remo *prime*, April 1970 (courtesy Mike Wood).

Rouaine, via two passage controls and miles of narrow alpine roads. Mike observed: "A number of accidents and breakdowns occurred on this stage as a number of the competitors had forgotten that trying too hard in the opening days was a recipe for disaster. We were fine and covered the distance without any problems." Fine they were, although slower than their four teammates by 15 minutes or more at the Rouaine control.

A very long transport section took cars west from France, across Spain, and into Portugal for the final European *prime*, the Portuguese, which would follow some of the TAP Rally route starting at Arganil and finishing 45 miles later at Pampilhosa. On this stage, both the Preston/Bailey car and the Hemsley/Easton car experienced difficulties, albeit in very different ways. Mike was driving this *prime* and all was well to begin with, but as they climbed a steep track, the Peugeot's manual transmission failed and they came to a stop—Mike could quite simply not change gears. Ever the ingenious problem-solver, Freddie removed the transmission tunnel cover and identified the problem: a broken link between gear stick and gear selector arm. With deft use of a tire iron and a Tirfor winch, he was able to get the gears to shift, but Mike cautiously decided that keeping gear changes to a minimum would be prudent. Next, in the midday heat, all windows were open and in flew a huge bumblebee. Both were determined not to be stung, not least because the buzzing creature would leave its stinger behind once the deed was done, so much flapping and swatting ensued with Mike all the while hustling the car along the section, anxious not to stop lest they wouldn't be able to get going again! In this chaotic fashion they completed the *prime*, picking up 90 penalty points, and nursed the ailing Peugeot all the way to Lisbon and the European section's finish control, 46th out of a total of 71 surviving cars, having amassed 205 penalty points.

For John and Wally, the continuously stressed shock absorbers on their car, cause still unknown, almost had them over the edge of a 600-foot drop when, about halfway through the Portuguese *prime*, a sharp right-hander required more maneuverability than the beleaguered suspension would deliver. John explained: "A kaleidoscope of earth, rocks, clouds, and trees flashed past the windscreen and, seizing the only available opportunity, we leant the car hard against the rock face, modifying most of the right-hand side of the car in the process. Fortunately, apart from a rather drawn-out noise of tinkling glass, little damage appeared to have been done as the car didn't stop." Despite this dramatic turn of events, John and Wally finished the *prime* 20 minutes down and got to Lisbon with 173 penalty points, putting them in joint 35th place with the women's team of Patricia "Tish" Ozanne, Bronwyn Burrell, and Tina Kerridge. For their efforts, John Rhodes and Joe Minto performed best on the Portuguese, 18 minutes down on the allowable time, which meant they had accrued 227 penalty points by Lisbon and were in 49th position. In doing so, they ensured that all three BAMA teams had booked their passage to Rio de Janeiro.

There was, however, much remedial work to be done, certainly to No. 6 and No. 72, before they could be craned onto the SS *Derwent*, the freighter that would take the cars across the Atlantic to the Brazilian capital. The Hemsley/Easton Peugeot needed some of its body panels straightened out, while the Preston/Bailey car received swift repairs to its transmission at Lisbon's main Peugeot dealer, where the mechanics were extremely impressed at Freddie's dexterity! In addition, with astute foresight, John and Mike had arranged for their respective wives, Sue and Netta, to fly out to Lisbon from England, carrying a host of spare automotive parts for the cars, including replacement shock absorbers.

From Lisbon, a number of the professional works teams flew on to Rio to undertake further survey work of the route out of Rio and the subsequent *primes*. But for the BAMA team it was an opportunity to explore the sights and sounds of Portugal's capital, which they did. Eventually competitors were required to board a jetliner bound for Rio, however, so on May 1, 1970, off they flew to begin the next part of the adventure, even if, after the thrills and spills of the European *primes*, Wally Easton needed just a little bit of persuasion to carry on!

5

Rules and Regs

While a basic tenet of stage rallying is that of setting time allowances between points A and B—a car is allowed a specified time period to complete a section, and for every minute exceeding that time limit, a penalty point is given—in order to ensure a fair, safe, competitive, and controlled rally event, the application of rules and regulations is key. For example, there would be little point in a rally if competitors could skip checkpoints or swap cars and crews along the way! Even local club rallies require the expectation that competitors will comply with agreed-upon rules and regulations.

In addition to mapping out and documenting the route around Europe and South America—no mean feat in itself—the World Cup Rally's organizing committee needed to consider a myriad of requirements in order to make the event occur within a controlled environment. This environment would need to challenge competitors but not carelessly put lives at risk. Competition rules needed to enable cars with a range of engine power to compete, to allow both professional *and* privately entered teams to participate. Organizers had to clearly specify how performance would be judged and recorded.

Tony Ambrose's view that the organizing committee was top-heavy with folks who had no motorsports experience brought into sharp relief the absolute requirement that any rules and regulations needed the careful attention of people with experience—rallying experience in particular. In other words, despite the luminaries—such as England national soccer team manager Sir Alf Ramsey and *Daily Mirror* director H.W. Atkins—involved, this would most definitely be a job for those who knew a thing or two about rallies!

It is therefore a testimony to Ambrose, John Sprinzel, John Brown, Dean Delamont, and undoubtedly Mary Smith, Sprinzel's secretary, that the official regulations were as comprehensive as they were. Made available from September 1, 1969, they gave prospective competitors a detailed insight into what to expect and what was required, both of them and the vehicle or vehicles they intended to enter into the competition.

All competitors would be required to hold a valid competitions license and an International Driving Permit. Crews could comprise two, three, or four persons, and the minimum age of a competitor would be 17, while anyone under 21 would need to provide written consent from a parent or guardian. Unlike the 1968 Marathon, this rally would be open to any four-wheeled passenger vehicle, regardless of drivetrain configuration. In other words, both two- and four-wheel drive cars would be eligible for entry. How competitors prepared their vehicles and what arrangements they made for servicing and support during the rally was up to them, but a car's engine block, body/chassis unit, and gearbox/transmission/differential casing(s) could not be changed or replaced during the event; organizers would ensure these items would be specifically marked at commencement of the rally and spot checks at undisclosed points on the route would be carried out to ensure compliance. In addition, all vehicles were required to carry a fully working fire extinguisher, a first aid kit, a red reflective warning triangle, and a crash hat for each team member. All cars would be required to have safety belts fitted for all team members.

All competitors would be required to follow only the prescribed route, as laid out in the official roadbook, and to ensure they would present their vehicle at each place listed in the order they were listed and within the specified times. All competitors would be required to present their vehicles at Wembley Stadium in London on April 18, 1970, to receive start formalities and undergo scrutineering to ensure crews and vehicles met all specified requirements. The following day, on April 19, the first car would be required to depart at 10:30 and the remainder at one-minute intervals thereafter; cars would run in order of the number they would be allocated at public ballot two weeks after the entry list closed on February 1, 1970.

All crews would be required to report at specified time controls as scheduled in the roadbook, and penalties would be incurred if a team reported in after this time. These penalties would be assigned in hours and minutes and would be applied as follows:

- A penalty point of one minute for every minute, or part thereof, that a team exceeded the time allowed between time controls
- A penalty point of one minute for every minute, or part thereof, that a team exceeded the time allowed for a *prime*
- Penalty points of three hours for failure to attend a control within its scheduled operating hours
- Penalty points of six hours for failure to arrive at or depart from a control in the specified direction or route
- Disqualification for failure to present at a time control, *prime* start control, or *prime* finish control within specified times
- Penalty points of three hours for failure to display official rally plates or numbers where required
- Penalty points of 12 hours for breaching *parc fermé* regulations
- Disqualification for replacing a marked component of a vehicle
- Disqualification for reducing, increasing, or replacing crew members, with an exception for emergencies where a team is assisting stranded competitors or injured persons
- Disqualification for failing to book out of a time control within 60 minutes of the scheduled time
- Disqualification for loss of a team's roadbook

Competing vehicles would be classified as per FIA formulae—1300 cubic centimeters (79 cubic inches) or less, 1301 to 1600 cc (79 cu to 97 cu), 1601 to 2000 cc (97 cu to 122 cu), 2001 to 3000 cc (122 cu to 183 cu), and 3001 cc (183 cu) or greater.

Due

(c) At SOFIA a competitor's time of arrival will also be his time of departure.

(d) At Time Controls competitors failing to restart within 60 minutes of their scheduled time will be excluded.

18. Passage Controls

(a) Passage Controls may be set up at any places named as being on the route to verify that competitors follow the official route.

(b) These Controls will always be in such a position as to be obvious to competitors who are on the correct route.

(c) These Controls may also check vehicle and crew identification marks and tags. No extra time allowances will be made for this operation.

19. Primes

(a) These will be of between 100 km. and 1000 km. in length, and will be timed to the minute. The time allowance for each Prime will be notified to competitors by the Organisers at the previous Time Control, and competitors will be penalised per minute taken in excess of this, but not for taking less time.

(b) Competitors may book into Prime Start and Finish Controls at any time that these are open. Opening and closing times will be stated in the Road Book.

(c) Competitors will not be booked into the start of Primes at less than one minute intervals.

(d) Primes in Latin America will be largely on controlled roads, but the Organisers cannot accept any responsibility for ensuring that any part of the route is free of local traffic and animals.

(e) No competitor will be permitted to start a Prime unless all crew members are wearing crash helmets and safety belts.

(f) Primes will generally include Passage Controls.

20. Control Points and Timing

(a) All Controls will be indicated by a control signboard.

(b) The Control area will extend for a minimum of 25 yards in each direction of the control signboard.

(c) No work of any nature other than washing of windows, lights and numbers and replacement of mud flaps may take place in any Control area.

(d) Only the official time declared by the controller will be recognised. No subsequent dispute or claim will be considered in this respect.

12

Rally rules and regs with John Sprinzel's handwritten notes (courtesy Ted Taylor).

Any entrant seeking eligibility for the Owner's Award would need to demonstrate documentary evidence, prior to February 1, 1970, that their vehicle was the personal property of one of the team members. Any vehicle that was privately owned but entered or sponsored by a commercial establishment, individual, or organization would still be eligible for the Private Owner's Award, as long as those institutions were not, nor the individual a representative of, manufacturers of motor vehicles. To be eligible for the women's prize, a team must be exclusively female.

Team entries would be categorized as manufacturers teams, national teams, and club teams. Manufacturers would be permitted to enter teams of up to five vehicles of their own manufacture. National automobile clubs and other clubs and associations would be permitted to enter teams of up to three vehicles.

Requirements for both standard and special *parc fermé* were specified, whereby when cars were placed in *parc fermé*, no repairs, changes, or renewing of consumables such as oil or brake fluid would be allowable. Crews would only be allowed to return to their cars 30 minutes before a given restart time. In special *parc fermé*, competitors would be allowed to undertake any required work on their vehicles, provided they only used tools, parts, and consumables that had been carried in the vehicle. Furthermore, no competitor could leave while work was being undertaken.

The rally's awards were defined within the regulations as being for competitors in general classification, i.e., prizes would be given to the crews that achieved first, second, third, fourth, and fifth place, as well as prizes for entrants who achieved first, second, and third place in their classification as private entrants. All-female crews would also be awarded first, second, and third place prizes. There would also be awards for classes, as described above, plus manufacturers teams, national teams, club teams, and for winning performances on stages and *primes*.

Other regulations related to documentation and legal requirements, crew identification, control points and timing, advertising, results and protests, and insurance and indemnities. Most prudently, the regulations also included an important warning: competitors were strongly encouraged to be aware that parts of the route would take them up to altitudes of almost 16,000 feet and that medical advice was highly recommended!

No fools they, the six British Army Motoring Association officers had taken heed of this warning and were ready for driving through the clouds in South America. First, however, they would have to get there!

6

Shocks and Surprises
(Part Two)

As competitors made their way to the docks at Rio de Janeiro to collect their vehicles, now unloaded onto the quayside, they began to recognize just what lay ahead. Mike Bailey recalled: "It was at this point that we began to realize what we would be confronted with over the next two weeks: the distances were huge, the average speeds beyond belief and the physical endurance we were expected to endure all came together at the same time." The hustle and bustle of the rally's restart, first ceremonial and then, some miles later, the real start, actually served as a distraction. However, as soon as they were flagged away, they stopped to fit all new tires as a precaution and, in doing so, managed to sheer a wheel stud, thus leaving only three studs for securing by lug nut on their front left-hand wheel. Without a spare stud in sight, it would be a risk they would have to take.

Cars were now headed southwest into Brazil, leaving asphalt roads behind and running instead on wide, flat dirt roads. Their destination was Ventania and the start of the first South American *prime*, the Parana, which would cover 125 miles of twisting dirt track. Mike recalled how this felt like a European section and that, although the time allowed—90 minutes—was impossible, Freddie completed it without incident, accruing 33 penalty points with the Rhodes/Minto car just one minute slower on 34. The Hemsley/Easton 504 was still misbehaving, however, which hindered their progress and cost them 43 points at the finish control at Bateias. Worse, however, was to come.

From Bateias, the route took competitors southeast to the coast and then south to Ituporanga, the start of the next *prime*, the Rio Grande. The stage was originally slated to stretch 240 miles to Canela, but surveys immediately prior to the rally's restart exposed flooding and associated obstacles, which forced organizers to cut it by half, running only to São Joachim. Shortened though it may have been, however, the rough going still knocked out a number of cars. John Hemsley explained: "All the Peugeot 504s were now beginning to suffer from rear suspension troubles due to weak shock absorbers, and, as a result, two of the 504s dropped out … with smashed rear differential casings." In fact, although reports differ about the demise of the 504s driven by the British father-and-son team Derek and Bob Currell, with Frank Bryan, and by the Argentinian team of Enrique and Juan Esteguy and Emil Ipar, both missing in action before the Parana *prime* finish control, by the end of the Rio Grande *prime*, the rear suspension malaise already reported by Hemsley had claimed BAMA teammates John Rhodes and Joe Minto. Given that the Royal Fusiliers' 504 of Moorat and Shaw had also experienced problems with its rear shock absorbers, it was clear that something was wrong with the cars. But what?

Perhaps with this in mind, Mike and Freddie tackled the Rio Grande with a certain amount of restraint, although Mike recalled that the biggest challenge here was actually the presence of civilian traffic, motorized and horse-drawn, which appeared without warning around every bend! In this fashion, No. 72 made it to São Joachim with a loss of 94 minutes, while John and Wally were just four minutes slower. Mike reflected: "Whereas the works supported entries could afford to go hell for leather in the knowledge that their support crews would keep them going, we had no such support other than arbitrary support from Peugeot agents in South America, of which we availed ourselves on a number of occasions."

The rally now moved on southwards to Porto Alegre before turning southwest to Rosário do Sul and then south again across the Uruguayan frontier to Tacuarembó and the start of the 125-mile Uruguay *prime*. While Mike and Freddie arrived at the start control without incident, the Hemsley/Easton 504 most certainly did not! The car continued to act up, this time requiring a five-hour stoppage while Easton stripped and repaired the fuel injection pump. Then, as they tried to make up for lost time, a simple navigation error took them speeding into a village not on the route. Quickly realizing his error, John searched for and actually found a roadside police officer, his intention being to request and receive corrective directions. Unfortunately, the BAMA duo had no Spanish and the Uruguayan policeman no English, and the universal language of sign and gesture also failed them badly. Concluding they were getting nowhere, John demonstrated thanks and farewell as best he could and drove away. A very big mistake as, the next moment, a hail of police bullets ricocheted off the beleaguered Peugeot, John desperately trying to speed off down the street. In standard cops-and-robber car-chase fashion, a bullet found a rear tire and the already heavy handling of the 504 got considerably worse and the car could go no further. Immediately, a swarm of police officers descended and John was swiftly escorted to the cells, Wally all but cowering in the passenger seat footwell! "Apparently the rows of oxygen bottles and various jack handles stacked across the back of the car looked to them like bombs and guns," John explained. "The local constable from whom we had innocently asked help had jumped to the conclusion that we were Uruguayan guerrillas who were apparently in the habit of hopping over the border to engage in the local week-end sport of raiding a Brazilian village!" Now, the language barrier that had enabled these proceedings compounded matters further as neither interrogator nor interrogated could understand the other and it was only after the intervention of the "local Police Commissioner's glamorous wife," who had a little English, that John was released from judicial clutches and allowed to get back to the stricken Peugeot and Wally who, not for the first time, was wondering what the hell he had signed up for! Later examinations of the car revealed "five more bullet holes in the rear body work. By some miracle none went into the fuel tank!"

Not surprisingly after all this excitement, undertaking an extremely difficult speed section on the South American leg of the London to Mexico World Cup Rally paled in comparison, and between Tacuarembó and Salto, John dropped 44 minutes to Freddie's 37. After all the drama, the transport stage to Uruguay's capital proved long and dull, albeit picturesque, and both BAMA cars made it safely to Montevideo, the arrival control, *parc fermé*. "There'd been terrific panic … and Peugeot sent an aeroplane with a whole lot of spares and there were … fuel injectors … complete fuel injector pumps, the whole thing," John recalled. "I think he flew out 20, we replaced ours and I still remember there were 18 fuel injectors, which in those days cost £380 [$770] apiece! … They were thrown in the ditch when we left!" Mike and Freddie would live to regret not grabbing a replacement set.

The following day, cars drove onto a ferry to cross the River Plate to Argentina and Buenos Aires. Out of 52 surviving cars, Mike and Freddie were sitting in 30th place, having lost 459 minutes. Primarily because of the errant fuel injector in Brazil, John and Wally were in 41st position with 785 penalty points.

From Buenos Aires, competitors were required to get themselves to Saladillo and the start of the 200-mile Pampas *prime*, which would offer up all-invasive dust, all-consuming mud, or both, depending on weather conditions, which were unpredictable at best. Despite a slight contretemps between Mike and Freddie and some local youths at a gas station (which the rally duo won), both BAMA teams arrived at the start control in good time and were met by a servicing team organized by Peugeot Argentina. Peugeot France had arranged for its Argentinian arm, primarily there to support the cars entered by Argentinians, to service and repair any of their products being run by other countries. Thus, the Peugeot service manager ensured resources were at the BAMA team's disposal, but it was here that a few marked differences between the British Peugeots and their South American counterparts were noted, including the fact that while the British-spec cars were fuel-injected, the Argentinian-manufactured cars were using standard carburation. Another subtle variation was that while the BAMA cars had four studs per wheel, the Argentinian cars had three. A third variation would reveal itself later.

At Saladillo, Mike noted that despite stocking up on Koni shock absorbers in Rio, the persistent issue with the cars' rear suspension had rapidly diminished their supplies to just two sets for front and rear, and it was with this niggling concern that both cars headed out into the Argentinian pampas for not one but two speed tests, the second being the 380-mile Trans-Argentine *prime*, which would deposit competitors at Bariloche, the ski resort in the foothills of the Andes. First, however, was the Pampas *prime*, which, for once, Wally and John completed without incident. Mike and Freddie were also going well; Mike recalled that, despite warnings of roughness and dust, the Argentinian authorities had obviously wanted to cast its road in a good light for foreign visitors and had been busy grading! Barreling along in a car they really thought was going well, 30 miles in a sudden realization had them doing a U-turn and speeding back the way they'd come! They'd somehow managed to forget their toolkit at the Saladillo control, and being caught without tools in the middle of Patagonia at night was a risk they didn't care to take. Hopeful the control would still be fully resourced, they were disappointed to find all but the service manager had packed up and departed, taking the wayward toolkit with them. Fortunately, said service manager managed to assemble a semblance of replacements and the duo was eventually back on the road, relieved but also frustrated that they had added 60 miles to the stage and therefore who knows how many penalty points!

Into the next *prime*, the Trans-Argentine, and they were again met with graded roads where there should have been rough going, yet now the car was devouring the last of the Koni shocks. Mike described the effects as "almost unmanageable, the wheels pumping up and down without any damping, rather like driving on marbles." The car was "slipping and sliding all over the place." The Peugeot service team had provided them with standard specification shock absorbers, not the enhanced Koni items, so these were duly fitted. They were, however, designed for normal road conditions, so how long they would last was unknown. Regardless, they made it within time thresholds to Bariloche, as did John and Wally.

The route now took them up and over the Puyehue Pass at 4,000 feet before descending into Chile and the long run up the Pan-American Highway to Santiago. Although military fit, both Mike and Freddie were now really feeling tired and fell into a half-hourly change of driving duties. "We were suffering from double vision and the loss of concentration," Mike recalled. "On one occasion I was driving and Freddie was asleep. It was dark and we suddenly came up behind a large lorry [truck] with only one taillight, how I managed to miss it I will never know. ... I awoke Freddie and at the first opportunity we changed over drivers. Unbeknown to each other at the time, we were waking each other up every 10 minutes or so telling each other that he had been asleep for over half an hour!"

Santiago offered competitors an enforced stop, time to work on battered cars, and, above all, rest! Both BAMA teams arrived within allowances, clocked in at the arrival control, found their hotel, and collapsed into bed. Forty-three cars had reached the Chilean capital, with Freddie and Mike in 37th place and Mike and Wally 41st. Rest was exactly what all competing teams needed at Santiago because, as John pointed out, what came next would be "some of the toughest stages ever devised in a modern rally"!

The Chilean *prime* was yet another casualty of meteorological intervention. Severe snow blocked what should have seen the stage traversing the Andes range at the 15,600-foot Agua Negra Pass—this was where Mike "Speedy" Broad was dispatched to single-handedly set up a hastily rescheduled finish control at Illapel. Upon receipt of the revised instructions, both BAMA teams set off from Santiago and headed north. Mike described the revised, 121-mile section as over "rough, undulating track at a planned average speed of 81 mph, quite impossible to achieve!" Nevertheless, both cars arrived at Illapel without anything untoward happening, Freddie and Mike losing 96 minutes and John and Wally 104. In fact, all but one car completed the revised Chilean, that being the Royal Fusiliers' 504 of Moorat and Shaw, tellingly taken out by a shattered differential casing.

From Illapel, the revised route took cars southwards again before turning east and up, ascending the slopes of the Andes to cross back into Argentina via a rail track tunnel, which authorities had suspended for its proper use for the duration of the rally transit. Cars climbed up and into the snowy landscape, some vehicles' engines struggling with depleted oxygen levels. "Entering the tunnel from the blinding light of the snow-covered mountains into the narrow unlit tunnel was quite unnerving,"

Mike recounted. "The combined effect of all the head- and spotlights made no difference to what we could see, which was not very much. The end of the tunnel was not visible and it was extremely difficult to see where we were going." Competitors emerged blinking into daylight and crossed the frontier back into Argentina. Now the really tough stuff would begin.

Further last-minute changes now meant competitors needed to make their way to San José de Jáchal for the start of the Gran Premio *prime*, 480 miles of narrow, rough, high-altitude, and extremely dangerous unsealed roads, which were little more than tracks, with sheer drops into oblivion, and all at an average set speed of nearly 64 miles per hour! To compound matters, much of the route would need to be executed in darkness, although this at least prevented competitors from really seeing what beckoned if a wrong move was made.

This stage was a real test for Mike and Freddie—or rather the rarified atmosphere was!—even with their altitude training. As "night fell and the track twisted and turned," Mike explained, "Freddie was driving and although I had told him we ought to be on oxygen, he chose to poo-poo the idea. I felt he was driving recklessly for, all at once, he was aiming the car at what appeared to be the track in front when I bellowed 'right!' We avoided a solid black rock face by the skin of the teeth, very scary!!" Despite this near miss, plus a slip-up that had the 504's front wheels all but hanging over the edge, *à la* the 1969 movie *The Italian Job*, Preston and Bailey endured the hardships and made it to the finish control at La Viña three hours and 24 minutes later than the desired target time but still within the allowable threshold. Mike and Wally thumped and bumped their way along the 480 miles, all the time aware that the car was ailing. Yet somehow, they too hung on and also reached La Viña within the limit, albeit as one of the slowest finishers.

Gritting their teeth, the two teams continued onwards and upwards to the Bolivian frontier and Villazón, the starting point of the next *prime*, the Bolivian Coffee, a 270-mile endurance test commencing at 11,300 feet and finishing at Potosí, at an elevation of 13,400 feet. Mike recalled that fatigue was now the enemy, and they both wrestled with weariness and the substantially reduced performance from the 504, its engine gasping for more oxygen! This heady cocktail of challenges saw them clock in at the finish control two hours and 26 minutes slower than the organizers' target time of five hours.

For John and Wally, the exhausting slog from La Viña saw their 504's problems begin to escalate. "We began to lose oil from a large crack in the rear gearbox casing and as this necessitated topping up the gear box every hundred miles or so, we had to take off the sump [oil pan] guard and rope it to the roof," John explained. They stopped and started their way to the Bolivian frontier, where they located a mechanic's shop and, sacrificing four hours, had the entire engine and transmission out, attended to, and reinstalled. In this fashion, they too clocked in at the Bolivian Coffee *prime* start control and, through sheer determination, arrived at Potosí within the allowable threshold. As with the Gran Premio, however, in unofficial results published immediately afterwards, there is no mention of No. 6's time, which suggests that if it was not *the* last car in before the control closed, it was certainly not far off!

Thus, two shaken and stirred BAMA Peugeots ascended to La Paz and a chance for their occupants to sleep in real beds. Mike recalled that, coming into the city and making for the airport, where Speedy had set up the arrival control, the welcoming crowds were enormous and the scene chaotic. "It was all very danger-ous when suddenly out from the crowd a young man rushed out. I was driving and it was quite impossible for me to miss him. He caught the front wing and spun off to the side. … I thought about stopping but others in the crowd waved us on and not to become involved."

Thirty-nine cars are recorded as having reached the elevated city, the fastest hav-ing incurred a total of just 232 penalty points, which meant three hours and 52 min-utes slower than the overall target time by this stage, with the slowest 44 hours and a minute beyond the target, which represented 2,641 penalty points! The slightly oxygen-starved cautiousness of Mike and Freddie placed them 27th here, with a total of 1,445 penalty points, while the extensive repairs required by No. 6 placed John and Wally in 35th place with 1,812 points. Once again, sleep was the essential ingredient here as there would be absolutely no letup for the BAMA four on leaving La Paz.

Most contemporary rally "special stages" were relatively short speed tests over challenging terrain, such as forest tracks or dusty desert trails or winding alpine passes, perhaps in snow. Seasoned rally professionals and experienced amateurs would have been familiar with a special stage through the mountains on the Monte Carlo Rally or muddy forests on the RAC Rally. Taxing of course, especially at night, but relatively short in design to offer the chance to use speed, as well as dexterity, to keep points to a minimum while showcasing the very best. For the London to Mex-ico endurance rally, even the European speed stages were relatively short with only one stretching for more than 100 miles. Now, here in South America, high in the Andes, as competitors made their way to the Peruvian frontier at Desaguadero and the shores of Lake Titicaca, they were faced with the almost unimaginable challenge. Beginning at Cusco, the Peruvian city synonymous with both ancient Killke and Inca civilizations, the rally now asked competitors to endure the Route of the Incas *prime*, a 560-mile, twisting combination of dirt, rock, and pothole, the trail winding back and forth and up, offering jaw-dropping views and nerve-shattering, unshielded drops into the abyss below—and all this to be completed in a target time of 11 hours. A very *special* speed trial indeed!

Although the rally was met for the most part by at worst curiosity and at best unbridled enthusiasm, not all local folks were thrilled with the prospect of nearly 40 cars hurtling across their terrain. "On the unsealed road" leaving La Paz, Mike recalled, "we were presented by a row of large rocks lined up across the road in such a manner as to suggest that the cars should follow the road to the right. The roadbook, on the other hand, indicated the road to the left. We followed the instructions in the roadbook which turned out to be the correct thing to do as we were told later that a group of local individuals had decided that they did not want the rally to go through their land and had tried to divert the cars in another direction!"

An uneventful end run to Cusco brought Mike and Freddie to the entrance of the *prime*, Mike wondering whether their supplies of oxygen would last all the way through. With their roadbook stamped and signed by British rally driver Donald Morley, they began the *prime*, a drive that felt like it would never end. Progress was

A perilous passage, Peru, May 1970 (courtesy Mike Wood).

without incident until, maybe slightly hypnotized by how the road snaked forward and back above and below them, Mike misjudged a bend and the Peugeot nosed over the edge and came to a halt. Scrambling out of the car, the duo surveyed the scene and realized they were resting on a rock, which had stopped the car from hurtling down the side of the valley! What to do? Utilize the trusty Tirfor winch! Quickly retrieving it from the trunk, Mike secured the cable to a rock on the other side of the track, attached the other end to the car, and began to pump the lever. Suddenly, with a burst of agony, Mike's back went and he collapsed roadside. Imploring Freddie to take over, he lay there waiting for the pain to subside. Gradually, the car shifted a little but then the pair became aware of a rumble. Searching for its source, they realized a bus was trundling towards them, right where the cable stretched and Mike lay prone! Frantic and painful maneuvers quickly ensued, man and chain safely removed from harm's way but, on sizing up the situation, the bus driver stopped and, with added assistance from no doubt fascinated passengers, the car was returned to the road, pointing in the right direction!

On they went, mile after mile, Mike gingerly testing his sore back in the confines of the car, and all was well until, as they drove through a small town, the severe camber of a crossroads took them unawares and they damaged the car when it briefly lifted off! The handling now substantially impeded, they limped on to Huancayo and the finish of the stage. But now disaster struck as the car began to lose power. They continued as best they could, and although provisional results do not reference No. 72 as a finisher of the Route of the Incas *prime*, Mike does recall clocking in and nursing the car down to Lima where investigations revealed a failed fuel injector.

"Because there had been no spares in the UK at the start of the event and no suitable alternative being available locally, we were out of the rally," Mike explained. "This was a great disappointment as the car had performed so well up to that point. We were left completely deflated." Freddie opted to fly back to the UK from Lima, but Mike's adventure wasn't quite over yet!

Now it was just John and Wally left to fly the flag for BAMA, which they continued to do, collecting 2,176 penalty points at Huancayo and reaching the rest stop and *parc fermé* at Lima in 28th position out of 30. "In Lima, we were greeted by the first rain that had fallen for 45 years, and a strong tremor at about four o'clock in the morning," John recalled. "The defence attaché who saw us off the next morning made a significant and unfortunate prophecy when he remarked that they were due for a major earthquake." In fact, three weeks after the rally departed, what has now become known as the Great Peruvian Earthquake caused unparalleled destruction to the north of Lima and claimed 70,000 lives.

The rally now took competitors 550 miles north to the border with Ecuador and the 250-mile Ecuador *prime*. John and Wally again hustled and scrambled the Peugeot along, arriving at the Cuenca control 27th out of 29 finishers. All that was left now was 730 miles of Pan-American Highway towards Cali in Colombia, where organizers had decreed that any car arriving within the time threshold would be classed as overall finishers of the rally, even if another 2,800 miles lay between there and Mexico City!

No doubt with this in mind, surviving cars and crews pressed on, determined to reach the finish point. John and Wally were no exception, making steady progress up to and across the border into Colombia and north towards Cali via Pasto and Popayán. Suddenly, somewhere beyond Pasto, all hell broke loose. "We rounded a corner in drizzling rain at dawn to find a landslide actually in progress," John recalled, "blocking the road with huge boulders, augmented by a large articulated lorry carrying out complicated avoiding maneuvers on the wrong side of the road." John was faced with a split-second choice—collide with a fast-moving landslide or with a slow-moving truck. He plumped for the latter: "In a last desperate attempt to dive underneath the trailer, we came to a dramatic halt underneath a pile of iron-mongery."

Reflecting on the accident almost 50 years later, John's militarily trained pragmatism is still evident; he actually sees the funny side to what could so easily have been a catastrophic event. As it was, while John crawled out of the wreck through the gaping hole where the windshield should have been, Wally had a number of cuts and contusions caused by broken glass and John had to help him extricate himself from the battered Peugeot. Wally "tottered off to the verge of the road to pick pieces of glass out of his shoulder," John explained, "whilst I went back to inspect the wreckage. It didn't look too promising: the roof at the front end of the car was squashed down to the level of the bonnet [hood], which had disappeared altogether. The front of the car had been completely demolished and all the electrical relays were squashed and emitting dangerous-looking sparks as the wiring was short-circuited by the crushed metalwork. The front left-hand suspension had been folded right back under the passenger seat and the battery had been thrown through the windscreen [windshield].

There didn't seem to be any glass left in the front of the car, and quite a lot of the body had disappeared as well. It was bad."

At this point, almost anyone else would have seen the accident, seen the car for what it was, and given up, resigning themselves to a long wait for a wrecking truck and all the complexities of getting body, soul, and crumpled metal home to the UK. Not Major John Hemsley, however, who retrieved hawsers from the crumpled 504's trunk and set about securing them to the front and rear of the car. Next, calling upon the assistance of two trucks that obviously had nowhere to go while both earth and steel blocked transit, John orchestrated a "push-me-pull-you" effort, one truck pulling the Peugeot's rear, the other dragging the car's front, until the bent 504 was looking, well, a little straighter! More ingenuity aligned a sagging suspension strut, but now Wally and John were faced with an almost insurmountable challenge. "We had no steering wheel and still 200 miles to go to qualify," John recalled, suppressing a chuckle. "Time was running out. Nevertheless, with the aid of a hammer kindly loaned to us by a Russian service crew, and some swift first aid on a rather second-hand looking co-driver, we managed to get going again, steering with the spokes of what remained of the wheel and refilling our highly modified cooling system at frequent intervals from streams along the route." Thus, as a testimony to determination and problem solving, No. 6 squeaked and rattled into Cali and qualified as a finisher of the London to Mexico World Cup Rally.

John, however, was not about to give up just yet! Determined as he was to not only get to Panama City via the sea and canal voyage but to then carry on to Mexico City, he set about shoring up the crumpled Peugeot. First, any panels that in their pummeled state might further interfere with onwards motion were beaten back into shape. Then, to support the car's front section, a length of railroad track was welded into the side of the car. Finally, as John explained, the tops of the MacPherson telescopic struts were joined by two parallel metal bars to hold the track constant. "The frame was so distorted that it was impossible to open the doors that were left, so we had to climb in and out of the windows. A 19-inch steering wheel requisitioned from a local lorry [truck] completed our repairs and we were all set for Mexico."

Meanwhile, with the Bailey/Preston Peugeot scheduled for shipping back to England and Freddie scheduled for jetting back, with farewells bade, Mike flew up to Panama City and then took a taxi along the route of the Panama Canal, rejoining disembarking rally competitors at Cristóbal. "Amongst the retirees heading home was a Canadian police Mercedes 220D crewed by Malcolm Wilson and James Walker," Mike recalled. "I knew both these guys from earlier times when we rallied in Scotland in the Scottish Internationals in the 60s. … They offered to give me a lift to Mexico City so that we could all attend the party at the end. There were no seats in the back of the car and I had to be content with the spare wheels and metal sub frame!"

Vowing to assist John and Wally wherever possible, Mike, James, and Malcolm, a.k.a. Jock, set off ahead of the rally in the big Benz sedan, and all went well until they reached David in Panama, about 35 miles east of the Costa Rican border. In the rear of the car, Mike was becoming increasingly aware of a knocking noise emanating from the right-hand rear wheel. Fearing it might be the suspension, Mike suggested they try and find a source of remedy. Spying a passerby, they asked if there was

No. 6—down but not out (courtesy John Hemsley).

a garage in the area that could assist. "Now bear in mind it was approaching midnight and the likelihood of finding a welder at that time of night seemed to be asking a bit too much," Mike recalled. "Surprise, surprise! The man directed us round the corner where he knew of someone who had an electric welding arc setup in his garage. Why not knock him up? The house was literally round the corner, about 100 yards off the main road through the town. The house was in darkness but a ring of the bell brought the owner to the door. He quickly understood our predicament and promptly opened up his garage and wheeled out the electric welding kit."

Quickly ascertaining that James and Jock were somewhat lacking in mechanical know-how, Mike set to work and welded a shock absorber bracket back onto the chassis. Then, just as they were finishing up, a second late-night "referral" to the welder arrived in the shape of the Timo Mäkinen/Gilbert Staepelaere works Escort! Mäkinen was in fifth place overall but a broken engine mount was threatening to ruin his chances. In double-quick time, Mike jacked the engine up from where it sat on the oil pan guard and welded the offending mounting plate back onto the remaining studs. "I was quite pleased with myself for keeping Timo on the road," Mike remembered. "At the party at the end of the rally Stuart Turner, head of Ford UK Rally Sport Department, approached me to express his gratitude for ensuring that Timo reached the finish in 5th position."

Meanwhile, John and Wally soldiered on in their mutant 504, pouring gallon upon gallon of oil into the transmission until, as John wryly commented, they "finally exhausted what must have been the total supply of gear oil in Costa Rica and seized the forward bearing of the prop shaft, at which point everything came to a juddering halt." Thus, somewhere along the penultimate *prime*, the Costa Rican, their rally came to an end. Mike and the Canadians followed the rally over the *prime* but failed to spot John and Wally so continued on to Mexico City. All were reunited at the celebrations before returning home.

John and Mike were of course disappointed to have broken down before Mexico, even if John and Wally had the distinction of being classed as one of the 23 finishers at Cali, but they also felt happy and privileged to have had the opportunity to compete on this extraordinary event. "Our only regret was that the remainder of our team had been forced to fall out through suspension troubles, and so many of the people who had given us their help at home had been unable to come with us to South America," John reflected.

As for the bug that appeared to afflict all the European 504s? The devil, as it turned out, was in the detail of the rear suspension's design, combined with precautionary measures—a skid plate—employed to protect the differential. No doubt as a significant evolution of suspension technology, Peugeot eschewed the conventional, tried-and-tested setup of coil springs with hydraulic shock absorbers up front and solid axle with Panhard rod at the rear, which had underpinned the 404 model, in favor of MacPherson struts and coil springs at the front and semi-trailing arms with coil springs at the rear. John explained: "At the engine end you had a gearbox, which had a long rear nose, … aluminium casing and from the nose of the gearbox was attached the driveshaft, which was a single driveshaft, there was no intermediate bearing of any sort, that went straight down to the back axle, to the UJ (universal joint) at the back and it was all enclosed within a steel torque tube. Now, the torque tube was attached to the aluminium casing … and the back of the differential. What happened was … we were coming down and we were hitting the skid plate on the ground and the shock was being transmitted all the way up the torque tube to the aluminium nose of the gearbox, which was then cracking." John became aware that the Argentinian 504s had not had this problem, however, and, upon enquiry, he learnt that the Argentinians were aware of the potential weakness and had stuck with the conventional 404 setup!

Hindsight is, of course, a wonderful thing.

7

If You're Not on the List…

From the summer of 1969 and into 1970, the *Daily Mirror* steadily stoked interest in the World Cup Rally. Prospective competitors were invited to obtain, complete, and submit application forms for the event from June 1969, and, working in partnership with the rally's organization committee, the *Mirror* launched their publicity campaign, announcing and reporting on expressions of interest from both professional teams and determined privateers alike as they arrived at headquarters.

In addition to Moskvič, Ford GB, and BLMC announcing their intention to field teams, such was the potential for global publicity leading up to and during the rally that, in September 1969, it was claimed that Ford USA also planned to enter. The *Daily Mirror* reported that "talks now underway in the US indicate that Ford of America are likely to enter a team of Mavericks—one crewed by women."[1] Talks obviously proved unsuccessful and there was ultimately no official Ford USA presence in the rally, although there would be a privately entered Ford USA product, to be driven by a co-ed team. As with the 1968 London–Sydney Marathon, there would also be a sole U.S. entrant, this time taking full advantage of the official allowance that both two- and four-wheel drive vehicles could compete.

In France, rally drivers René and Claudine Trautmann and Robert "Bob" Neyret began to investigate the possibility of independently entering the rally. Together with regular co-driver Jacques Terramorsi, Neyret had previously competed in the 1968 London–Sydney Marathon and, in 1969 and 1970, won the Moroccan Rally or *Rallye du Maroc*, the latter achieved while other competitors were exploring the delights of Lisbon during the London to Mexico Rally stopover! The Trautmanns were also hugely successful rally competitors—René was a former French rally champion while Claudine was a nine-time winner of the women's championship! It was obvious that the presence of these highly skilled professionals would bring considerable competitiveness to the event. Yet surprisingly, to begin with at least, René Cotton, head of Citroën's Competitions Department, wasn't interested in the World Cup Rally. It's safe to say that his ambivalence wouldn't last.

Among early private applicants for the rally were Ron Channon and Rod Cooper, who were to maintain the soccer theme as they invited fellow fans of their local team, Bristol City, to contribute $2.40 each to the Channon/Cooper effort; in return each donor would have their signature painted onto their Ford Cortina Lotus.

By the end of October, the *Mirror* was reporting that the entry list represented a truly international lineup, with applications received from entrants in 14 different countries. They also reported that at least five teams would be led by women. For fans of the 1968 London to Sydney Marathon, there would be some familiar faces: Australian rally stalwart "Gelignite" Jack Murray had thrown his hat into the ring, so those expecting to see fireworks at Wembley Stadium in April 1970 were not to be disappointed. Early reports that Kenyan Robin Hillyar, winner of the extremely tough East African Safari Rally in 1969, would be competing eventually proved unfounded, as did the claim that the British Royal Regiment of Fusiliers would be running a Ford Escort GT and that Peggy Preston, wife of British Army Motoring Association and soon-to-be competitor, Major Freddie Preston, would be taking on her husband and every other entrant in an all-women team. During the months that followed and even after the closing date had come and gone, the list of accepted applicants would shift and change as hopeful competitors hit their own roadblocks and insurmountable obstacles, which would eventually prevent them from lining up at Wembley. Regardless, by late October, almost half of the 120 places on offer had been filled, and there were still three months to go!

Despite the fact that Ford GB had now announced that hugely successful Finnish rally driver Timo Mäkinen as the latest member of their team for the rally, and the fact that British rally driver Tony Fall, who would go on to team up with soccer star Jimmy Greaves for Ford GB, had been reported as saying "It will be a man's rally. Any non-professional taking part will need to take a lot of advice … or he'll never reach South America,"[2] application forms from privateers continued to arrive at rally HQ. Bringing his experience of off-road racing and the Baja 1000 in California, Jeep dealership owner and Anaheim, California resident Brian Chuchua was determined to show how his expertly prepared Jeep Wagoneer would disadvantage other competitors, would "really come into its own on the rough roads of South America."[3] Chuchua teamed with Hertz car rental company employee and fellow Jeep Club member Richard Gould and Gould's acquaintance Bill Kirkland of West Coast Netting. Originally, motoring journalist and author John Thawley was to be third teammate, but his employer, Petersen Publishing, ultimately refused to release him. Chuchua prepared the Wagoneer himself. "It was standard, but we reinforced what we knew were the weak points of the car," he explained, mentioning the suspension in particular. "They used rubber bushings and we put in lubricated bushings where we could lubricate the car. We had the transmission gone through and had the shift points changed because it was an automatic and … didn't do anything to the engine that time." Perhaps an eyebrow raising sight on the starting ramp at Wembley, the "Yellow Buffalo" might yet prove itself an ideal automobile for traversing South and Central America!

Armed forces applications were also arriving, one of the first being from the British Royal Air Force (RAF) Motoring Association. Stating that their preparation had begun many months before and that they had identified a car to prepare, the RAF was trying to agree who would join Flying Officer Donald Soames-Waring in their Tecalemit fuel injected Ford Cortina GT. "This is a plum event and the crew will not only have to be experienced, they must have made some contribution to the association," Soames-Waring declared. "So far, we have not decided who will be the lucky men."[4]

The number of countries represented among the rapidly filling list of competitors

Brian Chuchua, California, 1969 (courtesy Brian Chuchua).

was increasing by the month, and just as British and Commonwealth Prince Michael of Kent would lend an air of royalty to the rally, so would Prince Bira of Thailand. Prince Bira began competing in motorsports in 1935 and drove in Formula One and Grand Prix events throughout the 1930s, '40s and '50s, driving for Maserati, Connaught, and Gordini. The prince was also an Olympic sailor. Newspaper reports announced Prince Bira's return to competitive motorsports in January 1970, stating that he would be taking up the role of technical adviser to one of two Thai-entered teams. Whether the Prince actually contributed to the entry or not is unknown, but the car, a BLMC 1800, would be crewed by Viscount Errington, 3rd Earl of Cromer, and Bill Heinecke, who had rallied together in the Far East. The World Cup Rally was to be their rallying "swansong," but, unfortunately, the noble 1800 failed to get to Wembley. Just a few weeks before departure, the viscount was involved in a serious automobile accident and the entry was withdrawn. Had it rolled down the ramp at Wembley, it would have had the distinction of being the only competing BLMC 1800 built from a brand new bodyshell; all other 1800s in competition were either rehabilitated entries from the 1968 London–Sydney Marathon or ex-dealership demonstration cars that had been rally-prepared from the ground up.

Perhaps more predictably, Porsche was by now making a presence in the growing lineup with two Italian brothers, Alfonso and Gianpiero Mondini, each entering a 911S. Initial reports that a third 911S had been entered by the British Royal

No. 27, the Porsche 911S of Alfonso Mondini (*driving*) and Giuseppe Bottaro, London, April 19, 1970 (courtesy Ted Taylor).

Navy came to nothing, although the proposed team, led by Lieutenant Commander Julian Mitchell, did go on to depart for Mexico City from Wembley in a BLMC 1800. The Italian Porsches were eventually joined by two more: British entrants Geoff Mabbs and Terry Hunter, both of whom had competed in the 1968 London–Sydney Marathon, Hunter in a Porsche, and French pair Eric Celerier and Michael Gauvain.

HRH Prince Michael of Kent's entry into the rally was officially announced in January 1970. Heralded as the first member of the British Royal Family to compete in an international motorsports event, Kent would compete in a Janspeed-prepared Austin Maxi with 1968 London–Sydney Marathon veteran Captain Gavin Thompson of the 17/21 Lancers and Captain Nigel Clarkson, who served with Kent in the Royal Hussars. Thompson had known Kent for quite some time, and when he found himself talking with Wylton Dickson about the possibility of competing, Thompson immediately thought of Kent and was thrilled when Kent enthusiastically agreed to the idea. However, when organizing committee member Tony Ambrose learnt that there was to be a prince among the rally men, he immediately feared that both the sponsoring *Daily Mirror* and the promoting Dickson could take advantage of the situation. "Dean [Delamont] and I felt it advisable to align HRH with the RAC," he wrote, "so as to minimize commercial exploitation."[5] According to Ambrose, he arranged for a private lunch with Kent, Thompson, London–Sydney Marathon competitor Andrew Hedges, and Delamont, in order to establish relationships and no doubt give every assurance that royal protocols and complete discretion were assured.

As the deadline for applications loomed, completed forms and entry fees continued to arrive, from all over the world. Competitors hailed from all corners—Kuwait,

Left: **Rodney Badham (courtesy Ken Green).** *Right:* **Rob Lyall (courtesy Ken Green).**

Thailand, Argentina, and even the small island of Antigua, which wholeheartedly and proudly supported their citizens Mike Tyrell and James "Jimmy" Fuller, who flew to England in January 1969 to collect their car, a Hillman Hunter, and embark on a recce of the European section. Also driving a Hillman, this time a GT, British entries Rodney Badham and Rob Lyall were receiving expert support in preparing their car from none other than Des O'Dell, former Rootes competitions team manager and one of the team behind the Hillman Hunter's victory in Sydney in December 1968. The Badham/Lyall entry would receive sole sponsorship from the electric fire and heater manufacturer Berry Magicoal; Badham and Lyall had known each other for many years and had previously competed together on a number of events. They had also competed in Rootes cars and knew most of the competitions department's fitters, so a Rootes/Chrysler vehicle was an obvious choice. Their car was prepared by Badham and the Midlands Rally Team following the 1968 London–Sydney Marathon-winning Hillman Hunter specification.

The closing date for applications came and went, and the committee embarked on the task of validating all entries in readiness for the draw to determine the rally's running order out of Wembley Stadium. The draw was made by England soccer team captain Bobbie Moore on February 12. Accompanied by Wylton Dickson, *Mirror* director H.W Atkins, and two young women in white mini-dresses, Moore used a tombola to indiscriminately select entries from its drum.

All in all, there were entries from 18 countries, and individual competitors hailed from many more. Alongside the manufacturer competitions team entries from Ford GB, British Leyland, and Moskvič, there were a host of privately and commercially sponsored entries as well as national teams. Not surprisingly, the country with the largest number of entries was Great Britain, but, representing South American countries, there were also six cars from Argentina, including three entered by Peugeot Argentina, an entry from Peru, a Bolivian national team entry, and four entries from Mexico, including three young men who decided that travelling all the way to London was the only way to drive home again—in an orange VW Bug.

8

El Vocho Abandonado

Among other things, a broken heart and a "little white lie" were instrumental in getting Mexicans Gabriel Maria Hinojosa Rivero, José Manuel "Pepe" Pérez Vega, and José Antoñio "Toño" Bárcena Compean to the starting ramp at Wembley Stadium in north London, England on April 19, 1970. The fact that these three young men were there at all was a testimony to determination, ingenuity, and simple generosity, not least because their attempt to compete in the London to Mexico World Cup Rally could so easily have failed at first refusal!

When he was eight years old, Gabriel and his family moved to Puebla's Calzada de los Fuertes, the road that leads to the forts of Guadalupe and Loreto, some 80 miles southeast of Mexico City. A mechanical engineer, Gabriel's father introduced him and his siblings to motorsports, often taking them to the motor racing at the Pablo L. Sidar airfield where they would strategically position themselves just where a tight bend led into the long fast straight that was, at other times, the runway! It was therefore with great excitement that Gabriel learnt that the Automobile Sports Club of Puebla, or CDAP, was to commence street races on the roads surrounding the two forts. Without a moment's hesitation, he and his friends José Manuel Pérez, affectionately known as Pepe, and Marco Arroyo volunteered their services to be official flag carriers. This in turn gave them the chance to attend the weekly CDAP meetings, listen to the stories, and bask in the club's revered atmosphere, complete with "hall of fame" photographs decorating the walls, commemorating countless Pan-American Race veterans including local Puebla hero Douglas Ehlinger who, at that time, had secured the highest place a Mexican driver had ever achieved on "The Pan American." Heady and evocative stuff, then, for Gabriel and Pepe, who were also afforded a degree of mentoring by the grown-up road-rally drivers.

At 17, Gabriel was invited to take a co-driver's position on a road rally and quickly established a reputation as a reliable and competent navigator. And so it was that, towards the end of 1969, at a CDAP meeting, talk turned to a rally of monumental proportions, a rally unlike any other. Organized in England, it would be run to celebrate the forthcoming soccer World Cup tournament, which was to be hosted by Mexico in 1970. Much excited discussion ensued, especially as the closing route of the rally would pass through Puebla. Imagine how it would be if members of the CDAP might actually compete! Gabriel recalled that suddenly, amidst the general chatter, one of the senior CDAP members, Mario González Cobián, turned his attention to Pepe, Marco, and him and informed them that he knew the senior executive of the

Puebla Volkswagen factory and intended to persuade him to provide a car for the rally. The three young men were even more astonished when Mario added that if VW wouldn't deliver, he would pay for a car himself!

Excitement quickly turned to cold, hard practicalities, however, as just having a car wouldn't instantly mean entry or qualification into the rally. Reconvening the following day, Gabriel, Pepe, and Marco considered the potentially insurmountable challenge of other costs: registration, plane tickets, expenses, and any equipment they might need. With little alternative, the young men agreed to call upon "the bank of mom and dad"—or at least Marco and Pepe did. Gabriel, being just one in a family of 11, was all too aware that spare cash was not a luxury at his parents' disposal. Instead, he offered the team his services as co-driver and navigator while also proposing to defer his imminent enrolment at university and instead use the time to scour Mexico City for commercial sponsorship. It would mean pounding the sidewalks, but surely one or two big corporations would be eager to highlight their profile in all the countries through which the rally would travel?

Unfortunately, the team's best-laid plans all but fell at the first hurdle. With great despondence, Marco informed the others that not only would his parents not provide any financial assistance, but they had quite emphatically forbidden him from competing at all! Better news came from Pepe's father, however, who felt that the rally might be the perfect antidote to his son's current unhappiness. Poor Pepe had wed his high-school sweetheart, but the marriage hadn't taken and his new wife had left him. What better way of distracting his son from heartbreak than sending him off on an international, 16,000-mile endurance rally? The fact that Pepe's father was a fairly wealthy businessman also didn't hurt, and he duly agreed to pay the rally registration fee.

Gabriel now had two tasks before him: post the money order to the Royal Automobile Club in London and hunt down some additional sponsorship. He placed the money order in an envelope, addressed it, and put it aside to be posted the following day. That evening he got a call from Pepe to say his father wished to see him. Gabriel was duly introduced to Pepe's father, who regretfully advised he could no longer meet the cost of registration. He then asked Gabriel whether he had already mailed the fee to London. With a split-second decision, Gabriel coolly explained that the money had indeed already been sent. In which case, said Pepe's father, there is nothing to be done and the men would just have to go ahead and compete! To this day, Gabriel's conscience still pricks … well, just a little.

There was no going back now, so thoughts turned to finding a third team member. What about Toño Bárcena? Gabriel had already navigated for Toño on a number of occasions; he was a good driver, so why not? Toño jumped at the chance, and with enthusiastic support from his brother and financial help from his parents, he joined the team. Next, Gabriel chose his moment and told his parents that he planned to miss a semester at university and instead relocate to Mexico City to drum up sponsorship. Of course, his parents were unhappy, but they had the resigned parental acceptance that he would go ahead anyway, so what could they do?

Full of hope, Gabriel began knocking on the doors of assorted oil, cigar, television, shock absorber, and other companies in the capital and met with any number

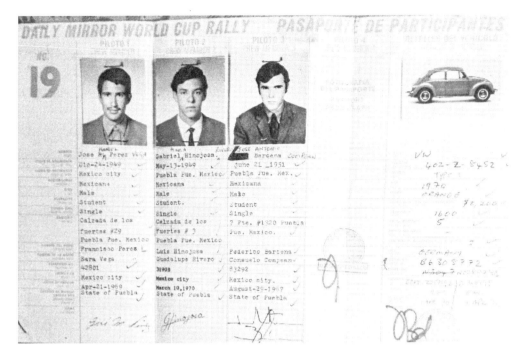

No. 19 Team Rally Passport (courtesy Gabriel Maria Hinojosa Rivero).

of marketing and advertising representatives. All were very interested and intrigued, but none were keen to put money where their mouths were. As Gabriel explained, other than for soccer, there was no tradition of commercial sponsorship in sport at that time in Mexico and he was thus met with no success whatsoever. Then, Volkswagen regretfully declined the chance to profile one of their products on this great rally. So that, it seemed, was that. But what had Mario said? If VW declined, he would pay for a car himself? True to his word, Mario did just that, which meant Gabriel really had no choice but to go, cap in hand, back to his father and ask if he could help. Fortunately for the team, his father decided to put his passion for all things automotive ahead of budgetary prudence and wrote a check, ruefully reflecting that Gabriel's mother would be less than happy. The team was now set. Next stop, VW's factory in Germany!

Gabriel was thrilled with his first ever time on a plane and full of anticipation for the next stage of the adventure. Landing in Frankfurt, they next needed to get to Wolfsburg and the VW factory where they would collect their car. Once again, good fortune shone upon the three young men: they were offered a ride with a couple of businessmen headed in that direction. Explaining upon arrival at the VW plant that they had come to collect their car, they were momentarily alarmed to hear that it wasn't ready. They were immediately reassured, however, that the car just needed some further preparation with special attention for the endeavor ahead; the automobile company explained that this was VW's gesture to support the rally team.

The following day, a VW Bug, in fetching factory clementine orange, was delivered to the team, with the express instruction to get the car to Munich where a workshop stood ready to add spot lamps, roll cage, and other assorted rally-fit necessities.

Once this was finished, the three set off on the road to England, with a quick detour to Paris, an opportunity they couldn't pass up! Driving all night, they emerged into daylight tired and hungry and were relieved to spy a restaurant open for business. Alas, the trio spoke no French and the proprietor had no Spanish; try as they might, their attempts to procure breakfast were thwarted. A sympathetic intervention by a young French student named Pierre revealed that, at this establishment at least, breakfast was over for the day! With a chastising rebuke directed at the diner's manager, the student hustled them away, taking them to purchase eggs and bread before inviting them to his apartment to eat and talk about student politics. Gabriel recalled that the apartment was full of Beatles records and photos of Che Guevara and that Pierre was fascinated by the trio's plans. The young Frenchman sent them, fed and watered, on their way to Calais and a ferry to the south English coast, but not before they that realized the file with all their necessary documentation, their passports, and all the international visas needed for the rally route was missing. Somehow, they had left them in a food store and, when they returned, were astonished to find the wallet still sitting there on the floor where it had been dropped!

The ferry departed in the cold, early hours of the morning, and Gabriel recounted that they had clearly not prepared for the chilly weather, their thin Mexican jackets offering little in the way of warmth. But, once again, good fortune intervened as Pepe struck up a conversation with a businessman returning from Switzerland. What were these three young Mexican men doing on a cross-channel ferry from Calais to Dover at three in the morning? Their explanation caught the man's imagination, and he promptly offered them welcome hospitality at his home in London. Gabriel marveled again at the kindness shown by strangers along the way.

Now, business turned to preparations for the rally itself and the documentation the organizers required. The registration fee was presented, and international rally permits, visas, and license plates all passed muster. Accordingly, the men were issued with their roadbook plus decals and metal plates displaying their entry number, drawn as they had been as No. 19. They then needed to source a Halda distance or trip meter and also decided to purchase a flexible map-reading light for nighttime navigation. The three were fascinated by the number of stores dedicated to the world of motorsports in London.

Not satisfied with the Bug's outward appearance, they determined that it needed a little bit extra, some references to who they were and where they had come from, like tattoos. Noticing some graffiti artists, they asked whether they knew of somewhere these painted adornments could be found. The artists went one better and set about painting the Bug's hood free of charge with the requested words and phrases— namely "Mexico," "CDAP," and best of all, and as a reference to how they came to be there at all, "*El Abandonado*," or "The Abandoned," an homage to Pepe's lost love! It wouldn't take long for the British print media to notice this sad story, which would have beneficial ramifications for the trio.

At last, the big day arrived and, joining the assorted highly tuned and meticulously constructed factory competitions team Fords and Triumphs, and expertly prepared privately entered BLMC 1800s and Citroëns, the orange VW Bug took its place in the holding area at London's Wembley Stadium, Gabriel feeling lifted by the car's

No. 19 leaves Wembley Stadium, London, April 19, 1970: (*left to right in car*) Gabriel Maria Hinojosa Rivero, José Antoñio "Toño" Bárcena Compean, José Manuel "Pepe" Pérez Vega (courtesy Guido Devreker).

fit-for-purpose spot lamps and the team's just-purchased rally jackets. Somewhat less confidence inspiring, however, was the simple fact that while the Bug had a full gas tank, the team had but $200 in their collective pockets and there were 16,000 miles yet to go! Undaunted, and cheered on by their graffiti artist friends who had come to see them off, they lined up the Bug in readiness, Gabriel reflecting on how they had been practically adopted by so many on their journey thus far and fascinated by the presence of four Russian teams, one of which presented them with pins of Lenin! Thus, with Pepe at the wheel, Gabriel in the navigator's seat, and Toño leaning forward between them from the rear seat, their entry was flashed up on the big screen, the flag went down, and *El Abandonado* pulled away and out of the stadium.

The VW made steady, unremarkable progress across Europe, the team getting their roadbook stamped within time limits at every passage control from England to Yugoslavia, as well as at the time control in Bulgaria. So far so good, but beyond Sofia lay a return into Yugoslavia, a trek down to Titograd, and the start of their first real test, the inaugural speed stage of the rally, the Montenegro *prime*, 50 miles of twists and turns, to be shared with civilian traffic, before a drop down to the Adriatic Sea by way of a series of perilous hairpin bends. And all this was to be achieved in a target time of 65 minutes, meaning an average speed of 54 miles per hour.

Driver Pepe and navigator Gabriel rose to the challenge, stewarding the little Bug to the finish control at Kotor only 18 minutes down, which meant they were quicker than 23 other cars on the *prime*. No doubt thrilled by their first experience of a European special stage, they set off on the 240-plus mile transport section towards the next *prime*, the Serbian, and the start control at Glamoč in the foothills of the mountains Staretina and Velika Golija. This stage would consist of 119 miles over unpaved roads, through forests and farmland, with a passage control at Sanski Most before heading on to Bosanska Krupa. Target time to complete was 135 minutes, which would require an average speed of 53 miles per hour.

The team found this more challenging now, the Bug bouncing and careening along the track, Gabriel shouting instructions to Pepe. Yet at the finish control they had lost just 40 minutes, meaning there were only 14 cars faster! The Mexican trio was definitely off to a flying start, no doubt taking by surprise all the dissenters who had sneeringly dismissed them as a novelty act.

The Mexican trio continued on towards Monza, which offered a nominal service point, i.e., an opportunity to attend to any issues with the Bug themselves, given they had no organized backup, before delivering the car to *parc fermé* and taking the opportunity to get whatever rest they could. Now, however, they were trying not to dwell on the simple fact that their cash reserves were dwindling, and, with another 1,700 miles or so before them, they would need to repeatedly refuel both the Bug and themselves! Things came to a head on the way to the Italian frontier. "We ran out of money and the gasoline was almost zero," Gabriel explained. "We said, 'Oh shit! We aren't going to make it any further, we're just going to have to stay at the side of the road!' So, we almost ended, the engine was turning off." Once more, providence was with them as they coaxed the spluttering Bug into a gas station, where another competitor was busy refueling his car. Feeling not a little ashamed, Gabriel approached the man, explaining their predicament. Without hesitation, the fellow competitor slipped $100 from his wallet and handed it to Gabriel, the consequence of which was that the young Mexican team was able to carry on towards Lisbon. Over 50 years later, Gabriel expressed regret that he could recall neither the man's name nor the car's number.

Replenished, the Bug arrived at the Monza control. The men were relieved and then thrilled to discover that provisional results put them just outside the top 20 fastest cars to that point! The VW was performing well, so little was needed in the way of servicing and maintenance before they deposited it into *parc fermé*. Given their precarious financial situation, they slept where they could. By 7:30 the following morning, they were off again, headed along the Italian Riviera before turning right and climbing up to Ville San Pietro and the start of the San Remo *prime*, a series of twists and turns over gravel. The route was eventually declared not as challenging as planned, owing to the ministrations of the Italian authorities, who had insisted on organizers revising their average target speed downwards. As a result, 23 cars cleaned the section into the finish control at Camporosso, while the Mexican Bug picked up 24 minutes.

Next up was the Alpine *prime*, including the Col de Turini, the French mountain pass familiar to anyone who had driven the Monte Carlo Rally. Cars crossed into France between Ventimiglia and Menton, before turning right and heading up into the mountains. Once again, the Mexicans performed well, losing just 21 minutes on the tricky section, which included two passage controls and innumerable snaking bends before arriving in Rouaine. Thus, points accumulated by the VW team on the *primes* so far were respectable, given their relative youth and inexperience, but there was also the challenge of getting from London to Lisbon in 126 hours, calculated from the VW's departure time at Wembley to Dover, then Boulogne to Sofia, Sofia to Monza, and Monza to Lisbon. If any car failed to arrive at these controls by their designated time, further points would be incurred, and this was the challenge now facing Gabriel, Pepe, and Toño: could they cover the miles and miles across France and Spain and into Portugal, complete the final European *prime*, the Arganil, and make it to Lisbon without accumulating even more penalties? Given their shrinking cash supply, could they get there at all?

Of the long transport stage from Rouaine to Arganil, the rally's official program declared: "Roads are faster, less demanding now. But drivers must maintain a stiff schedule."[1] Teams would need to make each of the five passage controls within their allotted times if they weren't to be penalized, but, for the VW crew, this was extremely difficult to maintain. Points began to add up as they headed for Arganil, while cash reserves plummeted, and although they completed the *prime* successfully, they added further to the points tally, 33 minutes slower than the target time of 65 minutes. Wondering whether they would make the budget stretch all the way to Lisbon, once again fortune shone on them. "At a control, or someplace like that, a guy came to us and said, 'I have some money for you from the Mexican coffee organization.' It was kind of a national monopoly for coffee … they controlled the Mexican coffee," Gabriel recalled. "They gave us $200 and a sticker for Mexican coffee! I said, 'Wow, we've got a sponsor! Mexican coffee is our sponsor for $200!'"

Feeling happy and relieved, the trio drove on to Lisbon, checking in at the arrival control and then leaving the Bug in *parc fermé* in readiness for loading onto the ship that would carry rally cars to Rio. In the final tally, taking into account points accrued on the *primes* and the amount of time they had exceeded the overall target of 126 hours, when results were announced, they found themselves in 51st place out of 71 cars that would be heading to Rio. Even though they had perhaps sometimes pushed the Bug to its limits through Europe, they had made it. So, with some extra funds at their disposal, and having worn the same clothes all the way from London, they purchased some pants to wear, not least because all finishers to the Portuguese capital were invited to a prize-giving function at the casino at Estoril, just along the coast. Kitted out in new pants and their rally jackets, they arrived at the casino, only to be met with a rather officious doorman who took one look at the three young men and refused them entry! It eventually took one of the rally organizers to intervene before they were allowed to take their place at the celebration dinner.

Somehow, word must have gotten around about the trio's somewhat shaky budget, so the next thing they knew, a collection was being organized among both other competitors and regular casino patrons! Although the ordinary gambling visitors proved less than forthcoming, the rally teams were in high spirits after their long and, for many, challenging trek across Europe and, by the end of the evening, the Mexicans were presented with another $200 or so to support their lively effort! Looking back, Gabriel still feels humbled by this act of kindness and stressed that, contrary to contemporary reports, this gesture was never solicited by the young men.

Gabriel recounted a final act of graciousness towards the VW team: "The *Daily*

Mirror knew about our history and somehow, they published a request for donations to help the Mexicans, so they made it possible for people to donate to us ... when we were finishing the European part, the *Daily Mirror* people came to us with $400 that was donated by British people. These poor guys, they need some gasoline! I have always been so grateful and surprised about the *Daily Mirror* people who took this with empathy, you know? These guys need help, we can help them collect some money!"

Almost two weeks later, after a spell in Lisbon and another in Rio, the rally got going again, headed for the wilds of Brazil and Uruguay beyond. Unfortunately, having had a providential passage from England to Portugal, the young men's luck finally abandoned them even as other rally cars snaked their way from

DEPARTURE CONTROL

RIO de JANEIRO

ADDRESS OF CONTROL HQ
Hotel Gloria
Praia do Russell 632
Telephone: 257272

TIME CONTROL

5b

OPEN FROM
19.00 to 23.00
8th May 1970
Local time is
BST —4 hrs

SCHEDULED TIME OF DEPARTURE CITY CENTRE	HOURS	MINUTES
	21	40
NEUTRALISED TIME ALLOWED TO KM 'O'	1	00
SCHEDULED TIME OF DEPARTURE 'O'	22	40
CONTROL STAMP & SIGNATURE		

OFFICIAL NOTES

TIME ALLOWED TO MONTEVIDEO 41 HRS. FROM CITY CENTRE CONTROL

5

No. 19's roadbook departure record at Rio, May 8, 1970 (courtesy Gabriel Maria Hinojosa Rivero).

the Rio dockside to *parc fermé* next to the Hotel Glória. The young men had made arrangements with a local VW shop to carry out repairs and maintenance—including replacing brakes and tires, fixing an oil leak, and adjusting the Bug's suspension height—immediately after they were flagged away from the start control. According to Gabriel, and contrary to contemporary reports, which stated that the Bug had gone AWOL before the start, the workshop took longer than expected. "We left late for São Paulo.... We followed the route as fast as we could because we knew we were running late. Near dawn, possibly 7:00 a.m. ... we meet the officers in charge of the Piedade checkpoint. They stamped us and signed the roadbook and we continued as fast as we could to make up time." It was, however, not to be as, on the way to Pilar do Sul, a simple driving error stopped the VW dead—they'd bent the front axle.

Hours passed before a tow truck finally roared into view, during which time the men's hope of continuing in competition slowly melted away. With the Bug secured to the truck, they bumped and lurched their way to Curitiba, where a local VW shop made the car roadworthy again—VW in Germany had sent out a wire, instructing their dealership networks to offer assistance to the men if and when required. Gabriel recalled that the workshop was tiny with just one mechanic and his assistant doing the work. They fitted a plastic windshield and straightened the axle as best they could, not quite properly aligning the front wheels. Somehow, while the VW was in the care of the workshop, the men's precious rally jackets were stolen and, even worse, their passports. But one last

OFFICIAL ROUTE

RIO de JANEIRO to BATEIAS

PLACE	CONTROL OPEN	PASSAGE CONTROL STAMP
SAO PAULO		
PIEDADE	00.20 to 07.20 9th May 1970	A.C. E. PIEDADE 38
PILAR DO SUL		
ITARARE		
ARAPOTI		
VENTANIA	PRIME	CONTROL
PIRAI do SUL		
BATEIAS	PRIME	CONTROL

No. 19's Piedade passage control record, May 8, 1970 (courtesy Gabriel Maria Hinojosa Rivero).

dose of providence shone on them and all items were recovered. Now, with absolutely no chance of catching the field or reaching any further controls before they closed, Gabriel, Pepe, and Toño made a decision: Why not take the quickest route to at least catch up with the competing rally cars and follow them to Mexico City? Careful calculations revealed that if they drove north and west out of Curitiba and then crossed the border into Paraguay and then on to Bolivia, the chances were that they would be in La Paz for when competing teams arrived. Thus, with the VW at least drivable again, the fearless three set off on the 1,800-mile journey.

The drive across Brazil and into Paraguay was fine, the trio making their way to Asunción, where a friend of Pepe's lived. They were welcomed with breakfast and then set off northwest, headed for the Bolivian frontier crossing at Villamontes, where things got a little challenging. At the border, stationed soldiers brought them to a halt, demanding to know what these three young men were doing trying to drive into such a dangerous part of Bolivia—bandit country! So concerned were these army men that they refused to let them pass, insisting that the trio wait until a suitable truck came by, onto which the Bug could be loaded, before they were able to proceed. Gabriel recalled that they were forced to wait here for three days, which all but ended their plan to meet the rally in La Paz. At last, a suitable means of transport drew up and the truck's driver agreed to assist once he had delivered his load across the border. With a price negotiated, the truck returned for them, as promised.

Into Bolivia now, and the unlikely cargo of Mexican students and German rally car were transported onwards across the Bolivian Chaco. About 12 hours into the journey, another squad of soldiers signaled the truck to stop. This time they were in no mood for discussion, instead ordering a group of smugglers or bandits onto the back of the truck at gunpoint! Having paid for their passage, Pepe began to protest, but Gabriel shut him up, gesturing at the weaponry on display. So all were resigned to an even more uncomfortable ride. Their driver seemed unruffled by these events, however, so Gabriel asked him how he was able to continue driving back and forth, day after day. "Well," the man said, "it's very easy, in a store you buy coca leaves and that's the way I keep on trucking!"

The VW and its team were deposited in the small Bolivian town of Muyupampa, also known as Villa Vaca Guzmán and notable as the place where Frenchman Régis Debray, close associate of Cuban revolutionary Che Guevara, was arrested and imprisoned in 1967. (He was released in 1970 after an international appeal to which, among others, support was given by Pope Paul VI!) With rather more apolitical priorities dominating the thoughts of the trio, and with the truck driver's words echoing in their ears, they took decisive action. "It was very late and we were very tired," Gabriel explained. "We had lost a lot of time and the rally could get ahead of us in the city of La Paz. If we did not hurry, we would not catch the rally…. So, we said we should buy some coca leaves! We stopped in a little store and for one dollar they gave us this big bag of coca leaves—you chew on the leaves, it doesn't taste good! It's kind of sour, so I was the first one driving, I took the road at about 10 o'clock at night and it was six o'clock in the morning and I was so happy driving! I didn't get tired at all, amazing."

In this fashion, they pressed onwards, becoming anxious to find a gas station. Miles passed, but still no sign of anything until, in another small town, they asked a passerby who told them to go to a particular house where they could buy fuel by the liter—like milk! All the while they were driving, they were listening to the Bug's radio and were able to keep up to date with the rally's progress. This is how they realized the rally was too far ahead. Thus, after their adventures across Brazil, Paraguay, and Bolivia, they reached La Paz just one day after competing cars had departed. With little alternative, they decided to carry on, follow the rally route, and see whether they could still catch up. First, however, they found the local VW distributor, who told them that he too had received word from Germany, and proceeded to further repair and service the Bug, this time replacing the axle altogether. Thirty-six hours later, they were off, ever hopeful they could catch the field in Lima.

Out of La Paz, the route book and maps took them towards Desaguadero and the Peruvian border on the southern edge of Lake Titicaca but, alas, on the shores of this famous stretch of water, their race to catch the rally came to an emphatic end. Having taken a wrong turn, Gabriel retraced their path, getting them back on the road close to the lake, but he overcooked a left-hand turn and, about 20 feet from the lake's edge, the car swerved and flipped, rolling over and coming to a mangled halt. Gabriel and Pepe crawled out relatively unscathed, but Toño was now bleeding from a head wound. Papers and possessions were scattered everywhere as a few local people came to their assistance in the darkness. The three were shocked and frightened, Gabriel and Pepe stumbling around trying to collect assorted items that had been flung from the Bug while also seeing what they could do to stanch Toño's bleeding. Out of the

The end of the adventure: (*left to right*) Gabriel Maria Hinojosa Rivero, José Manuel "Pepe" Pérez Vega, and José Antoñio "Toño" Bárcena Compean (courtesy Gabriel Maria Hinojosa Rivero).

darkness came a Jeep, driven by a local mining worker, who rescued them and took them to safety. Gabriel would regret the loss of information contained in books left in the car. "We lost a lot of names and addresses of people who had been extremely nice to us," he said, "which is something that really hurts me, you know, they never [heard] anything back from us. They think these guys never wrote back or anything like that."

The following morning, with Toño bandaged up, they returned to the site of the crash, only to discover the car was gone! After some frantic enquiries, they learnt that the wreckage had been recovered by local authorities. With the car beyond repair, the men arranged for it and themselves to be transported back to La Paz, where humble calls were made to parents in Mexico in the hope "the bank of Mom and Dad" was able to cover costs of flying home. The Bug was deposited at the local VW dealership where a promise was made to purchase it for $200. Gabriel never received the money.

Looking back on their adventures some 50 years later, Gabriel remained in awe of how much generosity was afforded them, how unconditional help was offered from so many people encountered along the rally route, from the French student to the London street artists, from the various rally competitors who took pity on them to the readership of the *Daily Mail* newspaper! His only regret was that he was never able to properly thank all those who assisted the three young Mexican men as they set off to drive home from London to Mexico in a mostly standard *Vocho*. He emphasized: "The important thing for the story is to make it clear that we never deserted, nor did we get lost, nor did we give up."

and a great deal of careful thought had gone into the make and model of car to enter and how to engineer it so that it would not only withstand the punishment it would have to endure on the way to Mexico, especially traversing South and Central America, but also be competitive enough to win. Both companies had a choice of product that they could develop, especially BLMC, which, by 1968, was manufacturing 11 brands and 21 models of automobile: Austin, Morris, Riley, Wolseley, MG, Rover, Jaguar, Triumph, Daimler, Land Rover, and Vanden Plas (the "Mini" brand wouldn't become a product in its own right until 1969). This enormous lineup of vehicles under one stewardship was a consequence of merger upon merger in the 1950s and 1960s, culminating in the formation, on January 17, 1968, of the British Leyland Motor Corporation, "the world's fifth largest vehicle producer, after the three American giants General Motors (GM), Ford and Chrysler, and behind only Volkswagen in Europe."[1] It was also producing the country's top-selling car, the 1100/1300 range. Many an article, essay, and book has been written about the wisdom, implication, and consequences of creating such a megalith of motor manufacturing, but this was the reality in 1969 when Peter Browning, head of BLMC's Competitions Department, began the process of considering which product best suited the 1970 London to Mexico World Cup Rally.

For 1969, the BLMC lineup consisted of a range of either face-lifted or enduring products that dated back to the early 1960s. The Mini was first launched as the Morris Mini-Minor and Austin Seven in 1959, followed by the 1100 range from 1962, which went on to include Austin, Morris, Wolseley, Riley, MG, and Vanden Plas brands during its lifespan. Moving upmarket, the 1800 range was launched in 1964 and adopted the Austin, Morris, and Wolseley brands—in Mk II guise, this was the car of choice for BLMC's Competitions Department when the London–Sydney Marathon became a reality two years previously.

The Triumph brand had been subsumed by Leyland Motors, a truck and bus manufacturer, in 1960 and was then additionally incorporated by the formation of BLMC in 1968. This meant that the British Leyland Motor Corporation now produced a range of Triumph-branded vehicles, including the Herald and Vitesse range, the TR6 and Spitfire sports cars, and the Giovanni Michelotti–designed 1300 and 2000 models. Presented as an up-market sedan at the British Motor Show in October 1963, the Triumph 2000 represented a new era in prestige motoring in Britain and abroad and was followed a few years later by a wagon version. In 1968, the car was further enhanced by the introduction of a 2.5-liter (152-cubic-inch), fuel-injected engine, which became known as the Triumph 2.5PI. Developed by Lucas Automotive in the mid–1950s and used in motorsports, this fuel injection system was further refined to use a mechanical metering system and, from 1963, it began appearing in production cars, eventually including the Triumph.

Taking on the role of chairman and managing director of BLMC in 1968, Sir Donald Stokes quickly determined that Triumph should be the company's sporting brand. However, when thoughts first turned to which vehicle would be prepared for the London to Mexico rally, the as yet still secret Range Rover model was initially the vehicle of choice. Officially launched in 1970, 40 development and pre-production models had already been produced, adopting the name "Velar" as a means of maintaining a smokescreen against ever-watchful motoring journalists while still being able to register cars for road use. When the head of BLMC's Competitions Department, Peter Browning, heard about the proposed SUV, it struck him that this would be the obvious choice for a 16,000-mile endurance rally. He took this idea to Ralph Nash, manager of Rover's Experimental Department, and persuaded Nash to allow him, rally driver Geoff Mabbs, and Competitions Department employee Doug Watts to take a test drive in the car. "Our first mistake was to stop for a bite of lunch at a pub on the way to the local Girling test track," said Browning. "We left the car in the pub car park but, unfortunately, had chosen the pub where the Rover directors had their lunch. They had a fit when they looked out of the window and saw the car surrounded by interested onlookers!"[2]

Browning managed to persuade the executives to accompany them to the test track where Mabbs took to the wheel. However, a bend on the track was tighter than expected. "As the lumbering Range Rover approached at unabated speed," Browning recalled, "I feared the worst."[3] Only Mabbs's expert reactions stopped him and the car from ending up in an adjacent ditch. Instead, the car slid sideways, tires screeching, and came to rest in a field. Mabbs emerged from the car and walked over to the group of spectators, commenting, "Not bad, but you've got to cure that bump steer!"[4] As a consequence of this apparent lack of agility, the Range Rover was summarily dismissed from competitive contention, at least as far as the London to Mexico World Cup Rally was concerned.

Following by now Lord Stokes's intention that Triumph be the sporting marque for BLMC, focus turned to the 2.5PI, although not necessarily for reasons that sat well with some. BLMC works driver Paddy Hopkirk wrote that "it was marketing trying to dictate what the Competitions Department used, rather than the other way around."[5] However, the car itself did meet with Hopkirk's approval, especially the fuel metering process, which drivers could control via a dash-installed lever, a crucial feature for driving at low oxygen at high altitude. The Competitions Department had already prepared a first-generation 2.5PI for the RAC and Scottish rallies and had learnt a great deal as a consequence, which boded well for development and preparation of four second-generation 2.5PI cars for the London to Mexico Rally. Motoring journalist and soon-to-be competitor Hamish Cardno reported: "The Triumph has the standard 2498 cc engine with a gas-flowed cylinder head, high-lift camshaft, and a compression ratio lowered to 8.5:1 to cope with low octane gasoline. For the same reason an advance/retard ignition control is fitted inside the car.... The four-speed box is augmented by a Laycock overdrive on third and top gears, operated by a toggle switch on the front of the gear lever."[6]

In addition to the four Triumphs, and with another whiff of a marketing opportunity, it was agreed that the team would also prepare a Mini 1275 GT for the rally. Launched in 1969 as a successor to the hugely successful—in terms of motorsports, at least—Mini Cooper S, the 1275 GT was actually slower than the Cooper but cheaper to buy and insure. Plus, it saved "Leyland the royalty being paid to the Cooper Company, which equated to a large slice of the profit on the vehicle."[7] It also sported the revised, squared-off front-end styling Roy Haynes had created for the Mini Clubman range, which had entered the market in 1969. What better way to demonstrate the 1275 GT's motorsports pedigree than have it haring across Europe under the scrutiny

9

Tortoises and Hares
(Part One)

On the evening of February 12, 1970, England soccer team captain Bobby Moore took his place at London's Café Royal and picked entries from a tombola to create the running order for the 1970 London to Mexico World Cup Rally. First out of the drum was a Triumph 2.5PI Mk. II, to be driven by London–Sydney Marathon veterans Bobby Buchanan-Michaelson and Roy Fidler, together with British *Daily Express* motoring correspondent David Benson. Sporting a very fashionable double-breasted camel-colored suit jacket, Moore patiently proceeded to select another 105 slips of paper from the drum, until all of the 106 entries were captured.

Not every successful entrant had indicated the vehicle they would be driving in the rally, but those that had shone a spotlight on cars that ranged from the fastidiously prepared manufacturer team machines to the fascinating, privately entered oddities like the VW-engine Beach Buggy entered by John Caulcutt, the Ford Escort camper van backed by Wilsons Motor Caravans (also a sponsor in the 1968 London–Sydney Marathon), the Rolls-Royce Silver Cloud entered by the Martin family, and the "sawn off" Ford Mustang backed by the British company Job's Dairy and to be crewed by a co-ed team including Job's Dairy-owning family member Lavinia Roberts. As with the rally between London, England and Sydney, Australia, 18 months before, the competing field promised an intriguing mix of professional and privately entered cars and crews with, as would be revealed, wide-ranging degrees of preparedness!

While amateur crews wrestled with financial and practical logistics, some of the premier motorsports divisions of British and European automobile manufacturers had been developing and fine-tuning both cars and crews for the fiercely competitive drive from London to Mexico City. During the second half of 1969, BLMC and Ford GB had been regularly issuing press releases confirming their chosen professional teams, with Ford particularly capitalizing on the PR dividends of having England soccer player Jimmy Greaves—a "household name" in the UK—as part of their competing arsenal. Certainly, throughout 1969, print media focused extensively on how Greaves was getting ready for the rally with, if not daily then certainly weekly coverage of his preparations, competing in domestic rallies when he wasn't either drilling a works Ford Escort around assorted training tracks and terrains or learning how to control a car on a skid pan!

Both Ford and BLMC were obviously attaching huge importance to the rally,

BLMC Team Triumph 2.5PI at Abingdon, England, 1970 (courtesy Mike Wood).

of print and broadcast media? Whether bosses had given much thought to how the sub-compact car, and its small wheels, might fare across South America remains to be seen.

A third marque to make it onto the competitions department's London to Mexico Rally worksheet was the Austin Maxi. Launched with much fanfare in 1969, the Maxi was the last car to be designed by the British Motor Corporation and was "BMC's gift to the newly formed BLMC."[8] The Maxi was an innovative and extremely contemporary concept on paper, but, as with so many BMC and then BLMC products, a combination of cost-saving measures and sometimes questionable build-quality meant that the car, as launched, was something of a curate's egg—good in parts!

Renault had upped the ante for family car design when it introduced its Renault 16 model in 1965, as it was the first factory mass-produced five-door hatchback. BMC's Italian division had experimented with a full hatchback design for the company's Pininfarina-designed Austin A40 a few years earlier, but this concept wasn't adopted by BMC in Great Britain before the A40 was discontinued in 1967, an aversion that would rear its head again and again for BLMC during the 1970s with models such as the Austin Allegro and Princess 18/22 series, both often criticized for not including an opening tailgate. The latter would only get a fifth door in 1982 when the redesigned Austin Ambassador briefly graced the showroom floor. However, in the mid–1960s, BMC had taken note of the Renault and set about working up a response, a five-door family hatchback that could offer all the interior versatility of its French competitor. The car would have a new 1,485-cubic-centimeter (90.6-cubic-inch) engine linked to a pioneering (for contemporary British mass family transportation)

Preparing a BLMC Team Austin Maxi at Abingdon, England, 1970 (courtesy Mike Wood).

five-speed manual box. However, what should have been a bold new direction for BLMC was met with disappointment by the motoring press, not least because of its styling. To cut costs, the design team had been given the brief of taking the doors from the BMC 1800 model and working from there (a precedented dictate as 1967's executive Austin 3-liter sedan had also suffered this indignity). That and the fact that the five-speed box really needed further engineering before launch meant that the Maxi had arrived promising much but delivering decidedly less than expected.

BLMC's Competitions Department had been given a Maxi for evaluation purposes, so department personnel Gerald Wiffen and Brian Moylan, rally navigator Tony Nash, and Peter Browning took the car to recce the Austrian Alpine Rally. "The recce didn't last long as the differential pinion wheel came adrift," Moylan explained. "We got the car to a BMC garage … to see if there was anything we could do—which there wasn't without removing the engine."[9] Moylan's adventure on the way back to headquarters in Abingdon, Oxfordshire, is a whole other story!

Undaunted, and perhaps already aware of the car's shortcomings as well as its strengths, the Competitions Department decided to prepare two Maxis for the World Cup Rally. The end results proved to be a testimony to the skills and experience of department engineers. To strengthen the car's shell, they welded the Maxi's unique hatchback tailgate shut and gave it a more conventional trunk lid. Shock absorbers were upgraded, and many of the body panels were manufactured from aluminum and glass-fiber to keep the weight down. Engine inlet and exhaust manifolds were upgraded, and power was increased from the standard car's 74 brake horsepower to 95 brake horsepower. Most notably, however, as Hamish Cardno wrote, "during tests on an Army tank proving ground, the Maxi had covered a greater mileage without trouble than any previous British Leyland competition car."[10] Undoubtedly a harbinger of things to come, as will be revealed.

Alongside the BLMC Competitions Department sat Leyland's Special Tuning Department, which had developed in response to increasing customer demand for parts and help with tuning Minis and other BMC products during the first half of the 1960s. Co-located with the Competitions Department at Abingdon in Oxfordshire, Special Tuning also set about preparing BLMC products—specifically six BLMC 1800s (including the ill-fated Viscount Errington/Bill Heinecke car)—to compete as privately entered vehicles in the rally. BLMC 1800s had been the competitive vehicle of choice for the 10,000-mile 1968 London–Sydney Marathon, both for the BMC Competitions Department and for a number of privately entered competitors and had proven to be a robust and reliable, if not particularly fast, rally car. Runner-up at Sydney in 1968 was a Competitions Department 1800 driven by works driver Paddy Hopkirk with co-drivers Tony Nash and Alec Poole. The 1800 was therefore an obvious choice for the rigors on offer on the way to Mexico, and eventually nine 1800s departed Wembley Stadium on April 19, 1970. In addition, and working to the same BLMC competitions specification, another Maxi was prepared by performance engineering firm Janspeed. Again, incorporating a strengthened, tailgate-less body shell, that Maxi would be a right royal affair!

One 1800 being prepared elsewhere was to be crewed by two serving British police officers and a police mechanic. Both Eric McInally and Hugh Penfold served with the London Metropolitan Police Force, or "the Met," and Eric worked with the Flying Squad, a branch of the Met's Serious and Organized Crime Command. Their chance to drive the roads and dirt tracks from London to Mexico City presented itself out of the blue!

10

A Policeman's Lot
Is Not a Happy One

It all started with an unexploded World War II bomb.

In 1969, 27-year-old Eric McInally was a serving police officer working for London's Metropolitan Police Force. Always interested in cars, especially driving them, in 1967 Eric had begun his Met Police driver training, an incremental course that lasted three years, trainees only being allowed to progress to the next module after periods of time during which they needed to prove themselves competent at the level to which they had been trained. Course phases were beginner, intermediate, and advanced, with the final training focusing on driving fast and driving safely in all environments, including busy urban areas. Much to the chagrin of some of his fellow officers, however, Eric was quite simply fast-tracked through the training, displaying such a natural aptitude for handling a car and extraordinarily quick reaction times that he found himself behind the wheel of very fast police Jaguars, Rovers, and Triumphs.

One Sunday afternoon, Eric and his radio operator colleague Hugh "Colin" Penfold received a call over the radio. Could they attend a disturbance? Standard operational procedure was for Scotland Yard to use "disturbance" as a generic description for any incident requiring urgent police presence as radio reports were usually monitored by the press! Thus, prepared for any eventually, they proceeded to the given location, a tony Chelsea townhouse in the last throes of construction. There they were met by the property's owner, accompanied by a friend, who was none other than Thomas Patrick John Anson, 5th Earl of Lichfield, more commonly known as society and glossy magazine photographer, and distant relative to HRH Queen Elizabeth II, Patrick Lichfield! Lichfield hung back while Eric and Colin accompanied the house's owner to the rear garden, not much more than a construction site still, and, upon suggestion, looked at what was causing all the fuss. They were confronted with an unexploded World War II incendiary device. Springing quickly into action, the officers piled construction sand onto the shell and immediately called the bomb squad, who promptly arrived and disposed of the problem.

The townhouse's owner was hugely grateful, of course, and proposed drinks as a thank-you. Obviously the two on-duty police officers, one responsible for a high-speed police vehicle, politely declined, but one thing led to another and, while declining an alcoholic beverage, they got talking to the man, who introduced himself as Michael Pearson. Pearson was, and still is, 4th Viscount Cowdray ("viscount" is a British peerage rank, just below that of "earl"). Pearson was interested in the life of a policeman, and the conversation was amiable and relaxed. Discussion turned to the previous year's London–Sydney Marathon endurance rally, Eric remarking that to drive in such an event would be wonderful. Pearson's interest was piqued, and he began asking questions. What would be involved? How would one prepare? What sort of car would Eric take on a long-distance motor rally? Then, as the men began to take their leave, Pearson suggested they come up with a plan to enter the recently announced London to Mexico World Cup Rally and then offered to fund them! Naturally, Eric and Colin were extremely grateful, but they knew that a serving officer in the British Police needed to be beyond reproach. They couldn't accept money, no matter how virtuous and honorable. Pearson smiled and suggested that matters be left with him, and so it was that the 4th Viscount Cowdray used his social standing and connections to persuade the Metropolitan Police's senior personnel to support the proposal, as long as Eric and Colin didn't handle any money!

The fact that Eric and Colin were to be entered in the rally soon became public knowledge within the Met, and interest quickly increased to the point where a few very high-ranking officers suggested that they, in fact, might replace them in the competition. The "offer" was respectfully declined, however, not least because Pearson had chosen Eric and Colin. Regardless, the media was intrigued, and it was Colin and his easy charm and obvious good looks who was made liaison, although it has to be acknowledged that his own police duties afforded greater flexibility than Eric's during this time. There were also many opportunities for the men to socialize with Pearson, and they quickly realized just what his social standing meant as they were afforded the chance to meet any number of "high society" folks, quite an eye-opener for them. They also put this time to good use, carefully organizing the necessary equipment, supplies, and documentation required to compete. They also visited the British Royal Navy diving school at Portsmouth, where they undertook decompression exercises, courtesy of ex–naval officer Colin's brother, who was a senior serving naval officer.

With a sizeable fund deposited by Pearson, and a financial administrator appointed, thoughts immediately turned to a vehicle. Pearson liaised with BLMC, purchased a standard, sand-colored 1968 BLMC 1800, and duly dispatched it to their Special Tuning department for rally preparation. Meanwhile, with approval for being "off pay," and with their domestic expenses covered, Eric and Colin attended rally briefings, lectures, and movies detailing the South American route and warning that, as some local people in some areas were so unused to motorized vehicles, they might try and lay traps just to see a car crash! They also invited a third member to the team, another policeman known to Colin, Peter Jones, who was a gifted mechanic if not an experienced driver. Surely Peter would come in useful if they experienced any mechanical problems, especially miles from anywhere with no service point in sight?

While the car was being prepared by Special Tuning in Abingdon, Oxfordshire, Colin and Eric decided to do a little recce work in Europe, at least along most of the transport stage across France, Germany, Austria, and into Italy, avoiding the immediate complexities of crossing into the Eastern Bloc on their run, just to give themselves a sense of the distance that lay ahead, if only in Europe. Their intention was

No. 34 Team Rally Passport (courtesy Ted Taylor).

simple: drive using all the professional skills and experience amassed, whether that was Colin on road sections or Eric on the *primes*, and just get to the end, even if they were the last car into Mexico City. Michael Pearson even said that should they arrive at the Aztec Stadium, even in last place, he would fly out, fly their wives out, and pay for them to watch all the World Cup soccer matches!

The McInally/Penfold/Jones 1800 was drawn No. 34 so, when their time came to roll out of Wembley Stadium, they followed the Peruvian BMW 2002Ti and were in turn pursued by the Yugoslavian Peugeot 504. Off and away down London streets familiar to Colin and Eric and then beyond to Dover, the ferry, and the start of the long haul across Europe to Bulgaria, Yugoslavia, and the first *prime*.

The 1800 performed impeccably, eating up mile after mile along the fast, rain-slicked *autobahns*, and they arrived without incident or penalty, first into Sofia and then via the drive to Titograd, the revised Montenegro *prime* start control. For Eric, a supremely skilled, very fast driver, this was where the fun would begin, even though he knew the route would be rough: they had been warned about boulder-strewn tracks in Yugoslavia during their briefings and knew that obstacles encountered would include, among other things, donkey and carts!

As with all the speed sections, and taking into account the hazards along the way, drivers were expected to maintain very fast times if they were to avoid penalty points. Eric, with a little experience of dirt track rallying from his younger days in Scotland, no doubt seized the opportunity (while also keeping in mind their mantra of just getting to the finish in one piece) and drove into the *prime*, which gave drivers the target of 50 miles in 65 minutes, meaning an average speed of 54 miles per hour. This was also Eric's first real opportunity to test the car and see how it handled over the rough stuff, and he performed well, just 13 minutes down on the target time, and faster than 43 other drivers, some of whom had a lot more experience than he did.

Roadbook stamped and signed, the police team continued on, enjoying the coast road along the Adriatic as it took them northwest through Yugoslavia, before ascending to the next *prime* start control at Glamoč, a treacherous approach that occasionally seemed to be at odds with the mapped route, teams frequently having to scour the terrain to see which was the right way. However, they arrived in good time and, in the mist and the darkness, began the second European *prime*, the Serbian, a speed section further complicated by inclusion of a passage control at Sanski Most, to be found in the middle of the night on an unfamiliar trail!

The going was much harder here, a mix of looming trucks and a plank bridge, which throughout the section appeared to be in different states of repair at different times, causing some competitors to hastily work out an alternative route! Thus, not a single car cleaned the stage, or completed it without penalty, and although most of the professional rally drivers lost mere minutes, Eric had picked up 119 penalty points by the time they arrived at the finish control at Bosanska Krupa. Much more than the Montenegro, this *prime* really drew the line between most of the professionals and most of the determined privateers. Was this reckoning just a taste of what was to come?

The next transport stage took the cars over the Italian frontier at Kozina and around the Gulf of Trieste, past Venice and the southern shores of Lake Garda. Eric and Colin shared the driving duties, and they took advantage of the fast roads. Eric recalled that they drove at speed through Yugoslavia and into Italy, perhaps over-exerting the 1800 as they went. Eric also recalled that, unlike some who could sleep anywhere, he found it difficult, and by the time the team reached Monza and its rest stop, service area, and time-controlled *parc fermé*, he was tired but unable to use the four hours available to recuperate.

On the morning of April 28, 1970, cars left Monza in their Wembley departure order and embarked on the 175-mile transport stage to Genoa, along the Ligurian coast and then up to Ville San Pietro in the foothills of Mount Moro, where the third *prime*, the San Remo, would begin. Here, Eric recalled that one of the rally professionals rather crisply, and not a little menacingly, warned them that should they see his car in their rearview mirror on the *prime*, they were to get out of the way immediately. Eric had no problem with the standard etiquette of ensuring that slower moving cars gave way to the faster drivers, but he was less sanguine about this particular individual's manner! Regardless, what lay before them was 65 miles of gravel, hairpin bends, and spectacular views, and although anyone familiar with the *Rallye Sanremo* or San Remo Rally, at that time one in the FIA's International Championship for Manufacturers series of events, would be familiar with the course, others—like Eric, Colin, and Peter—were not. Even so, the Met Police team incurred just 11 penalty points during their mountain maneuvers to get to the finish at Camporosso.

The 1800 continued with its spotless mechanical record as the team now headed for the French border and then on to Menton on the French Riviera, before turning sharply north and beginning the ascent to the Col de Turini, the magnificent Alpine mountain pass, where a passage control awaited. The technical centerpiece

No. 34, the Metropolitan Police team, on the way out of South London: (*left to right in car*) **Eric McInally** (*driver*)**, and Hugh "Colin" Penfold (courtesy Ted Taylor).**

of countless Monte Carlo Rallies, the pass comprises a breathtaking series of mountainous hairpin bends, twisting forwards and back with magnificent views to dangerously distract any rally driver or navigator following the route! From there, the route descended via Pont Charles Albert and Coursegoules, following the French D5 road to Les Quatre Chemins, literally "the four paths," a dot-on-the-landscape junction where the Alpine *prime* would begin, climbing up to another passage control at Sigale, perched on the mountain, and then upwards again to Entrevaux and the *prime*'s second passage control. From there, the *prime* twisted and turned down to the tiny hamlet of Rouaine. Demanding though the stage was, and although the Alpine claimed a couple of cars, Eric, Colin, and Peter made it safely to the finish, picking up 20 points for their troubles.

After all this exhilaration, the police team was now faced with an extremely long drive out of France, across Spain, and into Portugal, where they would head for Arganil and the final European *prime*, the Portuguese. Again, sharing the driving, they made trouble-free progress along the grinding 1,200-mile journey, poor Peter sitting in the back and probably wondering what he was doing there. Organizers had placed five passage controls through France, partly to keep competitors on the right track and partly to ensure shortcuts, if indeed there were any, would be avoided.

At last, after an undeniably grueling slog across southern Europe, the trio finally made it to the *prime* start control. Once again, Eric was behind the wheel as he gunned the 1800 into the stage, 45 miles of forest track similar to British rally sections in Scotland and Wales, with a target time of 65 minutes. While the professionals either cleaned the *prime* or dropped just a few minutes, Eric steered the car through the section in an hour and four minutes, safely managing to avoid one stranded rally car while accommodating any faster car coming up behind. Now, provided there was no mishap on the transport section to Lisbon, they knew that they had booked their place for Rio de Janeiro and, beyond there, the South American section.

In the final tally at Lisbon, of the 71 teams that made it, the Met Police Team was in 41st place. Making sure the 1800 was prepared and ready for shipping, the men took it to *parc fermé* and then went on to their hotel in Cascais, about 30 minutes to the west of the capital city. After 5,000 miles of driving, hard concentration, and very little sleep, they retired to their rooms. All competitors' luggage had been sent on ahead and should have been waiting in each room, so Eric was ready for a shower and some shut-eye. Upon inspection, however, he realized the suitcase wasn't his. Peering at the luggage label, Eric read "Mäkinen." Somehow, he had got the Finnish rally driver's baggage! Hopeful therefore that Mäkinen now had his, Eric called down to reception, obtained the number, and called his room. Explaining the situation, Eric volunteered to walk the case over as they were on the same floor. He knocked on the door and Mäkinen opened it, insisting Eric come in. Eric entered and was immediately offered vodka, and, despite polite refusals, the Finn insisted. Though not a vodka drinker—or any kind of drinker for that matter—Eric duly accepted the proffered beverage, drank it, and was left gasping. The alcohol nearly blew his head off! Eventually, feeling slightly the worse for wear, Eric made his excuses and departed unsteadily, ruing the intake of such strong liquor. However, he did get the last laugh as, while checking to see whose bag it was, Eric had noticed it wasn't properly closed. And what lay on top? Timo Mäkinen's route notes!

The following day was mostly spent sleeping, but there was time to discuss the state of the car, the very few concerns they had as the 1800 hadn't missed a beat, and reviewing pace notes. Then, for the next few days the trio seized the opportunity to explore Lisbon, finding a harbor-side fish restaurant where Eric fell into conversation with a fellow Scotsman who was living and working in the capital city. The Scotsman proceeded to entertain them through the next few days, suggesting they visit the casino at Estoril and inviting them to his home for drinks and dinner.

During the second week in Lisbon, the team focused on preparation for South America and on the car. They reviewed notes and documentation and reflected on their performance thus far—what had worked and what could be improved? They were also in touch with the BLMC works personnel to check on any issues or questions they had about the state of the 1800, but, apart from a wee bit of "pedal to the metal" on the route out of Yugoslavia and up to the San Remo *prime*, their driving had been careful, so there were no major causes for concern.

At last, it was time to board the jet that would take competitors to Rio de Janeiro. With amusement, Eric recalled some of the antics on the plane, card games with stakes and much consuming of alcoholic beverages. That said, not being an enthusiastic drinker himself, and aware that there would yet be time for socializing in Rio, Eric used the plane journey to rest, catnapping and dozing where he could until, eventually, the plane touched down at Rio's Antonio Carlos Jobim International Airport. This was Eric's first visit to Brazil, and as he disembarked the jet, he was immediately struck by the heat and humidity, even though they arrived at night! Sweating, he joined other competitors as they checked into the Hotel Glória, overlooking the Praia do Flamengo and Guanabara Bay beyond.

Eric gazed out of the hotel room window and was fascinated by the endless strip of grass that separated the road from the beach. As far as it reached, in either direction, it was floodlit and consisted of a long line of makeshift soccer fields with scores of players. He later learnt this was a weekend tradition, starting Friday evening and going on all weekend. So, this was how Brazil produced so many great soccer players!

Eric also noticed the extreme difference between wealth and poverty around him. The team had received briefings about the *favelas*, the low income and underprivileged communities in Rio, with the advice that these were "no-go" areas. Generally, they had been instructed to avoid walking the streets of Rio at night, especially alone, so when Eric recounted to a visiting British embassy official who had come to meet competitors how he had walked back from a bar in the early hours of the morning, he was roundly reprimanded with the caution that he had been lucky to get back to the hotel in one piece!

Eric was also amused by some of his fellow competitors' attitudes to them as "the police team." He recalled that poolside breakfasts at the hotel were relaxed and sociable occasions and many were interested and keen to ask them questions about a police officer's life. That said, when they in turn asked their own questions in response, maybe a few felt uncomfortable with police officers making enquiries!

The Rio downtime eventually came to an end, however, and thoughts turned to recommencing the rally. The SS *Derwent* docked in Rio and disgorged the rally cars ready for collection, so the team collected their 1800, refueled it after weeks at sea with a compulsorily drained tank, and drove it to the service point for a quick check over before depositing the car at the *parc fermé* located back at the hotel. Then it was over to the ceremonial start of the South American section, now departing in order of standing, followed by a brief drive to the actual start. Thus, on the evening of May 8, the Met Police team was back into the rally and the 11,500 miles that lay before them.

From Rio, a transport stage took competitors first west and then southwest to a passage control at Piedade, via the busy city of São Paulo, 340-plus miles of good roads. The 1800 appeared to display no ill effects from the lengthy ocean crossing, and all was well as they drove through the Brazilian jungle. By now, both Eric and Colin were aware that poor Peter had *ipso facto* become a passenger on the rally, so minimal had been the demands on his skills. Although the matter wasn't discussed, Peter must have felt slightly bemused by it all. However, there were many miles yet to go and, of course, anything could still happen that would instantly require Peter to be either under the hood or under the car, investigating and fixing.

As this stretch would be long and over good, paved roads, Colin took the wheel and, with any number of other competitors either in front or behind following the departure from Rio, Eric decided there was no risk of losing the route so, it being the early hours of the morning, he dozed off. Colin drove on and a few hours passed when, approximately 190 miles into the rally at the town of Resende, there was suddenly a loud bang and the hood, which was both locked and strapped down, flew up!

Crawling to a halt at the side of the road, Peter leapt out and, torch in hand, inspected the 1800's engine bay. With other competitors speeding by, some flashing headlamps or sounding horns, Colin and Eric joined him, asking what had happened. At last Peter turned to them and grimly announced that the car was done and they would go no further. What? How? Why? The horrible realization that the problem was way beyond Peter's ability to repair began to sink in. This was a major fault that would require extensive workshop attention and not something that could be fixed with a toolkit in the dark on the roadside. Other cars slowed, and then one of the Soviet teams stopped to see if they could offer assistance. All the Russians could do was take a message to the control at Piedade to ask that a recovery vehicle be sent.

After thousands of miles of faultless, problem-free driving, the 1800 had quite simply expired.

In misery and bewilderment, Eric, Colin, and Peter eventually waited five or six hours for a recovery vehicle to arrive and load up the stricken car. Then, with all three onboard, the truck returned to Rio and deposited its human cargo back at the Hotel Glória, where the team were able to book into their old rooms while the car was taken on to a holding garage. After getting some fitful rest, thoughts turned to letting their Michael Pearson-appointed intermediary know their adventure was over. Arrangements were thus made to get men and car back to the UK, with the agreement that no repairs be made to the car in Brazil.

When asked what the high point of the whole experience of the rally was, Eric said it was the moment their number came up at Wembley Stadium and they rolled down the ramp and away. After weeks and weeks of wondering whether something would arise that would prevent them from competing—perhaps the Metropolitan Police deciding to withdraw their support, perhaps a problem with the car, or paperwork, or any of the other complicated and detailed logistics necessary to deliver them to the start line—the high that he felt driving away through London and onwards down to Dover lasted all through Europe. He also recounted how the telephone switchboard, specially set up at the rally-sponsoring *Daily Mirror* newspaper to provide real-time updates on progress, was inundated with calls from police stations across the country, fellow officers so keen to check up on how No. 34 was doing! As far as he was concerned, the sad fact that their adventure came to an end so soon after starting the South American section was no fault of theirs. They had acquitted themselves admirably and, unhappy though it was, they would be able to face their benefactor knowing they themselves had not let him, or any of their supporters, down.

As for the 1800? The initial diagnosis was a broken connecting rod, the engine component that connects a piston to the crankshaft. The reason it broke? That, reflected Eric with an eyebrow slightly raised, will never be known for sure.

11

Tortoises and Hares
(Part Two)

The variety of cars accepted as entries for the London to Mexico World Cup Rally created an almost *Wacky Races* element. Running for just 12 months from 1968 to 1969, the Hanna-Barbera cartoon show featured an array of colorful and, in some cases, highly unlikely vehicles (and competitors!) that would race each week from points A to B, all the while experiencing perilous adversity and sometimes intentional obstacle. While it can't be said that the World Cup Rally would offer up a villainous Dick Dastardly and his sneaky hench dog Mutley, some of the event's *primes* and time allowances would definitely not be kind to unwitting competitors, and the road to Lisbon, let alone Mexico City, would surely be littered with casualties!

In addition to some of the other previously mentioned automotive novelties in contention, the starting lineup for the rally included a barely modified and rather long-in-the-tooth FIAT 2300 station wagon, an extremely modified Mini Cooper S that sported two additional doors, a Vauxhall Victor FD station wagon, and a Trident Venturer manufactured by the Trident Cars company, on offshoot of the high-end, independent sports car company TVR, which had collapsed in 1965. A few other independent entries of note that failed to materialize at Wembley Stadium on April 19, 1970, included a rear-engine NSU 120CS, an interesting choice given the German NSU's rally pedigree across Europe; a British Ford Zodiac IV; a French Simca 1501S; and a Japanese Isuzu Florian, a rarity on British and European roads in 1970. Why F.W. Hill, Humphrey Mead, Raymond Pontier, and London–Sydney Marathon veteran Kazuhiko Mitsumoto withdrew from the event is unknown, but their departures, together with a few other entries drawn from the tombola drum on February 12, meant that what had begun as a field of 106 entries had shrunk to 96 starters on departure day.

Proven to produce reliable, not to mention successful, vehicles with which to compete on endurance rallies, Peugeot the brand, if not the French manufacturer's Competitions Department, took up a number of places on the entry list. Eleven cars in total were set to compete, a combination of the tried-and-tested Peugeot 404, which had won the arduous East African Safari Rally in 1963, 1966, 1967, and 1968, and its intended successor the 504. During their lifespan, both cars were assembled in a number of countries around the world, including by the Argentinian company SAFRAR, the acronym for *Sociedad Anónima Franco Argentina de Automotores* or Franco-Argentina Auto Company. SAFRAR entered three Argentinian-built 404 models, one of which was crewed by French rally hero Jean-Claude Ogier, together with co-driver Claude Laurent. Ogier and Lucien Bianchi had had victory secured during the final stages of the 1968 London–Sydney Marathon when an inexplicable and devastating smash with a private car ended their extraordinary run so close to the end.

As described previously, the British Armed Forces had a strong presence, mostly driving 504 models. Also as described previously, the South American Peugeot 504s had been prepared differently from their European counterparts, with deeply frustrating results for the British Army teams. Adding a Yugoslavian-entered diesel-engine 404—complete with enormous, bed-sized roof rack—to the mix, Peugeot had the potential to be a force to be reckoned with.

Compatriot car manufacturer Citroën also had a presence at Wembley, albeit in the form of private entries. Just as had occurred with some of the Mercedes models on the 1968 London–Sydney Marathon, not everyone graciously accepted that the six Citroën DS21 automobiles ready to depart Wembley Stadium in April 1970 were not in fact factory-backed, Citroën Competitions Department-supported entries. In addition to the three *tricolore*—red, white, and blue—cars on display, three more cars had joined the field, including one entered by the *Societe d'Encouragement Automobile France* or the French Automobile Club, and crewed by Marathon veterans Patrick Vanson and Olivier Turcat plus Citroën Competitions Department mechanic Alain Leprince. With regards to the opinion that the Citroën entries were hardly privately entered, Vanson commented: "Well, of course they'd say that! They weren't really private entries; they were works entries but the way they did it … because they weren't doing any servicing … they entered us as private entries." Interestingly, in the April 16, 1970, issue of *Autosport*, the SAFRAR Peugeots were listed among the works, semi-works, or works-assisted entries, while the Citroëns were not. Regardless, being a private entry would very much work in the favor of *Messieurs* Vanson, Turcat, and Leprince, as we shall see.

Ford products were, not surprisingly, in abundance on the entry list, and despite the Ford GB Competitions Department's extremely disappointing performance with the Ford Cortina Lotus on the London–Sydney Marathon, the field included three privately entered versions plus two "Savage" V6 cars. One of these, plus the Cortina Lotus backed by JC Withers, had also competed on the road to Sydney in Australia, the Withers car being the re-engineered Ford driven by Rosemary Smith with co-driver Lucette Pointet in 1968.

Alongside these was Ford's "new kid on the block," the Capri. Launched in January 1969 and marketed by Ford as "The Car You Always Promised Yourself," the Capri quickly found favor among younger drivers—those with cash to spend, anyway. For the World Cup Rally, two privately entered Capris, a 1600-cubic-centimeter (98 cubic-inch) model and, in 1970, an unusual German 2300-cubic-centimeter (140 cubic-inch) car, joined their more motorsports-experienced stablemates—unusual because the 2300-cubic-centimeter engine was never fitted to the first-generation British Capri as a standard offering.

However, the Ford product to watch, the car of choice for Ford GB's Competitions Department, and for a number of other private entries, was the Escort. Introduced

Ford GB Team Escorts—working up from the bare shells (courtesy Stan Clark).

to buyers in Ireland and the UK towards the end of 1967, it very quickly became an extremely popular platform for both touring car races and rallying. Extraordinary to think, then, that for the 1968 London–Sydney Marathon, there was just a sole, privately entered Escort taking on the 10,000-mile endurance competition, whereas by the time the 1970 London to Mexico Rally was fast approaching just 18 months later, Ford GB had chosen the Escort to lead the assault on the prize and first place at Aztec Stadium in Mexico City. Under Competitions Department manager Stuart Turner's leadership, Ford entered a team of seven Escorts based on the Twin-Cam bodyshell and strengthened with a tubular steel enclosure, bolted to the front suspension turrets and up through the front wings, over the windshield and into the car where it was welded to the roll cage. Ever mindful of the severe shortcomings of the Lotus-made, eight-valve, overhead camshaft engine, which powered their London–Sydney cars, this time Ford selected the Cortina GT motor, a Ford Kent "crossflow" 1600 cubic-centimeter (98 cubic-inch) engine—"crossflow" because the carburetor was on one side and the exhaust on the other—which they considered much more durable for a 16,000-mile endurance event. Turner's team proceeded to bore and stroke the engine to 1838 cubic-centimeter (112 cubic inches), giving it approximately 140 brake horsepower, and link it to a five-speed ZF box. The team fitted three gas tanks, two normal rally tanks plus an extra 12-gallon tank over the rear axle, giving a total capacity of 33.5 gallons. Turner's strategy also included ensuring that weight was kept to an absolute minimum, the heaviest items being a 2.5-gallon drinking water container and two spare wheels to be bolted to the cars' trunk lids. The cars were prepared at Ford's Boreham rally engineering department, engineering company Stan Clark of Narborough, and Clarke and Simpson in Chelsea. Turner, as we shall see, meant business!

Preparing a Ford GB Team Escort (courtesy Stan Clark).

No. 77, the Thai-entered Toyota Corolla KE10-B of Jan Leenders and Preeda Chullamonthol (courtesy Ted Taylor).

Other automobile manufacturers represented as privately or commercially sponsored entrants were Mercedes-Benz with four cars, three 280SEs and a 220D; BMW with three 2002Ti models, General Motors' British arm Vauxhall with an HB Viva GT, an FD Ventora, and the FD Victor station wagon; and Porsche with four 911 cars, including a re-engineered veteran from the 1968 London–Sydney Marathon. Other brands in competition included SAAB with a privately entered 96 V4, skillfully prepared to rally spec; Volvo with a private 142S and a modified 132; a Toyota Corolla KE10-B; a privately entered but hugely rally-proven Datsun 1600 (1600s had just taken first, second, and fourth places on the East African Safari Rally, and this 1600 had previously been driven by Rauno Aaltonen on the RAC Rally); FIAT with a 2300 station wagon and a 124 Sport Coupé; an Alfa Romeo Giulia Super; and a Spanish SEAT 1430. All these plus two Rolls-Royces, including a Silver Shadow extensively and knowingly modified by hugely experienced British rally driver and 1968 London–Sydney Marathon veteran Bill Bengry, and the London to Mexico World Cup Rally really promised to be an enormously competitive and enormously entertaining event.

During the lead-up to departure, three teams were busy wrangling the mechanical, financial, and administrative requirements necessary to see their distinctly unusual vehicles take their places in the starting line up at Wembley Stadium in April 1970. Their chosen machines were a Trident Venturer, a GP Beach Buggy, and a V8-powered Ford Mustang. As they discovered, preparation is all!

12

A Series of Unfortunate Events
(Part One)

It is safe to say that if a 16,000-mile, international transcontinental endurance rally is announced, in which, as long as certain rules and regulations are met, any type of car can be entered by anyone with enough money (or financial backing!) to pay for both registration and end-to-end costs, any privately entered vehicle would no doubt stick to proven principles. This is why, among the professionally prepared, factory-backed Ford Escorts and Triumph 2.5PIs, the London to Mexico World Cup Rally saw any number of rally-proven BLMC 1800s, Hillman Hunters/GTs, Citroën DSs, Mercedes-Benz sedans, and Porsche 911s line up to depart London's Wembley Stadium on April 19, 1970. After all, whether having earned their stripes on the previous 10,000-mile London–Sydney Marathon endurance rally, or on countless, rugged Eastern African Safari rallies, or on fast, meticulous European competitions such as the Monte Carlo or Alpine, these were the cars that had pedigree. Yet, mixed in with those machines that day, there were a few more eclectic vehicles, more eyebrow-raising, perhaps completely unlikely as a choice for the rigors that lay ahead. Anyone enjoying the spectacle at Wembley must surely have pointed and cheered at the two Rolls-Royces—one modern, the other, if not ancient, then certainly mature. Spectators may have been amused to spot a compact Escort camper van in the lineup, or a modified four-door Mini Cooper! However, each of the teams that sat waiting in these cars that day was determinedly serious and some, as in the case of the more contemporary Rolls, had the motor rally experience to prove they had what it took!

Among the mean-looking Fords and sleek Triumphs and Citroëns, three cars that also bucked the trend were a hand-built Trident Venturer sports coupe, a slightly "sawn-off" Ford Mustang, and, perhaps most spectacularly of all, a beach buggy! However, regardless of novelty or, in the case of the buggy, possible impracticality, serious attempts had been made to ensure that these cars were prepared to endure the miles ahead. Whether these efforts had been enough would be revealed as competitors took to the roads and rough rally stages of Europe.

Eighteen months earlier, at London's Crystal Palace Stadium, among the teams lined up to start on the 10,000-mile endurance rally road to Sydney in Australia were two serving officers of the British Junior Leaders' Regiment of the British Royal Artillery, Lieutenant Martin Proudlock and Captain David Harrison. There to see them off was Lieutenant Arthur "Pat" Hazlerigg, a fellow serving officer of the regiment and the best man at Proudlock's wedding. The original intention had been for Pat to take "third chair" in the Harrison/Proudlock car but, it being a Ford GB-entry, the general consensus among the Ford team was that the preferred and approved configuration would be two-up. Pat therefore lost his place, but Proudlock assured him that if any further competitive rallying opportunities arose through the regiment, he would be first in line. Little did he know that, as he stood there on November 24, 1968, just a year and a half later, he would himself be sitting in a car waiting to begin his own endurance rally adventure!

The British Job's Dairy Company's roots go back as far as 1874, when Edward and Louisa Roberts established a dairy in Teddington, England. Over the years, the enterprise developed and expanded, adopting contemporary developments including pasteurization, setting up a laboratory and eventually contracting a large number of dairy farms to supply milk for processing and distribution. The business remained in the ownership of the Roberts family until they sold it in 1987.

In 1969, Lavinia Roberts was working for the family company, which at that time was managed by her father and uncle. At a party one evening, she got talking with Martin Proudlock. Proudlock knew Lavinia's eventual husband, James, and, as a thank-you for providing some help in his rally endeavor, Martin had brought him back a boomerang! The party chatter got onto the Marathon, and the recently announced London to Mexico World Cup Rally came up. Lavinia asked Martin whether he would do such an event again. Martin declined but suggested Pat Hazlerigg, not least because Pat had an international driver's license as a consequence of rallying Land Rovers, among other vehicles, with the Far East Army Motoring Association while serving in Singapore. Pat jumped at the chance, of course, and as Harrison and Proudlock had set the precedent, requested and obtained permission from his regiment to compete.

Lavinia told her father of her idea, and he suggested they get a mechanic involved. "Patrick knew a bit but…. I knew absolutely nothing," Lavinia explained. Fortunately, Lavinia knew a man who might just fit the bill so suggested David Jones to her father. "Okay," she recalled her father saying, "well we need a mechanic at Job's to service the vehicles. We'll employ him and then you can take him on the rally."

Jones's services duly procured, the next challenge was to choose and purchase a suitable vehicle. "We were heavily into polo and an American chap … was very, very rich and he wanted to get into polo in England, so he did it through my dad," Lavinia explained. "Dad said, 'Well, yes, we could probably manage it, we could probably have your horses here but, of course, my daughter is doing this.' … So he said, 'Oh, well I've got contacts in America who can get Ford Mustangs, I can get you a Ford Mustang sent over'…. So, it was all 'who knows who'!"

While waiting for the Mustang to be shipped over from the United States, Lavinia and Pat competed in a few club rallies, not only as an introduction to the sport for Lavinia but also to give them both experience of working as a driver/navigator partnership. Lavinia took a high-speed driving course and, as one of Pat's pastimes was racing a Formula Ford racecar, she even took his crash helmet and pretended to be him in a race!

Courtesy of the U.S. benefactor, a brand-new Mustang with a V8 engine

Lavinia Roberts and Lt. Arthur "Pat" Hazlerigg with the Ford Mustang (courtesy Lavinia Black).

and a manual box with Hurst shifter, in Ford factory dark bright aqua, was delivered to the Job's Dairy site at Hanworth, just west of London, where it was to be prepared in the vehicle maintenance workshop. As Pat had previously helped Harrison and Proudlock prepare their London–Sydney car, he was enlisted to inspect and assess the Mustang in order to determine what modifications and adaptations the car would need for the 16,000-mile run. "Well, you've got to raise the ground clearance to start with," Pat explained, "so we've got to change the size of the wheels … we've got to seam-weld the whole bodyshell, every single joint was seam-welded inside and out…. We chopped off two feet from the front of the car … and we put on that bumper bar." Intended as an overall weight reduction, that last modification would prove extremely prophetic, as the team would discover. Pat also specified a roll-cage and an additional 30-gallon fuel tank across the rear axle, fashioned from a Bedford van's, which increased the Mustang's range. "The Mustang," Pat noted, "was thirsty!"

Pat also specified that dash panel instrumentation be reconfigured, including the repositioning of the windshield wash-wipe switch, which would operate a one-gallon tank with dual pumps. The standard springs were upgraded, and an oil pan guard, Koni shocks, and anti-tramp bar were fitted. Jones did most of the work with Pat helping out at weekends. Pat was also determined to keep weight to a minimum and thus wasn't keen on the decision to carry an enormous—and extremely heavy—toolbox on the roof! Ready or not, on April 19, they took their place at Wembley Stadium.

They had been drawn No. 86 and therefore had a wait before their departure time came.

Another car with military presence that had less of an interval before rolling down the starting ramp was a striking, low-slung Trident Venturer V6 coupe. All set and ready to go, Captains Christopher Marriott and Jack Dill of the British 17th/21st Lancers Regiment sat and watched the clock tick down on the start of their rally adventure.

Neither Jack nor Chris was a stranger to the rigmarole and roar of the crowds with which they were presented that day as both were London–Sydney Marathon veterans, Chris having been one of a four-man army crew in a Land Rover in 1968, while Jack had teamed up with George Yannaghas in a Porsche 911T. Eighteen months later, their choice of vehicle was either brave or foolhardy, a work of sheer brilliance or a handmade folly, although its sleek, vaguely Aston Martin–like looks certainly had the crowd's attention and appreciation, if not that of the watchful press.

The British Trident Cars Ltd company was an offshoot of the independent sports car manufacturer TVR, which, in various guises and under various ownership, had been outputting either cars in kit form or, later, fully constructed vehicles since the late 1940s, all using a wide variety of pre-existing engines produced by other manufacturers. TVR's product evolved through the 1950s, but the ever-present specter of financial debt grew with each passing year. Into the 1960s, despite investment and regrouping, constant rancor at the director level saw the company undergo constant management changes and, by 1966, although a new project was well into the development cycle, further financial woes led to the project's reins being handed to TVR dealer William J. "Bill" Last, who duly established Trident Cars Ltd and worked the project to its conclusion, the Trident Clipper.

Trident launched a second model in 1969—the Venturer coupe, powered by a Ford V6 engine—and this was the car that Jack and Chris selected for the rally. "Well, it landed on Gavin Thompson's [radar], who I'd been on the London–Sydney with, and he was mad keen to get going, but he'd already got a team up with [Prince] Michael of Kent and Nigel Clarkson," Chris explained. "Then we found these lovely men Bill Last and Stephen Conlan, who were making the Trident Venturer, and managed to wiggle our way into them lending us a car!"

Chris had been friends with Jack Dill since childhood, and as he had also competed in 1968, he seemed an obvious choice as partner. Thus, the pair commenced on a severely time-limited program of activity to oversee the car's preparation, collate all the required documentation and maps, and generally plan for as many eventualities as possible. Jack listed what he thought were essentials on the trip, including warm clothes (in case they broke down in the Andes); ear mufflers for the co-driver; battery razors; hand and foot cream; pre-mixed coffee, sugar and dried milk; cigarettes; glucose drinks; currency; driving gloves; sunglasses; a map-reading lamp; a compass; and a full tool kit. Meanwhile, Chris devoted time to raising funds since while Trident, which obviously saw the event as excellent publicity, was providing the car and covering the cost of preparation, the captains needed to meet all other expenses, including the entry fee. Some help came from Marriott family connections. "My uncle … was a man called Humphrey Prideaux," Chris explained. "He ran Brooke

Bond Oxo for a bit, and he was a great friend of Hector Laing, of Laing's Biscuits, so he gave us some money, but other than that it was sort of the begging bowl was out, some chums lobbed in something."

Chris spent much time at the Trident factory in Ipswich, Suffolk, in the east of England, helping and advising on the car's construction and making requests for additional modifications. "I remember one night, half asleep, the gearbox suddenly falling on the floor with a hell of a smash," he recalled. "It took us hours to get all the wiring together and, to begin with, we could only start it by shorting it out with a spanner! I remember the first time we did it, it revved straight up to 4,500 revs and the oil pressure gauge was very slow ticking up and I thought we'd got no oil pressure so I turned it off and the looks I got from the guys who'd spent bloody hours trying to get the flaming thing started and I turned it off after five seconds!" He also specified that the instrumental panel be completely reconfigured so that each gauge was angled in such a way that, apart from the fuel gauge, all the needles pointed upwards so that any problem—temperature, oil pressure—could be spotted at a glance!

Time, however, was running out, and as late as a month prior to the rally beginning, the car was a work in progress. "We are still awaiting the flashing light, the air bottle clips, the jack and we would like a pattern oxygen cylinder," Bill Last at Trident wrote to Chris. "We also require the hand swiveling roof lights, the screen washer kit and anything else you realise we may need to fit in the car."

One issue that eventually proved decisive for the 17th/21st Lancers' rally effort was that of wheels and suspension. The standard Venturer had fairly thin wheels, so Chris requested that Trident make provision to fit wider tires. Attempts were made to widen the wheel width by welding steel discs onto the hubs, but, when tested, they completely threw out the wheel balancing and then broke so the team was forced to revert to the car's standard wheels. Chris also made attempts to obtain a set of small, inflatable rubber balls, which he would insert into the Venturer's springs, thereby limiting the travel and slightly increasing ground clearance. Unfortunately, time ran out, but not before the car was cleverly decorated with images of soccer players, plus an image of the soccer World Cup Trophy adorning the hood, courtesy of a local artist! Thus, taking their place in the heavily laden coupe at Wembley Stadium, they were all too aware that there was precious little allowance between tire and wheel arch!

Another team up against it during the months before the start was that comprising John Caulcutt, Noel Hutchinson, and David Stewart. A stockbroker in the City of London by profession, Caulcutt had also, by the age of 22, carved out quite a reputation as an inspired and ingenious racer of boats, competing in the inaugural Round Britain Powerboat Race in 1969 with an unprecedented rigid inflatable boat, a commonplace vessel today but unique in 1969—John still holds the worldwide design rights! The inflatable's rear engine also inspired him when thoughts turned to entering the London to Mexico Rally—why not procure an air-cooled VW-engine-powered beach buggy? Beach buggies were fast becoming an extremely fashionable vehicle in the late sixties in Britain, and contemporary motoring magazines issued copious articles and features on the variety of bodies and motors at the disposal of any budding enthusiast. To enter the buggy in the rally, however, John needed a team. Whom did he know who could get involved?

No. 30, the Trident Venturer of Capt. Christopher Marriott (*driving*) and Lt. John "Jack" Dill, Wembley Stadium, April 19, 1970 (courtesy Guido Devreker).

By late 1969, 22-year-old David Stewart was at a loose end. Back home with his parents after a job came to a close in Paris, France, a friend suggested he get a job with an English stationery and office equipment supplier that was selling its products in Finland. Thus, in January 1970, David found himself in Rovaniemi in the north of the country and confronted with severe sub-zero temperatures. On a whim, he decided to call his friend John Caulcutt, just to touch base, at which point John matter-of-factly asked him, "When are you coming back to fix this car?" According to David, John's first choice for a competing vehicle was a Mini Moke. "I said, 'That's crazy, not got a chance of getting there, small wheels, not rugged,'" David explained. "But John was always doing mad things…. I said, 'Well, what about a beach buggy?' They were very successful in the Baja rallies, so that appealed to him no end. A beach buggy? Absolutely up his street!"

David knew about a company that produced buggies not far from where his parents lived, GP Speedshop in Hanworth, so after initial enquiries, they were commissioned to produce a buggy for the rally. "Not with a great timeframe, I'm afraid," David observed. "We didn't give ourselves like enough time for the project so the testing of the vehicle didn't happen properly." This fact would rear its ugly head only a few months later.

For now, however, as initial plans for a transport company to back the entry had fallen through, John was now bankrolling the whole affair upfront, albeit with the proviso that all costs, and any benefits, should they win anything, would be split three ways. Thus, work commenced on creating a buggy fit for a 16,000-mile transcontinental endurance rally. While GP Speedshop manufactured the body and chassis and worked on the suspension, axles, and wheels, David put his knowledge of VW engines to good use. He knew that a standard 1500-cubic-centimeter (91.5-cubic-inch) motor could be stroked up to 1950-cubic-centimeter (119-cubic-inch) courtesy of a specialist German manufacturer, Autocavan, that was supplying special crankshafts with roller bearings, rather than the VW's standard white metal bearings, and these were duly purchased to upgrade the buggy's performance.

While the buggy was being worked up, thoughts turned to a third team member. John asked David if he knew any likely candidates, and David immediately thought of a friend of his, Noel Hutchinson, with whom he had attended Brooklands Technical College in Weybridge, Surrey. Noel was a keen club rally enthusiast, and David had co-driven for him on a number of events, rallies that would eventually show Noel he was more suited to navigating than driving. No doubt it was this fact that led David to make a phone call a month or two before the rally began. "It was quite out of the blue," Noel remembered. "Would I be interested in doing the World Cup Rally? As you can probably imagine I was somewhat taken aback by this sudden offer. Fortunately, I was in a position to accept without much hesitation because I was going to change jobs in July." Noel proceeded to relocate to Surrey, where he moved in with his brother; he recalled that both he and David were in fact stepping in as two friends of John's had dropped out.

Coming in at such a late stage, Noel had to hit the ground running and, with David taking charge of overseeing preparation of the buggy and John busy with his city job, Noel took on purchasing and organizing supplies. Time was now of the essence, and so it was that GP Speedshop was now racing to obtain and fit the two bespoke alloy fuel tanks, to be positioned pannier-style on either side of the car. Noel recalled that while there had been a plan to insert rubber fuel bags within each tank, time ran out. Frenetic activity continued during the final days and weeks before the off, with David putting together an extensive set of tools and spare parts for the buggy, the weight of which, Noel thought, would come at a premium for the admittedly light buggy.

Saturday, April 18, when all cars entered were required to be present at Wembley for scrutineering, was looming, and still David and GP Speedshop were wrestling with problems. Two anxious nights were spent attempting to solve an oil seal problem, which was eventually resolved. Finally all was ready, and the three joined up to deliver the car and their documentation for inspection at the stadium. The paperwork was in order, but the buggy most definitely was not. While it passed muster with the rally organizers, the two fuel tanks had both sprung leaks! What to do? Regulations expressly forbade any car to leave the holding area once checked in after assessment so the effort, in David words, "seemed doomed to fail even before the 'kick off.'" Rescue came in the form of David's friend Roger Miskin, a highly skilled mechanic, whom David had had the foresight to invite along. Roger gave the matter quick thought and promptly announced that, if the whole car couldn't be removed from the site, then they could instead remove the faulty parts! Thus, both fuel tanks were removed, stashed in Miskin's Austin A40, and driven back to his house in

Still working on the buggy, Wembley Stadium, April 19, 1970 (courtesy David Stewart).

Cobham, where he and David spent much of the night carrying out repairs. Noel recalled: "The night before the rally when we were packing, I can remember work was still being done on the car. Working until about 11 or 12 the night before the rally was bonkers, given the prospect of a long day followed by night driving across into Germany. The day of the start to the rally the car was ready, but there had been no time for any testing or shake down."

As dawn broke on April 19, Roger and David took the tanks back to Wembley to refit them and reunite with Noel and John. "We made the start line literally by a whisker, barge-queuing the line up to our nominated position!" David recalled. Yet made it they did. "It was an amazing feeling joining all the other competitors and their cars, into the briefing and then realising this is it," Noel reflected. "Then it was time to drive into the crowded stadium to the accompaniment of the sounds of Ginger Baker's Airforce [band]."

Now, after all the frenetic activity, all that was left for the teams in Nos. 30, 50, and 86 was the simple task of driving 16,000 miles to Mexico!

13

Cast and Crew (Part One)

At Wembley Stadium in North West London on April 19, 1970, the 229 men and 12 women who sat in their cars watching the clock tick, or who milled around among friends and family while watching the clock tick, or who checked and rechecked provisions and paperwork while watching the clock tick undoubtedly had no thoughts about what they represented within the field of competitors dreaming of, hoping to, or determined that they would get to Mexico, let alone win this 16,000-mile-long, 16,000-foot-high motoring odyssey. Yet, from this lofty and not a little anthropological perspective half a century later, one can categorize and classify these people, those dreamers or optimists, those experienced club rallyists eager to showcase their skills, or those cool professionals, regarding this as just another job, albeit rather more unusual than the competitive norm.

The first category has to be the men and women who lived and breathed motor sport, and more specifically rally, the automotive game of driving skill and navigational dexterity like no other. These were the people who, even if they had one or two professional sidelines, earned a buck or two working for the top-drawer automobile manufacturers' competitions divisions. These were the men and women who had been carefully selected to bring the chance of victory—whether class or category wins or outright victory—to the table. The depth and breadth of talent available to Ford GB or BLMC or even, indirectly, Citroën, was rich indeed, peppered with drivers and navigators who had performed to the limit throughout the 1960s, scoring class and outright wins throughout the rally calendar, whether on the fast and furious Monte Carlo Rally or the arduous and demanding East African Safari. Only the best would be backed by Peter Browning for BLMC, Stuart Turner for Ford GB and, in the end, René Cotton at Citroën. Even SAFRAR of Argentina was clever enough to invite rally and London–Sydney Marathon veteran Jean-Claude Ogier to the party!

By 1970, the competitions arm of BLMC was in a precarious position. Even though the London–Sydney Marathon had been won by a car prepared by the Rootes GB Competitions Department eighteen months previously, new company owner Chrysler USA had effectively folded up the motorsports division in the UK, and the now "Lord" Stokes was undertaking a forensic investigation into the competitive arm of BLMC. Yes, Paddy Hopkirk, Tony Nash, and Alec Poole had secured second place at Sydney in 1968, but, as BLMC Competitions Department's Bill Price recalled, "unless they're really rally nuts, no-one would have a bloody clue who came second or third or whatever."[1] This time, it would be all or nothing, no small pressure on

Uldarico "Larco" Ossio, River Plate Ferry, May 11, 1970 (courtesy Pat Smith).

chosen competitors, but considering the caliber of the men and women contracted to represent BLMC, there was absolutely no reason why they couldn't deliver.

Peter Browning assembled a formidable team of drivers and navigators, wisely allowing his A-list drivers Andrew Cowan, Paddy Hopkirk, and Brian Culcheth to select their preferred co-drivers. One of Cowan's partners for their winning performance in the 1968 Marathon was Brian Coyle. A proven combination, Coyle and Cowan had, by 1970, competed together more than 15 times on international events. Third team member would be Peruvian Uldarico Ossio, a shrewd choice, given Ossio's previous race and rallying experience in South America where, according to BLMC's October 1969 press release, "in 1967 he drove a McLaren Chevrolet and won the *Boliviariano*, a series of races held in Peru, Colombia, Ecuador and Venezuela."[2] Known as Larco, Ossio had also assisted BLMC with its South America recces in preparation for the World Cup Rally.

Hopkirk had also developed a proficient partnership with co-driver Tony Nash, who had effectively stepped in when Hopkirk's erstwhile co-driver, Ron Crellin, had retired in 1968, and had already taken second chair on the 1968 London–Sydney Marathon. To Neville Johnson the news that he was to be Hopkirk's second co-driver came as a surprise wedding present, arriving while he was on his honeymoon!

Johnson ran Hopkirk's Toyota dealership in Northern Ireland. For Culcheth, there was only one choice for his co-driver, and that would be long-time rally partner Johnstone Syer.

Joining these three teams would be Paul Easter and John Handley. Another London–Sydney Marathon veteran, Easter had made his international debut on the 1960 RAC Rally, which, as he explained, "ended straight on a T-junction into a large wall in Pateley Bridge in thick fog!" Naturally, this took his car, a Riley One-Point-Five, off the road, which led to Easter obtaining a Mini, entering the 1961 Tulip Rally, and effectively beginning a long relationship with Minis on the European international circuit, first as a privateer and then, upon invitation by then-BMC Competitions Department manager Stuart Turner, as a regular co-driver for Timo Mäkinen. By 1994, Easter and Mäkinen had competed together in more than 30 international events, the majority in Minis. Handley too was a seasoned Mini competitor, combining circuit racing, rally, and rallycross—he won the British Touring Car Championship in 1968—so Browning sent Easter and Handley off to compete in the 1969 *Tour de France* Rally in a Mini, which they led until the last day when they hit a wall and damaged the car's steering rack. Nevertheless, it introduced Handley to rally-essential pace notes and offered the opportunity for Easter and Handley to work together, good preparation for the London to Mexico World Cup Rally, although whether it would be as clever to enter a Mini in the event at all remained to be seen.

Rounding out BLMC's assault on the rally were three teams: one led by Rosemary Smith; one reprising veteran Australian rally partnership Evan Green and "Gelignite" Jack Murray; and one, carrying on the tradition set on the London–Sydney Marathon, comprising three British Royal Air Force "Red Arrows" pilots. The Red Arrows were, and continue to be, one of the world's premier aerobatic display teams.

Smith had already proved herself a clever and highly successful driver, winning many *Coupes des Dames*, or ladies' cups, plus the overall title on the 1965 Tulip Rally, much to the chagrin of many of her male competitors! Smith had also had a long-standing and, for the brand, tremendously successful relationship with the Rootes GB competitions arm, becoming forever associated with their Imp model. (The relationship, however, came to an unexpected end. "For whatever reason," Smith explained, "in 1968 it was decided my services were no longer required."[3]) Smith drove for Ford in the 1968 London–Sydney Marathon, and would be joined on the London to Mexico Rally by Frenchwoman Ginette De Rolland and Scotswoman Alice Watson.

De Rolland had been a frequent co-driver with nine-time French Women's Championship winner Claudine Trautmann, and also had form with Smith. On the 1968 Geneva Rally, Smith was paired with De Rolland and given a Porsche 911 to drive by Porsche PR manager Huschke von Hanstein ("mainly, I think, because he fancied me," Smith said[4]). Lying second overall, Smith had lead car, another Porsche 911, in her sights when, driving in the early hours, De Rolland commanded her to slow down as a sharp right-hand bend loomed. Smith braked. Nothing! "Once again, my father's words came back to me," she remembered. "'If you can't stop with your brakes, drop down through the gears.'" Judicious use of both hand brake (parking brake) and gear shifting slowed the Porsche, but it still slammed into a cliff face.

Ginette De Rolland (*left*) and Claudine Bouchet (courtesy Claudine Besanceney).

A glance across revealed that De Rolland wasn't moving. How badly was she hurt? Smith leapt from the car, ran to the passenger side, and found De Rolland throwing up but all right. The fact that De Rolland leapt at the chance to reunite with Smith for the London to Mexico Rally is testimony to her acumen plus Smith's driving skills.

Scotswoman Alice Watson, who had begun rallying with her husband in 1957, made her international debut on the Welsh Rally in 1965 and with Smith, had won the Ladies' Prizes on the 1969 Scottish Rally and the 1969 and 1970 Circuit of Ireland rallies, winning the latter just a month before the World Cup Rally began. This women's team was definitely one to be reckoned with.

The Green/Murray partnership had its roots in a friendship that stretched all the way back to the 1950s when Murray was scoring successes on the Around Australia Trials and journalist Green had begun dipping a toe into competitive rallying. Debuting in 1954 as a co-driver on a 995-mile rally in New South Wales, Australia, Green went on to (briefly) navigate for Murray, before capitulating to the extreme nausea that so often comes with high-speed map-reading and switching instead to driving. Nevertheless, his first choice for any endurance rally remained "Gelignite" Jack, despite Murray having "no knack whatsoever in map reading or finding his way."[5] Exploiting lessons learnt from the 1968 Marathon and its impact on print media, British *Motor* magazine journalist Hamish Cardno was embedded in the Green/Murray entry as third team member.

The Red Arrows team saw the return of 1968 Marathon veterans Terry Kingsley

"Gelignite" Jack Murray and Jean Denton, Wembley Stadium, April 19, 1970 (courtesy Pat Smith).

and Peter Evans, this time also joined by a motoring journalist, British *Autocar* magazine's Michael Scarlett, who would serve as reserve driver while also sending dispatches from the front line. This was a savvy PR coup, but whether Scarlett would be as good a rally competitor as he was a journalist remained to be seen.

The instability surrounding BLMC's Competitions Department had already chalked up a casualty in Timo Mäkinen and, by 1968, Rauno Aaltonen had also departed, albeit unwillingly. Together with Hannu Mikkola and Simo Lampinen, these four became the first of the "Flying Finns," with oil company Castrol even making a film of the same name in 1968 that focused on the competitive rivalry between Mikkola and Mäkinen during the Finnish 1,000 Lakes Rally of that year. During his tenure at BMC and then BLMC, Stuart Turner had already facilitated tremendous success by pairing Finnish drivers with British navigators, including two wins in 1965 and 1967 with Mini Coopers on the Monte Carlo Rally (the Anglo-Irish pairing of Hopkirk and Henry Liddon had already set the precedent for BMC and Mini by winning in 1964). Having resigned from BLMC and then spent a year working for Castrol, Turner was now in charge of Ford GB's competitions arm. Journalist and TV editor Brian Robins wrote of Turner: "Determined to win the biggest rally of them all, he had a budget of £60,000 ($144,300), his old proven Anglo-Finnish team, and a car, the Escort that had won rallies all the way from Aberystwyth to the Arctic."[6] Turner's account of financial matters differs slightly in that as Ford had rather lost control of their 1968 London–Sydney Marathon budget, "Anything we did in 1970 was under scrutiny," he remembered. "In the end I was allowed £40,000 ($96,000) and gave the go ahead."[7]

While still considering the exact lineup for Ford's assault on the rally, Turner and

Rally ID passport for Tony Fall and Jimmy Greaves (courtesy Ted Taylor).

Ford's PR team scored maximum publicity by announcing that England soccer ace Jimmy Greaves would be pairing up with another BMC alumnus, Tony Fall. By 1970, Fall had competed in more than 35 major rallies, mostly driving Minis, and had also gained experience of both endurance rallying, having competed in the 1968 London–Sydney Marathon with Mike Wood and Brian Culcheth, and rallying in South America, where he scored an outright win in the 1969 *GP Nacional de Carreteras Caminos del Inca*, or Rally of the Incas, with Gunnar Palm. According to Greaves, one of his regular watering holes was a pub near the Ford factory in Dagenham, Essex, where he got to know some of the folks who worked at the plant. "Unbeknown to me, Ford was looking for a high-profile driver to partner Tony Fall," he explained. "One of the Ford lads asked me if I would be up for it. I was in my cups, so to speak, and found myself saying 'Yes.'"[8] All forgotten in the cold, sober light of day, Greaves eventually found himself in training for the 16,000-mile rally by entering events in Great Britain, learning the art of the skid, and driving to Yugoslavia with Fall to see whether they could get on. Fortunately for both, they did!

For anyone even vaguely interested in the British and European rally scene in the 1960s and 1970s, whether at the time or in retrospect, surely there can only be one name more synonymous with Ford rallying, and the Ford Escort in particular, than any other: Roger Clark. By 1970, Clark had already driven for the Rover works team, for which he won his class on the 1965 Monte Carlo Rally in a Rover 2000. However, when Rover closed its Competitions Department that same year, Ford beckoned, and thus began a relationship that lasted decades and reaped both tremendous rewards and bitter disappointments. Much-favored to win the 1968 London–Sydney Marathon, Clark and his co-driver, Ove Andersson, were leading at the start of the Australian section at Perth, but, despite heroic efforts to solve their Lotus Cortina's mechanical problems, they eventually finished in 10th place.

David Campbell asserts that "Stuart Turner gave Clark grounds for anxiety when he arrived at Ford as the boss. Turner made no secret of his preference for Scandinavian drivers."[9] Regardless, despite initial discussions about what type of vehicle to enter and whether teams should be two-up or three-up, plus the fact that Turner dispatched Clark to compete on an Eastern European event in an unlikely Ford Zodiac IV as an exploratory test to determine whether a large Ford would be preferable for the run to Mexico City (it wasn't), Turner wrote in his autobiography that "Roger Clark became a key factor in our success."[10] Certainly, Clark shunned the idea that teams should be three-up and cars should be large and accommodating, instead insisting "that two drivers in each car were more than enough and that ... an Escort was exactly the right car for the job."[11] Thus, joining Clark in an Escort for the London to Mexico Rally would be London–Sydney Marathon veteran and 1969 British Touring Car Champion Alec Poole.

Turner added strength and depth to the Ford team with his favored Finns Mikkola, Mäkinen, and Aaltonen, pairing Mikkola with Sweden's Gunnar Palm and Mäkinen with another Marathon veteran, German co-driver Gilbert Staepelaere. For his part, Aaltonen took it for granted that Henry Liddon would be his co-driver. Aaltonen had previously enjoyed an extremely successful partnership with Tony Ambrose, but when Ambrose announced his retirement in 1965, he suggested Liddon as his replacement. Although Ambrose and Liddon were very different characters, Aaltonen quickly came to trust his new co-driver implicitly. It was this trust and

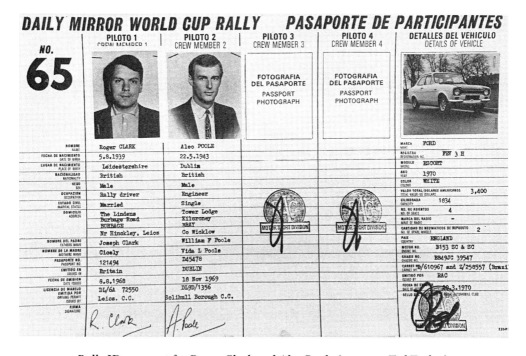

Rally ID passport for Roger Clark and Alec Poole (courtesy Ted Taylor).

working harmony that enabled the partnership to endure many a challenge on the road to Mexico.

Rounding off the Ford team were Polish duo Sobiesław Zasada and Marek Wachowski—Zasada was European Rally Champion in 1966 and 1967 and, with Wachowski, had blasted a Porsche 911 to fifth place at Sydney in 1968—and Colin Malkin and Richard Hudson-Evans. As well as being part of the winning Hillman Hunter team at Sydney in 1968, Malkin was also 1968's British Rally Champion.

Turner was taking no chances!

The Soviet Trading Company Avtoexport had established quite a presence on the 1968 London–Sydney Marathon, entering four factory-backed Moskvič 408s. All four made it to Sydney, the highest finishing in 20th position. This time Avtoexport had five 412 models in competition with a mix of two- and three-person crews. Emmanuil "Mischa" Lifchits and Victor Shavelev would be repeating their partnership from 1968, as would Sergey Tenishev and Valentin Kislykh, this time also joined by Valeri Schirochenkov. Yuri Lesovski was also returning, and a further eight Soviet competitors made up the Moskvič team. Contemporary reports refer to Stasys Brundza as a crewmember in Moskvič No. 21, but, as Russian Moskvič enthusiast Alexander Matveev was able to point out, he was replaced at the last minute by Gennadi Garkusha. *Autocar* magazine reported that "while the 412s may not be the fastest cars in the rally, they are probably the toughest, and according to Fedor Komarovski, of the Russian Trade Delegation in Britain, they have not needed any modifications."[12] According to Alexander Matveev, however, each car was driven for over 3,000 miles before being dismantled, inspected, and reassembled in readiness for the rally. Avtoexport had also prepared three Moskvič 427 wagons to serve as support vehicles along the 16,000-mile trail to Mexico City.

Perhaps if these principles had been applied to a certain GP Beach Buggy and a certain Trident Venturer, things might have turned out so very differently!

14

A Series of Unfortunate Events
(Part Two)

With a 20,000-strong crowd cheering from the grandstands and bleachers, competing cars were faced with a staggered getaway from Wembley Stadium during the morning of April 19, 1970. First up to depart were Nos. 1 to 45, and with the Triumph 2.5PI of British trio Bobby Buchanan-Michaelson, Roy Fidler, and Jimmy Bullough, a late replacement for original crew member David Benson, in pole position, John Caulcutt inched the beach buggy along the line, fuel tanks refitted, to take its place. Slotting in between the Bolivian National Team's BMW 2002Ti and the Australian BLMC 1800, Noel Hutchinson looked around at the spectacle of the stadium, the shouts and whistles of spectators vying with the lusty throbbing of the buggy's motor. Poor David was suffering from severe lack of sleep and thus took his place in the noisy rear of the car, hopeful he might get a bit of rest on the road down to Dover. As the minute hand ticked, the countdown to departure began and, with a roar from the crowd, No. 1 was away. No doubt the trio kept an eye on the display board and watched the cars in front as they gradually moved forward in line, the throaty growl of the stroked out motor a stark contrast to the more discreet idling sounds of the 1800 in front and BMW behind.

At last, it was their turn, and, as commentator Raymond Baxter expressed faux surprise that there was actually a buggy on the ramp, John gunned the engine and No. 30 took its leave out through the stadium arch and off into north London roads. Noel remembered streets lined with spectators: "They were virtually leaning over into the buggy shouting encouragement. I remember distinctly, John saying it's worth it just for this! It was such a zany entry and everybody seemed to know about the buggy, no doubt thinking, 'Who are these crazy people taking a beach buggy around the world?'"

Next up was the Trident Venturer, looking decidedly laden as it bounced and groaned up onto the ramp. It was too late to alter anything, and, with a wave of the flag, away it went, Chris Marriott and Jack Dill waving happily against one or two odds!

Last, after a musical hiatus, came the Mustang, probably the most fit-for-purpose of the three cars. Lavinia's long blonde hair no doubt got a few journalists hot and bothered; Lavinia was one of the very few women competing in the rally, and the only competitor in a co-ed team. The Mustang itself looked as if it meant business, and although Pat had reservations about the weight of the roof-mounted toolbox, the car wasn't alone in having assorted kit strapped on top: the diesel-powered, Yugoslavian

No. 50 sets off from Wembley, April 19, 1970: (*left to right*) **John Caulcutt** (*driving*) **and Noel Hutchinson (courtesy Guido Devreker).**

Peugeot 404 appeared to have a double bed strapped to its roof! With a fierce growl from the Mustang's V8 motor, the Job's Dairy team was away, following an intentionally convoluted route through London before heading off towards the south coast and the port of Dover.

The Mustang and the buggy arrived in Dover without incident, although poor David Stewart was having to cope with the realization that sleep in the noisy buggy would prove a challenge as he took over driving duties on the run south. Both cars checked in with marshal Peter Riley, ably assisted by young Mike Broad, who was on hand to answer questions and accompany vehicles and competitors onto the ferry to France. Waiting to drive onto the boat, the buggy team gave some attention to the car's carburetion. "The carburetors hadn't been balanced properly," Noel explained. "Fortunately, for us, along came Bill Bengry, who was driving the Rolls-Royce Silver Shadow with the exhaust passing over the roof, another car receiving much media attention—and by Rolls-Royce. It was an engine very familiar to him as he used to rally a Beetle. Admittedly, he couldn't spend long but after some careful adjustment the carburetors were far better."

Meanwhile, the members of the Venturer team were quickly realizing that the car, although extraordinarily powerful, wasn't happy with its payload, so a slightly apprehensive run south meant that, at the very first timed control at the channel port, they were 20 minutes late!

Aboard the ferry, competitors chatted, ate, snoozed, or studied maps and roadbooks until it was time to return to their cars in the hold. Then it was off and away

The Ford Mustang at Wembley, April 19, 1970: Lavinia Roberts (*foreground in car*) and Pat Hazlerigg (*background in car*). Hazlerigg's name is misspelled on the car (courtesy Guido Devreker).

into France towards Metz, via Arras, and then over the West German frontier to the passage control at Saarbrücken. The fast *autobahn* sped the vehicles onwards in the dark and rain, Noel now driving and really enjoying the powerful buggy, although he quickly learnt not to be too hasty balancing clutch and throttle, otherwise the car's front end threatened to rear up!

The Mustang was also making excellent progress, Lavinia and Pat enjoying the car's performance and handling on the fast highways, even if they were slightly less enamored by the constantly sleeping Jones on the back seat, knocked out perhaps by an abundance of travel sickness medication. Chris and Jack, however, were already in trouble as the heavily laden Venturer was just not coping with the lack of clearance between tire and wheel arch. "Early on, the back wheels were rubbing on the wheel arches, that's how much it had sunk," Chris explained. "So, we cut holes in the top of the wheel arches—they were fibre glass—which was fine until it started raining! Then it was thoroughly uncomfortable, to put it mildly, we had mud … on the route, half-way across…. We had already worn the tyres down quite a lot by then."

Onwards they sped towards Sofia in Bulgaria, via Munich, Vienna, and Belgrade. The buggy was powerful, which allowed for some deft overtaking of slower traffic, but somewhere between Vienna and Budapest, the team gradually became aware that they were losing fuel. "At first, we were not quite sure what was the source, but then realized that fuel was weeping from one of the fuel take-offs," Noel recalled. "They were at the rear of these long rectangular aluminium pannier tanks. The take-off was simply a stub of aluminium tubing welded to the tank body. Onto these take-offs were clipped plastic fuel lines going through to the pumps. But, with the vibration, the plastic was moving causing the welded stubs to start cracking around the weld."

They made it to the Budapest passage control, where excited spectators crowded around to see this unique rally car. Many a Hungarian held lit cigarettes as they pawed over the buggy, urgently prompting the team to ask an armed soldier, undoubtedly on crowd-control duty, to warn the throng back, which he duly did—with force! At the first available opportunity, John contacted GP Speedshop back in England to seek advice and was assured they would dispatch the originally proposed rubber fuel bags to Monza, where an enforced rest stop, service point, and *parc fermé* were scheduled. The team had no choice but to continue on to Belgrade in Yugoslavia, resigned to the fact that they would need to continue stopping to refill the tank. The leak, however, was getting worse, to the point where they were forced to stop in a small village. Did anyone have a spare fuel tank they could have? Extraordinarily, a local farmer obliged, so they strapped the tank to the roof and ran a makeshift fuel line to the motor. However, when they filled the temporary tank with gas, fuel spewed out through various holes! Using pieces of wood, they fashioned a setup whereby the fuel remained below the errant holes and thus proceeded onwards, making it across the border into Yugoslavia. Eventually they needed to stop for more gas and, spotting a station, they pulled in and went about topping up the roof-mounted tank. Finished, Noel fired the engine. Nothing. What? "It had a hydraulic lock from petrol entering the bores as the result of pressure from the head of fuel from the tank, forcing open the needle valves on the carburetors," Noel explained. "The next thing I knew there was an almighty whoosh, and all I could see through the rear plastic window was a sheet of flame coming up from the engine. Yelling fire, John and David bailed out instantly and managed to put the fire out with the extinguishers we were carrying. Meanwhile the petrol station attendant had run off down the road, completely abandoning his filling station!" Once calm had been restored, attempts to restart the buggy proved futile and, with heavy hearts, John, David, and Noel realized their rally was over. What to do next? Help came in the form of some local car enthusiasts who helped get the car to a local garage. Over an inspection pit, with the buggy's engine removed, they discovered that the roller crank had bent out of shape. How were they going to get the crank re-engineered? John decided to travel onwards to meet a girlfriend in Milan so Noel and David agreed to find a way to transport the crankshaft and meet up with John. Thus, via a number of hitchhiking adventures, the crankshaft was delivered to an engineering shop in Milan, where David agreed to take responsibility for the car, while John and Noel enjoyed a meandering and highly entertaining trip back to England. Meanwhile, David eventually got back to the Yugoslavian village with the repaired crankshaft, got the buggy running again, and drove it back to the UK, although not before breaking down again in the French town of Amiens, once more removing the crank and then taking it back to England for further repair before returning to France and getting mixed up in the local Rally of Picardy, spectators perplexed that a rally car was apparently going in the wrong direction!

Looking back, David had some ideas about why the fuel problem occurred: "The tanks were sub-contracted by GP Cars to another local firm and the pick-up pipes, I can't remember where they had been positioned. I seem to remember they came out of the rear end of the tanks, and they just fractured because they hadn't been given any mechanical support. They'd just been welded coming out of the side of the tanks or the end of the tanks."

Meanwhile, both the Mustang and the Venturer had made it to the Sofia control in Bulgaria, albeit with some discomfort for Jack and Chris, and had then about-tailed, as per the revisions caused by heavy snow, and retraced the way they had come before turning off and following the new course down to Titograd and the start of the foreshortened first European *prime*, the Montenegro. This was the teams' first opportunity to really test both their skills and their vehicles over 50 miles of mountain road and many hairpin bends, requiring an average speed of 54 miles per hour. The Mustang was in excellent shape, but how would the injured Trident fare?

Pat Hazlerigg, designated driver for the *prime* in No. 86, brought the Mustang home at the finish control at Kotor 18 minutes down on the target time, beating 23 other cars into the bargain. "The Mustang behaved absolutely brilliantly, you could power it around corners," Pat recalled. "Phenomenal torque and you could use that torque to power it, you could really dump it." Pleased with the result, Pat was weary so Lavinia suggested he get some rest while she would navigate for David to give him the chance to drive.

Jack Dill took the wheel for the 17th/21st Lancers' effort and was making decent progress. Until he wasn't. "We hit one of the corners and bounced down a bank, not desperately because the car was recoverable, and one wheel was doing that and the other was doing that," Chris explained. "So, we took the steering arm out and we put it on a rock and belted it with a hammer until it was about straight and then we screwed it back again. The car was fine until you hit a bump, when it went sharp left!" Unfortunately, although their army-trained "just get on and solve the problem" approach got the car going again, they were out of time and out of the rally. Defeated yet undaunted, Chris and Jack decided to continue at a leisurely pace to Lisbon, enjoying the delights of Cannes and the Côte d'Azur, the French Riviera, along the way. Rumor has it they even put the large windshield washer tank to good use, filling it with gin to take back to England, but this cannot be confirmed! The team's early exit from the rally was, from one perspective, a lucky break. "The awful thing to say, in a funny sort of way, it was almost a relief!" mused Chris. "We realised that actually we were fools to try it anyway and if we'd done what we did in [Yugoslavia], if we'd done that in Brazil, none of us had any money, we hadn't thought about what to do. It's never going to happen, we'll be all right! But it would have been a very big problem."

The Job's Dairy Mustang drove on along the Adriatic coast before heading upwards to the second *prime*, the Serbian. The route up to Glamoč was difficult and in some places extremely confusing, seemingly offering any number of potential directions to follow. Thus, whether it was from lack of experience, tiredness, or even an excess of travel sickness pills, David lost control of the powerful car and crashed off the road. Pat woke to "crunch, crunch, crunch bang! Get out, get out! Not easy to get out of the back seat, it faced across the car, a single seat." Shaken, the team examined the car and realized they'd need help pulling it back onto the road. One of the front wheels looked decidedly crooked, but when the car was finally extricated from its unscheduled resting place, a swift wheel change seemed to get the Mustang back into rally-fitness. Still within the time threshold for arrival at the start control, they carried on, Pat now driving, anxious to reach Glamoč. Suddenly, a hefty bump over a pothole brought everything to a grinding halt. The impact broke an already injured track rod connection, and no amount of welding, provided by a local garage, could get them to the *prime* entrance before it closed. After showing such early promise, the Job's Mustang was out.

Looking back, Pat reflected that the high point of the rally for him was arriving at Dover and being surprised by fellow members of Junior Leaders' Regiment, there to wish him well. And even though it was, for her, such an ignominious ending, Lavinia had no regrets. "It was a wonderful thing to have done, I wouldn't have missed it," she explained. "It was a wonderful experience and just a pity that we weren't better organized to have done the thing better.... I'd have liked to have done it better, in hindsight, but hey … we were young. It was a wonderful thing to have done."

15

Cast and Crew
(Part Two)

Examining the final entry list for the 1970 London to Mexico World Cup Rally, the roster of men and women who would ease their vehicles away down the starting ramp at Wembley Stadium on April 19, 1970, it's quickly apparent that, as well as the professional drivers and navigators in evidence, there were plenty of hugely experienced folks who would be driving commercially sponsored, privately entered, or armed forces–backed cars on the road to Aztec Stadium in Mexico City. The field could not be neatly divided into professional and amateur categories; some of these competitors were already rally-hardened with experience on the national and international circuit, including the 10,000-mile endurance rally that ran from England's capital to Sydney only 18 months before. Among the all-comers, the array of eclectic machines and perhaps naïve hopefuls, there were also a significant number of competitors who could potentially give the pros a real run for their money.

Back for another bite at the endurance rally cherry, after his endeavors on the road to Sydney in 1968, British driver Terry Hunter was again at the wheel of a Porsche, again backed by Swiss food supplement company Bio-Strath and this time supported by hugely experienced co-driver—and 1961 Tulip Rally winner—Geoff Mabbs. Hunter had progressed from club rallies to national events in the 1950s and early 1960s and had a first taste of the international circuit in 1962 on the *Coupe de Alpes* or Alpine Rally, driving an 850-cubic-centimeter (51.9-cubic-inch) Morris Mini Minor. Not to be messed with, during an altercation with a rally manager in the mid–1960s, Hunter took exception to a comment, picked the manager up, and hung him on a coat peg! Having been forced out by mechanical problems during the 1968 London–Sydney Marathon, Hunter was determined that he and Mabbs would bring some glory to Porsche and Bio-Strath in Mexico City.

Another competitor who posed a serious threat to the factory-backed teams was German-born Kenyan, Edgar Herrmann. Driving a Porsche 911, Herrmann and his co-driver, Hans Schüller, had secured the private entry award at Sydney in December 1968, and, just a few weeks prior to departure at Wembley, the duo had won the difficult East African Safari Rally outright in a Datsun 1600 SSS. This time opting for two co-drivers, Herrmann was joined by Dieter Benz and Horst Walter and would drive a Mercedes-Benz 280SE sponsored by the Ulm Racing and Rally Team.

Dutchman Rob Janssen was also back, this time swapping his compact DAF 55 for a tough, rally-proven Datsun 1600 SSS, and anyone running an eye over the

No. 2, the Porsche 911 of Terry Hunter and Geoff Mabbs (courtesy Mike Wood).

entry list at Wembley on April 19, 1970, may well have recognized a few other famil-iar names, especially if they had followed the London–Sydney Marathon 18 months previously. Back for more were British pair Peter Graham and Leslie Morrish, again in a Ford Cortina Savage V6, prepared at Race Proved Ltd by David Price, who would also join the team as second co-driver. Also returning was Kim Brassington, with a Cortina that he "'had left over from the Marathon' with a 3-litre V6 engine and Bullet gearbox"[1]; David Skittrall, this time in a Ford Capri with a Ford Cologne V6 engine, specially prepared by Ford GB's Research and Development department at Dunton in Essex; and two-time British Rally Champion Bill Bengry, this time in an exqui-sitely prepared Rolls-Royce Silver Shadow. Based on the prestige car manufacturer's U.S. export model, Bengry had undertaken all the modifications and adaptations to the luxury auto himself, including his hallmark vertical "tail-pipe" system, this time running the Shadow's dual exhaust out through apertures in the hood, up either side of the windshield, and along either side of the roof. Suffice to say, Rolls-Royce ini-tially saw the whole enterprise as beneath them, with *Motoring News* reporting that the luxury car company was "not in the least bit interested in what their customers do with their cars after they leave the factory."[2] However, this rather snooty attitude would change as the rally got underway!

Others giving endurance rally another go were British property tycoon Bobby Buchanan-Michaelson; former Formula One racing driver, author, and all round *bon viveur* Innes Ireland; and fellow former racing driver Michael Taylor. All three hoped to put the mechanical catastrophes of 1968 behind them. This time, Buchanan-Michaelson would be teaming up with 1966 British Rally Champion

The Rolls-Royce of rally cars: No. 52 at Wembley, April 19, 1970 (courtesy Guido Devreker).

Roy Fidler and 1967 champion Jimmy Bullough in a Triumph 2.5PI prepared by auto tuning company Janspeed to the BLMC Competitions Department's specifications. Keeping in character, Ireland would be competing with Taylor in another Mercedes-Benz 280SE, sponsored by the extremely fashionable, members-only London nightclub Annabel's. Joining them would be Annabel's proprietor, Mark Birley.

Other 1968 Marathon alumni included Cecil Woodley (no doubt hoping to avoid the indignities that befell his entry on the road to Belgrade in Yugoslavia 18 months earlier), Welshman Barry Hughes, British Army Captains Christopher Marriott and John "Jack" Dill joining forces in the Trident Venturer, Australians Tubman and Welinski, Colin Taylor in a SAAB V4, Bob Freeborough in a BLMC Special Tuning–prepared BLMC 1800, Freeborough's Marathon team member Dennis Cresdee in another 1800, and the founder of the Lydden Hill race track in Kent, England—William "Bill" Chesson—in an Escort GT.

Remaining first-time endurance rally competitors, who hailed from countries as diverse as Argentina, Yugoslavia, Thailand, the Netherlands, Canada, Kuwait, Italy, the United States, and Antigua, as well as the other British and Irish freshmen, no doubt comprised a mix of starry-eyed hopefuls and dangerous dark horses. Certainly German-born Peruvian Peter Kube had form, having already competed in the Rally of the Incas, achieving a formidable second place in that event in 1968, and he would again be driving a 2002Ti! West Germany's partnership of Alfred Katz and Alfred Kling had also achieved some impressive performances on the European circuit and definitely knew how to rally a big Benz sedan—Katz won the *Rallye Tour d'Europe* in 1962 driving a 220SE. Bolivian national team member William Bendeck had won at least five national titles going into the London to Mexico Rally, Argentinian racing driver Gastón Perkins had won Argentina's *Turismo Carretera* the previous year, and what Yugoslavia's Ivica Vukoja, driving one of the bullet-proof Peugeot 404s, or the Italian Mondini brothers, both entering a Porsche 911, could achieve was anyone's bet! British Mike Butler also had considerable experience, in both the driver's and navigator's seats, in the UK and mainland Europe, and his Ford Escort 1300GT had been superbly prepared by Ron Pellatt at the Auto Sports Center in Kent, outsourcing some of the work to Broadspeed. Pellatt had stripped the car to its shell, strengthened the panels, fitted a five-speed box to give the small engine better cruising at lower revs, and lowered the compression to accommodate variable fuel quality. He fitted a cable clutch unit to ease maintenance and replacement if required, and even opted to paint sponsorship and other details on the Escort's bodywork, thus avoiding the risk of souvenir-hungry spectators peeling off decals! Ron and friend Alan would also provide mechanical support for Butler and co-driver Doug Harris in Spain and Portugal, a move that earned some favors for Harris and Butler during the rally.

Among these experienced rallyists, there were also a number of entrants with only a little competitive pedigree under their belts, including British trio Brian Englefield, Keith Baker, and Adrian Lloyd-Hirst in an independently prepared Triumph 2.5PI. With financial backing provided by Lloyd-Hirst, Englefield had meticulously handled the car's preparation at his own garage, making sure that the Triumph had a fuel metering unit for altitude driving and even reengineering the position of the radiator fan to give more space. "I had rallied and … under heavy braking…. I had had the engine go forward on the mountings and the fan go through the radiator," he explained. Paying particular attention to balancing the engine and the crank,

The Triumph 2.5PI of Brian Englefield, Keith Baker, and Adrian Lloyd-Hirst heads out of South London, April 19, 1970 (courtesy Ted Taylor).

Englefield kept the car's original dark green color but added a gold roof and gold Minilite wheels, overlooking the fact that this combination was actually Australia's national team colors! Regardless, Englefield believes that his Triumph was just as well prepared and powerful as the professional BLMC 2.5PIs.

British Ken Bass was an ex–Formula Three racing driver, who decided to team up with his good friend and ex–Ford apprentice Graham Waring—Waring knew his way around a competitive automobile as his business was involved in preparing racing sedans. Bass's weapon of choice for the London to Mexico Rally was a BMW 2002Ti, ordered in left-hand drive form via the UK BMW distributor. On delivery from Germany, the car was taken to Waring's shop where he and Bass carried out all of the necessary preparations themselves to ensure it was rally-fit, double-welding its seams, fitting a roll-cage, detuning the motor's compression to meet the rigors of altitude driving, and upgrading the suspension and dampers. Knowing they would have little opportunity to seek BMW support along the route, they also included a carefully organized collection of spare components.

The relative newcomers to endurance rallying may well have felt intimidated at the sight of so many veterans of national, international, or transcontinental motorsports, or they may have simply stuck out their collective chins and resolved to try and beat the odds, reported by *Autosport* magazine on April 16 as "8–1, Paddy Hopkirk. 10–1: Clark, Aaltonen, Mäkinen. 12–1: Greaves, Mikkola. 14–1: Cowan, Green."[3]

One seasoned professional who knew her way around the European International Rally circuit was two-time *Coupe des Dames* winner Patricia "Tish" Ozanne. Recruiting two young drivers, Bronwyn "Bron" Burrell and Katrina "Tina" Kerridge, to join her in an independently prepared Austin Maxi for the London to Mexico World Cup Rally, it was all to play for as she released the handbrake and eased the dark blue Maxi down the starting ramp.

16

Puff the Magic Maxi
(Part One)

The island of Guernsey sits in the English Channel, just off the French Normandy coast. While not part of the United Kingdom, it shares its currency and English is its main language. Defense is also administered by the UK, as well as certain international relations. During World War II, Guernsey was occupied by German forces, the imminent threat of which led to a mass evacuation of islanders over to the UK. Taking her place on the very last boat before the invasion was 17-year-old Patricia "Tish" Ozanne. Ozanne spent the remainder of the war in England, and after peace was declared she decided to take "a two-year round-the world voyage, ending up on a sheep station in New Zealand. During this time, she was challenged to a duel by a woman who was sufficiently upset at Tish's interest in her boyfriend. Fancying herself with a .22, Tish agreed to firearms at dawn. Fortunately, the hefty brute was too inebriated to pitch up the following morning so Trish triumphed by default"[1]! Returning to England, she took up residence in the Suffolk countryside, which offered little in the way of entertainment and adventure. By chance, she came across a motoring magazine that announced a local motor rally. Her interested piqued, she decided to try her hand, and thus began her first miles towards what would be an international rally career that lasted 20 years, during which she competed as a British Motor Corporation (BMC) competitions team driver for a time, tackling events including the British Royal Automobile Club (RAC), Monte Carlo, Tulip, German, and Geneva rallies. She won the women's prize on the London Rally of 1961 and, just prior to the London to Mexico World Cup Rally, she drove a Mini on the Monte Carlo Rally with soon-to-be competing rival Pat Wright as co-driver.

During the second half of 1969, Tish read about the forthcoming sequel to the 1968 London–Sydney Marathon, this time to be a 16,000-mile endurance rally from London to Mexico City. Tish decided to enter and set about securing both a car and as much financial sponsorship as she could. Being a regular customer of Marshall, a large British Leyland dealership in the east of England, she got talking with the company's racing and tuning specialist, Peter Baldwin. "After speaking with the top men at Marshall about assistance, I was asked by the workshop manager Gordon Pluck if I would like to take on the project," he explained. "I could have my apprentice Ray Brand to help and we would be guided by British Leyland at Abingdon, who were building the works Maxis." No stranger to competitive racing, Peter had been racing a Mini since 1967. Work got underway at Marshall's Jesus Lane depot in Cambridge, with Peter in regular contact with BLMC at Abingdon, Oxfordshire, to make sure the Austin Maxi would be prepared to their specification.

Having secured a car for the rally, Tish's thoughts turned to building a team for the event. As she had competed with female co-drivers throughout the 1960s, creating an all-women team was the only option, so she began looking around the area to see who might fit the bill. She also put the word out among rally and motorsports friends and acquaintances, one of whom was Peter Cooper, a former rally driver now working for the RAC. Peter gave the request some thought and decided to pay a visit to young rally driver Bronwyn "Bron" Burrell at her workplace in Haslemere, Surrey. Bron recalled: "I said, 'I missed the London–Sydney, of course, '68, and I was really quite upset about that, I hadn't been rallying that long to know about it.' I said, 'I hear there's another rally coming up, the London to Mexico, is that right?' … 'Yes,' he said. I said…. 'I wish I could do that.' He said, 'Funnily…. I know someone who needs a co-driver, I'll put you in touch with her, you'll like her.' I said, 'Oh Peter, would you? That would be brilliant.' He said, 'I'll ring her up and get her to contact you.'"

Originally from New Zealand, Bron was bitten by the motorsports bug as soon as she had learnt to drive as a 17-year-old. Initially preferring horses, on her mother's instruction she took her first lesson and discovered that she really liked being behind the wheel of a car, even if was just a driving school's dual-controlled Morris Minor!

Puff with (*left to right*) **Tish Ozanne, Bron Burrell, and Tina Kerridge** (courtesy Katrina Kerridge-Reynolds).

All things equestrian, including horse trailer, were soon replaced by a desire to really get to grips with driving skills, so Bron begged and pleaded with her mother to let her borrow the family car so she could drive over to the Brands Hatch racing circuit and take some racing lessons, her heart set on getting behind the wheel of single-seat racing car. Thus, she began to attend lessons, sneaking out of her secretarial school every Friday so she could get over to Brands Hatch.

A New Zealand compatriot and friend, Nancy Wise, got wind of Bron's new ambition and, being a television producer working on the BBC show *In Town Tonight*, she suggested running a piece about this young woman who was learning how to be a racing driver. The production crew descended on Brands Hatch, filmed an interview with her, and took some footage of her doing some laps. With the show scheduled to go out two weeks later, the following week she encountered 1963 Formula One World Champion Jim Clark and thought nothing of asking his advice. "I said, hi Jim, I'm going on the television," she remembered. "He said, well that's good … what are you going to be doing? I said…. I've been driving the Formula 3 car around but…. I'm not sure I got the right line."[2] (In all kinds of circuit racing, from carts to bikes to cars, the racing line or simply 'the line' is the optimal path around a racecourse.) Jim promptly offered to take Bron around the circuit in a Ford Cortina Lotus, the same model of car in which he would win the 1964 British Saloon (sedan) Car Championship. Bron studied the form, and over 10 laps she noticed how smooth the travel was. On completion, she thanked the champion and then suggested perhaps he'd held back a bit, given that she was a passenger. With a raised eyebrow, he suggested she go and ask what the lap times were. "Well," she recalled, "he'd only unofficially broken the lap record for that particular car by point eight of a second or something! The thing that got me was that it was so smooth. No screaming tires, no chucking the car sideways … which they all do nowadays, it seems. It was just so smooth, so easy and I thought, that's the way to do it."

Buoyed by the experience, Bron was determined to get some lap practice in on the day of the TV show as she had her first proper race scheduled for the following Sunday. Once again cutting class—claiming she had a dental appointment—she was back at the racing circuit and out on the track, trying to improve her times. She was definitely improving, but, remembering Jim Clark's approach, decided to try again, this time really going for speed. Waking up in the hospital, she had no recollection of hitting a marshal's post. "I think I locked the wheels up," she explained. "I'd torn the wheel off, the linkage had come past, hit me on the head and I crashed into the bank. Didn't damage the car that much, it was racing on the Sunday, but I'm now, for the next six weeks, flat on my back and they think I've broken my neck!" Fortunately, this was not the case, but in light of the BBC TV show, she did make headline news, which in turn exposed her extracurricular activities to the secretarial school.

Thinking perhaps that circuit racing might not suit her, she turned to rallying, inspired by Rosemary Smith's achievements, and spent the next few years competing in club events, which led to goes on a few national and international rallies, including the International Rally of Great Britain in 1968, driving with Joan Pink. This got her noticed by Peter Cooper, and, true to his word, during the tail end of 1969, Bron received a call from Tish Ozanne to ask whether she might be interested in co-driving in the London to Mexico Rally. Bron didn't need to be asked twice!

Tish now needed a third crewmember and didn't have far to look. There was a local woman who obviously knew her way around cross-country rallying and endurance trials, so, in February 1970, Tish gave Tina Kerridge a call.

Katrina "Tina" Kerridge was no stranger to the rigors of rally motorsports when she was invited to join Tish and Bron and compete in the 1970 London to Mexico World Cup Rally. By the mid–1960s, she was juggling the challenges of raising two small children with accompanying her then husband around the British autocross and rallycross circuit in which he regularly competed. Usually with a movie camera in hand, she was fascinated by the thrills and spills on offer and the obvious love of the sport on show by the various competitors. Not content to just be a supportive bystander, she decided to get behind the wheel and was soon taking the co-driver's seat on a number of long-distance trials, which invariably included a section where cars would be required to make one or more non-stop climbs up invariably muddy and steep hills. As a consequence, Tina learned the skills required to coax a car upwards and through thick, wet mud which, in essence, combines reducing tire pressure, revving the engine, and, if the car begins to slow and spin its wheels in the greasy dirt, spring up and down in an attempt to use gravity to assist forward motion. Bouncing up an Exeter Trial in southwest England in 1966, she didn't know that four years later, these skills would become a cause for contention somewhere in the middle of the Argentinian pampas!

Tina quickly moved on to competing in 12-car rallies, local club events, this time taking the wheel in her rear-engine Hillman Imp, before progressing to national

Tina Kerridge rallying her Hillman Imp, 1969 (courtesy Katrina Kerridge-Reynolds).

rallies. "I decided I would change the Imp for a Honda S800, such a pretty car, she certainly did me proud … being way out in front on trials and rallies," she remembered. "Unfortunately, I did put her into an ice-covered pond on a trial!" Thus, with the generous support of family and friends providing childcare, she continued to hone her competitive driving skills over a variety of rough and rugged terrain.

Tina was quite taken aback by Tish's offer but, given her family commitments, immediately gave a grateful and gracious no. Tish wasn't about to give up that easily, however, and suggested that she might send over information about the rally. She encouraged Tina to give it all further consideration before making a decision. "As I read through the various documents detailing the route of the rally," Tina recalled, "I realized that this would be an adventure of a lifetime. Could I go on this rally…? After family discussions and finally being convinced that my ability to be part of their team could be an asset, I… agreed to participate." Family mobilized to organize childcare for elementary school-age Karen and Kelsey during the potentially six-week period their mother might be absent, and Tina was amused that both children saw the whole thing as adventure they could follow at school!

With work underway by Peter and his team at Marshall to get the Maxi ready, the three women set about getting the vaccinations required to enter the various countries along the South American route and obtaining the necessary visas, currency, and documentation needed to enable both car and competitors to enter, and then leave, each country. They were also drilled by Peter on basic mechanics. "He was brilliant in getting us to understand the mechanics," Tina explained. "One of the things which was important was how to change a wheel quickly. We practiced and practiced until we actually managed to do it in under two minutes." Tish was also busy securing additional sponsorship from various sources, including clothes designer Jean Allen, who provided the fashionable white catsuits they wore to publicity shoots. Other items of clothing were provided by department store C&A and Husky. "One sponsor provided us with paper knickers, pink, white and blue," Tina recalled. "They were a godsend, how were we going to do our laundry on the road?"

Local garage owner and club rallyist Tim Reynolds knew Tina and was well aware of her impending London to Mexico adventure. With an idea, he approached Marshall's PR person, Colin McCullock, and proposed the idea of putting together a service crew to follow the dark blue Maxi across Europe and assist with any servicing and mechanical issues as needed. Again, Marshall saw the publicity opportunities for the Austin Maxi product and sanctioned the use of an ex-demonstrator Maxi as service car, while Tim's garage would pick up fuel costs. Tim had done his mechanical apprenticeship at British automobile manufacturer Rootes and thus knew his way around a motor. As Peter and his apprentice Ray Brand had been preparing the rally Maxi, there wasn't much they didn't know about the car, so they were obvious choices to form the team. Thus, with Peter and Ray taking vacation pay, the women would now have a three-man service wagon at their disposal, at least between London and Lisbon.

BLMC were holding briefings about the rally for anyone entering a BLMC-manufactured automobile, so the three women attended and received information about the potential hazards of South America. The issue of weaponry was

The Jean Allen catsuits—(*left to right*) Tina, Bron, Tish (courtesy Katrina Kerridge-Reynolds).

raised—should they take firearms? The women opted against this, Tina suggesting that they could always use a tire iron to get out of danger! Driving at altitude was also discussed, with the recommendation that competitors carry small oxygen cylinders for driving over the Andes. While Bron couldn't make it, Tish and Tina visited the British naval training base at Portsmouth to get some experience of reduced oxygen supply using their decompression chambers. "Another thing BL told us: 'Don't drink the water or even clean your teeth in it, use bottled water,'" Tina recalled. "If we had to stay in a lodging somewhere, beware of cockroaches. If nature calls then stamp around on the ground, just in case of snakes!"

At last, the Maxi was ready, and Marshall, under Peter's supervision, had done an exceptional job. Gone was the car's signature feature, the tailgate, replaced with a trunk lid attached to a reinforced brace panel across the back of the car per BLMC's specification. Some steel panels were replaced with fiberglass to reduce weight, and a John Aley roll-cage was fitted. Wheel housings were bolted into the roof, and a bull-bar, or llama bar, as Bron described it, was attached to the Maxi's front end. It also had a 29-gallon gas tank to increase range, especially for the long stretches in South America. The rear bench was replaced with a single seat, the remaining space to be taken up with parts, equipment, and personal items. Tish, Bron, Tina, and Peter took the Maxi to a nearby field for a little testing over uneven terrain, and Tish was challenged to get the car airborne for a photo op. However, the sheer weight of the car proved too much, even with hugely experienced Tish behind the wheel! Bron said she

Tish trying to get the Maxi airborne (with Bron Burrell, *backseat,* **and Tina Kerridge) (courtesy Bronwyn Burrell).**

couldn't remember who said "she has no puff in her," but at the time the Peter, Paul and Mary song "Puff the Magic Dragon" was very popular. "Mind you, we did not at the time know what it referred to, as none of us were on drugs, etc., of any kind! So, we nicknamed her Puff."

On Saturday, April 18, 1970, Tish took Puff up to Wembley Stadium for scrutineering, and all was well. Mechanical components specified in the event regulation were duly marked, and then the car was placed in the holding area ready for the next day. All retired for the night in anticipation of what was to come—Bron recalled that she and her partner, Rob, stayed overnight in a small hotel nearby, and all of Tina's family had travelled to see her off. Peter, Tim, and Ray were also staying overnight, ready to take their place behind the Marshall Maxi once it departed the stadium. "I think of all of us, Tish had more idea about what might be ahead," Bron recalled.

Departure day dawned, and the three women, plus family, friends, and service crew, arrived at Wembley. There to greet them was Marshall's PR person, Colin McCullock, so they all joined in a champagne toast to the team and generally milled about chatting and sizing up the competition, no doubt intrigued by the Russian Moskvič parked on one side of the Maxi and the orange VW Bug, together with the three young Mexican men who made up its crew, on the other. Puff had been drawn as No. 20, which meant they were in the first group of teams to depart. As the time to line up for entry into the noisy stadium drew near, hugs and farewells were the order of the day and the service team got their red Maxi ready to be on hand outside so they could slot in behind as the women drove off into north London.

With Tish at the wheel, No. 20 took its place in the departure queue, all enjoying the festive atmosphere but ever watchful of the countdown clock. Tina spotted and waved to her two young children in the crowd, reminding herself that, all being well, she would see them in just six weeks. Finally, the Mexican VW drove up onto the ramp and was flagged away, so Tish released the parking brake, depressed the clutch, put the five-speed manual box into first, and edged up in the Bug's wake. "We're flagged down the ramp by Sir Alf Ramsey, John Sprinzel was there—bye John!" Bron remembered. "We trundle out of the stadium and I remember the crowds lining the street around London, it was extraordinary, they wouldn't do it today, I'm sure. The whole route was lined with people … there was that wonderful AA [Automobile Association] sign, how many miles we had to go to Mexico—16,173, or something like that, which was clever of them."

After the ferry crossing to Boulogne in France, Bron recalled the journey as long, rainy, and boring, although beyond the German border and on to the first passage control at Munich, breakfast at the city's BMW factory was most welcome and the red service Maxi narrowly avoided being taken out by a truck that changed lanes without signaling on the dark, rain-slick *autobahn*! Austria saw competitors arrive at Vienna's Schönbrunn Palace, where coffee and cake was on offer. Then the field continued on to Budapest in Hungary, where a Russian rally team shared food with the hungry trio, and then on to Belgrade in Yugoslavia, before arriving at Sofia in Bulgaria, where competitors were given a specific departure time from the control—anyone arriving early would be held there until that time. Some of the savvier competitors had booked hotel accommodation, but Tish, Tina, and Bron had to get two

Tina (left) and Bron waiting for the start, Wembley, April 19, 1970 (courtesy Ken Green).

or three hours of rest where they could before an unpleasant breakfast. Then it was Bron's turn behind the wheel. "We took a rota," she explained. "If I was tired driving, I'd say, 'I'm tired now, whose turn?' Just purely because you didn't want to get over-tired and the best thing is, three-hour stints are good, longer than that, you know, silly, unless you're on a *prime*, of course, in which case you just keep going."

As the first European *prime* had been revised to account for heavy snowfall, competitors now drove back part of the way they had come before turning left and making for Titograd. The road was now a little more challenging—gone were the *autobahns* and decent pavement—but the team made it to their first *prime* control, where Peter, Ray, and Tim were waiting in case Puff needed any attention. All was well, however, so Tish took the wheel—it was agreed that she would drive all the speed stages, given her experience. Off into the Montenegro *prime*. "We found the road turning into a narrow path," Tina recalled. "It was the mountain pass with a huge drop on one side, lots of hairpin bends and all the time we were trying to avoid the oncoming trucks, what a nightmare!" At the finish control at Kotor, they were 18 minutes beyond the target time but still faster than 23 other teams— definitely a satisfactory start.

The next *prime*, the Serbian, was a tougher task for Puff and the women, not least because it gave the team their first opportunity to put their wheel change drill to the test. "This was the *prime* that would see a lot of damage done to the cars," Tina explained. "Punctures were going to be one of the main problems. Our teamwork came together here as we had two punctures on this *prime*. This was when we found out how good we were at changing wheels!" Negotiating the 119-mile mix of asphalt, rough track, potholes, and unreliable plank bridges, not to mention wheel changes, Tish got the Maxi home safely but was 83 penalty points down as they got their road-book stamped and signed at Bosanska Krupa. To compound matters, the Maxi's drive shaft had been damaged, but the attendant BLMC service team, there to sort any of the professional entries' problems, came to the rescue, thus enabling the women to continue on to the enforced rest stop at Monza in Italy, where their own service team would meet them. On arrival, one of their sponsors, Cambridge Steroscan, wired Marshall: "Dirty birds have arrived safely. Running out of drive shafts. Please send more."

Twenty-five-year-old Bron Burrell was no stranger to mischief, even under the watchful eye of forty-something Tish Ozanne, and Monza gave her the chance for some fun. On inspection, Puff needed some welding repairs to one of the roof-mounted spare wheel housings before the car was locked up in *parc fermé*, but, when Peter Baldwin looked around, neither the women nor his fellow service team were there to assist. Finishing the task, he went to the hotel where they were staying, got cleaned up, and went off for dinner by himself. He recalled: "I was asked by reception to go to room 21 as Bronwyn wanted to ask me a question. On knocking on the door, Tina answered and said that Bronwyn was in her room and was expecting me. I knocked and entered only to find her already in bed with the lights down low. I sat on the edge of the bed and said, 'Peter here, you called?' and a squeaky voice told me to get in and, not needing a second invitation, I squeezed under the covers only to find Tim Reynolds! Bronwyn burst out from the wardrobe laughing her head off!"

Needless to say, the ensuing giggling summoned Tish, who firmly suggested they all get some rest as the following day's start would be early!

Early it was—the departure control opened at 07:00—and away cars went, headed for the Italian frontier and the start of the San Remo *prime* at Ville San Pietro in the foothills of Mount Moro. Running to Camporosso, the stage offered drivers 65 miles of loose gravel surfaces that twisted and turned—all to be achieved in two hours, if penalty was to be avoided. Looking back, Tina reflected that Tish was brilliant, so experienced. "When we got to the end of the San Remo Prime," she recalled, "I got out and said, 'What the hell am I doing here? I've got two young children at home!' I thought I might never see them again. I needn't have worried, Tish drove those *primes* brilliantly although it still didn't stop me thinking about the sheer drops, hairpin bends, and the very slippery surface!" The San Remo behind them, there would be no rest for Tish since the same day competitors would need to endure another *prime*, the Alpine, which required crossing into France to Menton on the French Riviera and then climbing up to a passage control at Col de Turini, the mountain pass that plays such an integral part in the Monte Carlo Rally and was therefore familiar territory to Tish Ozanne.

Beyond the pass, the route continued to a small rural junction, Les Quatre Chemins, and the start of the *prime*, zigzagging into the mountains and then down again to Rouaine, via two passage controls at Sigale and Entrevaux, 62 miles of twists and turns, with a target time of 90 minutes. With pure concentration and Tina's navigational commands, Tish completed the course without a hitch, the Maxi performing beautifully. Over the two *primes* in Italy and France, No. 20 incurred a total of 72 penalty points. Both Bron and Tina were now seeing all of Tish's rallying experience come to the fore and had begun to believe they really could succeed in getting to Mexico.

Beyond Rouaine, there lay a very long transport section that stretched out of France, through Spain, and into Portugal, miles and miles of continuous driving before competitors would arrive at the start of the final European *prime*, the Portuguese at Arganil. "It was such a boring drive, that was dreadful," Bron recalled. "We were getting fed up with driving for the sake of driving, you know, there was nothing to do … we'd stop, because we'd have to get petrol, obviously, and we'd have something to eat but we never ate anything proper. Drink, probably mostly Coke…. We had a lot of fruit but we were always told by British Leyland…. 'Don't drink the local water, wherever you are … drink something that's bottled, don't eat any fruit that you don't peel, so bananas, oranges'…. And packets of biscuits [cookies]." However, as Tina explained, the mission came first: "We were getting closer to our goal, we just had to make it and prove that three girls can compete with the men."

At last, they reached Arganil and the 45-mile forest stage to Pampilhosa. Anyone familiar with the Portuguese TAP Rally would recognize this speed section, although this was to be completed at night for many, through swirling mist, the scent of pine trees strong in the air. By now, however, Bron was decidedly unwell, stomach pain worsening over every bump, so she hunkered down on the rear seat and tried to sleep as Tish tore around the stage, getting Puff to the finish control 35 minutes down on the target time.

Finally, they were on the road to Lisbon and the end of the European section of the rally. Approaching the capital city, a man stepped out and flagged them down. To their surprise, it was Sir Michael Marshall, managing director of the Marshall dealership, who had flown in to welcome them. With many congratulations, he suggested taking them to dinner while in Lisbon, which the women happily accepted. Then it was to the finish control at a SACOR gas station at Lisbon's city limits, before delivering Puff to *parc fermé*, where they were reunited with Peter, Ray, and Tim who, not being allowed to work on the Maxi in the closed area, yelled instructions through the fence so that the women could check and re-check everything before grabbing personal belongings and making arrangements for the gas tank to be drained before the car was pushed onto the quay in readiness for loading onto the ship bound for Rio de Janeiro. Out of the 71 cars that made it Lisbon, Tina recalled, "the ... surprise was that we were lying 35th overall."

While the rally cars were being shipped across the Atlantic, the women had a chance to relax and enjoy Lisbon, but not before hearing about their trusty service squad's own adventures on the road to Portugal. "As we travelled in Yugoslavia to the next service area, we were passed by Timo Mäkinen, who flagged us down to ask if we had any hose-clips with us," Peter Baldwin recounted. "His prop shaft was out of balance and had caused the gearbox to leak oil. I supplied him with two large hose-clips, which he fitted round the prop-shaft and went up the road to test it and returned saying they needed moving round. Ray slid underneath the car and moved them with their heads together to act as a weight. This happened once more before he returned with a thumbs up and sped off!"

All too soon, Peter and Ray had to drive the service Maxi back to England so, with many hugs, thanks, and farewells, and with Colin McCullock accompanying them, they set off, making it safely home but not before an altercation with Spanish law enforcement in the early hours of the morning. With no traffic around, they had overlooked a stop sign, and the police almost manhandled poor Ray out of the car! Needless to say, he refused to drive again until they were safely over the border into France!

Tim happily remained in Lisbon and accompanied the women to the awards ceremony at the casino in Estoril. The remainder of the time was spent relaxing and recharging batteries—Bron even got the opportunity to go horse riding with fellow competitor Prince Michael of Kent! However, all good things had to come to an end, and it was time for Tish, Bron, and Tina to jet off to Rio, leaving Tim to make his way back to England. "What an experience we had all shared," Tim remembered. "It was just a pity that we could not go on to South America with the girls. If only it had been discussed earlier, we might have been able to have organized a service crew for them. We wished them luck."

17

Miles to Go Before the Start

The online Collins English Dictionary defines "recce" as both a verb and a noun. Collins explains the verbal usage as follows: "If you recce an area, you visit that place in order to become familiar with it. People usually recce an area when they are going to return at a later time to do something there."[1] Collins offers the following example of "recce" used as a noun: "Uncle Jim took the air rifle and went on a recce to the far end of the quarry."[2] Notwithstanding Uncle Jim's motivations, reconnaissance or recce is an essential element in planning and then preparing for a rally, especially a long-distance event that will take competitors from England through 23 countries before arriving in Mexico!

With the rally route finalized, frenetic recce activity commenced and advance parties of rally drivers and navigators were dispatched by BLMC, Ford, Moskvič, and Citroën to follow and notate the trail from Boulogne in France to Lisbon in Portugal and/or from Rio de Janeiro in Brazil to Mexico City. Many of the recce parties comprised drivers and co-drivers who would actually compete in the event, such as London–Sydney Marathon veteran Paul Easter and co-driver John Handley, a competitive Mini specialist with much experience in rallycross, the motorsport that combined the rigors of a stage rally with the jostling and speed of circuit racing. Easter and Handley were dispatched by BLMC competitions head Peter Browning to survey some of the European section, including the first European *prime*, which would run from Peć to Titograd after a transport stage from Sofia. "We did the route through Austria, Hungary, into Sofia, and this stage was one of the old Liège-Sofia-Liège routes," Paul explained. "On the Liège, that was diabolical, that was still grim, snowing like hell. We eventually managed to limp into Dubrovnik … we couldn't get out of Dubrovnik for three hours; we were snowed up." Eventually, leaving their recce Mini behind, they took a complicated series of flights to get to Titograd, picked up the Mini courtesy of BLMC mechanics, and continued their survey. They then flew on to Lisbon, rented a car, practiced the Portuguese *prime* from Arganil, returned to Lisbon for a flight to Nice on the southern French coast, and practiced the French *prime*.

Ford's Stuart Turner was less concerned about the familiar European section than the challenges posed by South America, so he began sending out teams to investigate the route. Team members Hannu Mikkola and Timo Mäkinen "both came back looking worried and shaken," Roger Clark remembered. "'Much too long for a two-man crew. Need three men. Need big cars, Need oxygen. Awful roads,

Paul Easter's and John Handley's recce Mini, Glamoč, Yugoslavia, 1970 (courtesy Paul Easter).

terrible mountains, big drops.'"[3] In response, Turner dispatched Clark himself to South America. "I wanted to know," he said, "how he was going to cope with *Primes* that were more than 500 miles long, and sectors of more than 50 hours between time controls, without rest *and* at altitude."[4] As previously stated, Clark's response was that two-up in an Escort was the obvious solution. Another person drafted in to undertake recce work in South America was Henry Liddon, co-driver of choice for Rauno Aaltonen. Aaltonen explained how Liddon did most of the recce alone, hiring cars and paying for them from a bag of money he had with him—he eventually worked his way through 17 rentals! At one point, when Liddon couldn't find a rental car to replace the one he had exhausted, he called Turner back in England. "'Buy something then,' I suggested. 'I'm glad you said that because I already have,' he replied!" Turner recalled. "Unflappable and very resourceful was Henry."[5]

For BLMC, a number of South American recces were undertaken prior to the event itself, the first in November and December 1969, when Tony Nash and Brian Culcheth joined Uldarico Ossio to investigate the route from Rio de Janeiro to Lima, using a local Triumph 2000. This gave BLMC the chance to assess some components they had been developing. "This Triumph 2000 had rather weak shock-absorbers so, to give the car some chance of lasting, the recce crew phoned Abingdon for some of the uprated shock absorbers which we had been testing," BLMC Assistant Competitions Manager Bill Price explained.[6] Subsequent recces proved a logistical headache, eventually involving a case of whisky, the near destruction of three rental VW Bugs, and the help of a certain *El Chueco*, at time of writing the only Argentinian ever to win the Argentinian Formula One Grand Prix!

After the woes that befell the poor local Triumph 2000 on the first BLMC recce,

BLMC decided to send out a couple of ex–RAC Rally 2.5PIs to South America to support further explorations of the route. While this was being organized, Culcheth returned to Rio, this time accompanied by Paddy Hopkirk, Andrew Cowan, Culcheth's co-driver Johnstone Syer, and Cowan's co-driver Brian Coyle. Together with Ossio, they rented three VW Bugs and set off on the more than 2,000 miles of rally trail to Montevideo, which included two *primes*, the 125-mile Parana, which promised fast straights and twisting turns, and the 120-mile Rio Grande, offering rough road and sudden narrow wooden bridges. So rough was the trip that the bugs needed structural repairs before they could be returned to the rental company in the Uruguayan capital.

The plan was for the two Triumphs to be collected in Buenos Aires and then used to recce the route all the way from Argentina, into Chile, back into Argentina, and up through Bolivia to the Peruvian capital, Lima. This 4,900-mile section would include the two longest *primes*, the 510-mile Gran Premio in Argentina and the 560-mile Route of the Incas in Bolivia. However, before the team could get started, there was the small matter of retrieving the two 2.5PIs, which had gotten entangled in the red tape of Argentinian import customs. Not making any headway, Hopkirk suddenly recalled that Buenos Aires was the home of a certain Juan Manuel Fangio, the legendary Formula One racing driver. Hopkirk had met Fangio during the 1964 Monte Carlo Rally. One phone call to Fangio's offices later, two men called for the team at their hotel and took them to buy a case of whisky. They then accompanied Hopkirk and Co. to the docks and, as Hopkirk explained, "they went into the customs house with the whisky. Ten minutes later the cars appeared at the back!"[7] Ironically, Mr. Fangio would later tell the Argentinian press that, in his opinion, not a single car would get all the way to Mexico. He would most certainly be proved wrong!

The recce from Buenos Aires to Lima would take the team almost two months to traverse. As Bill Price explained, the Gran Premio route "took them five days to complete, with delays from punctures and other minor problems (Brian Culcheth completed this stage in 12 hours on the rally)."[8] Arduous indeed but, for BLMC and the team, extremely useful as much was learnt about driving at altitude: whether modifications would be needed to maintain efficient fuel combustion, whether the crews would need oxygen, and whether two- or three-person teams would be the necessity.

Soviet Moskvič representatives also spent considerable time surveying the South American route and, despite the fact that the six Citroëns were all privately entered, Citroën competitions team chief René Cotton nevertheless undertook his own investigations of the South American route. Accompanied by his wife Marléne and local Citroën representatives, Cotton encountered landslides blocking the path and, crossing the Argentinian pampas, flash flooding that all but swept away a Citroën 2CV survey car, forcing the team to strip to their underwear and wade out into the fast-moving torrent to rescue its occupants! Nothing short of a large tractor was able to drag the stricken 2CV out of the deluge.

Of course, apart from automotive testing and the practical benefits of exploring the physical and environmental challenges that lay ahead for competitors, the key deliverable from all of this reconnaissance work was the intelligence needed to create the essential tool for any rally crew—the route notes. These pages and pages of meticulous text and diagrammatic instructions were often referred to as "tulip" notes, each page containing symbols, arrows, advice, observations, and warnings to ensure a car is kept on course mile after mile.

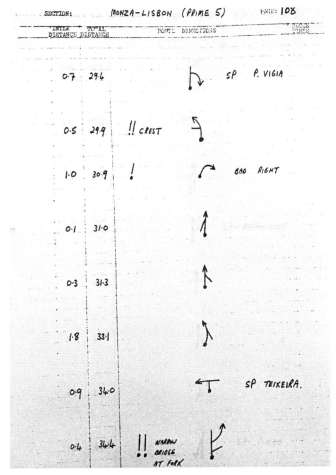

Rally route notes (courtesy Ted Taylor).

18

Puff the Magic Maxi
(Part Two)

Tina laughed as she recalled the antics on the jetliner as they headed for Brazil, remembering how, with movie camera in hand, she was allowed onto the flight deck and even sat in the pilot's lap while he casually smoked a cigarette! Meanwhile, first time flyer Bron had not enjoyed the labored takeoff at all but was soon joining in with the ribald songs and partaking of alcoholic beverages towards the back of the plane. The fun and games had to come to an end, however, and competitors were soon disembarking at Rio into the sultry evening heat. They were taken by bus to the hotel overlooking Flamengo Beach, and most spent the remainder of the time sightseeing, enjoying the newly released movie *Butch Cassidy and the Sundance Kid*, and enjoying the sun and sea.

At last, the *Derwent* docked and unloaded 71 rally cars. Tish retrieved Puff, sorted the required paperwork, and no doubt took the Maxi for a quick checkup at the BLMC service point, the needs of the professional BLMC and Special Tuning cars allowing. Then it was back to the hotel for the women to tick off contents and load their personal belongs before getting ready for the ceremonial start just opposite the hotel. Cars would be waved away and were then given one hour to arrive at the "zero mile" start control and the beginning of the South American adventure. The first section would be to Montevideo in Uruguay, with an allowance of 41 hours and to include three *primes*.

Puff hit the road on time and drove down through Brazil. Bron recalled the asphalt road eventually giving way to dirt track, seeing bright orange mud through green trees. Fuel stops were a rudimentary affair, gas just being siphoned from large drums into the tank. The women made the first speed stage control without incident, arriving on time for the start of the Parana *prime*. Here, competitors were faced with 125 miles of challenging bends and fast straights over dirt and loose rocks, all within a time allowance of 90 minutes.

Tish gunned the Maxi away from start control at Ventania, negotiating a number of precarious-looking plank bridges, all three women remaining vigilant for the sudden looming of oncoming trucks and other civilian vehicles. Suddenly, they were lost! Spying a small truck, they flagged it down and, using signs and gestures, pointed at their map. The Portuguese-speaking driver understood and beckoned them to follow him until they were on the right track again. Thus, they made it safely to Bateias, although their navigation error cost them 41 minutes.

The swimming pool at the Hotel Glória, Rio de Janeiro, May 1970 (courtesy Pat Smith).

On to the next *prime* now, the Rio Grande, which had been hastily shortened because torrential rain had either submerged or completely taken out a number of bridges along the original route. From the start at Ituporanga, Tina recalled, "Puff was flat out, Tish concentrating hard in the dark, looking out for oncoming trucks. At least we could see them coming lights blazing away.... There were now 56 cars still going. They were quickly falling by the wayside. Another night we made it through. Tish drove the *primes* again brilliantly, us doing what was needed to get her through. We were tired but somehow the adrenaline kept us going. We would certainly be gaining places after the two *primes*." Although the three women now had changing wheels down to a fine art, a flat tire here, combined with all the inherent challenges, meant that at the revised finish at São Joachim, Puff was 65 minutes over the target time of 80.

The section to the next *prime* was long and tiring, out of Brazil and into Uruguay. Running 125 miles from Tacuarembó to Salta. The Uruguay speed section "would be a fast drive over open countryside," Tina recalled. "We lost another three rally crews here. There were a few nasty accidents. The locals had said it was mad to do the *prime*, they obviously knew what they were talking about. We had now been driving for 40 plus hours nonstop, how we managed to keep going I will never know but it was the same for all."

The next destination was Uruguay's capital, which offered the competitors a rest stop before they took a car ferry over the River Plate to Buenos Aires and the next country on the list—Argentina. Out of the 52 cars that survived the severities of the route from Rio, No. 20 was in 39th place at Montevideo. On arrival, the tired trio drove to the allotted *parc fermé* overlooking the River Plate and, as per regulations, began checking and servicing the Maxi as best they could, prevented as they were from seeking outside assistance. This didn't stop assorted service personnel and others, including Ford boss Stuart Turner, from yelling advice and instructions through the fence! Having done what they could, and after double-checking the car's contents, they retired to their hotel accommodation for dinner, baths, and bed, eager to be as well-rested as possible before embarking on the long drive south and west across Argentina and over into Chile toward the South Pacific coast.

The following day's river crossing took three hours, so there was time to catch up with other competitors and swap war stories. Bron was amazed that the river was actually wider than the Bristol Channel between England and France, which made the notorious World War II battle of the River Plate seem to make more sense.

The ferry and its passengers were greeted at the Argentinian capital's port by large crowds and a band playing in their honor. Once the business of disembarking cars from the ferry was done, they joined a police escort out of the city, outriders eventually peeling off as competitors continued towards Saladillo, 155 miles or so from Buenos Aires and the gateway to the next *prime*, the Pampas. The rally's official program booklet, on sale to enthusiastic members of the public back in the UK, described this speed section as tricky whatever the conditions: "Depending on whether it's wet or dry, drivers will have to cope with glutinous mud or thick dust."[1] Most of the departures—overseen by Jim Gavin—occurred under the latter conditions, but for Puff it was a different story. Earlier, driving down to Montevideo, Tish had begun to notice something not quite right with the Maxi, but without recourse to servicing, she had been compelled to continue on. However, the women knew there was a BLMC service point before the Saladillo control and sought assistance as soon as they arrived. As per protocols, the professionals' Triumphs and Maxis took precedence, followed by cars prepared by BLMC's Special Tuning department. "They said to us, 'Oh, it will be 10 minutes,'" Bron remembered. "Three hours later they still hadn't serviced us and we're now running out of time to get to the control." Hours crept by and still the service team had their hands full. Finally, they turned their attention to Puff and diagnosed a damaged exhaust manifold. No problem, they had another and thus set to work replacing the damaged unit, but then discovered it wasn't the right one, so they then had to weld-repair the existing manifold and refit it. Time had now really caught up with the women, and, to their dismay, they realized that all other competitors had set off for the *prime* control. They had to get to the start before it shut, but the repair work wasn't yet finished and now it had begun to rain.

Someone then had an idea: if they could get Puff to the start control by towing the car, they might be able to get a start time recorded and then return to complete repairs. Sadly, at the control it was pointed out that each car must be able to depart a control under its own power. Tina ran back through the rain to the service point and asked the mechanics to come and at least get the Maxi started, which they did. Thus, they were able to have a start time recorded within the time the control was operational and then return to the service mechanics for completion of the work. Now, with heavy rain falling and the hour very late, Tish had to decide whether to retire or carry on. Then the car was ready so, with decision made for them, they set off, into not dust but driving rain and an increasingly muddy trail.

Bron recalled how the stage seemed to weave between paddocks, the route first heading two miles to the left, then taking a 90-degree turn to the right and continuing for three miles, then repeating. The mud was getting worse, it was quite dark, and the Maxi's windshield wipers were beginning to struggle with the falling deluge. On they plugged, knowing that they had to cover 200 miles with a target time of three-and-a-half hours—crazy at the best of times, and these were definitely not the best. Since watching *Butch Cassidy and the Sundance Kid*, Tina hadn't been able to get the song "Raindrops Keep Falling on My Head" out of her brain, but these weren't drops, these were golf balls! Knowing that other competitors would be hours ahead and there was no one behind them, Tish focused on the track, gingerly guiding the Maxi forward, then left, then right, the turns getting trickier each time as Tina and Bron watching the Halda meter, counting the miles down. Then, with perhaps about 50 miles to go before the finish at Espartillar, almost in slow motion, it happened. On another turn, despite Tish's efforts, the Maxi lost all grip and slid sideways into a wet, slippery ditch.

The three women clambered out into the mud, the water rising, to survey the situation as best they could in the darkness and the rain. They had the winch, prudently packed as an essential tool, but where could they attach the end if there were no trees, just pampas grass, some of which was taller than Tina? The drainage ditch was mud over concrete so there was no way they could attempt to drive the winch stake into the ground. So, with Tish at the wheel, Bron and Tina tried to push, but they just got covered in mud for their troubles. Tucking coats under wheels made no difference either. Bron had a go at the wheel, trying to get even a little forward momentum to gain enough speed along the channel to try and get the Maxi up the side. The idea seemed to work for a moment, but, alas, Puff just slid back down. Drawing on her mud trials experience, Tina wondered whether deflating the tires might help, but Tish opposed the idea, thinking the risk too great. Defeated, the women climbed back into the car and waited, knowing that, eventually, the Argentinian Car Club's big sweeper truck would arrive, which it finally did. "They pulled us out and on we went and finished the *prime*, but the control had closed earlier," Tina recalled. "If only it hadn't rained, if only the car had been ok. If only…. We did cry. This was tough rallying. Our rally was over like it had been for many other drivers earlier, all so very disappointing."

At Espartillar, these intrepid women now had a decision to make. Go on and follow the route, even though they were out of the running, or drive the 400 miles back to Buenos Aires? After discussion, they opted for going back, not least because Tina felt that, not being a competitor anymore, she might as well fly back to her children in England. Eventually arriving in the Argentinian capital, they made contact with the BLMC agent who arranged hotel accommodation for the three disheveled women. There they met Commander Julian Mitchell and the rest of the crew of No. 55, the British Royal Navy-entered 1800, which had also retired from the rally. After getting cleaned up and some food in their bellies, Tish, Bron, and Tina considered their options. Tina opted to spend a night at the hotel and then travel up to Santiago in Chile the following day, accompanied by the navy team. Thus, with an emotional farewell for Bron and Tish, Tina boarded a flight and landed in the Chilean capital after an extremely uncomfortable trip. Bron and Tish, meanwhile, had decided that they wanted to get to Mexico City by car, so they pointed Puff in the right direction and set off.

In Santiago, Tina met up with more retired teams, this time No. 94, the British RAF Cortina of Donald Soames-Waring, Andrew Thwaite, and George Crichton, and No. 9, Rosemary Smith's ex–London–Sydney Marathon Cortina, entered by J.C. "Cal" Withers and crewed by Ian Harwood, Frank Pierson, and London–Sydney Marathon-veteran Barry Hughes. Not satisfied to see their perhaps once-in-a-lifetime South American adventure come to an end, their plan was to drive up the edge of the Atacama Desert to Lima, 2000-plus miles along the South Pacific coast, where they hoped to meet up with teams still in competition. What should Tina and the navy team do? They all opted to join the Cortina convoy so, squeezing person and possessions into the two cars, they set off, Tina now wondering whether she should have stayed with Tish, Bron, and Puff!

The two Cortinas had taken a pounding on the rally and were, to various degrees, battle-weary, the Withers car especially. However, apart from stops to check and adjust various things or for comfort breaks and refueling, the convoy pressed on and eventually arrived at the port city of Antofagasta, where a small hotel was found and the Withers Cortina team received mechanical attention at a local shop. Rested and repaired, the following day they pressed on to Lima, via the Peruvian border, just beyond Chacalutta, and Arequipa.

At last, they made it to Lima, bedraggled but happy to arrive, only to discover that the hotels were full. A British journalist came to Tina's aid, suggesting she use his room as he would be on the road to cover the arrival of the rally and saying he would only need to collect his baggage later on. With gratitude, Tina bathed and collapsed into bed. The following morning, she stumbled into the bathroom to discover a hastily written message in lipstick on the mirror. It seemed the journalist had crept into the room to retrieve his baggage while Tina slept and left the scribbled note as a joke, although the thought of a stranger sneaking in left her somewhat unamused!

The following day, the British consulate stepped in, offering food and accommodation to Tina and the navy team, and then it was time to board a flight back to the UK. At the airport, little more than a collection of sheds and outbuildings, they were taken to a hut alongside the runway. Two other people were there, and Tina realized they were actors Peter O'Toole and Siân Phillips, husband and wife, who had just completed filming the movie *Murphy's War*! O'Toole got talking with Tina and was hugely impressed by her rally achievement, insisting she should be proud of what she had done. Then, they boarded the plane and, 23 hours later, she was reunited with her children.

Tina didn't realize until later just how close she had come to bumping into Tish and Bron on her trek up the coast. Having decided to drive Puff to Mexico City, they charted a route and set off, determined to eventually catch up with competitors in Buenaventura in Colombia. Looking at the map, they realized that they would pass through Salta in Argentina, just north of the finish control for the long Gran Premio *prime*, so they decided to stop there to see the cars pass through. A long drive followed, but at last they arrived, stopping to find overnight accommodation and shop for warmer clothing. The next day, competitors were due, so Tish and Bron found a good place to watch. Thus, they were witness to the arrival of the injured Andrew Cowan who, with teammates Brian Coyle and Uldarico "Larco" Ossio, had crashed into a deep ravine along the *prime*. Coyle and Ossio were hospitalized, but Cowan thought he was all right. "'[I'll] book a flight back but my neck's a bit sore,'" Bron recalled him saying. "'I think I'll go have a massage.' So, he finds somewhere to go have a massage but it still doesn't really help him." It was only later that Cowan discovered he had actually broken his neck!

Bron and Tish moved on, driving at higher and higher altitude, constantly adjusting the Maxi's gas to oxygen ratio, but the car began to increasingly splutter and cough until, in a small town, Puff gave up altogether. What to do? They managed to seek assistance from an English-speaking mine owner, who linked them up with a mechanic. The Maxi's rotor arm had broken, and although they had catalogued a set of replacement components and parts onboard the Austin, there was no rotor arm! All they could do was contact the Argentinian Automobile Association and arrange for Puff to be recovered back to Salta and then put on a train back to Buenos Aires. Meanwhile, an overnight stay in the town involved attending a party and, the following morning, lunch with the mine owner.

The two women now needed a revised plan of action and decided to fly back to Buenos Aires and then fly up to Buenaventura, not least because they had tickets for the ship crossing to Panama. The flight from the Argentinian capital stopped at Santiago and then Lima. For Bron, this was only her second time in a plane, and this was so much smaller than the Boeing 707 from Lisbon to Rio! At Lima, the plane made three failed attempts to take off—Bron was white-knuckled and queasy—but at last they were airborne and landed at Cali in Colombia without issue. Finally, a short flight to Buenaventura and they were there to board the ship, although not before some argument about not being able to use their tickets without their car, which involved much perspiration as they trudged to the dock's shipping office in the heat, wearing the warm wool suits they had purchased in the mountains.

The SS *Verdi* afforded continuing and defeated competitors the chance to let off steam, which they did with much enthusiasm, even holding an impromptu party for rally leader Hannu Mikkola's soon-to-be birthday. Bron, of course, joined in the fun and got talking with Russian driver Victor Schavelev who, together with his teammate Emmanuil Lifshits, had seen their assault on Mexico City come to an end on the endless Incas prime. Neither Tish nor Bron was very keen on flying to the Mexican capital when they might be able to hitch a ride with one of the retired cars that would follow the rally route. As Emmanuil had previously departed, Victor grinned and offered them a ride in his Moskvič, which Bron accepted, telling Tish they would be able travel by car rather than plane. No doubt Tish raised an eyebrow but agreed with the plan.

The road from Cristóbal in Panama to Mexico was long, crossing six frontiers and covering 2,100 miles. Often the road was riddled with bumps and potholes, which wasn't doing much for the already battered Moskvič, and by the time they crossed into Nicaragua, it was obvious the Russian car's bodywork needed attention. Its A- and B-pillars were beginning to crack, Bron recalled. Somehow, they found a

No. 84, the Moskvič 412 of Emmanuil Lifshits (*driving*) and Victor Schavelev (courtesy Guido Devreker).

shop that could provide welding, so the local mechanic set to work, refusing payment on completion, just happy to have helped a rally car! The Moskvič restored, they continued, Victor always attempting to have Bron ride up front, which Tish thought not always the best idea! Occasionally, they took turns driving, anxious to get there on time for the rally to arrive at Mexico City, but by the time they got to San Salvador, the car needed more repairs, more welding. Spying a Peugeot garage, they pulled in and were immediately met by the English-speaking manager. When they explained the situation, the manager mobilized his team and then, while work was underway, insisted they come back to his home for a meal. Once again, he refused any money. "It's amazing," Bron recalled, "the kindness we were shown, unbelievable."

At last, they drove into Mexico City, disappointed to have missed the rally arriving at Aztec Stadium but still in time for the ensuing festivities. Victor bid them farewell, and the two women checked into a hotel, tired but happy that their disappointing but highly unusual rally had finally been run.

"We were so pleased we'd made it," Bron reflected. "We wouldn't have seen half of Latin America if we hadn't tried to go on. Trouble is, when you're doing it at speed, you get an impression of the country but you don't … you're concentrating or asleep, it is long-distance endurance rallying. Not like the modern endurance when you stop every night and have a really good meal and a comfortable bed, this was proper endurance rallying and you slept when you could."

"What an adventure we had," Tina remembered. "16,000 miles, three girls, and a Maxi. We didn't finish but we had given our all, we had driven on tracks with large rocks strewn about, sheer drops on either side, encountered earthquakes, tropical

Together again—Puff and team after the rally: (*left to right*) **Tina Kerridge, Tish Ozanne, and Bron Burrell (courtesy Katrina Kerridge-Reynolds).**

storms with torrential rain, and we had come through all of this. Unfortunately, we just couldn't get out of that deep water filled ditch in Argentina."

Puff was eventually shipped back home, where Tish had the car's engine and gearbox upgraded before entering the Portuguese TAP Rally later that year with Pat Wright, for which they won the women's prize. Her last rally was in 1973 before she retired to focus on other pursuits. She died on February 11, 2009. She was 85.

In 2016, Bron Burrell purchased a mostly restored Puff and proceeded to bring the car back to road and classic rally standard. Since then, a reunited Bron and Tina have taken the Marshall Maxi on a classic car rally to Portugal and continue to take great pride in accompanying Puff to many events and shows in the UK as interest in the endurance rallies of the 1960s and 1970s deservedly increases.

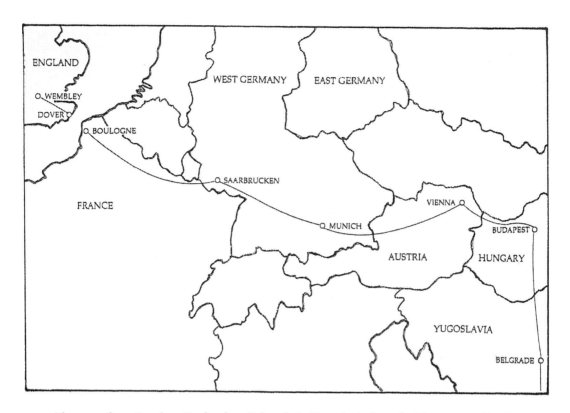

The route from London, England, to Belgrade in Yugoslavia (map by Martin Proudlock).

19

And They're Off!

Each team intending to compete in the London to Mexico World Cup Rally was provided with a specific time to present themselves and their vehicles on Saturday, April 18, 1970, for start formalities, or scrutineering, at Wembley Stadium. These formalities would include formal registration of all crew members; checking and verifying the required classifications of driving licenses; issue of ID tags and roadbooks; marking the relevant mechanical parts for each vehicle with paint to prevent attempts to replace core components such as engine block or chassis unit on the road to Mexico City; and scrutinizing of safety belts, crash helmets, mud flaps, fire extinguishers, first aid kits, and reflective safety triangles. Entrants could then depart, but were required to return on April 19, position their cars in the assigned paddock area at the stadium, and be ready to attend a drivers' briefing at 09:30. The rally was scheduled to start an hour later, with cars departing at one-minute intervals.

Scrutineering no doubt gave many competitors their first opportunity to size up the competition. It also highlighted a few examples of frenetic, last-minute activity to ensure rally-readiness for the following day. In addition to the fettling required by the beach buggy, the Ford works Escort of Zasada and Wachowski suddenly needed a replacement engine "with a piston packing up in a bore. A spare engine, already on its way to Portugal … was hastily hauled back from Southampton."[1] Drawn as No. 39, the green-and-gold Triumph 2.5PI was also giving Brian Englefield, Keith Baker, and Adrian Lloyd-Hirst more than a few anxious moments. "The guy that had collected and put the battery in hadn't put any acid in it," explained Englefield. "It was a dry battery, a special battery, that Lucas did and he had only put distilled water in it…. I couldn't start the car so we actually did the rally on a tiny little one!"

Elsewhere, many crews frantically arranged, studied, and re-arranged the contents of their cars. Lists of spare parts and tools were examined with forensic detail. Maps, route notes, and essential documentation were checked and stashed, and toiletries, blankets and pillows, and changes of clothing were crammed wherever they would fit. No doubt a few eyebrows were raised at the sight of the Yugoslavian Peugeot 404, complete with what appeared to be a double-bed box on its roof, wider even than the car itself, and the Ford Escort "Elba Motor Caravan," an Escort van conversion complete with extendable "pop-up" roof to create standing space! U.S. competitor Brian Chuchua recalled that the Jeep Wagoneer, nicknamed the Yellow Buffalo by some American newspapers, was "kind of a laughingstock, but they were very curious." On the way to the stadium, No. 70's Captain Gavin Thompson was involved

No. 16, the Wilsons Motor Caravans Ford Escort Elba camper van: (*left to right in car*) Laurie Ritchie and James Gardner (courtesy Guido Devreker).

in an automobile accident, which, on arrival, required medical attention and thus required HRH Prince Michael of Kent and Captain Nigel Clarkson to attend to all start formalities. "I cut my lip and got a black eye, most unpleasant, just before the rally!" Thompson recalled. "I got there looking slightly sorry for myself."

With cars securely placed in *parc fermé* to be guarded overnight, crews and officials finally departed the stadium. For competitors it was the last opportunity to sleep either in their own beds—or at least in a comfortable hotel room—before everything kicked off the following day. As motoring journalist and competitor in car No. 3 Mark Kahn wrote, "one more night at home and then…."[2]

April 19, 1970, dawned bright and clear in London, and it wasn't long before Wembley Stadium began to see a flurry of activity, with competitors arriving to attend the scheduled 09:30 briefing and spectators gathering to watch and admire the colorful machinery on display. Competitors' friends and family milled around as drivers and co-drivers attached their allotted rally numbers to their cars or found last-minute space on bodywork for one more sponsorship decal. No doubt a few butterflies in stomachs were felt as the clocked ticked down to the time when all cars had to leave *parc fermé* and line up in the departure order selected by England soccer captain Bobby Moore a few months earlier. Originally 106 entrants were accepted, but because of last-minute withdrawals, although entrants were numbered up to 106, there would be only 96 cars in competition. While entries 1 to 45 queued up in the stadium, entries 46 to 106 were instructed to line up in order in the collection paddock.

The likes of Bobby Buchanan-Michaelson, Terry Hunter, and former Le Mans

Competitors Enclosure, Wembley Stadium, April 19, 1970 (courtesy Guido Devreker).

24 Hours racing driver Peter Jopp wouldn't have long to wait as numbers one, two, and three in the grid, but for those at the rear it would be a long and alternately fretful or boring couple of hours or more before they would get on the road. In a bid to keep them and the spectating throng of 20,000 entertained, live music was on offer and popular British TV presenter and motorsports enthusiast Raymond Baxter provided live commentary. In his inimitable style, Baxter calmly bid the live music quiet in order to get things underway. Bobby Moore was on hand to ceremoniously cut out a square of the stadium's emerald green turf for safe passage to, and re-laying at, Mexico City's Aztec Stadium, to be presented by fellow soccer star—and rally competitor—Jimmy Greaves.

Then, at precisely 10:00, having been ushered to the ramp by one of a plethora of young women wearing then fashionable capes and waving the flags of countries represented in the field, England national soccer team manager Sir Alf Ramsey flagged away No. 1, the Buchanan-Michaelson Triumph 2.5PI. The watching crowds cheered as the Triumph eased away, turned to the left, and drove through the tunnel to be met and led down the Olympic Way by one of a convoy of little blue and white Austin A35 RAC vans. Except it wasn't! Moments after emerging into the sunshine, Buchanan-Michaelson delivered the Triumph into the waiting arms of the mechanics to fix a fuel injection problem, which cost them 35 minutes of delay. It transpired that the car's fuel-to-oxygen ratio mixture was incorrectly set for altitude driving! Therefore, No. 2, the pale blue Bio-Strath Porsche of Hunter and Mabbs took over as *de facto* lead car, followed in rapid succession by the white Jopp 1800 and the Berry Magicoal–sponsored, grey and orange Hillman GT of Rob Lyall and Rodney

Badham. No. 3 crewmember Mark Kahn wrote: "Somewhere in Westminster, a girl ran out into the road and to the Porsche. Hunter pulled up. While he and Mabbs were chatting to her, we, for a glorious few minutes, headed the rally."[3]

Meanwhile, as planned, once No. 45 had departed, a second musical entertainment began with Ginger Baker's Air Force jazz-rock band and "a stage full of imitation Mexican guitar players"[4]! Allegedly, Mr. Baker and his musicians overran their set, although suggestions that someone pulled the plug on an amplifier or two cannot be confirmed! Then, dispatch of cars 46 to 80 began. Paul Easter, driver in No. 59, recalled: "At Wembley they play football, and I don't know much about it but I believe they have studs on the bottom of their boots. I had got shoes like this on and happened to put a foot on the grass. Some official … went mad—you mustn't stand on that grass…. I thought God! They run around with studs on their boots, don't they?" Suitably chastened, Easter and John Handley were flagged away while the remaining cars lined up outside the stadium. Finally, cars 81 through 106 were summoned for the third wave of departure.

Throughout the morning, organizing committee member and secretary of the rally John Sprinzel smiled knowingly at each competitor as he counted down the second hand on his stopwatch and waved them off. "Gelignite" Jack Murray let off his customary firecrackers, and the Martin family's stately, 13-year-old Rolls-Royce Silver Cloud almost beached itself departing the starting ramp. Eventually, the British Lydden Circuit-entered Escort GT of Chesson and East and the Mexican FIAT 124 coupe driven by Enrique Lamas-Fortes were flagged away. Ninety-six cars, bedecked with bull bars, spare wheels and tires, tool kits, and sponsorship decals aplenty, were off, out into the congested, spectator-lined London streets and onwards towards the ferry port at Dover on the south England coast.

A champagne toast on the way to Dover. No. 45 and (*left to right*) Doug Harris, Mike Butler, and John Whitehouse, Hollingbourne, England, April 19 (courtesy Brian Millen).

Organizers had allowed three hours for cars to reach the Dover control, a journey of approximately 100 miles. This sounded achievable enough, but the crowded roads through central and southeast London and the main A20 road—and briefly the short section of M20 motorway—meant competitors were not experiencing normal traffic conditions. After the Buchanan-Michaelson Triumph's debacle at Wembley, they were once again briefly delayed after a contretemps with the police in London's West End. Nor were they the only car to experience first-night nerves. "Coming out of London, we are fluffing and fouling plugs and changing plugs, just to get out of the London traffic," Paul Easter recalled. The Tony Fall/Jimmy Greaves works Escort was briefly sidelined while a wheel bearing was investigated, and Doug Harris and Mike Butler stopped at a service point specially convened by Ron Pellatt at Leeds Castle in Kent, complaining of a misfire. Pellatt diagnosed a speck of solder on the carburetor's main jets, which took precious time to fix. So it was that, while 92 cars— including No. 1, with a minute to spare—arrived at the control at Henley's Garage in Dover in good time, four cars somehow managed to achieve penalty points for lateness. As duly noted by marshal Peter Riley, the Vauxhall Viva GT led by Peter Garratt was seven minutes late, the Tenishev-led Moskvič was penalized with 18 points, Chris Marriott's Trident Venturer received 20 penalty points, and the Harris/Butler Escort GT amassed 28 points as a consequence of their carburetor issue.

While everyone waited to be summoned onto the Boulogne-bound British Rail ferry, more crowds jostled with competitors, eager to look at the rally cars and maybe get a few autographs. Representing the *Daily Mirror* newspaper, a battalion of young women dressed in soccer shorts and shirts handed out complimentary travel bags and other goodies as competitors arrived and seized a few photo opportunities with HRH Prince Michael of Kent. Australian filmmaker Rob McAuley, in No. 32, and British London–Sydney Marathon veteran Colin Taylor, driver of No. 51, busied themselves with movie cameras, both making films of the rally.

The ferry crossing gave teams a few hours rest and the chance to grab a meal before getting back into their cars, guiding them off the ferry, and offering up their roadbooks for the required stamp and recording of departure time at the Boulogne control. Then it was off into the rainy night to attempt to cover the 1,300 miles to the Bulgarian capital, Sofia, in the 37 hours allowed for the journey.

There were five passage controls between Boulogne and Sofia, all designed to ensure that cars were keeping to the prescribed route and maintaining allowable times. The first, at Saarbrücken in West Germany, just beyond France's northeastern border, expected competitors to arrive, get books stamped, and depart between 02:15 and 06:15 on April 20. The road through France posed no particular challenges other than rain and darkness, yet No. 95, the 1800 driven by Dennis Cresdee, somehow managed to miss Saarbrücken altogether, therefore incurring an automatic 180 penalty points.

Onwards then on fast *autobahns* to Munich in southern Germany and the next passage control with six hours and 30 minutes allowed for arrival. The Englefield/Baker/Lloyd-Hirst 2.5PI took a wrong turn and then had to do a lengthy detour to get back on the right road again and, as previously stated, No. 30, the Trident Venturer, wasted 60 minutes having forgotten a vital document at the Saarbrücken control.

Rauno Aaltonen and Henry Liddon on their way through South London in No. 46, one of the Ford GB team Escorts (author's collection).

However, the Munich control, located near the BMW factory and the stadium that would host the Olympics two years later, was eventually reached by all except one car without incident. Driving a seven-year-old FIAT 2300 station wagon, which appeared somewhat lacking in rally preparation, the two Kuwaiti tugboat pilot brothers, Joseph and James Sherger, were beginning to succumb to their lack of experience. They failed to clock in at Munich, earning the automatic 180 penalty points; a wrong turn took them to the Austrian city of Linz, where they decided to pause in favor of food and sleep!

The first casualty of the rally.

From Munich, the field sped on to the Austrian control located at Vienna's Schönbrunn Palace, an extremely stately and hugely historic backdrop to the rally cars. The vast majority of competitors were able to feast their eyes on the Rococo architecture as they steered their machines towards the control point, but not, sadly, Cecil Woodley, Bob Locke, and Phil Waller. Their Vauxhall Ventora developed brake problems after Munich, and the resultant wait for repairs earned them 180 penalty points. No. 79, the Dutch Datsun 1600 SSS, needed mechanical attention for a broken piston at Vienna, a portent of what was to come, and was thus delayed two hours, while the Rolls-Royce Silver Cloud of Mr. Martin and sons had a short circuit, which took out its starter motor. Fortunately for them, representatives from Lucas, the automotive electrical company, were on hand to make the repairs. Car 85, the *Sunday Express*–sponsored Ford works Escort of Colin Malkin and Richard Hudson-Evans, required expeditious work to its alternator pulley, lest it spin off and puncture the

Ready to go: (*second from left to right*) **No. 84, Moskvič 412; No. 85, Ford Escort 1850; No. 86, Ford Mustang; and No. 90, FIAT 2300 station wagon (author's collection).**

radiator, prompting fellow team members Rauno Aaltonen and Henry Liddon to inspect theirs.

At this point it's probably worth clarifying the difference between a car being "entered" in a rally and a car being "sponsored." BLMC and Ford entered seven cars each: four 2.5PIs, two Maxis, and a Mini for BLMC, and seven Escorts for Ford. However, each car was specifically sponsored: five Fords by British national newspapers; one by the London-based Springfield Boys Club, an organization aimed at supporting less advantaged children, which had developed ties with motorsports in the early 1960s; and one by competitor Sobiesław Zasada himself. For BLMC, three cars were sponsored by the Football Association, two by motoring magazines, one by a London evening newspaper, and one by the BBC TV sports show, *Grandstand*. Most of these sponsors effectively offered financial support in return for the publicity of having their logos emblazoned on a rally car traversing country after country. Motoring journalist and car No. 3 competitor Mark Kahn summed it up, explaining that while teammate Peter Jopp bought their car and entered it in the rally, the *Sunday Mirror* newspaper financed the effort. "If you say that this is a purely legalistic distinction," Kahn remarked somewhat laconically, "I will not argue."[5]

Now the field was heading for the Eastern Bloc and Hungary. The next control would be located in Budaörs, approximately seven miles west of Budapest, and the time allowed to arrive from Vienna was four hours and 45 minutes. Before the Austro-Hungarian frontier, the Lydden Circuit–backed Escort GT suffered a broken fuel pipe and could only continue after 30 minutes of diagnostics and repairs, while along the route to the Hungarian control, assorted minor niggles afflicted a

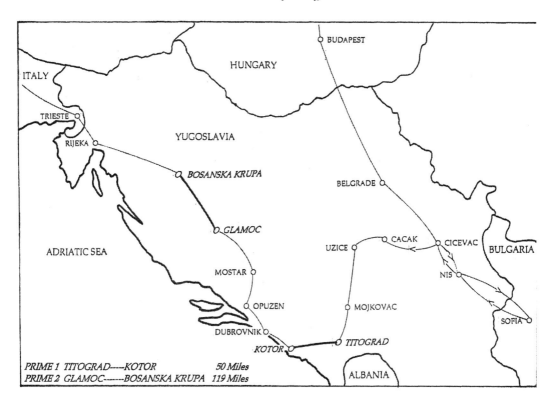

PRIME 1 TITOGRAD-----KOTOR   50 Miles
PRIME 2 GLAMOC-------BOSANSKA KRUPA 119 Miles

The route from Budapest in Hungary to Trieste in Italy (map by Martin Proudlock).

few other competitors. The J.C. "Cal" Withers–backed Cortina Lotus, driven by Ian Harwood, had prop shaft issues, while the Porsche 911S of French duo Celerier and Gauvain picked up a cracked windshield. For others it was perhaps their first experience of Eastern Europe, with barbed wire fences, watchtowers, tanks, and armed soldiers all very visible. On approach to the control, competitors were met with thousands of people lining the road; *Autosport* magazine reported that 4,000 spectators were crowded into the control's garage site alone. With roadbooks stamped by Chris Belton of the British Royal Automobile Club, cars moved on toward the Yugoslavian capital, Belgrade.

The roads were becoming increasingly pot-holed and muddy. No. 54, Reg Redgrave's Special Tuning–prepared 1800, survived having a brick lobbed through its windshield, while the orange and white striped Maxi of Rosemary Smith seemed increasingly unwilling to keep in fifth gear. The Jopp 1800 made the best of a difficult run, as its windshield wiper motor failed, and No. 89, the highly unusual "Mexi-Mini," an extended Mini Cooper S that now had four doors rather than the customary two, narrowly escaped being obliterated when a tank fell off a hauler up ahead.

Into the Belgrade control came the Aaltonen/Liddon Escort suffering all manner of gearbox problems that required extensive repair. They would have to struggle on to Monza before all would be put right. Also, at the Belgrade control, Ford and BLMC teams were given revised route notes to allow for the fact that snow had rendered

Reg Redgrave (*right*, with an unknown individual) celebrates sponsorship by Standwood Radio Ltd., Essex, 1970 (courtesy Teresa Jensen-Redgrave).

the original route from the Yugoslavian capital to Titograd, via the first prime starting at Peć, impassable. Ford had deployed Roger Clark's regular co-driver Jim Porter and his London–Sydney Marathon co-driver, Ove Andersson, to map a revised route from Sofia to what would be a new prime between Titograd and Kotor. Expert co-driver Mike Wood had provided the same service to BLMC. The fact that these hasty corrections and revisions were achieved so efficiently and effectively really was a testimony to all involved in the rally's organization. Porter would go on to map out the new special stage route, still to be known as the Montenegro *prime*.

Although still a way off, talk of a *prime* undoubtedly emphasized to competitors that their mammoth transport section from London to the start of the first special stage was almost done. First, they just had to get to Sofia and then return the way they had come, back across the border, before turning off beyond Niš for Titograd.

Whether the six Citroëns that lined up at Wembley Stadium on April 19, 1970, could be considered factory-backed competition department entries or not depends upon the letter of the rules and regulations for the rally. Nevertheless, after the DS19, driven by Lucien Bianchi and Jean-Claude Ogier, had assured victory snatched from them on the final stretch before Sydney in 1968, someone somewhere within the French rally motorsports world must surely have determined a rematch. What began as three independent entries offering up the *pièce de résistance* of French rallying eventually evolved into an *assaut formidable*, or great assault, on victory at the Aztec Stadium.

No. 6 at Wembley Stadium, London, April 19, 1970 (courtesy John Hemsley).

Major John Hemsley giving way to llamas, South America, May 1970 (courtesy John Hemsley).

C2

No. 6 under repair, Colombia, May 1970 (courtesy Mike Wood).

The remains of No. 19, Lake Titicaca, Peru, May 1970 (courtesy Gabriel Maria Hinojosa Rivero).

No. 89, the "Mexi-Mini" of Allan Keefe and James Conroy (*left*), and No. 90, the BMW 200Ti of Ken Bass and Graham Waring, Wembley Stadium, April 19, 1970 (courtesy Ted Taylor).

Rosemary Smith (*left*) and Alice Watson with their Austin Maxi—the Red Arrows' Maxi in the background (courtesy Mike Wood).

The Trident takes a bow with Capt. Christopher Marriott (*left*) and Capt. John "Jack" Dill, Ipswich, England, 1970 (courtesy Chris Marriott).

Paddy Hopkirk and unidentified flight attendant, Caledonian Airways Bristol Britannia bound for Rio via Recife (courtesy Mike Wood).

Reunion with Puff: (*left to right*) Pat Smith, Katrina Kerridge-Reynolds, and Bron Burrell, Warwickshire, England, 2016 (courtesy Katrina Kerridge-Reynolds).

No. 59, the Mini 1275 GT of Paul Easter and John Handley, Wembley, April 19, 1970 (courtesy Pat Smith).

Patrick Vanson (*right*, with an unknown individual) and the ill-fated MGA (courtesy Patrick Vanson

Guy Verrier (*left*) and Francis Murac (courtesy Ted Taylor).

No. 17, the Hillman GT of John Bloxham, Peter Brown, and Robert McBurney (courtesy Andrew Bradbury).

No. 100 between Cali and Buenaventura (courtesy Patrick Vanson).

Running out of time: No. 99, the Ford Cortina Savage V6 of Kim Brassington (*pictured*) and Don Carslaw, southern Yugoslavia (courtesy Kim Brassington).

Rosemary Smith at Ville San Pietro, April 23, 1970 (courtesy Andrew Lees).

Ford GB service point, Ville San Pietro, April 23, 1970 (courtesy Andrew Lees).

The Annabel's nightclub-sponsored Mercedes 280SE of Innes Ireland, Michael Taylor, and Mark Birley, Italy (courtesy Andrew Lees).

Logan Morrison checks a control sign before Kotor, Yugoslavia (courtesy Mike Wood).

Rally cars loaded on the SS *Verdi* (courtesy Pat Smith).

The BLMC Triumph crews: (*left to right*) Brian Culcheth, Neville Johnson, Johnstone Syer, Paddy Hopkirk, Tony Nash, Andrew Cowan, Uldarico "Larco" Ossio, Brian Coyle, Evan Green, Hamish Cardno and "Gelignite" Jack Murray (courtesy Mike Wood).

Artist's rendition of No. 39 (courtesy Brian Englefield).

The Red Arrows Maxi: Peter Evans (*left*) and Terry Kingsley (courtesy Mike Wood).

The Royal Maxi: (*left to right*) Capt. Nigel Clarkson, Capt. HRH Prince Michael of Kent, and Capt. Gavin Thompson (courtesy Mike Wood).

Evan Green (*left*) and "Gelignite" Jack Murray, April 1970 (courtesy Brian Culcheth).

No. 32 at Mexico City, May 1970 (courtesy Mike Wood).

No. 54 in Reg Red-grave's driveway before the rally (courtesy Teresa Jensen-Redgrave).

Getting ready: (*left to right*) Jean Denton (*blue jacket*), Liz Crellin, and Pat Wright checking the maps (courtesy Pat Smith).

No. 29, the Bolivian National Team BMW 2002Ti of William Bendeck, Dieter Hübner, and Jorge Burgoa (courtesy Pat Smith).

Pat Wright's rewritten instructions for the start of the Grand Premio *prime* (courtesy Pat Smith).

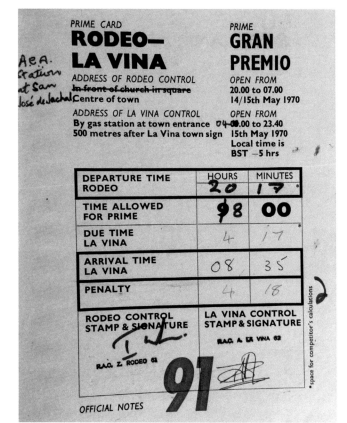

On the way to Cusco, Peru (courtesy Mike Wood).

Artist's rendition of No. 88 (courtesy Brian Culcheth).

Brian Culcheth at the end of the Gran Premio *prime*, on which he averaged 104 miles per hour (courtesy Brian Culcheth).

No. 88, motoring above the clouds in Ecuador (courtesy Brian Culcheth).

Johnstone Syer (*left*) and Brian Culcheth on the Scottish Rally in June 1970—which they won (courtesy Brian Culcheth).

Costa Rica (courtesy Mike Wood).

Opposite, top: No. 54 gets a going-over before the start of the last *prime*, the Aztec (courtesy Mike Wood). *Opposite, middle:* Victory in sight: No. 18, the Ford GB Escort of Hannu Mikkola (*driving*) and Gunnar Palm, on the Aztec *prime* (courtesy Mike Wood). *Opposite, bottom:* Against the odds: the privately entered BLMC 1800 of Redgrave, Freeborough, and Cooper at Mexico City (courtesy Mike Wood).

Post-event Ford GB Press Conference: (*left to right*) Gunnar Palm, unknown, Hannu Mikkola, and Stuart Turner, Mexico City, May 1970 (courtesy Mike Wood).

The winning Escort at Mexico City: (*left to right*) unknown, Gunnar Palm, and unknown (courtesy Mike Wood).

20

A Private Enterprise
(Part One)

It could be said that, as with the law, there is the letter of a rally's regulations and then there's the spirit. Motoring journalist and London to Mexico World Cup Rally competitor Hamish Cardno wrote that "it is grossly unfair that the Citroëns, which (at Lisbon) are crowding the leader board and taking almost all the private entries' prizes, should be there…. Several of the crews are works drivers, the cars are works prepared, they have service crews all over the place and competitions manager René Cotton keeps turning up to see how things are going."[1] However, one suspects that for Claudine Trautmann, Patrick Vanson, and the rest of the Citroën crews, the intricacies of entry definition were furthest from their minds as the six DS21s lined up at Wembley in readiness for departure for the longest rally competition ever.

By 1970, Frenchwoman Claudine Trautmann had established an extraordinary record at the top of the French women's rally championship, taking the title nine times between 1960 and 1968. Reflecting on her unprecedented success, Claudine joked: "My maiden name is Bouchet and I was champion in '60, and '61 under the name of Vanson. Then Bouchet (again), then Trautmann. It's true that if you look on the internet … some years are missing. I think they couldn't keep up with me!" This extraordinary record had its humble beginnings in 1957 when, skiing for her local club, she took a tumble on a slalom. One of the spectators began to laugh and asked her to go for a drink, once she had recovered herself. He turned out to be the local Simca dealer, the French automobiles produced from 1934 until the brand itself disappeared from showrooms after the PSA Group bought Chrysler Europe in 1978. The man explained he had been rallying a Simca in club events and asked whether she, a Simca owner herself, had thought of competing. This intrigued her, so she decided to enter the *Rallye du Mont Blanc*, surveying the route on weekends. A highly successful start, she finished fourth outright and took home the *Coupe des Dames*, the "Ladies' Cup." She was very proud, she recalled. "I decided I am going to do this. I did several rallies until 1960, when Mr. Cotton from Citroën took me." "Mr. Cotton" was René Cotton, then president of the Paris Île-de-France club, which supported privately entered Citroëns in rally events, and who would, by 1965, become the head of the Citroën Competitions Department.

Claudine began to drive for Cotton, piloting Citroën IDs to great achievements during the first half of the 1960s, shared a roster with successful French women co-drivers, including Lucette Pointet, Françoise Vallier, Marie-Claude Beaumont,

Claudine Trautmann (*left*) and Colette Perrier, Wembley, April 19, 1970 (courtesy Guido Devreker).

and Ginette De Rolland, who would eventually share co-driving duties for Rosemary Smith in the London to Mexico World Cup Rally. She also began taking the co-driver's seat for another of Cotton's drivers, René Trautmann, again scoring success after success. By 1960, Claudine had married another driver in Cotton's team, Patrick Vanson.

Patrick's introduction to the world of rally motorsports happened by pure chance. In 1951, as a young salesman for Colgate-Palmolive in France, he was dispatched to Morocco to assist the local importer in promoting the company's products. During his visit "the importer's son-in-law said, 'Oh look, in the paper, there's a rally on here from Casablanca to Marrakesh next weekend, why don't we do that, it would be a nice change,'" Patrick explained. "I said, 'Yes, that would be fun, we've nothing else to do. But,' I said, 'we don't have a car. Well, I don't!' He said, 'No, but my father-in-law will lend me his Citroën.' It was a Light Eleven. … We were number 11 and we finished 11th. … It was a fun day. And that started it off."

In 1955, Colgate-Palmolive sent Patrick to the United States for a year, but on his return another chance encounter with a colleague led to both of them entering the *Rallye des Routes du Nord*, or Northern Road Rally, using Patrick's Simca Aronde in standard road condition. "It was a difficult rally to start with. We even went up one hill backwards because we couldn't get up forwards in the snow," Patrick recalled. "It was fun! We lost the dynamo and the lights went out. We ended up in one of the horse-trough ponds. We got pulled out by the farmer with his old mare. We finished 56th, or something like that, out of a hundred. It wasn't a question of winning."

Patrick Vanson, 1970 (courtesy Patrick Vanson).

Having worked in the United States, Patrick had U.S. dollars to spend, so he treated himself to an MGA, using it to compete in two or three rallies. Then, in 1957, he decided to enter the ill-fated *Mille Miglia*, the "thousand miles" Italian road race on public roads, from Brescia to Rome and back. Patrick surveyed the entire route with his co-driver in the MGA and then parked outside the Brescia hotel where they were staying overnight, asking the night porter to keep an eye on it. The next morning it was gone—stolen—and, when asked, the porter feigned surprise and puzzlement! What to do? There was no way Patrick could just rush out and purchase another MG, so now they had no car. Eventually, he was able to join forces with someone who had a modified Peugeot 403, and they went on to finish 134th out of 310 entries and second in class. This *Mille Miglia*—the 24th—would be the last carried out in its original form. Forty miles before the finish, Ferrari driver Alfonso De Portago, a Spanish aristocrat, and his American co-driver, Edmund Nelson, had a blowout. De Portago lost control, and the Ferrari careened off the road, ploughing into a crowd of spectators before bouncing back across the road into more onlookers. The catastrophe took the lives of 12 people, including those of De Portago and Nelson. As a consequence, the famous Italian road race was banned, resurfacing briefly as a highly regulated rally-type event before relaunching as a classic car race in 1977, into which only cars manufactured during the period up to 1957 could be entered.

More rallies followed for Patrick; he tackled, for one, the 1959 8,700-mile

Algiers-Cape Rally in a DKW automobile at the invitation of Herr Trubsbach, head of Auto Union's Competitions Department (Auto Union being the precursor to Audi). Then, at the beginning of the 1960s, Patrick began rallying Citroëns with the Paris Île-de-France club, where he met Claudine Bouchet. The two married soon after, and Patrick moved to Annemasse in eastern France. The marriage, however, was short-lived, and at his mother's suggestion, he returned to Paris, which set in motion a chain of events that eventually led him to begin working for the then-fledgling Swedish seatbelt manufacturer, Klippan, a working relationship that lasted 23 years.

Patrick continued rallying when he could and was eventually noticed by Stuart Turner, then head of the British Motor Corporation's competitions team. "Stuart Turner called me and said, 'Patrick, I need you,'" Patrick explained. "I said, 'What can I do for you?' 'Oh, we've entered a Mini for the Monte. We've entered Timo Mäkinen, a top Finnish driver, but he only speaks two words of English and no French. Now, can you go with him?' I said, 'Of course, I'd be delighted!' So, we did the Monte Carlo together and finished fourth. Timo was not at all interested in driving all these kilometers from here to there, he was only interested in special stages. So, I became his driver." This was the year Paddy Hopkirk and Henry Liddon took the title, also in a Mini Cooper S. It's worth noting that Citroën's best showing that year was 12th overall for René Trautmann, then married to Claudine.

Patrick continued to compete, while also continuing to work for Klippan, replacing his DKW with an MGB that was prepared at the Abingdon BMC works in Oxfordshire, England. He competed in the Le Mans 24-hour race and, not being tied down to a specific manufacturer's team, continued to rally Citroëns, entering a DS19 in the 1965 East African Safari Rally with Guy Verrier and taking 8th place overall. Then, in November 1968, he took his place with Jean-Louis Lemerle and Olivier Turcat in a Citroën DS21 for the start of the 10,000-mile London–Sydney Marathon. "'The A.C.F [*Automobile Club de France*] has entered a car for the London–Sydney 1968,'" Patrick recalled Turcat saying. "'They've entered Lemerle and me and neither of us have driven a Citroën and they want us to drive to Sydney. Would you like to come with us?' I was working for Klippan. They were delighted! I mean car producers would say you can't buzz off for a month or two, you can't do that, but the succession of lucky times, lucky moments." The trio successfully made it from London to Bombay in India and then over to Australia, but mechanical problems brought their Marathon adventure to an unfortunate end crossing the Flinders Ranges in South Australia.

Not long after he returned to France, rally organizer John Sprinzel told Patrick about the proposed 16,000-mile endurance event from London to Mexico City, scheduled to commence in the spring of 1970. Patrick leapt at the chance, but not before three other French rally drivers, and their co-driver/navigators, had thrown their hats into the ring. Claudine explained: "With my husband [René Trautmann] and Bob Neyret, the three of us decided to do the World Cup Rally. [René] Cotton was not interested at all at the start. Did you notice that we have a blue car, a white car, and a red car? Because we were certain we would reach Mexico! Finally Cotton thought I must do something for them so the factory decided to give a car to Verrier, Vanson and the third … [Paul Collteloni]. … Then there were six Citroëns."

The first three cars were prepared in Paris and Grenoble in Switzerland, although Claudine recalled that very few adaptations were actually needed. On his recce of South America, René Trautmann became acutely aware of the great length of stretches and sections and decided that, for these, cars should be able to cruise at lower revs. Thus, he requested an extra gear be added to the DS21's standard four-speed box. The other challenge for the initial three was that of cost, given that René Cotton and his competitions department remained ambivalent about the endeavor. With fellow entrant Robert "Bob" Neyret's assistance, they were able to secure a degree of financial sponsorship from *Le Figaro* newspaper; watch manufacturer Herma via a Bouchet family connection; and Aseptogyl, the toothpaste company also familiarly connected to dental surgeon Neyret.

At this point it's worth reiterating the rules of entry into the London to Mexico World Cup Rally. For a car to qualify as a private entry, that car had to be owned by and registered to a private individual, rather than to a manufacturer's competitions department. Cars could be backed or sponsored by commercial enterprises but needed to be entered by a private owner. Whether purchased by or presented to the Citroën drivers, each car was in fact registered to them, hence the classification and the consequential detractors in 1970, journalist and competitor Hamish Cardno included!

Thus, the *tricolor* Citroën squad of three had increased to six by the time cars lined up for departure on April 19, 1970: joining the two Trautmann cars and that of Neyret were those of Vanson, Guy Verrier, and Paul Coltelloni. Of the 13 crewmembers—all were two-up except the Vanson team, which was a trio—five were veterans of the 10,000-mile London–Sydney Marathon endurance event of 1968. Joining Neyret was fellow dentist and regular co-driver Jacques Terramorsi—the duo had a long history or competing together and had scored ninth place in Sydney in '68. Coltelloni had won the 1959 European Rally Championship and had driven a privately entered Volvo in the London– Sydney Marathon. This time he was joined by old friend and frequent co-driver Henri "Ido" Marang. The two were considered Citroën's "elder statesmen," given their ages of 49 and 51! Besides regular co-driver Turcat, Vanson also teamed up with Citroën ace-mechanic Alain Leprince—a judicious choice, given the frequent *parcs fermés* planned for the route, where only team members could work on their cars. René Trautmann was teamed with racing and rally competitor Jean-Pierre Hanrioud, while sports all-rounder Verrier was joined by regular partner Francis Murac. Completing the lineup with Claudine was Colette Perrier, who had co-driven for Claudine in the past. As Claudine recounted, "she had done a few rallies on her own. She could drive as well. She could sleep very well also!" Not an ability to be dismissed!

The Vanson car was drawn No. 100, so it was their plan to get past as many other cars as possible before the first special stage in Yugoslavia. They managed to get by some 50 competitors by the time they reached Titograd and the revised Montenegro *prime.* All the Citroëns made effortless progress through Europe. "We … were old rally lads," Patrick commented. "You don't need to go flat out from here to … Munich, down the motorway, didn't matter if you were late." Claudine even went so far as to describe the European section as tame, citing too many built-up areas and

René Trautmann (*second from right behind car*) with No. 93 (courtesy Guido Devreker).

good roads with just the 570 kilometers (374 miles) of the five "special stages" to keep the competitors awake. Anyone familiar with the major European rallies of the day would recognize these speed sections, so it's perhaps no surprise that the experienced Citroën crews quickly established themselves on the road to Lisbon, throwing down the gauntlet to the British Ford and BLMC teams.

Happy with their standing, Patrick decided not to push it on the Montenegro *prime* and picked up four penalty points at the finish control at Kotor. Claudine collected five points, while Trautmann and Neyret received just one penalty as they tore into the control. Best of all, Guy Verrier cleaned the stage; i.e., No. 101 incurred not a single penalty. Now they had all had their first taste of the European speed sections, so it was onwards towards *prime* number two, the Serbian, another potentially familiar stretch for most of the French drivers. Patrick recalled that the road through Yugoslavia was easy and brought them to the Glamoč start control at around three in the morning. While other timely arrivals tackled the *prime* as soon as they could, Patrick calculated that waiting until daybreak would offer benefits, not least because, in his view, there was still plenty of time to reach the rest stop at Monza—organizers had allowed cars a total of 35 hours to get from the Sofia time control to the famous Italian racetrack.

Daylight meant that fog during the first 50 kilometers (31 miles) wasn't the hindrance it could have been in darkness and, wryly, Patrick recalled that the trail was awful—ideal for the Citroën's hydropneumatic suspension system! Even so, they were 15 minutes late at the exit control at Bosanska Krupa, which Patrick initially thought was a lot. However, they were thrilled to discover that they were lying fourth by the time they rolled into Monza. Of the other Citroëns, only Verrier and Trautmann had done better, while poor Claudine and Colette had suffered a puncture on the Serbian, Claudine recalling that she couldn't get the offending wheel off, forgetting that on the DS, the parking brake effectively locked the front end. Momentarily baffled, Colette came to rescue by releasing the brake, and all was well. Unfortunately, this rookie error by such an experienced Citroën driver contributed to No. 25 amassing 105 penalties by the time Bosanska came into view. To make matters worse, all three of the French women's rivals for the women's prize—Tish Ozanne, Rosemary Smith, and Jean Denton—were faster to Bosanska. This battle within the fight was now well and truly on!

Perhaps blurring the lines between factory-backed and independently supported, René Cotton had finally sat up and noticed what was happening before the rally got underway and had consequently organized Europe's extensive Citroën dealer and workshop network to provide servicing at designated sites, including Monza. Once checked over, cars were locked away into *parc fermé* and, arrival times allowing (and hotel arrangements being made in advance!), competitors had the chance to get some rest before the next onslaught to Lisbon.

A transport stage led competitors to the third *prime*, the San Remo in Italy. Patrick described it as 100 kilometers (62 miles) of narrow and tortuous road. However, No. 100 cleaned the section, although not before a puncture and the slow-moving SAAB of Colin Taylor and Bert Jennings threw up a couple of obstacles. Many other competitors also cleaned the San Remo, the consensus being that this *prime* had not been quite as challenging as it could have been. The next, however, was decidedly not one Patrick was looking forward to as the Alpine *prime* would cover some of the Monte Carlo Rally route, including the legendary Col de Turini mountain pass. Accordingly, Patrick took no chances and accepted the 12-minute penalty at Rouaine.

All the Citroëns made incident-free progress on the very long transport stage through France, receiving a welcome reception and additional checks and servicing from the Citroën dealership in Pau, before crossing Spain and into Portugal, where the final European *prime* at Arganil would offer one last trial before Lisbon. On this forest stage, both Patrick and Claudine encountered Argentinian Peugeot team Gastón Perkins and Jack Forrest Greene, who had misjudged a bend and bumped off the road into a gully. Their efforts to drag the 404 back onto the track involved running a taut cable from the car up and across the road, with the express purpose of winching the Peugeot out of its resting place. Fortunately, Claudine and Colette were signaled by one of the Argentinians to stay as close to the left as possible and avoided any danger. Patrick was not quite so lucky as the Citroën hit the stretched cable, which somehow spared the windshield but destroyed one of the spotlights attached to the driver's door. After the event, Patrick drolly reported that he would have been rather bored had the cable taken his head off!

Once again, the Citroëns excelled: Neyret collected six penalties; Coltelloni eight; Vanson three, despite the dance with disaster; Verrier one; and, once again, Trautmann cleaned the *prime*. Furthermore, dropping just 22 minutes, Claudine now consolidated her lead over Smith, Ozanne, and Denton. Provided the Trautmanns made it to Lisbon within limits, they were headed for the double—René Trautmann

No. 51, the SAAB 96 of Bert Jennings and Colin Taylor (courtesy Guido Devreker).

as leading car at the close of the European section and Claudine Trautmann as leading woman.

Lisbon loomed, and cars made for the designated control at a gas station on
the city's limits before heading for *parc fermé* at the Alcántara docks. Time allowing,
cars could be checked over, and then they needed to be made ready for the planned
ocean crossing by ship. Much attention was given to René and Claudine, both being
awarded prizes at the ceremony at the casino at Estoril, and there was a general sense
of satisfaction for all the Citroën entries. René and Hanrioud were in first place; Verrier and Murac in third; Vanson, Turcat, and Leprince in fifth; and Neyret and Terramorsi in seventh. Claudine and Colette were just outside the top 20 but had beaten
their nearest rivals— Rosemary Smith, Ginette De Rolland, and Alice Watson—by 15
points, putting them three places ahead on the finishing board. Could the Citroëns
bring the same performance over to South America? There was all to play for!

While most of the Citroën crews took some time to relax in Lisbon before
boarding the flight to Rio de Janeiro, there was no rest for Neyret and Terramorsi.
René Cotton had entered them into the *Rallye du Maroc* or Moroccan Rally, not least
because they had their 1969 title to defend. After 4,500 miles across Europe, they
journeyed to Morocco and, astonishingly, despite the previous rigors, won the event
again! For other competitors, most if not all were more than ready to jet off to Brazil
when the time came, although Rio represented yet another time of tourism for many,
indulging in a little sun, sea, and sand, visiting the sights and being entertained by
various embassy personnel. Fun though it was to hang out with other competitors at
the city's famous Hotel Glória, all were soon restless and itching to get going on the
next stage of the London to Mexico World Cup Rally.

21

Three Wheels on My Wagon

The Sofia control, marshaled by John Brown, former co-driver to, among others, John Sprinzel, was located at the Balkan Hotel in Sveta Nedelya Square, and would be open between 08:00 and noon on April 21. From Belgrade, competitors followed the *autoput*, which took them through Niš and over the border into Bulgaria just after Gradinje. Two hundred and forty-plus monotonous miles through the night—as long as concentration was maintained, surely all would be well?

Making steady, untroubled progress thus far, about 25 miles out of Belgrade, calamity struck one of the Ford works Escorts. Backed by the British *Sunday Express* newspaper, No. 85 was being crewed by London–Sydney Marathon winner Colin Malkin and motoring journalist and rally competitor Richard Hudson-Evans. As they drove at around 80 miles per hour, oncoming headlamps appeared in the opposite direction, coming closer and closer. Rather than approaching as if to pass the Escort, the lights appeared to be aiming directly at it. A truck was bearing down, apparently determined to collide head-on, and, despite heroic attempts, there was nothing Malkin could do to prevent a smash. "I saw stars and things," Hudson-Evans reported, "losing my breath and nearly having my head torn from my shoulders with the violent retardation."[1] The car spun on the dark road and gasoline spewed everywhere. Frantically unbuckling safety harnesses, Colin and Richard managed to extricate themselves from the wreckage, miraculously unhurt, only to be faced with a new danger. The mangled Escort had ended up facing the way it had come. In the middle of the two-lane highway. In the dark! An easy target for a speeding car or distracted truck driver. (The offending truck had, in fact, crashed off the road and out of sight.)

After some initial assistance from the Rolls-Royce crew, Bill Bengry and David Skeffington, the first competitors to arrive after the collision, there was nothing for it but for Malkin to remain in situ and warn traffic while Hudson-Evans hitched a ride back to the Belgrade control in search of help. His adventure on the way is a story in itself, but suffice to say he was able to arrange for a ride back to the crash site and get the wreck pulled off the *autoput*.

It was eventually determined that the errant truck driver had dozed off at the wheel; he was duly prosecuted. No comfort to the crew of No. 85, however, as they were out of the event, so Colin Malkin returned to England while Richard Hudson-Evans continued onwards, no longer as a participant but as a journalist covering the rally.

Elsewhere, Englefield, Baker, and Lloyd-Hirst in No. 39 were experiencing some

155

of the tricky logistics that can so often impact progress and performance on an endurance rally. They had adopted a driver rotation approach for the long transport stage: first Baker, then Englefield had done their stints, and now it was Lloyd-Hirst's turn. He declined, explaining that Englefield had been driving so fast that he had been unable to sleep and thus wasn't ready to take over! Englefield was therefore forced to continue, a risky move. "I suffered very badly from motion sickness," Englefield explained. "I went to see a doctor … He said, 'You need to take these [pills], but they can make you drowsy.' I said, 'I can't have that!' He said, 'Well, you need to take these to counteract that.' The second lot were amphetamine! He said … 'Don't go over about 11 hours' … about 11 hours I was driving on the *autoput* … on the way to Sofia and I just drifted off and … whoa!" Baker quickly took over and all was well, although they had also noticed something not quite right with the car. With both logistical and possible mechanical issues in mind, they made it to Sofia where Englefield got to work under the car, discovering that the prop shaft had been attached using standard nuts and bolts, not what he had specified to one of his mechanics. These had worked loose and put the quill-shaft bearing under stress. This was not something that he could quickly fix, so they were forced to continue with just a rudimentary repair.

Ninety-three cars arrived at the Balkan Hotel, and of those, only two picked up points for lateness. In addition to the Sherger's FIAT and the obliterated Escort, as previously reported, the beach buggy had also gone out with a bang! Still nursing their Escort, Aaltonen and Liddon received penalty points, as did Cecil Woodley's Ventora. A number of other entrants that did arrive within the threshold had all sorts of mechanical and other problems, however, with the Trident now in need of replacement suspension bushing and the Royal Maxi also now experiencing fifth gear problems. Perhaps surprisingly, the rally had seen only two privately entered Volvos appear on the starting grid, and now, the 132 entered by Colonel J.W. Weld was struggling on soft shock absorbers while No. 104, the V6-engined Ford Cortina Savage, was in need of alarming quantities of transmission oil. Crews who arrived with time in hand seized the opportunity to tend to machines or get, as Red Arrows' team member Michael Scarlett reported, "some welcome horizontal sleep in the huge Balkan Hotel."[2] Anyone able to get some rest would be grateful as now, with just a 360-mile hop down to Titograd via the Biogradska Gora national forest on the way, competitors would at last get their first taste of a London to Mexico World Cup Rally *prime*, even if it was to be a hastily rerouted and therefore foreshortened stage.

Competitors departed Sofia and sped off back towards Niš, turning left at Ćićevac, many suffering the extortion of a "pop-up" policeman, who took great pleasure in fining drivers for "speeding"! Yet, even as cars followed the revised route, hours after the control had closed, in came a certain FIAT 2300 wagon, the sheepish Kuwaiti Sherger brothers arriving in the hope that they might be allowed to continue! Sadly, this was their final confirmation, if they had needed one, that their Mexico dream was over.

The revised route from Sofia to Titograd took competitors west and south, taking in the cities of Kruševac and Titovo Užice, before arriving at the start of the first *prime*, the Montenegro. Located on the Citinje Road exit from Titograd, the control would be open between 17:00 on April 21 to half-past-midnight on the 22nd,

The No. 39 Team: (*foreground, left to right*) Adrian Lloyd-Hirst, Brian Englefield, and Keith Baker (courtesy Brian Englefield).

and competitors were expected to complete the 50-mile expanse of asphalt mountain road in 65 minutes. Drivers had been warned that the road was open to normal traffic and made aware that there were innumerable hairpin bends with unshielded drops, some 1,000 feet down, especially on the way to Kotor, overlooking the Adriatic, and the finish control. Competitors were no doubt also bemused by local reports that

The Sherger brothers' FIAT 2300 station wagon (courtesy Guido Devreker).

southern Yugoslavia had experienced a number of earth tremors, potentially with more to come!

For the inexperienced and the uninitiated drivers, this would be first real test. For the professionals and other seasoned competitors, it would be their first chance to show what they could do. Cars lined up to have their books stamped and their start time recorded by jovial Jim Gavin and then accelerated away, some less than happy that they might encounter donkey carts, buses, even trucks on the fast run. French rally professional René Trautmann and Finnish maestro Rauno Aaltonen were especially critical, but only because they both knew the speeds required to "clean" the *prime*, i.e., complete it without penalty. Ultimately, despite still suffering from transmission trouble that rendered all but the top gear unusable, Aaltonen put all of his experience and skill to good use and lost just three minutes at Kotor, while Trautmann put concerns aside to lose just one minute! Better still, six cars cleaned the stage, with plaudits going to Andrew Cowan, Terry Hunter, and Guy Verrier in one of the Citroën DS21s, and Mikkola, Fall, and Clark in the works Escorts. Only a broken camshaft gear during the very last moments of the section prevented Mäkinen from joining his teammates, instead picking up seven penalty points.

Of the remaining field, 19 drivers acquitted themselves with aplomb, losing less than 10 minutes. These included Paul Easter and John Handley in the BLMC Mini 1275 GT (despite continued mechanical problems, which the BLMC service team attributed to breather issues from the Mini's centrally mounted rear fuel tank) and all three privately-entered Hillmans, with Rod Badham, John Bloxham, and Mike Tyrell at the respective wheels. They certainly posed a threat to the Citroëns' aspirations of winning the private entry prize! Perhaps not surprisingly, slowest to Kotor was the Martin family Rolls.

The *prime* did not pass without incident, however, as, after assorted misfortunes that had already afflicted No. 10, the Ventora of Cecil Woodley, it failed to complete the stage. As previously reported, the Montenegro also finally dashed the aspirations of Captains Marriott and Dill, who learned the hard way that ground clearance is all! The green-and-gold 2.5PI had a puncture to add to their quill-shaft woes, and although they were given a replacement assembly by the BLMC service team at Kotor, complexities of refitting, which involved isolating the rear suspension, proved extremely time consuming, and they had to race to reach the next control.

Competitors were now required to get themselves to the start of the next *prime*, the Serbian. Following the Bay of Kotor, they made for Risan and then along the Adriatic coast to Dubrovnik before turning inwards and upwards via Mostar, Posušje, and Livno to Glamoč in the foothills of Staretina and Velika Golija. The road to Dubrovnik was asphalt and easy, the track up to Glamoč the complete opposite, offering up dust, rocks, and, in places, the fear that a competitor might not be on the right mountain track, or any track at all! Added to this, fatigue would surely now kick in, especially for those less than experienced in endurance rallying.

A matter of days before, and because winter snow had prevented the likes of Paul Easter and John Handley from completing survey work in the Mini in Yugoslavia earlier in the year, Ford boss Stuart Turner dispatched rally driver Chris Sclater to notate the Serbian *prime* route. With the instructions that he should get to London's Heathrow Airport, collect a ticket, fly first to Zagreb and then onwards to Split, pick up a rental car, drive up to the control start at Glamoč, and then tape-record his notes and comments along the route, Sclater set off just a few hours after competitors departed Wembley on April 19. The first sign that this was not going to be a straightforward reconnaissance was when he discovered that there was no ticket awaiting him at the airport! Then the flight was delayed, which meant he missed the connecting flight to Split and had to get an overnight train from Zagreb. Time was of the essence, with only a day-and-a-half before rally cars would arrive, so he collected a rental car and set off on the 80-mile drive up to the start control location.

It took Sclater two hours to reach Glamoč. "I realized by the time I got there that this was going to be a fairly lonely trip," he explained, "not only because I was flying solo, but even on the 'main' roads there were not many cars and very few petrol stations."[3] At Glamoč, he checked into the only hotel there was to get some rest in readiness for surveying and notating the 120-mile *prime* the following day. He also purchased a couple of plastic containers and filled both car and them with gasoline.

The little Peugeot wagon he had rented wasn't exactly suitable for the recce, but there had been little choice, so he checked tire pressure, lights, oil, and water and set off. All was well, albeit challenging, for the first 40 miles or so, along rough country lanes, but then a puncture brought the Peugeot to a halt. Sclater retrieved the spare tire. It was also flat! What to do? He climbed back into the car and sat, hoping another vehicle might come along. Nothing. As he hadn't passed any garages thus far, and because the car was front-wheel drive, he swapped tires around so the flat was on a rear wheel and pressed on, continuing with the recorded notes and ever hopeful a repair shop would materialize along the way. It didn't, and eventually rubber gave way to rim and the wheel stopped turning. At a junction, a sign suggested civilization, so he limped the car into a small village, confirmed the lack of a garage or workshop, and, also confirming that there was no transport back out of town, left the car behind. He set off on foot in the hope a passing motorist might take him back to Glamoč. Cars went by, but no one stopped. "After about half an hour a Dutch couple in a campervan took me about 15 kilometers (nine miles) to the nearest big town," Sclater explained. "They told me that hitching was illegal in Yugoslavia, which explained why the locals wouldn't stop."[4]

Eventually, after finding another hotel and discovering that there was no transport willing or able to take him further, Sclater got a ride back to Glamoč courtesy of a couple of friends of the hotel concierge and the emptying of his wallet. He wrote up the pace notes and got the hotel to make copies. Although they only covered the first 70 or 80 miles of the *prime*, they were ready for distribution when the Ford works competitors arrived.

Sclater's adventure on the road back to England is a whole other story, but suffice to say Ford managed to avert any legal action threatened by the Peugeot's rental company for damaging and abandoning their car in the middle of nowhere, and Sclater eventually had all of his out-of-pocket expenses reimbursed. He also received "a very curt letter from Stuart [Turner] saying it was a pity [he] hadn't gone a bit further along the Prime because there was an unsafe bridge."[5]

Although the entrance to the *prime* was at a gas station on the edge of the town, the encroaching mist caused former Rootes works driver Ian "Tiny" Lewis to establish the Serbian control at the hotel. The control was open from 01:00 to 11:00; provided competitors had time in hand, they could decide when to depart. In trouble at Glamoč, and in need of every minute they had at their disposal, were Brian Peacock and Dave Skittrall in the 2.3-liter (140 cubic-inch) V6-engined Ford Capri. The car had been developed and built at Ford GB's research and development center at Dunton in Essex where, according to the car's current owner, Michael Ryman, 22 employees volunteered to work on the Capri, which was gifted by Ford Cologne in Germany as an early face-lift model Capri 3000GT in January 1970. "Team Dunton" worked tirelessly to transform the car into a rally machine, no doubt benefiting from the Ford "parts bin" at their disposal, plus any design and development secrets coming down the pipe! Ryman emphasized that, although the Capri was entered by Team Dunton, it was a legitimately private entry, receiving no formal endorsement or sponsorship from Ford itself.

Peacock had upgraded the joint between the steering column and rack and was now annoyed with himself as it had failed. Once the works Escorts were on their way, the Ford service team, including Chris Sclater, set to work fixing the ailing Capri with Ford auto electrician Pat Sullivan helping Peacock and Skittrall to improvise a solution. "I can't remember how but I think there was a fair bit of grinding, filing, drilling and welding,"[6] Sclater wrote. Very late, the Capri was therefore able to continue off onto the *prime*. Not so fortunate was the Conroy Motors' four-door "Mexi-Mini" of Allan Keefe and James Conroy. The unique Cooper S arrived after the control closed and was therefore forced to retire.

The broken bridge on the Serbian *prime* (courtesy Mike Wood).

Any competitor familiar with the many European Liège-Sofia-Liège rallies of the 1960s would have recognized the terrain generally and the *prime* route from Glamoč to Bosanska Krupa, with a sneaky passage control at Sanski Most, specifically, as they sped off from the control. Others would get a first taste of "real horror, with a diabolical mixture of tarmac, smooth dirt, very rough tracks, villages and occasional road works ... trucks and people on the un-closed roads."[7] Whether competitors chose to depart as soon as they arrived at Glamoč or waited a while, the Serbian took no prisoners; Richard Hudson-Evans suggested it was the *prime* that most influenced the final standings at Lisbon. It was also the *prime* that saw not a little dexterity and initiative involving the bridge, or lack thereof, to which Stuart Turner had tersely referred in his letter to Chris Sclater. Upon encountering the offending construction, early competitors attempted to replace missing planks of wood, but as quickly as they were laid, they would disappear again. Reports that Hannu Mikkola decided not to let a little problem like the absence of a bridge get in his way and simply jumped the car across the offending gulch are still disputed to this day. Needless to say, a hastily routed diversion was deployed to keep things moving, with organizers chalking the whole thing up as simply a taste of what South America would bring.

Predictably, the Serbian created any number of incidents, both major and minor. As per previous explanations, the British Job's Dairy Mustang, crewed by the only co-ed team in the rally, met its end, while British bar owner Dennis Cresdee's team required medical attention when their 1800 came off the worse in an argument with a tree. The Antiguan Hillman of Mike Tyrell, Bernard Unett, and Jim Fuller

The ill-fated BLMC 1800S of Dennis Cresdee, Bob Eaves, and Frank Bainbridge (courtesy Ken Green).

was taken out by a truck, the team fortunate not to be injured but unfortunate to see their Mexico dream expire, while No. 22, the Dutch Alfa Romeo Giulia of Bob de Jong and Christiaan Tuerlinx, lost an axle and thus their chance to proceed further. The Ron Channon/Rod Cooper Cortina Lotus's engine mountings broke, necessitating more rally-improv involving a leather belt to secure the engine, and a comedy moment of pants-dropping Whitehall farce proportions at the end control! The Buchanan-Michaelson 2.5PI was driving with hardly any shock absorption, a very uncomfortable experience for him, Roy Fidler, and Jimmy Bullough. The first taste of how trailing dust can impact a high-speed competitor occurred when Roger Clark was momentarily unsighted and rolled the *Shoot Football Weekly* magazine-sponsored works Escort, although the fact that he and co-driver Alec Poole only incurred 68 penalty points as a consequence is extraordinary. Rob Lyall recalled that, having gone into the prime to immediately refuel before returning to the start, they encountered Clark coming back up the track, having lost most of his gasoline during the accident. Clark and Pool had no cash to pay for gas, so Badham and Lyall footed the bill. They didn't get reimbursed until South America and then only with Yugoslavian currency, completely useless on the road to Mexico City! Regardless, Rob was unhappy with both conditions and their performance on the Serbian, citing no relationship between route map and the actual route plus the offending bridge, or rather its absence, as previously mentioned. These frustrating obstacles led to No. 4 picking up 67 penalty points by the finish.

The Easter/Handley Mini was still misbehaving, and now John Handley had begun to feel unwell, asking Easter to take driving duties again. Poor performance

No. 4, the Berry Magicoal–sponsored Hillman GT of Rod Badham and Rob Lyall (courtesy Ken Green).

meant that, despite Easter's experience and skill on this familiar stretch, the 1275 GT picked up 27 penalty points by the finish.

More successfully, French duo René Trautmann and co-driver Jean-Pierre Hanrioud lost only four minutes, with compatriots Guy Verrier and Francis Murac losing six, Mikkola and Gunnar Palm seven, and Aaltonen and Liddon eight, still running in fifth gear only! Others doing well were the bright yellow JCB construction equipment-sponsored Hillman GT of John Bloxham, Peter Brown, and Rob McBurney, Peter Garratt's Viva GT, and No. 19, the Mexican VW Bug. For the women's teams, the gauntlet was truly thrown down as both the Smith/De Rolland/Watson Maxi and the Denton/Wright/Crellin 1800 "Beauty Box" clocked faster times than the Claudine Trautmann/Colette Perrier Citroën DS21.

Having had their route books stamped and times recorded by rally driver Erle Morley at the finish control at the Bosanska Krupa hotel, surviving teams were then required to make their way to Monza in Italy and its famous *autodrome* for a special *parc fermé* and the chance of rest, repairs, and regrouping!

22

A Private Enterprise
(Part Two)

At last, the ship arrived and unloaded its rally cargo in readiness for the start of the South American section. Competitors wrangled their vehicles out of customs, brandishing the required paperwork, and hastily checked the state of the cars. After René Trautmann's success across Europe, all eyes were on him, but something was amiss. No. 93 did not appear quite as it had been when left for loading onto the ship; Claudine explained that René believed someone had put water in his fuel tank! Whatever the malaise, the car wasn't running correctly, but there was little time to properly repair any problems before the start. Now, instead of starting in numeric order, competitors would depart in line with their position at Lisbon. Thus, Trautmann and Hanrioud were expected to be first away from the ceremonial departure control close to the Hotel Glória where competitors had been staying. With time at a premium, the ailing Citroën had to receive remedial work even as cars departed, meaning that No. 93 missed the first away spot.

Going was slow out of Rio, with throngs of spectators anxious to catch a glimpse of the multi-colored rally cars as they crept along and, if possible, grab a decal or two off a vehicle's bodywork! Then, once checked in at the "zero mile" start, they were away into Brazil, making for the first South American *prime*, Patrick and his team starkly aware that the ensuing 11,500-plus miles represented five Liège-Sofia-Liège or four East African Safari rallies put together!

The route south took competitors through São Paulo, which Patrick recalled as being worse than Rio for clamoring crowds, but all managed to negotiate the busy city and pressed on towards Ventania and the Parana *prime*, which nearly took out the Vanson Citroën when, driving a straight line through a village, it hit a bump at around 40 miles per hour and momentarily took flight! Sudden gasps all around, but the car deftly landed on all four wheels and on they went, 28 minutes beyond the 90-minute allowance. Of the other Citroëns, Verrier was just three minutes quicker, much-favored Trautmann collected 24 points, Coltelloni 26, Claudine 46, and, fastest of all, but only just, was Neyret with 23.

Next up was the truncated Rio Grande *prime*, half of which had been dismissed as it was waterlogged. While the 120-mile section saw the end of a few competitors' dreams of reaching Mexico, all the Citroëns survived the tricky stage, although they had all lost between 43 and 51 minutes at the finish control at São Joachim. In fact, so tough was this *prime* that the fastest car, the Escort of Rauno Aaltonen and Henry

Liddon, was still down 35 minutes on the target time. Even tougher conditions and challenges were yet to come.

Competitors now headed south, then west, then south again and across the border into Uruguay, making for the third South American *prime*, running 125 miles from Tacuarembó to Salto, close to the Argentinian border. The Vanson Citroën had lost its muffler on the Rio Grande, and its three occupants had to endure the resultant roar as they sped towards the speed section. Event organizers had set yet another trial for surviving crews here, insisting on 90 minutes for a penalty-free finish over terrain that was teasingly described as being like the Scottish Highlands. Yet more seemingly makeshift bridges required judicious approaches here, but Verrier, Vanson, and Neyret hung on to pick up just 23, 25, and 27 points, respectively, with Coltelloni and Claudine slower for 38 and 49 points. Claudine's closest rival for the women's prize, Rosemary Smith, had now managed to claw back some of the Trautmann/Perrier lead, 12 minutes quicker across the three *primes* thus far in the *Evening Standard* Austin Maxi. One Citroën would not be joining the others at Salto, however, as disaster struck for René Trautmann and Jean-Pierre Hanrioud. Whether because of a momentary lapse of concentration or a split-second navigation error, Trautmann overcooked the approach to a bridge and crashed, rolling over and severely damaging the red DS. Escaping with a few cuts and contusions, the pair frantically tried to get the car back on track and going again, but it was hopeless. The car leading at Lisbon, the team that had reigned supreme across Europe, was out.

Of course, the international print media exclaimed the calamity all over its pages, but, for the surviving Citroën teams, the matter at hand was to get to Montevideo, the

On the road to Montevideo (courtesy Pat Smith).

Uruguayan capital, and an overnight stop and *parc fermé* before taking a car ferry across the River Plate to Argentina's capital, Buenos Aires, the following day. Patrick recalled the transport section to Montevideo as fast over asphalt roads and the city itself as not especially attractive. However, it did offer the chance to rest before pushing on to Argentina and the long 1,200-mile stretch south and west to the Chilean border, via the Puyehue Pass. This section would take cars across the flat Patagonian pampas and would include two speed stages, the 200-mile Pampas *prime* and the 380-mile Trans-Argentine *prime*, the distances just a taste of what was still to come.

At Montevideo, Trautmann and Hanrioud notwithstanding, the Citroëns had performed well. Verrier and Murac were lying in third place out of 52 surviving teams with the Vanson team and Neyret and Terramorsi in equal eighth. Claudine and Colette were 21st fastest, and Coltelloni and Marang 32nd. The French women would now need to bring all of their experience and prowess to bear across Argentina if they were to improve on 17th-placed Rosemary Smith, supported by Claudine's onetime navigator Ginette De Rolland, and close in on the women's prize.

From Buenos Aires, a police motorcycle escort had been arranged for the rally cars, but, as Patrick recalled, they set off at such a pace that half the competitor convoy got left behind and had to rely on route notes to navigate their way beyond the city limits and down towards Saladillo and the Pampas *prime* start control. Out into the pampas, all but any stragglers were met with dust and a zigzag of wire fences, right-angle turns, and the thump-thump of crossing rail tracks. Dust nearly caused calamity for the Vanson car when Patrick was wrong-footed on a slight bend and ended up in a pond. Fortunately, the team was able to extricate the blue DS, and they were safely on their way again. Catching up with the dust-spewing vehicle ahead, they were amused to discover it was not, in fact, another competitor, but a civilian van! All was well, however, although towards the end of the stage, rain turned dust into the mud that would see the end of Puff the Magic Maxi's challenge further back.

After the finish control at Espartillar, the route stretched ever onwards, miles and miles of desert and scrub, taking cars to the next *prime* start at San Antonio Oeste. "We had a very good drive," Patrick recalled. "It suited the Citroën perfectly there, across Argentina to Chile. We were 120, 130, 140 kph [74, 80, 87 mph] all the time, it's the sort of surface which suited [the Citroën] very, very well." On this stretch, in darkness, a drowsy Colette suddenly came to her senses at the sight of glaring headlamps ahead, certain they were about to be set upon by members of the *Tupamaros*, the militant left-wing guerrilla group that was extremely active in the late 1960s and early 1970s. Whether the lights did belong to the rebels or not, they weren't especially interested in the rally and the women continued unimpeded.

The Trans-Argentine *prime* set a target time of six hours, which called for an average speed of over 60 miles per hour, if competitors were to arrive at the Bariloche ski resort, some 3,000 feet above sea level, without penalty. After the flat desert, Patrick recounted how they climbed to Bariloche and the contrast of beautiful lakes and pine trees, ascending further to the Puyehue Pass at 4,000 feet and into Chile, before tumbling back down again towards the Pacific and a right turn to join the Pan-American Highway at Osorno and a long slog to Santiago. The fast road

Citroën in the dust: No. 100 in South America (courtesy Patrick Vanson).

allowed Patrick to arrive in the city in good time to carry out much-needed maintenance on the DS before delivering it into *parc fermé* and then collapsing into bed for a well-earned rest.

All the Citroëns made steady, trouble-free progress, and by the time they reached the Chilean capital, of the 43 surviving cars, Verrier and Murac were still in third place, 21 minutes adrift from the leaders Mikkola and Palm in their Escort and just one minute behind second-placed Mäkinen and Staepelaere in theirs. Vanson and Neyret maintained their joint eighth place, and Claudine and Colette had achieved what they had set out to do: lying in 16th place, they were now 61 minutes ahead of Smith, De Rolland, and Watson. Coltelloni and Marang rounded off the Citroën entries, 23rd overall. After Santiago, however, what was to come represented the toughest, most challenging section of the entire rally. If cars were to successfully reach Buenaventura and the ship that would carry them up to and along the Panama Canal to Cristóbal, they would have to endure the harshness of driving at oxygen-deprived altitudes and five punishing special stages, two of which would cover some 500 miles, all against the clock!

Once again, the weather intervened, forcing John Sprinzel and his co-organizers to hastily reroute the next *prime*, the Chilean, which would now take competitors into Argentina via a rail tunnel at an elevation of 10,500 feet, instead of the original border crossing at the 15,600-feet high Aguas Negras Pass. Thus, cars departed Santiago and headed north, making for Putaendo and a speed section that would weave its

Llamas on the way across Argentina (courtesy Mike Wood).

way along a disused rail track, gently climbing 121 miles to Illapel with an allowance of 90 minutes. On the way to the start control, the Vanson car struck a dog at speed, the damage from which took out the Citroën's headlamps. Fortunately, the *prime* was to take place during daylight so they continued, collecting 68 minutes at the finish control compared to 57 for Neyret, 63 for Verrier, and 70 for Claudine. The Chilean proved extremely unkind to Coltelloni, however, as all manner of problems befell him and co-driver Marang, resulting in a huge 199-point penalty at Illapel. Frustrated but unbowed, they continued onwards and upwards to yet another slightly revised speed section, the Gran Premio *prime*, a mere 480 miles at elevations of up to 15,000 feet—and all to be tackled in eight hours!

Rattling and echoing through the Cumbre Tunnel at Las Cuevas, competitors entered back into Argentina and headed eastwards and then north to the new *prime* start control at San José de Jáchal. Patrick explained that this stage, this unprecedented endurance challenge, became increasingly difficult the further they progressed. The route offered up a concentration-sapping series of high-altitude straights, hairpins, and stomach-turning drops, all swathed in thick dust, a peril that would spell disaster for a very high-profile and much-favored competitor. So taxing was the sandy trail that the Citroën repeatedly skidded and skittered across the road, and not even Patrick's none-too-shabby driving skills could prevent the DS from finally striking the rocks that haphazardly punctuated the roadside, damaging the driver's door. They pressed on, but now noticed that something wasn't quite right with the car's fuel supply. First, the car's reserve tank appeared to be empty, so they switched to the main tank, but then, after only 60 miles, they seemed to have used up half of that tank! Anxiety gripped the team as they tried to calculate how many jerry cans of gas they would need at the next fuel stop if all the DS could achieve

Mike Wood's recce car at the Argentina-Bolivia border (courtesy Mike Wood).

was 60 liters (16 gallons) per 60 miles! At last, a gas station loomed, and, with huge relief, they pulled in and busied themselves with the business of replenishing supplies. But wait, the reserve tank was now completely full! It then dawned on Alain Leprince that, for reasons unknown, the pump serving both tanks had begun to work in reverse, drawing gas from the main tank to the booster. Thus, purchasing as much fuel as they could carry, they continued, forced to manually manage the fuel pumps back and forth. They made it to La Viña but lost 151 minutes in the process, a real dampener compared to Verrier's 94 and Neyret's 95 penalty points. Although collecting 213 points here, Claudine and Colette continued to consolidate their lead over Rosemary Smith, even though the Maxi was just six minutes slower at the finish control.

From La Viña, the route climbed and climbed to La Quiaca at over 11,000 feet before crossing the border into Bolivia and the next *prime*, the 270-mile Bolivian Coffee, starting at Villazón just the other side of the frontier. Ever conscious of the potential effects of oxygen deprivation, Vanson and his team remained on guard, but, as Patrick recalled, taking aspirin kept resultant headaches at bay. Patrick also reported that the *prime* start control was somewhat chaotic as so many competing cars had arrived in advance that organizers had to play fast and loose, marshaling cars onto the stage in a disorderly fashion. Accordingly, the Vanson Citroën found itself behind a number of much slower vehicles spewing dust clouds, which made overtaking a real task during the first 60 miles or so. Once again, the trail twisted and turned and climbed, demanding determined and unbroken attention by driver and navigator alike, only this time, apart from anyone running at the rear of the field, it was all to be achieved in darkness!

At last, the approaches to Potosí and the finish control were reached, Patrick reporting that thousands of people had gathered to welcome the cars, many of which were almost overwhelmed, so exuberant was the reception. A combination of oxygen-depleted slow-going and the early hindrances of slower cars meant No. 100 incurred 104 points here, further separating them from teammates Verrier, third fastest on the stage with 54 points, and Neyret with 66. Claudine and Rosemary continued their battle, No. 25 picking up 115 points compared to the Maxi's 123. Meanwhile, Coltelloni and Marang continued to struggle, second slowest with a not inconsiderable 254 penalty points accrued.

From Potosí, the field headed for the promise of a hugely welcome rest stop in Bolivia's capital, La Paz, some 330 miles hence. The route offered no respite for the internal combustion engine, however, Patrick observing how the car seemed to drag itself along with 40 percent reduced efficiency. Thus, whenever the road allowed, he let the Citroën use gravity to accelerate on the sporadic downhill stretches, smoking the brakes on corners. However, in his view, the long drive was relatively easy, and they reached La Paz four hours ahead of schedule, enabling the team to carry out essential repairs and maintenance before depositing the car into *parc fermé*. Priority was given to replacing a rear passenger window, which had been destroyed by a rock thrown by a young boy, perhaps thinking these strange interlopers needed a few warning shots across their bows, or sterns in this case! Also, in La Paz, Claudine was presented with a record of Bolivian music and reported that this was the only time altitude sickness threatened when she dashed up the hotel stairs, queasily collapsing onto her bed, half exhausted, half faint! Drifting or plunging into sleep, the Citroën crews could reflect on their overall standing thus far: Verrier and Murac had dropped to fourth behind a barnstorming Brian Culcheth and Johnstone Syer in their works Triumph 2.5PI, while Neyret and Terramorsi had successfully defended eighth position. The aforementioned problems cost the Vanson team one place; they were now in ninth position, 90 minutes slower than Neyret. Claudine and Colette still had the women's prize in their sights, 13th place overall and 79 minutes quicker than Rosemary, Ginette, and Alice, who were 15th at La Paz. However, there were still miles and miles of punishment ahead, including the extraordinary Incas *prime*, perhaps the rally's centerpiece stage, an unimaginable 560-mile slog that would snake its way along rocky trails with bleak drops into oblivion left and right and appalling terrain combining impacted dirt, loose rock, and teeth-juddering washboard. No coincidence, then, that competitors were allowed to sleep in actual beds in readiness for this Peruvian feat of endurance from Cusco to Huancayo.

Cars departed La Paz in darkness and a snowstorm, which gradually turned to rain, and made their way west to the Peruvian border at Desaguardero on the southwest corner of Lake Titicaca. Any hopes of viewing this famous stretch of water were dashed, however, save for glimpses by moonlight, as competitors followed the route northwest. Cold, dark, and dusty, the drive to the *prime*'s start control stretched for 330 miles, but one of the Citroëns didn't make it to Cusco on time. After having maintained such an impressive pace and performance across Europe, won a completely separate and very grueling rally as a sideline, and then successfully endured mile after mile of whatever terrain the South American section had thrown at them, Bob

Neyret and Jacques Terramorsi ground to a halt when a piston blew in their blue DS. They eventually waited 36 hours to be recovered, without heat in the car! The remaining four French cars pressed onwards, Patrick recalling how local people had lit fires at the side of the road and had even used impromptu firelight to prevent wrong turns as competitors sped by.

Everyone was aware of the sheer length of the Incas *prime*, not only its distance but also the amount of time in which organizers expected cars to complete it. Patrick reported that they set off at dawn and arrived at the finish control in darkness. During the stage, the sun was fierce, adding to the already extreme environment with which competitors were required to contend as the route snaked back and forth. As the road wound its way up the mountainsides, there were stretches where one crew could see another high up ahead or following below, close as the crow flies but difficult to catch (or be caught by). At one point, traversing a valley that appeared covered in dusty sand, Patrick was astonished at the sight of flowering trees and shrubs, wondering how anything could grow in such conditions and at this altitude.

Starved of oxygen, the Citroëns felt like they could average just 40 miles per hour, braking at each hairpin and then accelerating to the next, ever onwards and upwards, back and forth, but at last, after what felt like days, the *prime* came to a close in an endless canyon, the road barely the width of a single car, Patrick amazed that any vehicle could survive without falling to pieces over the rough and rugged ground. Tired, tense, and nursing low-grade headaches, as much from concentration as altitude, three DSs clocked in at Huancayo—the Vanson car, Claudine and Colette, and, battling onwards despite previous woes, Coltelloni and Marang. But Guy Verrier and

Roadside memorial on the way to Lima, Peru (courtesy Mike Wood).

Francis Murac— consistently in the top five and running in third place at La Paz—
were missing in action. Their "engine exploded," explained Claudine, and they "were
out." Patrick's report differs: "*Ce fut vers la fin de cette étape que la voiture de Verrier
sortit de la route lorsque son coéquipier s'endormit en conduisant* (It was towards the
end of this stage that Verrier's car rolled off the road when his teammate fell asleep
while driving)."[1] Regardless of cause, one of the real contenders for a podium position was gone.

There was absolutely no letting up for those who had endured and survived
the Incas *prime* as now they needed to drive another 190 miles to the scheduled rest
stop at Peru's capital, Lima. For the most part, the road was relatively fast asphalt,
although Patrick reported that it was extremely rutted and uneven on the approaches
to the city. In addition, as if weary crews needed even more reason to focus, many
were met by huge mining trucks as they descended from 11,600 feet to sea level, and
as the journey was through darkness, it felt like every truck driver had lost the ability to dip the head-lamps! Attempting to pass, let alone overtake, these mechanical beasts of bur-den proved a challenge for none but the brave.

At Lima, by the time each car had clocked in and been deposited into *parc fermé*, all told there were 30 teams still in the mix. With the loss of Verrier and Murac and another extraordi-nary charge by Brian Cul-cheth and Johnstone Syer in No. 88, there were a few changes on the leader board. Patrick, Olivier, and Alain were now in sixth place overall with Claudine and Colette in ninth. Coltelloni and Marang languished in 29th position, but they were, at least, still in com-petition. Claudine and Colette had also now built up a 196-minute lead over

Colette (left) and Claudine go shopping, Lima, Peru, May 1970 (courtesy Claudine Besanceney).

Rosemary, Ginette, and Alice and, barring disaster, the women's prize was assured.

Getting whatever rest they could, competitors then hit the road again, heading north along the coast towards the frontier at La Tina before crossing and a short drive to the Ecuador *prime* start control at Macará. As Claudine inched forward to make their departure, an excited spectator reached into the open window on the passenger side and snatched Colette's sunglasses. Her loud cry of protest served simply to make the crowds laugh and cheer all the more! The asphalt road from Lima stretched ahead, a drive of more than 700 miles, but the women's progress soon halted. "I had all the red lights on. The engine seized," Claudine explained. "Patrick was right before me or right behind me, I don't know. I stopped and his co-driver came to see the car, we opened the bonnet (hood) and it was steaming. We opened the radiator and no water, not a drop. I'm sure that at the service in Lima—not on purpose of course—the mechanic opened the radiator drain and I lost all the water. I'm sure that's it because there is no reason for this to happen." Alain Leprince retrieved some of their water supply and slowly, carefully refilled the radiator tank. The women were mobile again so both cars continued on to the *prime*, to begin just after the border at the Ecuadorian customs point.

Patrick reported that the 250-mile speed section was heavily guarded with armed soldiers and that this was also to be another test of nerve and ingenuity. No. 100 developed another fuel problem. It appeared that gas was escaping from the secondary tank. Using a block of soap, Leprince fashioned a make-do seal, but, to make absolutely certain, the team decided not to use the backup tank. Then, however, the pump on the main tank began to fail so they had no choice but to revert to the reserve. In a small village, they found a fuel dump, a site where gas was available out of barrels. They set about siphoning gas into the reserve, needing an hour to fill the tank with 13 gallons. Finally replenished, they set off again, but now the tank's welded seam breached and hard-earned gasoline began to spill into the DS's trunk and onto the exhaust. They stopped immediately, anxious that heat from the tailpipe would ignite the gasoline, and nervously emptied both tank and trunk. Now, however, they were faced with another problem—how to use the fuel in the main tank with the reserve's pump? Once again, the decision to add Leprince as a third crew member paid off as he was able to jury-rig a length of rubber tubing from the main tank, around the back of the car, and connect it to the auxiliary pump. Were they ready to get going again? No! Now, because they had been forced to administer to the Citroën's maladies at over 11,000 feet above sea level, the water in the radiator had heated to boiling point. Despite delicate attempts to remove the radiator cap, pressure spat it into oblivion and boiling water sprayed all over the motor. Eventually, having allowed the engine to dry out and accepted a generous donation of precious water from the Argentinian duo Gastón Perkins and Jack Forrest Greene in No. 66, they were finally back on the road to the Cuenca finish control, picking up 287 penalty points as a reward for their pain, although they still kept their sixth place overall and were ninth fastest out of 29 survivors.

Despite earlier mechanical troubles, Claudine and Colette were seventh fastest on the Ecuador Coffee *prime* and, as a result, had all but guaranteed the women's prize, almost an hour quicker than Rosemary and now seventh overall compared to 12th for their nearest rivals. Meanwhile, Coltelloni and Marang kept soldiering on, 28th fastest at the finish control and 28th overall. Now, all competitors had to do was complete the 737-mile transport section to Cali in Colombia and they would be classified as finishers of the London to Mexico World Cup Rally. At a prize-giving ceremony to mark the occasion, while the leading team of Hannu Mikkola and Gunnar Palm were presented with pairs of emerald cufflinks, Claudine and Colette had to settle for sets of wooden bookends—Claudine for one was not a little jealous!

The route took teams north via the Ecuadorian capital, Quito, Patrick reporting that some of the road felt like it been paved a hundred years before, it was so uneven and broken. However, all three Citroëns finally crawled into Cali and *parc fermé*, their occupants collapsing into hotel beds to sleep before a very early morning departure to Buenaventura on the coast and the sea and canal voyage to Panama. Rally organizers had worked with local authorities to arrange for the army to guard the locked-away cars but this didn't prevent liberal pilfering. Patrick reported that on return to No. 100, they discovered assorted items of clothing and automotive parts missing with other crews also discovering evidence of theft.

The Colombian seaport was just 72 miles from Cali and, after the exertions of the previous *primes* and transport stages, it seemingly appeared to be a relatively quick and easy jaunt. The reality, however, proved anything but as rally cars encountered veering truck after careening bus. The Vanson car was one of the teams that were fated to endure this obstacle course to the limit, the crew quickly realizing why Sprinzel and Co. had allowed four hours for the section. Having successfully negotiated bends and skirted perilously close commercial wagons, they were not far from Buenaventura when, around another bend, they were faced with impending obliteration. A bus driver had decided to overtake a slow-moving truck and, at that moment, not even a bicycle could have slipped through the space remaining. The three Frenchmen stared in horror, Patrick flooring the brake and wrenching the wheel to minimize the inevitable collision, convinced that the 13,000 miles they had come since London were all for nothing! At the very last moment, however, the bus managed to swing in front of the lumbering truck, although it still managed to make contact with the DS, shattering its left-hand rear passenger window and crumpling the rear fender and trunk lid. Patrick, Alain, and Olivier clambered out to survey the damage, gathering up pieces of twisted metal and then making a hasty departure before the bus driver knew what had happened.

At Buenaventura, the men began trying to beat out the damaged bodywork, ever hopeful that one of the local assistance cars would arrive and possibly donate a rear window at least. However, when the service DS finally did draw up, the team could only laugh as the very parts they had hoped for had been destroyed when it too had encountered a wayward bus!

Claudine and Colette also had troubles on the road from Cali when a steering rod broke. Coltelloni and Marang were not far behind and even offered to donate a replacement from their car, but it proved too difficult to remove. With a stroke of luck, a local mechanic living right where the car had stopped came to their rescue and welded a repair, allowing both teams to proceed to Buenaventura.

All that was left was for the teams to wait in the steamy heat, under armed guard in a decidedly down-at-heel hotel, until the time came for cars to board the Italian ship *Verdi* and crews to surrender to the delights of sleep, chianti, pasta, and air conditioning aplenty, although not necessarily in that order!

Having sailed up the Panama Canal to the docks at Cristóbal on the Atlantic coast, the *Verdi* deposited its human and automotive cargo into a deluge of rain for the neutralized section to Panama City and then the beginning of the last, long slog to Mexico City, via six international border crossings and two final *primes*, the Costa Rica Coffee and the Aztec. Thus, on the evening of May 24, 1970, surviving cars departed the control and headed southwest before curving west and then northwest towards the Costa Rican frontier and the penultimate *prime* start at Paso Canoas. Not far out of Panama City, however, the unthinkable happened.

Longstanding friends Paul Coltelloni and Henri "Ido" Marang had had their fair share of mishaps and delays on the road across Europe and from Rio to Buenaventura but had determinedly carried on regardless, still competing when so many others had retired. They were among the last to leave Panama City, and about 95 miles into the journey, at Penonomé, a car cut across them without warning and collided with the speeding Citroën. The crash was devastating, with reports stating that the DS was cut completely in half. Both men were pulled from the wreckage moments before the car caught fire, but, although Paul Coltelloni recovered, Ido Marang sustained fatal head injuries and died on the way to the hospital.

Whether or how this appalling tragedy was reported to the two other Citroën crews as they progressed on the rally is unknown, but it threw a grim shadow on the event. Remaining teams had come this far, however, and all continued onwards. Patrick reported that the Costa Rica Coffee *prime* was 220 miles of filthy road, climbing up and over a mountain. They were now driving slower and slower, determined to make it to Mexico City, which is borne out when the 85 penalty points that they collected at Cartago are compared to fastest finisher Paddy Hopkirk, who lost just 40 minutes. Claudine and Colette were also slowing down, but the reason was cause for concern. The car was beginning to struggle and consume ever-increasing quantities of oil. On Colette's insistence, on the *prime*, Claudine began cutting the engine on the downhill sections to try and preserve the motor, ever mindful of the cushion of time they had over Rosemary, Ginette, and Alice. Careful calculations suggested they could still take the prize in Mexico; all they had to do was take it easy. Thus, it was Rosemary Smith who was faster to the finish, 71 minutes over the target time compared to Claudine's 104.

There was one last speed section before the finish, a 106-mile dash between Oaxaca and Tuxtepec in the last country of the rally, Mexico. This was the Aztec *prime*, reported by Patrick as perhaps the hardest they had encountered since setting off from London. Reminiscent of the Serbian *prime*, between Glamoč and Bosanska Krupa in Yugoslavia, this time they were taking absolutely no chances, focused intently on just hanging in there until the end, more than happy to accrue 98 points at Tuxtepec. However, No. 100 would be the last Citroën standing, or driving, as just before Oaxaca, despite receiving the attention of local service mechanics, Claudine and Colette were devastated to realize that, with little more than 200 miles to

Paul Coltelloni (*driving***) and Henri "Ido" Marang leaving Wembley, April 19, 1970 (courtesy Guido Devreker).**

go before the official finish at Fortín de las Flores, their rally was over. As Claudine explained, "I think it was the first time in my life that I cried, I really cried."

Thus, of the six Citroëns that set off from Wembley Stadium in London on April 19, 1970, a single DS cruised into Fortín de las Flores during the evening of May 26. Greeted by young women in regional costumes who hung garlands around their necks, Patrick Vanson, Alain Leprince, and Olivier Turcat joined other tired but jubilant finishers and, to the music of a mariachi band, enjoyed the knowledge that, out of 96 starters, they had taken seventh place overall. And, given the classification of the six teams ahead of them, they had also won the private owner's award!

As for the detractors, those who disapproved of the classification of the six Citroëns as privately entered when, it was claimed, the might of Citroën the company and its competitions arm was supporting every mile, perhaps the point is that, at the beginning, Bob Neyret, René Trautmann, and Claudine Trautmann quite simply decided to enter the rally. Yes, they secured financial support from various sources, but, as Claudine explained, the competitions boss René Cotton was quite simply not interested. He only sat up and took notice when entry was confirmed and then three other teams threw their hats into the ring. The detailed and complex event regulations left no room for interpretation when it came to classification so, like it or not, all six cars and teams qualified as private entries. The fact that the teams were hugely experienced drivers and navigators and the fact that they had the wherewithal to compete and, in Trautmann's case, recce the South American section, just added substance to the effort. Being an international distributor of automobiles, Citroën was

(*Left to right*) Olivier Turcat, Alain Leprince, and Patrick Vanson, Mexico City, May 27, 1970 (courtesy Patrick Vanson).

able to mobilize local networks and dealerships across Europe and in South America and, as the rally advanced, decided to support the six teams, organizing local service crews and backup where they could. Even if this provided an advantage over completely independent entries like the hugely successful British team of rally freshmen Reg Redgrave, Phil Cooper, and Bob Freeborough, who were the only other privateers among the top 10 finishers in their Special Tuning–prepared 1800, the might of BLMC's travelling team of service mechanics was always on option, time and demand allowing.

In the end, Patrick Vanson, Alain Leprince, and Olivier Turcat were awarded the private entry prize because, as specified by the regulations, they qualified as a private entry. None were more delighted than the committee members of *L'Automobile Club de France* or the Automobile Club of France, who had approved and lent their name to No. 100's entry. For their trouble, a dinner was held for Leprince, Turcat, and Vanson at the French car club's lofty headquarters on the *Place de la Concorde* in Paris (where Patrick had been haughtily reprimanded for referring to their dining room as "a restaurant"). Perhaps more heartfelt and meaningful was the surprise party held in Patrick's garden on his return home, guests wearing t-shirts emblazoned with the words *Viva el Rey del Mexico* or "Long Live the King of Mexico"!

Reflecting on her adventures on the 1970 London to Mexico World Cup Rally, Claudine smiled and said, "Well, time flies and London-Mexico remains an exceptional memory, unbelievable, fantastic. Well, anyway, magnificently mad!"

23

Two Primes in One Day

From Bosanska Krupa, the field went west to Senj on the Adriatic and then northwest along the coast to Rejika before heading inland towards Kozina and the Italian border near Trieste. The Italian authorities insisted that competitors cover up their rally numbers at the frontier so hasty arrangements were made to conceal the prohibited items before teams followed the *autostrada* to the exit ramp for Monza and signs for the *Autodromo Nazionale*, the historic racetrack and venue for the Italian Formula One Grand Prix.

Monza was classified as a special *parc fermé*, whereby once a car was placed in the specified secure enclosure, only competitors would be allowed to carry out servicing or repairs and only with tools and parts carried within the car. Therefore, provided a car arrived before 18:00 on April 22, they could use that time to receive help from service crews. Competitions team service personnel were ready and waiting within assigned areas to work on their cars, and privately entered competitors no doubt presented themselves also, on the off chance of a few *ex gratia* helping hands!

At Monza, Ford was ready to at last repair the Aaltonen/Liddon Escort's gearbox, rebuild the Mäkinen/Staepelaere Escort's engine, within regulatory parameters of course, and carry out bodywork repairs to the Clark/Poole Escort after it somersaulted on the Serbian *prime*. The BLMC service crew tended to the Mini 1275 GT, which had now begun to experience water and fuel leaks, and transmission overdrive problems with Andrew Cowan's 2.5PI. The Moskvič team had their travelling service wagon on hand, and, elsewhere, local servicing had been organized for some of the other marques, including Citroën and Mercedes. Along with the continuing raised eyebrows over the entry status of the French cars, Richard Hudson-Evans remarked of the big Mercedes sedans that, "upon seeing these cars all lined up together, it was fairly obvious where they had been prepared."[1]

For other competitors, it was all hands on deck to solve problems and make good. The British Army 17th/21st Lancers regiment-backed 1800 of Jeremy Rugge-Price, Philip Beaver, and Charles Morley-Fletcher required extensive repairs and made it into the control with just 30 minutes to spare. The Lydden Circuit Escort GT needed its oil pan straightened to prevent what had become very noisy contact with the crankshaft, while No. 51, the SAAB 96 of filmmaker Colin Taylor and co-driver Bert Jennings, required work to an engine mounting. Late in, and therefore straight into *parc fermé* for competitor-only repair work or an anxious wait until the morning, were the Donner brothers' Ford Capri, the Argentinian Volvo 142S of José Araujo and

179

Escorts get the works at Monza: (*foreground, left to right*) Gunnar Palm, Hannu Mikkola, unknown, Stuart Turner, April 22, 1970 (courtesy Guido Devreker).

John Batley, and the Buchanan-Michaelson 2.5PI, which required extensive repairs after a catalogue of mechanical disasters had hindered—but not ended—their run all the way from London. They would have to wait until cars were allowed to leave *parc fermé* in the morning before all would be well.

At Monza, the Porsche of Terry Hunter and Geoff Mabbs also needed attention, but, as with so many other private or independently entered cars, there was no team of expert Porsche mechanics waiting to do what was required. Hunter and Mabbs therefore parked the car and went for a wander, eventually finding a lone Italian Porsche agent. Hoping for perhaps a slight service or adjustment to the Bio-Strath–sponsored sports coupe, they were astonished when the agent immediately got to work, actually removing the engine for careful examination! Hunter attempted to explain that the car needed to be back in running order for depositing into *parc fermé* by a specific time, but the agent simply shooed them away. As competitor and motoring journalist Mark Kahn noted, "Porsche cars are not the cheapest in the world to work on. It looked as if there would be a formidable bill. They wandered back.... Their car was ready. The engine was perfect. The bill: just the equivalent of £9 ($22)"[2]!

Sadly, not everyone made it to Monza, and to the roll call of valiant heroes who had fallen along the way needed to be added the Italian Porsche 911 of Gianpiero Mondini and Mario Contini, which retired shortly after the Serbian *prime*; No. 7, Peter Garratt's Vauxhall Viva GT; the James Gardner/Laurie Ritchie Ford Escort Elba Motor Caravan, sponsored no doubt for maximum international publicity by Wilsons Motor Caravans, which made it to Venice before an electrical short circuit ended its run; and No. 99, the V6-engined Cortina of Brassington and Carslaw. Kim Brassington had previously competed in the 1968 London–Sydney Marathon in the Cortina and had re-engineered the car for the World Cup Rally, discarding its original motor and replacing it with a Ford V6 block, a Ford V4 clutch housing, and Atlas rear axle, a mistake in his opinion as the original set-up had offered much more low-down grunt. Across Europe, they had had to stop and re-torque the heads as the V6 motor bedded in, but the car had flown on the first *prime* until they got stuck behind a big truck on a single-lane stretch. The car had then begun to run hot, which gave much cause for concern, and, to make matters worse, on the transport stage to Monza, Kim couldn't keep his eyes open so pulled over and dozed off, prodding Carslaw awake so he could take over. Fifteen minutes later, Carslaw properly came to, got behind the wheel and drove on. Alas, the queue of latecomers at Monza meant they were out of time at the control—by 15 minutes! Perhaps saddest of all was, despite the herculean attempts at improvising a solution to its steering problems back at Glamoč, the Team Dunton Capri missed control closure by a meager 14 minutes, again caught in the last-minute rush to check in. But rules, as they say, are rules on any rally event!

Monza departure control opened at 07:00, so 83 cars departed and headed back onto the *autostrada*, headed for the third *prime*, the San Remo. The route took competitors south to Genoa and then along the coast of the Ligurian Sea before turning right between Imperia and San Remo and up to Ville San Pietro in the mountains. The *prime*, described in the regulations as "loose-surfaced, slow and twisty,"[3] would run over the Passo Della Teglia mountain pass to a passage control at the village of Andagna before descending to Montalto Ligure and a second control, then heading west, cross-country to Camporosso, not far from the French frontier. Competitors would be allowed no more than two hours to cover the 65 miles. The start control, overseen by rally driver Peter Harper, would be open from 12:00 to 18:00 on April 23, and competitors were required to reach the finish control by 23:05. However, *Motoring News* reported that "San Remo was too easy really, perhaps because the Italian authorities had been strict about target times."[4] Certainly not as challenging as the two previous *primes*, ultimately 23 cars got to Camporosso without penalty.

Obviously, ensuring supplies of automotive consumables like tires was an essential part of supporting the rally, and so it was that 18-year-old Goodyear employee Andrew Lees found himself at Ville San Pietro, having the time of his young life. Goodyear "had a small rally team, based in Watford, that used to service on rallies, and what they needed was a significantly larger group of people to go out and look after the European *primes*," he explained. "One of the criteria was having a passport. …my father was always working abroad because he was in the gun trade … and he always swung holidays on the back of a meeting he had to attend, so I was well-used to travelling and I had a passport." Goodyear asked Andrew if he was interested in helping out, and within a few days he found himself riding shotgun in a big Goodyear Tires truck towards the South of France and onwards to the Italian Riviera. He explained that his role was to help make sure the truck arrived in good time and then help recce the potentially tricky road up to Ville San Pietro to ensure no nasty surprises for the big vehicle.

Once in situ at the start of the *prime*, a tire fitter would actually do the work,

The Martin family's Rolls-Royce Silver Cloud departs the Monza control, April 23, 1970, with the Martin family, David, William, and Julian, inside the car (courtesy Guido Devreker).

which left Andrew to watch cars arrive and depart. "We had a number of other competitors stop to seek help," he explained, "mainly because we were clearly Brits, we were in the middle of nowhere, and we had obviously got some tools. So, we looked after a few cars, there were people who weren't really fully equipped, and anybody we could help, we helped. I was helping one guy rewire a starter motor, because he was having to bump start it. I looked at the wiring and said I know a bit about what it should look like, so I thought right, we'll have a go at this. I wasn't there to fix tyres, I was really there as a companion, I wasn't going to do any tyre fitting…. So, I went across and helped this guy, I think he was in a 504. That was quite pleasing."

Unfortunately, even with this impromptu help on hand, not all competitors found the San Remo *prime* easy, and a few more dreams expired in the mountains that day. In addition to the hazards on offer—winter damage to the road surfaces, wandering livestock, inexplicably parked cars, and sheer drops with nothing but low walls to prevent going over the edge—a few entrants also faced mechanical challenges. The Mexican FIAT 124 was one of the 23 that cleaned the *prime*, but it promptly broke down beyond repair at Camporosso. No. 28, the Volvo "Amazon" 132, went out with a broken prop shaft, and even though the car had had a thorough going over at Monza, the BLMC works Mini 1275 GT dropped a piston, and that was that for Paul Easter and John Handley. Thinking back about the car, Easter reflected: "I had it run in, got some miles on it, and I took it back to Abingdon and I said, 'There's a piston playing up.' … 'No, no … it's a newly built engine, it hasn't got enough miles, the bores are a bit tight, the crankshaft…' I said, 'No, it's piston trouble.'" Piston trouble indeed.

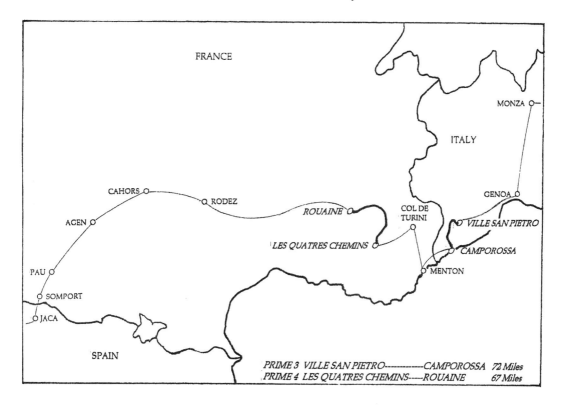

FRANCE

ITALY

MONZA

CAHORS   RODEZ

ROUAINE

COL DE
TURINI

GENOA

AGEN

VILLE SAN PIETRO

LES QUATRES CHEMINS

CAMPOROSSA

PAU

MENTON

SOMPORT

JACA

SPAIN

PRIME 3 VILLE SAN PIETRO----------CAMPOROSSA 72 Miles
PRIME 4 LES QUATRES CHEMINS-----ROUAINE   67 Miles

The route from Monza to Jaca (map by Martin Proudlock).

Down but not quite out was the Bolivian 2002Ti as, even in the experienced hands of William Bendeck, it still managed to incur 90 penalty points. No. 83, the Washington James–backed Hillman Hunter, ran out of fuel a mile or two before Camporosso and then had to be pushed back the way it had come to find a suitable place to allow other cars to pass! A do-it-yourself siphoning of gasoline from a parked car got them to the end just in time. Meanwhile, the J.C. "Cal" Withers Cortina, an extensively re-engineered incarnation of Rosemary Smith's ill-fated London–Sydney Marathon car, limped to the end without steering bushing.

April 23, 1970, was to prove an extremely busy day for the remaining 90 teams as it offered not one but two *primes*, the next being the Alpine, a 67-mile stretch along some of the European Monte Carlo Rally, in the French mountains. First, however, another transport stage, this time via Ventimiglia, where Roger Clark sought help to fix a broken axle, then across the border into France to Menton before turning north and upwards via Sopel and Moulinet to a passage control at the Col de Turini mountain pass, a prominent part of the Monte Carlo Rally route. From there, it was down via La Bollène-Vésubie to the start of the Alpine at Les Quatre Chemins, the control being open from 17:31 to 01:31 the following morning.

Even though all of the European professionals were extremely familiar with this section, only five cars actually cleaned the *prime* by the finish control at Rouaine, although many others only incurred low-figure penalties. Monsieurs Trautmann and Hanrioud continued their very fine form with a points-free run, as did Neyret and

Terramorsi, no doubt determined not to be penalized on their home ground. The Escorts of Mikkola, Mäkinen, and Tony Fall also joined the exclusive "no points" club. Aaltonen and Clark incurred just one point each, even though the Clark/Poole Escort's axle began leaking oil again, while Guy Verrier collected two. Elsewhere, Madame Trautmann and Madame Perrier picked up just four points in their DS21, thus stamping their authority on the women's competition.

Fortunes elsewhere were mixed for experienced and novice teams alike. The privately entered Peter Jopp 1800 and Channon/Cooper Cortina GT both put in nice performances. The Annabel's nightclub Mercedes sedan developed severe brake troubles, forcing racing driver Innes Ireland to rely on the big car's parking brake. They picked up 25 penalty points at Rouaine. "We've got absolutely no brakes left and we can't get any help," Ireland told a *Daily Mirror* reporter. "We even stopped by a waterfall and used our crash helmets as jugs to catch the water to throw on the brakes to cool them."[5] After the monumental effort to get the Buchanan-Michaelson 2.5PI roadworthy again at Monza, all was for naught as it failed to arrive at Rouaine. Dust was again a hazard on this *prime*, with the Taylor/Jennings SAAB 96 refusing to go on as a result of a clogged carburetor, forcing the crew to push the little Swedish sedan to the finish!

Among the travelling marshals setting up and staffing *prime* start and finish controls was Jim Gavin. Regardless of Roger Clark's test activity and subsequent rallying with the newly released Ford Escort in 1967 and 1968, Gavin was the first competitor to drive an Escort in an endurance rally event, the London–Sydney Marathon of 1968. His adventures as a marshal on the 1970 London to Mexico World Cup Rally are a story worth telling.

24

Potatoes and Emeralds

Jim Gavin, Martin Maudling, and John Maclay drove a very early model Ford Escort to 45th place out of 56 finishers on the London–Sydney Marathon in 1968, despite leaving an oil slick all the way through the Australian city on the victory parade! The car was sponsored by Jim's company, Super Sport Engines, which upgraded customers' Cortina GTs for competitive motorsports events. Although Jim had had some previous local club rallying experience back in his native Ireland and had done a few races in England, he didn't really consider himself a dedicated rally or motorsports competitor. Back in England, after the Marathon, he decided to sell his share of the Super Sport Engines to business partner and soon-to-be World Cup Rally competitor Rod Cooper and began making a living via various commissions from the British Royal Automobile Club (RAC) and a few local motor clubs. "I was very lucky and I was also doing magazine articles, which didn't pay a lot but they paid enough," he explained. "I was getting all these jobs … [they] would ask me would I help plan things and they said, 'Look, we'll pay you good expenses.' Fine, I was making enough. So, I was existing in my contacts."

During 1969, through both his association with the RAC and from reading the British *Daily Mirror* newspaper, he became aware of plans to hold a 16,000-mile endurance rally from London to Mexico City as lead-up to the forthcoming soccer World Cup championship in 1970, to be hosted by Mexico. This was definitely something with which he wanted to be involved, but not as a competitor. With his experience taking commissions from Dean Delamont, the RAC's head of competitions, it made sense to contact him and offer his services. "Dean was away so I rang up [John] Sprinzel and said … 'Can you put me down to do something on the London Mexico?'" Jim recalled. "'Oh,' he said, 'there's about 600 people have already phoned up.' 'Right, well put me down anyway….' I said, 'Look, I've never been to South America.' He said, 'Well, that's what they all want to do. We can certainly find you a control job or something in Europe, but South America…'" Never one to take no for an answer, Jim came up with a plan!

Through the work he was doing for Delamont, Jim was a regular visitor to the RAC's motorsports division, based in London's Belgrave Square, and was therefore known and recognized by concierge personnel. "They knew me well enough for me to pass in through the door and down into the basement, which was where all the planning went on for big events, lots of tables and stuff on the wall," Jim explained with a smile. "I looked in and a couple of them looked up and said, 'Hi Jim.' I went straight in and went over to a table and stood and looked at a wall or something and somebody put his hand over a phone and said, 'Has anybody worked out the exact mileage yet? They keep asking.' 'No, we will, we will.' I said, 'I'll do that,' and immediately started measuring on a map. Didn't wait to be asked. I said, 'I'll know in a few hours,' and they left me at it! The end of the day came…. 'Will you be there tomorrow morning?' 'Yes, sure.'"

Thus, Jim made himself indispensable, working away almost in the background, running errands and helping to fix problems as they arose. Seeing what he was doing, Dean Delamont offered him the same financial remuneration package as others supporting the effort, and Jim found himself rostered to help at the departure event at Wembley Stadium and staff a few European controls. The prospect of being sent to South America was, it seemed, out of his reach, although he had secured the necessary travel visas, just in case! Thus, he busied himself with tasks such as going to London's premier map supplier, Stanfords, and collecting various officials from London Airport.

About two weeks before the rally was scheduled to begin, Delamont called Jim with a problem. The planned route for the first *prime* in Yugoslavia was blocked by snow, so could someone go and help with the revised plan? Immediately, Jim offered his service and thus found himself, with fellow marshal Logan Morrison, on a plane to Belgrade. William Logan Morrison was a regular competitor on the European rally circuit and had driven or co-driven with Roger Clark, Timo Mäkinen, and Johnstone Syer. During the 1964 Liège-Sofia-Liège Rally, Logan Morrison and co-driver Syer had elected to retire their Rover 2000 and help fellow competitor Gunnar Blomqvist when his VW had overturned, rendering the driver unconscious.

From Belgrade airport, Jim and Logan hired two Mercedes and drove up into the mountains to confirm the blockage. This, Jim recalled, was the first time he saw a wolf. Then the pair drove to Titograd and checked into a hotel. From there, Jim called the RAC office and explained the situation, repeatedly emphasizing—despite protestations from the other end—that the route was impassable as consequence of both snow and a landslide. Jim and Logan had also got talking to folks at the hotel and had therefore begun to work out a solution, a revised route for the *prime*.

There was little point in flying back to London now because the rally was about to begin, so the pair spent their time getting to know a few local people and generally entertaining themselves while also driving the proposed new route from Titograd and Kotor, "up over the mountain through a place called Citinje and down the other side, down 16 hairpin bends to the finish control." Between them, they decided Jim would marshal the start control and Logan the finish. Officially the role of a marshal on a rally is "to stamp a route book, the route notes of a car when it comes in to say when it arrived and maybe sign it and put a copy of that time into the record you keep yourself," Jim explained. "You then get that information back to wherever the headquarters are as soon as all the cars have gone through. But, the most important thing is initiative, because you'd be told you arrive at that spot, it's right there but, when you get there, it's now a building site so you have to make it over there and how do I tell the guys to turn right at this corner when they're coming in? You've got to chat up people."

Ford GB team members Jimmy Greaves (*left*) and Tony Fall (courtesy Mike Wood).

Jim opened the Titograd control at 17:00 on April 21, 1970, and made himself ready to sign and stamp competitors off into the speed section, warning them that they should have their windshield wipers on during a short section of the *prime* that tunneled through rock where there was a steady flow of water running. The control would remain open until 00:30 on April 22, to allow for latecomers and, during this time, it began to rain. Jim beat a hasty retreat into the gas station immediately adjacent to the control point. "I remember Tony Fall," he recalled. "It had started to rain so I'm inside in this petrol station, with my little books and clock, those wonderful clocks you had, and he said, 'Aren't you coming out?' I said, 'No, it's raining, you come in here'—I made everybody come in. 'You should be out standing in the road!' Bollocks!"

Control duties complete, Jim and Logan now needed to get themselves to Lisbon. Back they drove to Titograd and checked their travel itinerary before heading to the hotel bar where they got talking with two aircraft pilots. As luck would have it, these would be the pilots flying the marshals back to Belgrade, and as Jim and Logan would be the only passengers booked on the flight, did they want to sit in the DC3's cockpit for the journey? Thus, the men were given a bird's-eye view to Belgrade from where they plane-hopped to Vienna, then Paris, and finally the Portuguese capital, Jim recalling that the Caravelle aircraft was actually held for them in Paris, other passengers eyeing them with a mix of interest and irritation as they clambered aboard. Jim also made a point of emphasizing the role of "Speedy" Mike Broad in all of this, such were his skills with analogue flight planning in pre-digital 1970!

From Lisbon, Jim hired a car and drove up to marshal the finish control for the Portuguese *prime*, stationing himself at a schoolhouse in Pampilhosa. "When I left the schoolhouse, they gave me one of those straw bottles … full of red wine," he recalled. "I could hardly carry the frigging thing!" Then it was back to Lisbon and a plane to London for a week or so before flying back to Lisbon, via Madrid, in order to jet off to Rio de Janeiro. His hope of getting to South America had been realized after all, but his attempts at readiness were in part misdirected. "I'd bought myself 'One Day Spanish,'" he recalled. "*Donde esta la playa?* Where is the beach? *Donde esta el autobus?* I arrived there and they said, 'No, it's Portuguese.' Oh, right!"

The competitors who had made it to Lisbon had already arrived in Rio and checked into the Hotel Glória. After finding his room, Jim "looked out the window, looked down [at the] swimming pool and there's Rosemary Smith in a white swim-suit looking gorgeous!" Work was at hand, however, and Jim was charged with help-ing make sure that the rally cars were properly unloaded from the SS *Derwent* at the Rio docks and administered into *parc fermé*. Then, after a little entertainment involv-ing a German flight attendant, a trip up to the Corcovado in her VW Karmann Ghia droptop, and an introduction to *caipirinhas*, he was off to Buenos Aires, where he was met by a car hire representative who delivered him, plus car, to a hotel where a few other marshals were staying, including London–Sydney Marathon veteran Peter Harper. Harper regaled Jim with the hair-raising experience of driving their own hire cars. The first had almost lost a wheel when it came out from the half-shaft, forcing them to make an impromptu right turn to get the thing back in place. Then the sec-ond had begun to smoke from the dash panel and eventually combusted, causing the horn to go off and, inexplicably, the starter motor to engage! They laughed, telling Jim they half expected the burning car to take off without them!

With this in mind, Jim set off for his next task, that of setting up the Pampas *prime* start control at Saladillo, some 115 miles southwest of Buenos Aires. Upon arrival, he consulted the map drawing he had been given that indicated where the control needed to be—placed adjacent to the railroad station. He thus began to arrange the huge *Daily Mirror* control banner and checked off his list of equipment, including the prerequisite marker cones that delineated the arrival and departure zones for clocking cars in and out. Once complete, Jim sat and waited for the first car to arrive.

Presently, a few local people arrived and, using a combination of broken Span-ish, broken English, and hand gestures, pointed out that the control had been estab-lished right next to a huge pothole and that it would be better if it was moved to another spot close by. Accordingly, the equipment was relocated to a site less peril-ous, and Jim returned to his vigil atop a trailer borrowed from the railroad station. Now, more people began to arrive, eager to witness the unprecedented spectacle of various rally cars thundering into, and then out of, Saladillo.

It was getting dark by the time the first cars arrived and the crowd was growing. The rowdy spectators "were having a blast," Jim recalled, "and every time a car came in, they were blowing horns, flashing headlights, and standing in front of the con-trol, and the poor bastards were like, 'Where's the fucking control?' … I kept bringing my little cones closer in so that the control area was shorter. Originally, I started off with a grand hundred yards but now it's about 25." By this stage, Jim had been joined by another marshal, and when one of the teams edged their car into the control, then stopped and proceeded to check something under the hood, Jim's colleague promptly announced that the team would need to be penalized. With a sigh of irritation, Jim grabbed a cone and positioned it in such a way that the car was now outside the control zone. When his colleague remonstrated with him, Jim shrugged, took the team's details, and sent them on their way!

Jim also remembered when another team arrived, one member of which was a good friend and business associate. "He was in a terrible state," Jim explained. "I wandered down to him and he said, 'I've had it, I can't' … He was sitting on the ground in front of the car, leaning against the bumper. 'I can't go on, I can't, I can't stand [his co-driver].' … I spotted Stuart Turner, who'd turned up, and I knew him reasonably well, so I went up and said, 'I need a favour,' so I told him. He said, 'I'll go and see what I can do.' He went and sat down beside [the competitor] and put his arm around his shoulder and chatted to him for a while. [The competitor] carried on and they eventually finished. I thought that was very nice of him. To people like us, me and [the competitor], he was it!"

The last car out from Saladillo was Puff, Tish Ozanne's ill-fated Austin Maxi, after which Jim closed the control and headed back to Buenos Aires, from where he flew on to Santiago in Chile, Lima in Peru, and finally La Paz in Bolivia, from where he was required to travel to his next control duty, this time at Potosí, the end of the Bolivian Coffee *prime*. However, with a few days to kill before making the long trip south, he got talking with the concierge of the hotel where he was staying, who asked him if he had visited the authentic German *Gasthaus*, a guest house close by. Of course, Jim went to see it and stopped for lunch, fascinated by the very German menu and young women serving tables dressed in *dirndls*! Operated and owned by a German, Jim could only imagine how the man had ended up running a restaurant in the Bolivian capital!

The late Jack Sears played a hugely instrumental part in planning and organizing the London–Sydney Marathon, so he was an ideal person to join the team for the London to Mexico World Cup Rally, not least because his diplomacy and negotiating skills were superb. A former touring car champion in the UK, Sears was now being called upon to problem-solve along the rally route. Sears "arrived the next day and saw me and he ran up the steps and dropped," Jim recalled. "The altitude! He was out for about 20 minutes. What happened? It didn't affect me, to my knowledge." Order and oxygen levels restored, Sears explained that there was a potential problem with the Bolivian border crossing, and it fell upon Jim to meet the appropriate officials to smooth things out as Sears was needed further along the rally route. Thus, with the assistance of the British consulate in La Paz, Jim found himself dressed up in shirt and tie, equipped with an assortment of rally souvenirs, and on his way to the Bolivian President's offices!

With an excuse that water for tea is difficult to boil at altitude (!), Jim was served gin that afternoon and was treated to questions about the British Royal Family and Queen Elizabeth II's daughter, Princess Anne, in particular! He was also introduced to his pilot for the forthcoming flight to Potosí, some 300 miles from La Paz. Jim recalled: "In came this guy, and when I was growing up there were various *Beano* and *Hotspur* magazines, *Eagle* magazine, and there was a character called Rockfist

Rogan, he was a pilot. This guy must have been reading these magazines and look-ing at old war cartoons because he came in and he had the boots, fur-lined boots, he had the proper jacket, he had a little moustache, he had a Colt .45 with the cap open on his holster, his trousers were tucked into the boots and he wore a sheepskin flying jacket!" Jim was told the pilot would be flying to Potosí in a DC3 and that he would need to be at the airport early for the flight the following day so as to avoid any turbu-lence caused as the sun rose. All was thus agreed and Jim gave his thanks and farewell and returned to the hotel.

Daily Mirror photojournalist Kent Gavin was accompanying Jim on the trip to Potosí, so they arrived at La Paz airport, as instructed, in readiness for the flight. However, unbeknown to them, their pilot had arrived earlier and somehow managed to strike a hangar door with the DC3, putting it out of action. Thus, as Jim and Kent looked around, the only plane they could spot was a small red Cessna and no pilot! Finding someone to talk to, they managed to explain the situation and were alarmed to learn that the pilot had arranged for the Cessna to be provided but that a miscom-munication meant that Jim and Kent were expected to fly the aircraft themselves! A few phone calls later, two replacement pilots arrived, but by that point Gavin had got-ten cold feet. "Kent Gavin said, 'I'm not going,'" Jim remembered. "I said, 'Why?' He said, 'It's only got one engine.' It was a Cessna 190 or 140. He said, 'I was in Nigeria during the Biafran war and I was on one of the last planes out that wasn't shot at and I made a promise to myself then that I would never, ever fly in anything that had less than two engines.' 'Well, how are you going to…?' 'I don't give a shit,' he said. 'I'm not going in that thing.' The taxi was sitting there and he took the taxi back to town!"

Not entirely convinced that the pilots knew how to operate the Cessna, Jim climbed in the back and they taxied off across the tarmac to the runway, running a few practice drills until they were satisfied with the controls. Eventually, the Cessna accelerated and took off, the pilots happily pointing out a condor, a bird Jim had never seen in his life. Jim refused to allow the pilots to take shots of the vodka he had tucked into his bag, and eventually they began to descend to what appeared to be a small grass patch below. This was the Potosí landing strip, which required a couple of flybys to chase off the sheep that were happily munching away!

At the small hotel in Potosí, Jim naturally got talking with the concierge who, once he learnt that Jim was from Ireland, went to great lengths to extol the virtues of the city's historical sights. Jim remembered the concierge talking up the region's renowned silver mining—and the potato museum. "'All the potatoes in the world, they came from Bolivia and Peru and Walter Raleigh took them back to England and he gave them to the queen and he took them to Ireland and now the Irish eat all of these potatoes and you should know!'" True enough, there was indeed a museum dedicated to the potato, with examples kept under atmospheric control, a curator, and regular visits from people researching the humble tuber! Jim was told there were 20 or 30 basic types of potato, and the visit made an impression. "I bet you've never met a curator of a potato museum in your life!" he crows.

Despite the distractions of what Potosí had to offer in the way of historic enter-tainment, however, Jim had a job to do, so he found the designated location—another small schoolhouse with just two rooms and a rudimentary restroom out back—and went about setting up the finish control in readiness for pummeled rally cars and weary crews as they came off the tortuous 270-mile *prime*—the checkpoint would open at midnight and run until 18:00 that evening. Once again opting to arrange the control paraphernalia inside, Jim was now joined by a local radio journalist with a formidable-looking power generator, the idea being that the journalist would report back to a station in La Paz, reading out the entry list and providing an as-it-happens account of cars coming through, with Jim making wry contributions as and when requested. Once again, enthusiastic spectators were gathering outside and, with a roar, it was they who alerted Jim to the approaches of the first car. "This was Mikkola and Palm," Jim recalled. "When they arrived, they were flying, and the last straight was about a quarter of a mile. They must have been flat out in fifth and you could hear the gravel. As they screeched to a stop, in front of this schoolhouse, the door is open and Palm is out with the book—'sign that you bastard!' The crowd erupted. They thought that was the best thing they'd seen in their entire lives! The speed that he arrived and the pumping of the brake and the tyres were locking and gravel flying!"

Cars arrived and departed, Jim stamped books and recorded times, and the clock ticked onwards. Then, predictably, he realized he needed to use the ramshackle restroom. There was nothing for it but to retire to the outhouse, clocks and book and stamps and all, and continue administering to competitors' urgent demands for ratification under the restroom's door! "Someone Irish, I can't remember who," Jim recounted, laughing, "they said, 'Is that you in there?' 'It is.' 'I'll tell your mother! Who've you got in there with you?'"

At last, it was time to pack up and close the control. People came and went until one man somehow tripped or stumbled and made contact with the power generator, taking both him and the radio out. Jim, who never found out what became of the poor man, remained ever hopeful that he survived to tell the tale! However, with all his equipment stashed in his standard issue kitbag, Jim returned to the hotel for a welcome sleep before flying back to La Paz the following day and then heading onwards to Cali in Colombia, at which any surviving team would be classified as a finisher of the rally.

In Cali, Jim joined Jack Sears, representatives from the local car club, and other officials to discuss any problems relating to the ship that would carry cars and competitors from the seaport at Buenaventura into and along the Panama Canal before unloading them at Cristóbal. With communications apparently broken down between rally organizers and seaport authorities, Jim and Speedy volunteered to go down to Buenaventura and problem-solve. Before that, however, Jim and Jack Sears had a lunch appointment with a local Bank of America representative and were whisked off to a smart country club, complete with a golf course, tennis courts, manicured lawns, and a doorman!

After lunch, they returned to downtown Cali and, at a sidewalk café, sat waiting for Speedy to join them. One of the reasons why they had been entertained by the banker was because the bank was to present the lead finisher into Cali with a valuable prize—pairs of cufflinks set with large Colombian emeralds. Sitting at the café, the cufflinks were surreptitiously shown to Jim and Jack. "Sears and I didn't look at each other," Jim recalled. "We were both thinking, they've got three sets but there will be only two people in the car. I could see his brain working just like me, how can I get hold of the third set? Fords were the leading cars and they only had two people, and here he's got three sets of cufflinks!" Sadly for Jim, at that moment the car arrived to take him and Speedy to Buenaventura, so he never did find out what happened to the third set.

The Colombian seaport city was hot and humid, with an ever-threatening heavy rain cloud hanging overhead. Jim and Speedy were dropped at the main hotel, which proved rather less than polished, and then proceeded to the Italian shipping company responsible for the vessel scheduled to carry rally cars and crews to Panama. The problem, it transpired, was that the police authorities demanded that all teams be officially cleared for departure. After some thought, it was agreed that police representatives would be invited to the hotel where Jim and Speedy would have all competitors' passports for processing and inspection, all the while priming the officials with assorted rally-related items!

Jim stood and watched cars being loaded onto the ship, the crane operators using nets to haul each vehicle into the air and then down onto the vessel. It quickly became clear that the automotive cargo was a wee bit oversubscribed. "There was one car, hovering over a space on the ship and it wouldn't fit," Jim recalled. "Why? Because of the door handles or the wing mirrors or something. 'Oh, just drop the bloody thing.' The car belonged to Gastón Perkins and much later … he was yelling at me, 'You told them to drop my car!' I said, 'Well, if they didn't, they would have left it on the dock! Now, you can have no wing mirrors or have it left on the dock!'"

According to Jim, any suggestions that he secured the best cabin on the *Verdi*

Sailing up the Panama Canal (courtesy Pat Smith).

for himself are unfounded. Whatever arrangements he did make for his shipboard accommodation, he recalls spending much of the time either on deck or in the bar. Seeing his first pelican or witnessing the ship's entry into, and then its mechanically drawn passage through the Panama Canal, were highlights for Jim during the voyage to Cristóbal, as was the party atmosphere onboard no doubt!

At Cristóbal, Jim's duties with the rally were done, so he began thinking about what to do next. He decided that, without a specific job to do, he wouldn't go on with the others to Mexico City. Instead, he talked with a travel agent in Panama City and, determined to be on one of Boeing's new 747s operated by Pan Am, booked a plane ticket that would take him back to the UK with stops in the Caribbean and New York. His rally was done.

Jim Gavin went on to play a pivotal role organizing the 1977 London–Sydney Marathon, working with Wylton Dickson. That, however, is another story altogether!

Jim Gavin passed away in January 2022. His contributions to my books, his generosity, irrepressible good humor and endless supply of irreverent anecdotes held a price above rubies.

25

All in the Family

After the excitement—or frustration, depending on performance—of the Alpine *prime*, with their roadbooks stamped and time recorded by Austin-Healey rally specialist Donald Morley, the contestants moved on. What lay ahead was a very long transport section, taking cars 630-plus miles across and out of France at Somport, via passage controls at Moustiers-Sainte-Marie, Le Chalet Reynard, Rodez, Tournon-d'Agenais, and L'Isle-de-Noé. Into Spain, they would head west for 440 miles to the Portuguese frontier at Vilar Formosa and then up to Arganil for the beginning of the last European *prime*, the Portuguese, with the start control opening at 03:05 on April 25.

For most, the slog west was uneventful, although it was not completely without drama. No. 49, the Mercedes-Benz 280SE sedan sponsored by trendy London nightclub and discotheque Annabel's, had been struggling with steadily deteriorating brake capability. Despite valiant improvising using parking brake and gears, on the road from La Chalet Reynard, with Annabel's proprietor, Mark Birley, at the wheel, the Benz went off the road, smacking into some trees. "The first part of the car to touch the ground after flying off the road was the back bumper,"[1] team member Innes Ireland explained later. Luckily, all escaped without serious injury, and at least Ireland could say he had won a bet that they'd get further than friend and former co-driver Bobby Buchanan-Michaelson—just!

French duo Eric Celerier and Michael Gauvain suffered the indignity of having their Porsche 911S break down beyond repair on home soil, little more than 50 miles from the Spanish frontier, and somehow, the Martin family contrived to miss two of the five passage controls along the way in their genteel Rolls. No. 73, the BLMC 1800 sponsored by British department store Grants of Croydon, lost a wheel bearing cotter pin in northern Spain, but, in another instance of rally-ready ingenuity, driver Tony Petts repurposed a wire coat hanger for a temporary fix. A proper replacement was secured en route. "The trouble is Tony used the coat-hanger on which my best suit was hanging," co-driver David Franks explained. "Now I won't have any sharp clothes to wear when we reach Mexico."[2]

Axle problems were continuing to plague Roger and Clark in their works Escort, despite the hasty welding work done in Italy on the way to the French border, and again at Rouaine. On the transport section through France, things got worse and worse, as the axle began to disintegrate. Against all odds, the pair made it to the Ford service point at the L'Isle-de-Noé passage control where, six hours later, the

No. 39 receives some attention from Keith Baker (*bending*) and others (courtesy Brian Englefield).

axle casing was repaired, strengthened, and refitted. Suffice to say, Clark had a very heavy foot on the gas pedal for the remainder of the journey, determined to get across Spain, into Portugal, and to the *prime* start control in time.

Someone else needing to up the speed was Brian Englefield in No. 39. Asleep in the rear of the 2.5PI, he awoke to find co-driver Baker encouraging third team member Lloyd-Hirst to get a move on. Acutely aware of the time they had already used for the quill-shaft repair, Brian took over driving duties and quickly got them back on track by the time they reached Arganil for the last European *prime*.

The Portuguese *prime* followed the forest sections of the TAP Rally, TAP being the national Portuguese airline, *Transportes Aéreos Portugueses*. Starting as an internal airline employee competition in 1963, the TAP Rally eventually became a European Rally Championship event in 1970. The *prime* would wind its way along 40 miles of forest tracks, and the completion time was set at 65 minutes. All but the very fittest would be really fatigued by now, some having only been able to snatch a few hours of sleep here and there since departure from London nearly six days before, so this particular 40 miles had the potential to be especially arduous.

No doubt Citroën and Mercedes again had local dealerships out in force to provide servicing before the last *prime*, and the Moskvič service wagon was still chugging along behind the Avtoexport cars. Factory teams Ford GB and BLMC had plans to undertake extensive repairs and maintenance at Arganil as they both wanted their cars to be match-tough and ready for the final dash, both teams all too aware

The Harris/Butler Escort 1300GT prepared by Ron Pellatt (author's collection).

that Citroën drivers Trautmann and Hanrioud were still leading, albeit by just two minutes.

Decisions were made that all work would take priority over any other activities before sunup and cars would then proceed to the beginning as dawn was coming up, so that Jim Gavin could stamp books and record start times.

Ford and Citroën set to and worked on cars steadily through the early hours of the morning, Ron Pellatt recalling that, being on hand to carry out whatever work was needed on the Butler/Harris Escort GT, he was also called upon to utilize his skills on one or two Ford GB Team Escorts. As a *quid pro quo*, given that Ron didn't have the financial wherewithal to travel to South America, Ford promised to keep an eye on the Escort GT, prepared by him, on the road from Rio to Mexico City! Ron returned to England after Lisbon, ever hopeful that he and his mate Alan, in their trusty Ford Thames service van, wouldn't encounter the same alarming armed police reception they had received on the road down through Spain to get to Arganil!

BLMC had a problem, however, as their service trucks had been delayed by red tape at the Spanish port of Bilbao and no diplomatic intervention or incentive could get them released. Fortunately, the BLMC cars were, on the whole, in relatively good shape in Portugal, and the parts stuck in Spanish customs were not, in the end, the deal-breaker they could so easily have been.

The Portuguese *prime* offered up its fair share of thrills and spills over its short, fast, forest track, drops, and, of course, more hairpin bends. All works Escorts except Zasada's roared into the Pampilhosa finish control without penalty, as did Trautmann, which meant that, barring disaster on the transport stage to Portugal's capital city, he and Hanrioud would be the victors of the European section. Others were not so lucky, with Edgar Herrmann letting the Ulm Racing Team Mercedes 280SE get away from him, hitting trees and bouncing back to block the track. Nursing a cut lip, he and teammates Dieter Benz and Horst Walter received help to move the stricken sedan from Porsche duo Terry Hunter and Geoff Mabbs, if only so the Bio-Strath–sponsored car could proceed onwards, unlike the Mercedes, which was out.

The Silver Shadow of Bengry, Skeffington, and sponsor Ray Richards, making steady, stately, and speedy progress thus far, began to suffer a disintegrating rear hub, while its older cousin, the Martins' Silver Cloud, had a front brake pipe break, meaning the family was reliant on parking brake only for the rest of the European section.

Movie-maker Colin Taylor's SAAB 96 was now struggling with more than just a congested carburetor as the car's clutch was failing and refusing to make the opening incline. Rapid repairs at Arganil eventually got them to Pampilhosa. Another entrant lucky to get to the finish control, and indeed to escape serious injury, was Argentinian racing driver Gastón Perkins in one of the SAFRAR works–prepared Peugeot 404s. With his teammate Jack Forrest Greene, he careened off the track and bounced down a deep drop. There the 404 languished for more than six hours until, using a cable winch, a Peugeot service truck was able to extricate the car and get it back on the road, but, as reported, not before a catastrophe was narrowly averted for a certain Citroën team. The *prime* also saw the demise of the Italian Porsche team of Mondini and Bottaro.

Now all that was left was for the remaining cars and crews to drive the 155 miles or so to Lisbon, the arrival control, and then a neutralized jaunt over to the special *parc fermé* at the Alcantara docks, from where cars would be loaded onto a ship for the sea crossing to Brazil and Rio de Janeiro. Total time allowed between Monza and Lisbon was 51 hours, so if a car were recorded as having left Monza at 08:00 on April 23, they would need to get to Lisbon by 11:00 on April 25. Therefore, the earlier a car arrived at the SACOR gas station within the city limits of Portugal's capital city, the more time the crew would have to seek professional assistance to undertake any repairs before being required to drive the 40 minutes over to the docks and enter *parc fermé*. In other words, a car required to arrive at the SACOR gas station at 11:00 would need to present itself at the docks by 11:40.

In *parc fermé* only competitors would be allowed to work on their cars; they could carry out last-minute repairs or preparations for the long sea crossing up until 15:00. During this time, and of course benefiting from assorted rally management and service personnel whispering or bellowing instructions and advice through the chain link fencing, crews were required to drain tanks and disconnect batteries. Organizers had been assured that the Automobile Club of Portugal would make suction equipment available. Between 15:00 and 17:00, cars would need to be pushed to customs on the quayside and loaded onto the ship.

The majority of cars made it to Lisbon without issue, although the rear hub on Bengry's Rolls finally broke about 35 miles shy of the control, taking the rear brake with it. The British *Sunday Mirror* newspaper reported: "Bill Bengry … carried out an astonishing temporary repair with a block of wood, allowing the Rolls to crawl forward. In Lisbon, a millionaire, Alberto Pombo, provided the spare part … from his

The Rolls-Royce Silver Shadow of Bill Bengry, David Skeffington, and Ray Richards (courtesy Guido Devreker).

own Rolls."[3] Somewhat embarrassingly for Rolls-Royce, it transpired that the reason for the hub disintegrating was that it had not been lubricated at all!

After their misadventures from the Alpine *prime* onwards, the Triumph 2.5PI of Messrs. Green, Murray, and Cardno received much additional repair work at Lisbon before presenting itself at the arrival control, just five minutes before their expected time, and *parc fermé* with 19 minutes to go! Another 2.5PI experiencing the excitement of trying to beat the clock here was No. 39. Brian Englefield recalled that his team had difficulty finding the port. "So, we stopped a taxi to take us," he said. "'No, I'm not going to do it unless one of you gets in.' So, we tucked Adrian in, quite illegally because we were supposed to be all three of us together. We hung on the tail of this taxi, got him to stop outside, Adrian got back in and we just made it."

So it was that on April 25, 1970, 71 cars in varying states of repair were pushed and rolled to the loading area and winched aboard the Royal Mail Lines Ltd vessel, the *Derwent*, a 13,500-ton steam ship that plied its way between London and Buenos Aires, via Cherbourg, Vigo, Lisbon, Las Palmas, Rio de Janeiro, Santos, and Montevideo. The ship was scheduled to arrive in Rio on May 7, leaving competitors to their own devices for two weeks, a week in Lisbon followed by a week in Rio.

The frontrunners, having accumulated only five penalty points, and winners of not one but three prizes, were Citroën team René Trautmann and Jean-Pierre Hanrioud. In second place were Ford team duo Hannu Mikkola and Gunnar Palm with seven points, and third was another Citroën entry, Guy Verrier and Francis

Murac with nine points. In honor of category winners, a prize ceremony was held at the Estoril Casino on the evening of April 27, where Trautmann "received £2,000 ($4,800) for being first in the general classification and £500 ($1,200) for heading the rally from London to Monza. He got another £500 ($1,200) for being the first private entrant to arrive in Lisbon."[4] Bemusement continued, at least in journalistic circles, as to whether the Citroëns really were privately entered. Brian Robins wrote: "Trautmann told me he had paid for his DS21 out of his own pocket and given Rally Secretary John Sprinzel the receipt."[5] However, the Citroëns had also been entered as a manufacturer's team, thus qualifying for that category's classification and potential prize, and had therefore been supported by a network of Citroën mechanics. Regardless, rally organizers had accepted the classification at entry and that was that. An excellent performance by the Citroëns then, made all the more impressive by Claudine Trautmann and Colette Perrier taking the leading women's prize—and another $1,200 for the Trautmann household—in their DS21 with 96 penalty points!

Other little pockets of controversy and confusion popped up here and there. As well as the rather insulting attitude some journalists had towards the young Mexican VW Bug team, slightly more serious was the suggestion that, in line with Supplementary Rally Regulation 3, stating that certain specified "component 'containers' may not be changed or replaced during the event, although they may be removed and dismantled for repair and refitted," the axle-casing on the Ford works Escort of Rauno Aaltonen and Henry Liddon was minus its paint mark "branding," applied back at scrutineering at Wembley. The fact that it was also clear that the casing had at no time been removed caused a degree of consternation, but the Ford team and car remained in competition, suggesting matters were resolved. In addition, some of the professionals were expressing dissatisfaction about the European *primes*, suggesting they had been too easy, given the number of cars that had cleaned all but one. They'd all be in for a wake-up call in South America!

The cost of entering the rally included bed-and-breakfast accommodation in Lisbon and a flight ticket to Rio, booked for May 1 on a Brazilian VARIG airlines flight. Many competitors relaxed, taking in the sites of Lisbon and its environs, visiting traditional bullfights, exploring the city, or just collapsing on the beach. For many, this was also a time of reflection and review of progress and performance thus far. Privateers who had seen their cars loaded aboard ship were probably just happy to have made it this far, while some of the professional teams were taking stock of how their machines had managed across Europe. Ford GB personnel returned to England to look at remedies for the Escort's axle issues, experienced by Clark, Tony Fall, and Rauno Aaltonen, while BLMC sent some of their competitors on ahead with service crews to undertake further recce work before the restart in Rio.

Eschewing the promise of a little R&R, other competitors also put the time at hand to good use. Lying seventh at Lisbon, Citroën duo Robert Neyret and Jacques Terramorsi promptly climbed aboard a plane and flew over to North Africa to compete in the *Rallye du Maroc*, or Moroccan Rally, a 3000-mile slog from Rabat, Morocco's capital city, out into the desert and Marrakesh and then back up to Casablanca. Neyret and Terramorsi won the event in 1969, and despite having just completed 4,500 miles from London to Lisbon, back they went to defend their title. Which they did!

For one crew, however, the European section proved an extremely inauspicious event. The Anglo-Australian team of rally veterans Evan Green, "Gelignite" Jack Murray, and motoring journalist Hamish Cardno was competing in a BLMC works prepared Triumph 2.5PI. After their bad luck in the Australian outback during the London–Sydney Marathon 18 months previously, Green and Murray were undoubtedly looking for a happier experience this time around.

26

Bangs and Whimpers
(Part One)

Hamish Cardno began working for the British *Motor* magazine in 1966, after a brief stint with the Royal Automobile Club. Always a keen motoring enthusiast, he had started out with motorbikes in his native Scotland before migrating to local car club meets, enjoying being behind the wheel on competitive events. Starting as news editor at *Motor*, he quickly noticed that the magazine had a rather relaxed attitude toward coverage of the British and European rally calendar; while a dedicated correspondent was assigned to report on Grand Prix motorsports events, rallies were given as a kind of company bonus, depending on where the competition was to take place. Hamish viewed this as puzzling, and eventually he went to magazine editor Dick Bensted-Smith and pointed out that rally was getting more and more technical, more and more difficult to understand. "You really need to have somebody who has a feeling for it and will get to know all the people if you've got the coverage," he argued, "rather than somebody who turns up once a year and says, 'Oh, I remember you, you're Timo Mäkinen.' So, he bought into that idea and of course I was the obvious choice."

Through the late sixties, Hamish covered all the major rally events for *Motor*, including the Monte Carlo, the *Coupe des Alpes*, and the Acropolis. He also wrote a lot about the London–Sydney Marathon, though he only went to the start of it. "And then I was in constant touch with the headquarters and things, doing bulletins all the time. I didn't actually get any further than [the rally's start at] Crystal Palace!" Thus, when the London to Mexico World Cup Rally was announced during 1969, he got talking with BLMC competitions supremo Peter Browning, learning that he had decided to add regular Australian rally duo Evan Green and "Gelignite" Jack Murray to the rally effort. Hamish had never met Green and Murray, though he knew of them from his coverage of the London–Sydney Marathon. And he was aware of the reason for Murray's nickname: Murray had a habit of throwing fireworks on rallies, usually at the start, not something that found favor with everyone! Green and Murray had been friends for many years, rallying together for a time and then getting involved in various trans-Australia exploits, including racing a car against a light aircraft around the continent! They had had their fair share of misfortune while crossing Australia in 1968 but were proven competitors, having first met in the 1950s, and had gone on to regularly compete on many Australian events. Theirs was an enduring partnership, despite, or maybe because of, their inherent differences. Before Hamish could even process this piece of information, however, Browning told Hamish he wanted him to take third chair in the car.

Evan Green's recollection of events leading to the three becoming an official BLMC team entry in 1970 includes almost having a genuine movie star in the car. The British Ford Competitions Department had achieved a major PR coup by adding England soccer ace Jimmy Greaves to their rally roster, so BLMC responded by trying to raise the stakes. BLMC "offered the spare seat in our car to Steve McQueen," Green reported. "He was keen to go. As the films *On Any Sunday* and *Le Mans* demonstrated, the American actor was enthusiastic about motor sport, and knew a thing or two about high-speed driving and travelling on rough roads."[1] In fact, filming on *Le Mans* didn't occur until June 1970, which was probably why Warner Bros. balked at the idea of having their star putting himself at risk on a 16,000-mile endurance rally across Europe and South America, which wasn't scheduled to finish until just a month before shooting began! Needless to say, instead of McQueen, it was Hamish who joined the Aussie duo.

Motor magazine was, of course, thrilled with the idea of having one of their own embedded in the rally, as was its sister magazine, *Autocar*, which had secured a place for one of their journalists, Michael Scarlett, with the experienced British RAF Red Arrows team of Terry Kingsley and Peter Evans, both also veterans of the London–Sydney Marathon, who would be driving a BLMC works–prepared Austin Maxi. Thus, Hamish reported to BLMC's Competitions Department HQ in Abingdon, Oxfordshire, for a first-time meeting with Murray and Green, who had flown in from Australia.

Things didn't exactly get off to a promising start. "I was in the workshop talking to Robin Vokins, who built the car," Hamish recalled. "He was the mechanic in charge of building the car. They appeared and Jack's first gesture was to pick me up, he grabbed me around the waist and hoisted me up and said, 'He's a fucking jockey!' Turned out that they both had this complete obsession about weight, anything that they could discard from the car or the luggage or anything to make the car lighter. To my mind, that makes even less sense now than it did then! We were talking about thousands and thousands of miles, so a second or a minute saved was just not going to affect any difference at all." However, with the ice not so much broken as smashed, they laughed and joked and got on well. Murray's larger-than-life personality would remain conspicuous as the three took their places in the Triumph 2.5PI prepared for them by BLMC.

As part of preparation, according to Hamish, BLMC had developed a prototype 2.5PI, which BLMC works driver Brian Culcheth had been testing at the British Army tank proving ground at Bagshot in Surrey, a standard location for putting any proposed rally car through its paces. Now, BLMC wanted the car to accumulate high mileage over a relatively short period, to see how it fared, so it was rostered for use among a number of drivers and mechanics. Hamish's turn came over the Easter weekend, so he decided to drive the car from London up to see his parents in Scotland, a thousand-mile round trip. Not far from the Scottish border, Hamish was pulled over by highway patrol. Initially he thought he had done something wrong, but no: the officers just wanted to have a look at this unusual 2.5PI, their own cruiser being a similar Triumph. After hearing about his rally plans, they wished him luck, and he was off on his way. On his trip back south, however, law enforcement was not so impressed with Hamish or the Triumph, noticeable by the roof-mounted spare wheel and assorted other visible modifications. Coming through a village, Hamish was a little lead-footed on the gas pedal, and it wasn't long before a rather irate motorcycle cop loomed in his rearview mirror! "I said, 'Terribly sorry, didn't realize,'" Hamish explained. "I think I'd gone through in about second gear! Anyway, he then started going around the car, which had all sorts of modifications, spare wheels in odd places, extra fuel tanks and extra lights and brackets here and there, all sorts of things. He took my license and took my details and said, 'Right, I'm cautioning you that you're being charged with speeding through the village. Also, this car has got 32 contraventions of the Construction and Use Regulations!'" Eventually, Hamish was allowed to continue and didn't give the caution, or the ticket, another thought.

BLMC continued work on their rally cars, occasionally adjusting equipment and cabin specifications to meet the needs of individual teams. For the Green/Murray/Cardno car, the challenge of team members' height needed to be addressed; although Hamish and Jack were similar average height, Evan was much taller. BLMC had struck a deal with Morlands, the longstanding British sheepskin supplier, to provide seat coverings that would afford both improved comfort and hygiene. However, with the thick sheepskin in place and his crash hat on, Evan's head was jammed up against the car's ceiling! Green and Murray "ripped the sheepskin cover off the driver's seat and started hauling out the foam to gain an extra couple of inches so that Evan's head wouldn't hit the roof," Hamish recalled. "We suffered from that for the rest of the event because all they'd done was take away the padding and so we were sitting on sheepskin cover and a bit of plastic and the springs. Wasn't ideal but these things happen."

The 2.5PI was one of four Triumphs prepared by BLMC for the rally, effectively hand-built at their Abingdon works. "Jack and I spent two weeks helping to finish the car," Green reported. "The men at Abingdon were magnificent: not only skilled and vastly experienced but dedicated to their work and prepared to do whatever you asked. They seemed surprised and pleased that a couple of drivers were taking such a practical interest in the preparation."[2] Green was less impressed with the state of affairs at BLMC, and its impact on the Abingdon works in general. BLMC had only recently been formed out of a merger between the British Motor Corporation, which included the brands Austin, Morris, and MG, among others, and Leyland, which offered Rovers and Triumphs to the car-buying public. Thus, what had been rival brands, especially Triumph and MG, were now uneasy bedfellows, with the competitions mechanics and engineers being called upon to prioritize Triumph development over MG. "It was made known that the future of the competitions department—the best in the world—was uncertain," Green said. "The word was out that the only cars to be rallied or raced, were Leyland models and, if they weren't suitable, then competitions would cease."[3] Within this extremely difficult working environment, work progressed on the cars, plus three non–Leyland cars, despite the general missive, two Maxis and a Mini 1275 GT. Whether this apparently toxic situation contributed or whether it was a simply a case of too much to do, not enough time, and a lack of manpower, Green said their Triumph did not receive a properly prepared motor. "It was supposed to be balanced, checked for cracks or flaws in the metal, and then assembled with meticulous care," he explained. "But because our car was lagging in so many jobs, the engine, a 2.5 litre fuel-injected six, had come straight out of the crate."[4] True or not, the experience of Green, Murray, and Cardno would differ hugely from that of the other Triumph teams once the rally got going.

Departure day arrived, and the team lined up for a photo op with Lord Stokes, BLMC supremo, who was there to nominally cheer on the BLMC effort, despite his apparent misgivings about his company's financial investment in motorsport. The team, drawn as No. 92, had a lengthy wait before being called to the stadium, and Hamish braced himself for "Gelignite" Jack's predictable plan to honor his nickname. With the car apparently misfiring, they coaxed it onto the ramp, Murray miming the throwing of a firecracker to unnerve Stokes, and then they were flagged away. Out of the stadium, Murray did produce a firework, lit it, and lobbed it out of the window. A small boy rushed forward to see what it was just as it exploded.

With Hamish nursing a heavy head cold, the Triumph continued to misfire through London, and Green reported that acceleration was sluggish. However, they made it to the control at Dover without penalty, at least in terms of time. Less certain was the fact that police officers were waiting for them, enquiring about incendiary devices being thrown in London and informing them that a boy had received burns to his hand as a result. Somehow, the police accepted the explanations offered, and since the boy's injury was minor, no further action would be taken. Mulling on this,

No. 98, with a team of Paddy Hopkirk, Neville Johnson and Tony Nash, gets underway (courtesy Guido Devreker).

Green was nevertheless unsettled by it all, an injured child and a problematic vehicle boding ill for what was yet to come. A BLMC mechanic assured them that someone from Lucas, the manufacturer/supplier of the Triumph's fuel-injection system, would be on hand at the Sofia control and advised the best course of action until then was to run the car hard across Europe. Which they did.

The long, fast trek to Sofia was wet but uneventful, save for an impromptu dinner stop in Germany, where Royal rally competitor Prince Michael of Kent organized the ordering of food, given he was the only German-speaker in attendance! At Sofia, they found the Lucas rep and explained the problem before heading to the hotel pre-booked by BLMC. Sadly, a breakdown in communications meant that, instead of rooms being allocated to British Leyland rally competitors, the hotel concierge had allocated their rooms to the first British people to present themselves! Grumpy and frustrated, they found rest where they could, Green reporting that he eventually slept in a bathtub!

Under a welcome sun, rally cars departed the Bulgarian capital and retraced their path for a while before heading west and south to Titograd and the revised *prime* start, the first in Europe. Hamish was driving. "On the way to the start of the first *prime*," he recalled,. "Paddy Hopkirk and I realized about the same time that if we really got a move on, we could get to the first *prime* and do the whole thing before it got dark. So, in the mountains of Yugoslavia, two Triumph 2.5PI's are going like a bat out of hell down to the start, where there was a service stop."

At last, the rally's inaugural speed section was upon them so, with Green behind the wheel, they sped away. The Triumph was using new Ferodo competition brake pads, which offered superb stopping capability but only once they had been faded, i.e., after they had been subjected to normal pressure at lower speeds over specific periods of time. According to Hamish, this piece of information hadn't been imparted to Green, with what could have been dire consequences. Hamish was barking out navigation instructions as the car traversed a long straight approaching a sharp right. "As we approach it," Hamish recalled, "he puts his foot on the brake and it goes straight to the floor so instead of going 90 right, we go through the gate! We turned around in the field and back out of the gate and carry on. I'm sitting there thinking bloody hell! Anyway, the brakes recovered and we got through the rest of the stage, it was all right. We realized what had happened and had a good laugh about it afterwards but it wasn't the best of starts." Green's account differs, with the claim that the Triumph's brakes failed as a result of a broken seal, caused by repeated fading as described above, and resulting in brake fluid escaping. Regardless, Green wrangled the car to the finish control just nine minutes down on the target time. The next *prime*, the Serbian, would prove considerably less forgiving!

The last few miles on the way to Glamoč and the start control were particularly rough. "The *prime* itself was a bit of a nightmare," Hamish reported. "It was so dusty some cars were starting at ¼ hour intervals and for the first few kilometres there was thick fog to contend with. Later on, there were greater nightmares. We came down a hill through some very rough roadworks to find the road completely blocked by three large trucks."[5] One of these had broken down, which effectively obstructed the route. Behind the Triumph, more rally cars came to a halt until there were enough competitors to manhandle the errant truck out of the way, the clock ticking to the detriment of all involved. And problems kept coming. First there was the unplanned bridge closure that forced many to detour (although not Hannu Mikkola, who was reported to have taken a flying leap in his works Escort and made it safely to the other side), and then two of the Triumph's shock absorbers began to give up. A service point at the finish control provided a single replacement, which was fitted, but then, only a few miles further on, the other one collapsed completely. Adding insult to injury, the various delays had cost them an hour and 48 minutes, and they still had to get to the Monza service point and *parc fermé* in Italy.

All the way to the famous *autodromo*, the Triumph's woes worsened. The motor was still misbehaving, running unevenly at low revs, and then a whining sound from the rear began getting progressively louder the further they went. To the team it sounded like the limited slip differential, the mechanism that ensures both driven wheels receive the same amount of power regardless of whether one wheel has traction or not. In Monza BLMC mechanics diagnosed a failed quill-shaft bearing, an issue that would impact at least two other 2.5PIs on the rally, so they set about replacing the errant part. One of the fuel injectors was also replaced, the service crew working with great dexterity to get the car safely into *parc fermé*.

Late leaving Monza, the team had to battle with heavy traffic as they made their way west towards the third European *prime*, the San Remo, and by the time they arrived at Ville San Pietro, the Triumph was misfiring again. Regardless, they completed the speed section without penalty, thanks to Green's expert driving skills. At the service point beyond the Camporosso finish control, mechanics again attended to the troublesome Triumph, now discovering a broken valve guide. But without a replacement, there was little they could do. While they set about repairing a broken strut, Hamish and another mechanic drove into the town to try to arrange for a replacement part to be sent on to the next *prime* finish control, but without success. Thus, again leaving late, they were forced to push hard to the next stage, the French Alpine *prime*. For Cardno, Green, and Murray, all hell was about to break loose!

Having negotiated the tricky route to get to the start control at Les Quatre Chemins, that dot on a map, Green gunned the Triumph away from the control. With Murray dozing in the back, Cardno and Green fell into the regimented relationship of driver and navigator. They were making good progress over the snaking section, negotiating small settlements and tight bends. "Suddenly, you're out of the village and running along a ridge," Green reported. "Then a few dips, a short climb, a turn. 'Right!' Hamish calls. He's been working hard, and well. We're a happy team. The three of us may have been plagued with poor luck, but we're starting to have fun."[6] The fun didn't last, however: on a fast mountain descent, a loud rumble caught Hamish's attention. As quickly as it had sounded, it disappeared, so Green continued, pushing the Triumph to 80 miles per hour on a straight section. Suddenly, there was a very loud bang, and, to Green's horror, the steering was gone. He slammed down on the brake pedal, but there was nothing; the car careened left and right, its occupants completely at the mercy of forward propulsion. One moment they were on the track, the next they were airborne, tree trunks brought into stark relief by the car's powerful headlamps and auxiliaries. The side of the car smacked a tree, knocking a rear passenger door open, and finally came to a violent stop, settling sideways on a couple of bent-over tree trunks, about 15 feet below the road. With Murray pummeled every which way in the back, Hamish and Evan both went for the car's master switch, knocking out the power and motor. They were plunged into darkness and silence.

During the car's tumble from grace, Green had momentarily noticed an ominous drop right next to his side of the car, so as Hamish began to extricate himself from the car, he gave a note of caution. Then, realizing Murray was about to slide out of the open rear door, Green grabbed him and managed to haul him back into the rear, Murray cursing the stinging nettles that formed a hostile border next to the abyss. Green followed Cardno out of the front passenger door, and together they surveyed the damage. A wheel was gone and the spots were smashed. Murray confirmed that the rear door wouldn't close and, on closer inspection, they saw that the oil pan guard was buckled. Although the radiator had been pushed backwards, the lower half making contact with the fan, there was no sign of a water leak. Green gingerly tried the starter motor, and they were relieved to hear the motor spring to life. Now, if they could get the stricken Triumph back up onto the road…

Clambering back up the way the car had come, Green flagged down the first competitor to come along, the Rolls crewed by the Martin family, and asked them to send for assistance with the message that they had gone off, miraculously uninjured but utterly incapacitated. Finally, a recovery vehicle arrived and dragged the car back up, local mechanics aboard the truck managing to carry out rudimentary repairs so that they could at least drive the car to the control. Thus, with unpredictable steering, reduced braking capacity, and barely 15 minutes to cover nine miles, Green wrestled the car to the finish, making it with just three minutes to go!

At Rouaine, they managed to rouse a sleeping band of service mechanics, who set to work fixing the damage and replacing components destroyed or disabled in the crash. Thoughts then turned to the challenge of driving out of France, across Spain, into Portugal, and up to the last European *prime*, the Arganil. "We decided to miss the next two passage controls (collecting three hours penalty for each)," Hamish explained, "and go by main roads across the south of France to Rodez, just north of the Spanish border."[7] Definitely a quicker route, but far from comfortable as now gasoline fumes and exhaust fumes were drifting into the car's interior and, somehow, they had all picked up some sort of stomach bug, Murray suffering much worse than his younger teammates. He was asleep in the back as they drove through Spain, but as they navigated their way around Pamplona, he awoke, urgently needing to use the bathroom. Ahead they saw a hotel and brought the ungainly Triumph to a halt, instructing Murray to go in and find the restroom. Murray dragged himself out of the car, hobbled across the road, and collapsed. Evan and Hamish rushed to his assistance, joined by folks from the hotel, and an ambulance was summoned, arriving quickly and loading Murray into the back. Evan and Hamish followed the van to the hospital where Murray was cleaned up and given a shot to settle him and his errant digestive system, his attending physician advising the men that their teammate needed to remain for a day or two under observation. Naturally the pair protested, explaining that they were on their way to Mexico! Against advice, with Murray wrapped in a blanket and deposited back in the Triumph, they headed onwards, making for Arganil.

They were, of course, even more behind schedule now, and the complaint that had felled Murray had also left the other two very fatigued. They took up a short-order rotation system for driving and even a slightly rejuvenated Murray took his turn. The car eventually consumed both front tires on the approaches to the start of the Portuguese *prime*, but these were replaced at the service point just before the start control. Mechanics also sent a message to Lisbon containing a list of what the tired Triumph required before loading onto the Rio-bound ship. Despite severely impaired performance from the sickly motor, the trio made it through the speed section and then coaxed the car all the way to Lisbon, where they delivered it straight into the hands of the awaiting BLMC service team. A flurry of expert activity ensued, and the Triumph received a replacement cylinder head, driveshafts, and a suitably straightened front end. They then dashed to the finish control, with seven minutes to spare, before returning to the mechanics for finishing off. Then it was into *parc fermé*, just 19 minutes before it closed. They had accumulated 1,011 penalty points and were 69th out of 72 surviving teams, but, against all the odds, they had booked their passage to Brazil.

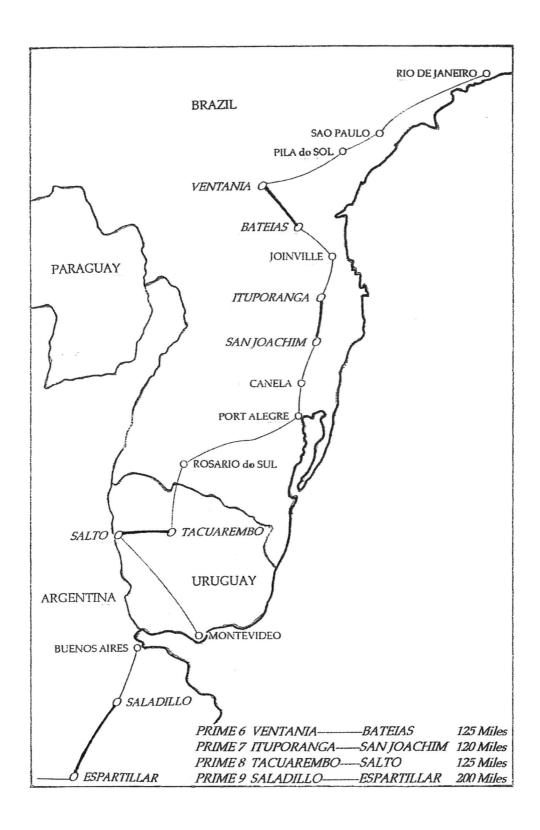

The route from Rio de Janeiro to Espartillar (map by Martin Proudlock).

27

There Go My Pants!

Looking back from the ultra-strict, ultra-controlled national and international flight regulations of today, with their stringent restrictions on what a traveler can and cannot take aboard a jetliner, whether in checked or carry-on baggage, the shenanigans that allegedly went on as rally competitors joined civilians on the non-stop flight from Lisbon's Humberto Delgado Airport to Antonio Carlos Jobim International Airport in Rio de Janeiro have adopted almost mythical proportions in motorsports circles.

It's all about supplies of replacement components!

Unlike Europe, the almost unimaginably long stretches between controls in South America would mean, especially for surviving privately entered teams, a lack of service points and therefore sources of assistance. Accordingly, even with cars stuffed full of components and consumables on their way aboard the *Derwent*, no opportunity could be wasted, so rally teams boarding VARIG flight RG829 on May 1, 1970 were toting whatever they could cram into their carry-ons, including radiators, shock absorbers, torque convertors, springs, even, as suggested by journalist Brian Robins, complete cylinder heads! Suffice to say, such automotive equipment comes with a consequence, and that consequence was weight!

Some of the competitors had a habit of timing takeoff when jetting off to various locations for rallying or other activities, and they generally had a good idea of the point from acceleration when a plane would rotate or lift off from the runway. Among others, Rauno Aaltonen watched the second-hand reach 45 seconds, then 60 seconds, and still the jet stayed resolutely on the ground. Not one for emotional responses, Aaltonen was just beginning to contemplate the imminent arrival of the end of the runway when, at last, the plane lifted and began its climb.

To entertain themselves on the 10-hour flight to Rio, competitors took full advantage of complimentary beverages and generally congregated towards the rear of the plane, talking and drinking until, it is suggested, they "drank the bar dry"! Given that probably more fuel was consumed at takeoff than was usual, thanks to the jet being a little heavier than the norm, it is also alleged that the plane's pilot eventually called for passengers to return to their seats as crowding the rear of the fuselage was causing the plane to fly slightly more "nose-up" than was fuel-efficient!

Regardless, the plane eventually touched down at Brazil's capital city, and as they disembarked, competitors were struck with the heat and humidity of a late Rio evening. At first, they were also impressed at the warm welcome of a steel band playing and crowds cheering, until somebody pointed out that this was actually in support of the Brazilian soccer team, flying off to Mexico City to begin preparations for the World Cup! Once baggage was reclaimed, they were transferred to the Hotel Glória, from where they had another six days to sight-see, lounge on the city's famous beaches, including Copacabana and Ipanema, or carry out further reconnaissance work. As Rob Lyall recalled, time in Rio was governed by three things: keeping out of the strong sun, never taking one's eyes off one's personal possessions, and, given the prices of everything on offer, spending as little money as possible! U.S. trio Brian Chuchua, Bill Kirkland, and Richard Gould eschewed the delights of Rio, however, choosing instead to fly back up to California until it was time to restart the rally.

On Monday May 3, seven competitors flew from Rio to São Paulo to survey the first South American *prime*, the 125-mile Parana, which would run from Ventania to Bateias. Competitor and journalist Hamish Cardno joined his teammates Evan Green and Jack Murray, plus Paddy Hopkirk and Royal Maxi competitors Captains Gavin Thompson and Nigel Clarkson, to make notes and explore the route. Their experience gave all a taste of what was to come—the ever-changing terrain of road works and complicated signage bore no resemblance to previously compiled notes. The *prime* itself was too much for the two rental cars. The track was "made of very hard-packed clay," Cardno remembered. "When it is dry this is like driving over a cobbled road with half the cobbles missing…. When the rains come it is equally rough but as slippery as sheet ice."[1] And come the rains did! BLMC works competitors Brian Culcheth and Johnstone Syer had flown over with the BLMC service crews on a chartered flight from Lisbon before other competitors and, on May 1, had flown out to investigate the second *prime*, the 120-mile Rio Grande between Ituporanga and Canela. A tropical rainstorm delayed them for hours as the route turned to mud. Cardno wrote: "The organizers have now sent the Morley brothers down to … make sure that the whole Rally will not grind to a halt there."[2] Hopkirk also flew on to Costa Rica and Mexico itself to further investigate the route.

Without the means, resources, or even necessity to undertake their own recces, most other competitors whiled away the hours and days with tourist-type activities and general good humor. HRH Prince Michael kept a few fellow competitors entertained while, as Brian Robins reported, "Tony Fall and the Ford factory team challenged the Russians to a football match, but the Moskvitch [*sic*] men insisted it had to be played *before* Jimmy Greaves arrived from Lisbon."[3] (Soccer ace Greaves had made his own arrangements to get to Rio.) Dublin-born rally champion Rosemary Smith continued her wily publicity drive, for BLMC if not for her own profile in international rallying. After courting the press with a photo op of removing her hose to provide a makeshift filter for another competitor's carburetor and, with co-driver Alice Watson, posing for cameras in bikinis and holding fishing rods during the Lisbon break, Smith took advantage of the media presence at the Hotel Glória. "As I stepped into the hotel swimming pool in my white bikini the flash-bulbs were popping," she explained. "No doubt that's what British Leyland was hoping for and I didn't let them down!"[4]

British competitor Peter Jopp asked teammate Mark Kahn to try to purchase some maps for their impending slog through Brazil, so he teamed up with fellow

British trio Bob Freeborough, Phil Cooper, and Reg Redgrave to scour the local cartography outlets, which proved surprisingly fruitless. They finally found what they wanted among the wares of a tourism street vendor!

With a nod to Rob Lyall's abovementioned recollection, hanging out at the beaches, however, was not without its own risks. British RAF Red Arrows team member Peter Evans was enjoying the sun, lying face down with his clothes and personal possessions close by. A sudden flurry of activity caused him to look up and witness his things heading off to the main road, snatched by a young thief. The busy traffic was no match for the runner, and he expertly disappeared with everything Evans had had with him! Evans wasn't alone as a victim of theft on the beach, however, as Rod Channon lost £170 and his pants.

Elsewhere, a British competitor almost bought it at Ipanema Beach. The British Army cavalry regiment, the 17th/21st Lancers, had entered an 1800 in the event. Lying in 68th place at Lisbon, two of the team and another competitor were enjoying a swim off the famous beach when driver Jeremy Rugge-Price got into difficulties with cramps. At first Rugge-Price thought he could swim it off but quickly realized the severity of the situation. His co-driver Philip Beaver immediately swam back to the beach to get help while the other competitor worked to keep Rugge-Price's head above water. However, his fellow competitor began to tire and, for a few moments, Rugge-Price began to accept the inevitable. Moments later, he was grabbed and dragged back to the beach by a couple of teenagers who had been playing handball and whom Beaver had summoned for assistance. A very lucky escape!

For Porsche driver Terry Hunter, a surprise awaited him on return to the hotel on the final day of the rest break in Rio. He was handed a message by the concierge, which had been sent by the captain of the *Derwent*, the ship that had carried the rally cars across the Atlantic. The ship had sailed from England to Lisbon, and Hunter's father had been the tugboat captain that had piloted the ship out of the River Thames. Upon learning that Hunter's son was competing in the rally, he said he would make contact on arrival in Rio and invite him aboard. Sure enough, the message invited Hunter to come aboard and have dinner!

Eventually, boredom and the oppressive humidity began to get the better of competitors, and by the time the *Derwent* berthed at the Pier Mauá in Rio's docks on May 6, crews were ready to get going. First, however, the cars had to go through the rigors of Brazilian customs formalities, which took the whole of May 7, so they were not released or ready to be collected until the afternoon of May 8. "We went down to the docks," wrote Mark Kahn of No. 3. "Here the sky was smoggy, a haze of grime hovered in the air. And there she was, our 1800.… I felt almost as though we were greeting a long-lost friend."[5] From the docks, cars needed to be taken to *parc fermé* at the Hotel Glória, to be booked in an hour from collection. The departure control would be open from 19:00 on May 8 and cars would then move over to Rio's Museum of Art for a ceremonial start, where they would be flagged away by Brazil's minister of transport in order of their standing at Lisbon, for a 60-minute neutralized passage to the real start at a gas station on the city's limits. Rob Lyall, competitor in No. 4, recalled that the short run from the docks to *parc fermé* was hindered by traffic and by a police-attended incident further along the road that prompted

Corcovado in the mist (courtesy Pat Smith).

Rosemary Smith to tuck in behind the Lyall/Badham GT so they could travel in safe tandem.

For the most part, cars were in good order after their Atlantic crossing with just a few flat batteries or tires to contend with or the odd scratch and ding to bodywork. A noted exception was Trautmann's Citroën DS21. First it wouldn't start, but that was remedied by tightening a battery connection. Then, Trautmann discovered that the car's hydropneumatic self-leveling suspension wasn't working properly. Whispers of sabotage were hardly backed up by concrete evidence, but the fault certainly impacted the leading car's departure. While Trautmann and team attended to matters, it was actually second placed Mikkola and Palm who took the ceremonial "first away" honors. Unfortunately for Trautmann and Hanrioud, there would be worse to come.

Another car requiring attention was the Brian Englefield Triumph 2.5PI. He had been able to replace the quill-shaft assembly back in Europe, but this had left the rear wheels steeply cambered and remedy was required. The ever-helpful BLMC service crew were able to assist, time and professional teams' needs allowing, and work was carried out, Englefield and co-driver Keith Baker all the while keeping an anxious eye on the clock. While they waited, Brian recalled needing to have a pee, going in search of a suitable place to the rear of the workshop, and coming upon the biggest cockroaches he had ever seen in his life. "When you stood on them," he remembered, they "went pop with a bang like a 12-bore [shotgun] going off!"

As with other long sections in the rally, the total allowable time from Rio to Montevideo was 41 hours so, as before, if a car departed at 21:52 on May 8, they would need to reach the Uruguayan capital by 14:52 on May 10. Along the way, they would need to cover 2,000 miles, negotiate three *primes*, and make sure they were stamped through a passage control. What immediately lay in wait for competitors departing the Brazilian capital was 24 hours of what Brian Robins described as "the most destructive day and night of the entire event."[6]

One team that was probably just grateful they would be able to face this ordeal at all was that of Evan Green, Hamish Cardno, and "Gelignite" Jack Murray.

28

Bangs and Whimpers
(Part Two)

While many of the other competitors immersed themselves in the delights of Rio de Janeiro, Hamish carried on with both journalistic and rally duties. Even during the rigors of No. 92's European escapade, he had continued to send dispatches back to *Motor* for their weekly editions, and now, in Brazil, he found himself with his team-mates, plus rally competitors Paddy Hopkirk, Gavin Thompson, and Nigel Clarkson—Prince Michael of Kent's fellow team members—flying down to São Paulo and then hiring cars to recce the first South American *prime*, the 125-mile Parana, which would run from Ventania to Bateias.

Piling into a standard Ford and an equally standard VW, they headed through busy São Paulo and then, using the route notes previously prepared by BLMC, they headed south. The first thing they noticed was that the instructions for encountering an intricate set of roadworks and signage had been superseded by changes on the ground. This required them to spend time investigating, rerouting, and notating so that the rally could follow revised directions. Once done, they headed off for Ventania, both rental cars being put through their paces, mechanically and physically. "After only 700 miles on these roads we had punctures, exhaust systems falling off, windscreen wipers packing up, and the suspension systems of both cars got a bit tired," Hamish reported.[1] No doubt the rental company would be billing for the repairs and maintenance required once their automobiles were returned!

Competitors were required to collect their cars from the Rio docks, process all the necessary customs paperwork, and then take their vehicles to a *parc fermé* adjacent to the hotel where the teams were staying, overlooking one of Rio's renowned beaches and the sea beyond. Green, Cardno, and Murray were now desperately hoping their European ordeal was behind them and that the expert work undertaken by BLMC's excellent service team in Lisbon meant they would be able to make steady, untroubled progress into South America, keeping a gentle pace and just making sure they got to each control within limits. Having extricated the Triumph from the docks, they began to drive towards the hotel, but something was wrong. Was that a clattering sound coming from the front of the car? With heavy hearts, and more than a little annoyance, they took the car to an emergency service point that BLMC had fortuitously established on the way to *parc fermé*, where a missing locknut from the right-hand suspension tie bar was identified. No nut being available, No. 92 was forced to depart the Rio controls first before it could join the queue at the next service point, waiting on necessary and time-consuming work being done to their teammate Andrew Cowan's 2.5PI. At last, the mechanics turned their attention to the Green/Cardno/Murray Triumph, but by the time all was well, they had lost two hours on the rest of the field.

The route took cars southwest to São Paulo, a run of approximately 275 miles on asphalt roads, which should have been an easy section. Unfortunately, as they sped to catch up with the field, even after all the attention the Triumph had received at Lisbon, the motor began to misfire again. Gritting their teeth, they carried on, eventually hitting roads that were less forgiving. Wooden bridges presented an added challenge. They were "like a Bailey bridge so there was a structure, a platform … with lateral wood slats going across it and two runners down the side, approximately the width of the car's track, that you were supposed to drive over," Hamish explained. "Whenever Jack was driving, and we came to a bridge, he would contrive to get only one or two wheels onto those tracks and the other two wheels would be crabbing and pulling the car sideways until Evan eventually joked, he said, 'You know the next bridge, maybe Jack you could get … three wheels on there, or four?'" Hamish's recent recce experience paid off, however, and Evan successfully negotiated the Parana *prime*, losing 31 minutes at the finish.

The next *prime*, the Rio Grande, led cars to Ituporanga, via Curitiba, where they were beckoned across a junction by a policeman, straight into the path of a VW, which gently but firmly T-boned the Triumph. The VW came off considerably worse, but the police officer insisted on form-filling, adding further delay. At another service point, immediately before the start control, a mechanic examined the motor and wearily informed them that a piston was failing, yet they got to the start control and completed the stage, this time losing 78 minutes by the time they finished at São Joachim.

No. 92 struggled on, crossing the border and making for the third *prime*, the Uruguay. Hamish was fascinated by the lack of modern cars. "You could see Model-T Fords driving around, things like that, there were some very antiquated cars driving around," he recalled. Import duty on cars into Uruguay was prohibitively high so, without a domestic automobile industry, drivers simply kept old cars going for as long as possible. Despite mechanical hindrances, Green was able to wrestle the Triumph along the speed section from Tacuarembó to Salto, the imperfect car forcing another 36 points onto their tally. Enough was enough, however, and at the final service point before Montevideo, they reapplied the running method they had adopted in Europe—disengaging a fuel-injector, losing a cylinder, and putting up with the steady trickle of gas out of the side of the car. Thus, they made it to the Uruguayan capital. "We were lucky to arrive," Green recalled. "By now, we knew the Triumph's engine was mortally damaged…. Power was poor, and the engine had developed a raging thirst for oil. The piston, damaged by the metal droppings from the broken valve guide, had begun to break-up … and for the last 36 hours Jack, Hamish and I nursed that ailing, groaning, shuddering car."[2] Owing to their lateness into the Uruguayan capital, they learnt that that any mechanical assistance was denied to them until Argentina, so they deposited the car into *parc fermé* and unenthusiastically noted that they were now in 51st place overall—second to last in the field. All they could do was screw their courage to the sticking place and carry on.

After a fitful night's sleep, they arose to find a message left by two members of the BLMC service team, Den Green and Doug Watts, who they had gotten to know back in Abingdon during the cars' preparation phase. If No. 92 could get to the service point beyond Buenos Aires, their next destination via ferry from Montevideo, they had the parts ready to sort the Triumph. Thus, they coaxed the sickly 2.5PI onto the boat, spent a few hours gazing out across the River Plate and catching up with other competitors. Then, once disembarked in Argentina's capital, they joined a crazed convoy of rally cars and police Harley-Davidsons and headed southwest towards Saladillo, where hoped-for salvation awaited in the form of the promised service stop. Once again, things didn't go according to plan.

At a gas station in Saladillo, BLMC had negotiated dedicated space to service their teams' cars, plus any Special Tuning–prepared vehicles and, if time allowed, any other competing BLMC products. "Such an arrangement had been normal procedure throughout the event," Green reported. "Ford, Citroën, Peugeot, Leyland—anyone with a number of competing cars staked out a specific service area for their mechanics to work on their vehicles…. All the teams, that is, except the Avtoexport squad of Moskvitch [*sic*] 412s."[3] Hardly in keeping with fair play, according to Green, the Russian service team arrived and, without request, commandeered part of the BLMC section, dismissing protests and unloading equipment in readiness to tend to their own. According to Green, things quickly deteriorated into pushing and shoving until "the Russians drove through the service bays, deliberately running over rows of equipment. Back and forth they went, leaving the site a shambles."[4] Thus, when No. 92 chugged in, apart from a complete oil change, there was nothing Green and Watts could do. Green, Cardno, and Murray would just have to complete the run to the Chilean capital of Santiago, a distance of almost 1,700 miles, where full repairs could be carried out. Ignoring the elephant in the room, hands were grimly shaken and the terminal Triumph headed out into the Pampas *prime*, storm clouds ominous overhead.

Somehow, they made it through the 200-mile speed section from Saladillo to Espartillar, despite mud and ever-dropping oil pressure, which required frequent stops to refill the precious lubricant. They were now equal parts anxious and fascinated that the car was still going, Hamish recalling that they were "running sometimes on four cylinders, sometimes five, very rarely six, absolutely drinking oil, oil smoke pouring out the back of it, but we carried on…. The only good thing was that nobody could overtake us because the cloud of smoke was so thick!" Having clocked in at the finish control, the map indicated a 555-mile drive south, then west, then south again to San Antonio Oeste on the San Matias Gulf, which marked the start of the Trans-Argentine *prime*, 380 miles with a target completion time of six hours across the Argentinian planes before climbing to Bariloche in the foothills of the Andes.

Onwards they went, out into the *prime*, stopping every 40–50 miles to fill up with oil, straining to hear even the slightest change to the noise of the motor. Then, about halfway to Bariloche, near the town of Los Menucos, it happened. "I was lying in the back at the time, trying to sleep," Green remembered. "The engine emitted a deep gurgle, as though it was an animal choking. The car shuddered and made a noise

On the road to Bariloche (courtesy Patrick Vanson).

like gravel being shaken in a bucket. Then came a deathly silence, as Jack slipped the gear lever into neutral and let the car glide to a halt. 'And that, gentlemen,' said Hamish, in a soft Scottish burr, 'is that.'"[5]

Attempts to send a message to the BLMC service team at Bariloche proved fruitless, but help came in the form of two rally volunteers, who had been assisting with an emergency service point not far away. They helped arrange overnight accommodation in Los Menucos, and, the following day, with a little welding assistance from a local garage, the car was attached to the volunteers' truck and towed all the way to Bariloche. Hamish recalled that the three of them took turns in riding in the truck, so utterly cold was the Triumph's powerless interior. After a hair-raising dash, the truck driving much faster than was prudent, given its trailing cargo, they arrived at the popular ski resort and sent a message to Peter Browning. With little else they could do, they took a plane to Lima, from where Hamish travelled point-to-point, assisting BLMC and continuing his *Motor* magazine dispatches.

After many adventures, involving an uncomfortable encounter with gun-toting Guatemalan soldiers, the irony of being hit by a wild horse in a Ford Mustang in the Mexican desert, and managing to get 65 ticketless competitors and service crew onto an international flight from Mexico to Canada, Hamish finally returned home. Awaiting him was a card from the post office notifying him that an attempt had been made to deliver a letter that required a signature. Hamish was pretty sure it was the speeding ticket and fine for contravening regulations from all those weeks ago in

The flight home from Mexico via Canada—Paddy Hopkirk facing the camera (courtesy Pat Smith).

Scotland. To his credit, he presented the card at his local collection office but was told that, after a certain period, any item not delivered was returned to the sender. "I got away with not only speeding but 32 contraventions of the Construction and Use Regulations," he explained, smiling. "And I still have a clean license!"

As for Green and Murray, they were to appear again further down the rally trail, a not altogether welcome sight for another Australian team. Making steady progress thus far were London–Sydney Marathon veterans André Welinski and Ken "Tubby" Tubman, together with moviemaker Rob McAuley. McAuley had already had an adventure on the Marathon 18 months earlier. This time he was actually competing.

29

Driver, Navigator, Filmmaker, Spy
(Part One)

In 1968, 34-year-old Australian moviemaker Rob McAuley was one of only two people to drive the entire London–Sydney Marathon in the opposite direction! Accompanying soon-to-be Marathon competitor Bob Holden, they set off from Sydney in a Volvo 142S, the very car that Bob planned to use in the actual event, and followed the route across Australia to Perth, before loading the Volvo onto a merchant ship bound for Bombay. From there, they drove out of India, through Pakistan, Afghanistan, Iran, Turkey, Bulgaria, Yugoslavia, Italy, France, and, via ferry, across the channel to England. All along the route, Rob shot film footage, which he eventually edited into a movie produced by the Australian division of the American oil company, Amoco.

Bob's experience of the actual Marathon is a whole other story, but Rob was assigned to leapfrog the event in a small plane, again filming the action from various vantage points along the way. During this time, he became great friends with a number of the many Aussie competitors, including Volvo drivers Ken Tubman, Jack Forrest, Gerry Lister, and his co-driver, 35-year-old André Welinski, a Polish-born, French-educated Australian, described by Rob as a complex, highly intelligent, extremely adventurous, and dynamic entrepreneurial character. "Truly a man of the world, he was also a warm, passionate person, the likes of whom I have never met before, or since," Rob said. "He was also very much a 'mystery man' if ever there was one!" Rob's friendship with André continued after the Marathon when, back home, Amoco further commissioned Rob to undertake promotional work with the Marathon movie. "This included some very pleasurable socializing with André. Lots of laughs—lots of experiences shared—lots of tales to tell," he explained. "There was very much a sense of kinship amongst those of us who had been associated with the Marathon." André even loaned his yacht when Rob's British wife-to-be, Anne Grundon, visited Australia to see if it was a country in which she would want to live!

One day in May 1969, Rob received a phone call from André, inviting him to lunch. During the meal, André announced that they were not only going to enter a car in the following year's London to Mexico World Cup Rally but also be the very first to have their entry received and registered. He believed that this alone would generate the financial sponsorship necessary to meet all the costs involved. Stunned into silence, Rob listened as André continued, explaining that Rob's primary role would be to film the rally from the car, which would undoubtedly attract broadcaster interest and therefore more sponsorship. André even had a plan for getting ahold of a couple of cars, one to be used to recce part of the South American route and the other for the rally itself. He told Rob that BLMC Australia had four 1800s in storage, left over from the London–Sydney Marathon, and he was pretty sure that rally driver, Marathon competitor, and BLMC Australia's PR man, Evan Green, could be persuaded to use his influence to allow André to purchase two of them, thus qualifying the proposed team for the private entry category. And there was more: André had spoken to Ken "Tubby" Tubman, who was very interested in taking on the job of main driver if the finances could be secured.

"Bloody hell! Why me, I thought? I'm not a rally driver," Rob recalled.

The Aussie team: (*left to right*) Rob McAuley, André Welinski, Ken "Tubby" Tubman (courtesy Campbell McAuley).

"I couldn't believe what André was proposing. I had never driven in a rally, nor did I have any great passion for the sport. Now, if it was a yacht race he was thinking about—that would have been a different proposition altogether. But me, driving in a major international car rally? No way. It all sounded absolute nonsense. But André had it all planned out!"

André took a sip of his drink and then asked Rob whether he was up for it. Despite gut-reaction misgivings, Rob could see that, somehow, it all made sense and that it had the potential to be a great adventure. He grinned and said yes. They shook on it, and, with that, André said he'd be in touch, paid for lunch, and disappeared into the Sydney lunchtime crowds. What had Rob gotten himself into? "I went back to the flat to tell Anne," he recalled. "That day, a chain of events began that was destined to change all our lives."

Before the rally, however, Rob had filming commitments that would take him to Tahiti, Easter Island, and Chile, making a movie about Swiss-Australian yachtsman Vic Meyer, who was sailing his yacht *Solo* around the world—suffice to say, the voyage actually came to an abrupt end off Punta Arenas when *Solo* was dashed against rocks during a storm, during which Rob was flung into the icy sea and very lucky to escape serious injury or worse! Before all of this, however, Rob told André about his schedule, at which André exclaimed that this fitted perfectly with the plan to take one of the purchased 1800s and recce a section of the South American rally route! Thus, recovered from his encounter with the Strait of Magellan, Rob found himself on a plane from Punta Arenas in southern Chile to Buenos Aires, to where the car had been shipped, in late January 1970. He explained: "We'd pick up the car, do a survey of the Rally route—Buenos Aires to Lima, Peru via the Andes—leave the car there full of spare parts, fly to London to carry out final preparations to the car we'd shipped direct to the UK. Then, on the 19th of April, we'd head off on the World Cup Rally. It was all that easy—or so it seemed at the time."

André's plans, however, came with a huge cost, so he was hot on the sponsorship trail. In the weeks leading up to Rob's departure for Tahiti, he got a call from André, requesting his presence at one of Sydney's exclusive dining and function clubs, the City Tattersalls, or City Tatt's, where they would be meeting journalist Mike Kable for lunch. Kable had accompanied Rob on his leap-frogging flight to follow the London–Sydney Marathon a year before, proving himself a very anxious passenger as their small plane swooped and dived to enable Rob to film another rally plane at close quarters. He had also been on the Amoco plane that took André and the other Australian Volvo competitors to London for the Marathon's start, during which André had tormented Kable with stories of aviation disasters! At the lunch, Rob could see André's mischievous mind at it again as he launched into his pitch, explaining that Kable could have the scoop on their plan for Rob to film the recce and then use the film, via a dash-mounted screen, as a navigation tool on the rally itself. Rob knew this was technically impossible but went along with the ruse. Kable appeared impressed, asking Rob whether this could actually be achieved. "'Well, we've got a few technical details to overcome, but we're working on it. I'll certainly be filming during the survey,'" Rob remembered improvising. "It was the most truthful reply I could conjure up. It seemed to satisfy Mike. He soon headed off; I assume back to his office to begin writing the story." Later, Rob confronted André about this cock and bull story, but André just grinned, dismissing Rob's concerns with the adage that all publicity is good publicity, especially if it generated sponsorship!

Calls from André came more frequently, some without offering any real substance, to the point where Rob was becoming frustrated. Then, one evening, another call came: could Rob get himself over to André's home urgently? With an irritated sigh, Rob motored over to André's tony waterfront house in Seacrest, noting that André's car was backed into his covered parking bay instead of the usual front-in-first. André buzzed him in and, as Rob entered the building, he was confronted with a very surprising sight: "There was André, pacing backwards and forwards across the room—pistol holster under his left armpit," Rob remembered. "As he paced, he pulled the pistol out of the holster, slid the firing mechanism backwards and forwards, replaced the pistol in the holster, then repeating the whole routine over and over again. As he paced and practiced, he glanced up and acknowledged my presence." Rob was at a loss for words as André looked at him, commenting that Rob knew very little about what he actually did. Rob gestured his acknowledgment, eyes fixed on the gun as André loaded bullets, only looking up when André went on to explain that he worked for the Australian Security Intelligence Organization, the nation's security service, and that he was shortly to facilitate a serious defection. Rob recalled that André slipped the pistol into its holster and, as Rob recounted, connected the imminent diplomatic exchange with the rally: "'You've met my friend Jack Tier, Editor of the *Sun* [Sydney's afternoon newspaper]?' I nodded agreement. We'd met him in a pub in Broadway for a few beers some weeks before. 'Well, I've offered Jack the exclusive rights to the defection story, and in return, if it all goes according to plan, his paper will sponsor us in the World Cup Rally.'" He went on to advise Rob that he would be out of contact for a while, for obvious reasons, but that he should keep an eye on the next day's *Sun* headline. If it was about the defection, they had a major sponsor! With that, André was out the door and gone, Rob close at his heels.

Any doubts about this story were dispelled the following day when, sure enough, the newspaper had a piece about an important defection, which in turn meant that the team now had a powerful sponsor—the Australian World Cup Rally 1800 would be adorned with the *Sun* newspaper logo. This soon led to further sponsorship, from the P&C Life Insurance Company; international airline UTA Air France, which meant their flights were covered; and Overseas Containers Limited, assuring shipping of the recce car to Buenos Aires and the rally car to England.

As per the schedule, Rob met up with André and Tubby in Buenos Aires towards the end of January 1970. Their recce car had been delivered to the local BLMC distributor, Pruden and Sons. "We were made extremely welcome by old Mr. Pruden himself," Rob recalled. "His was a small showroom in a wonderful old building that featured lots of wooden beams and a wonderful, wooden floor, all beautifully varnished. At the far end, a raised polished wooden display platform was truly the jewel in the crown of this remarkable showroom. And in pride of place on this platform— the absolute star of the show—our … 1800 sat gleaming in all her glory." Unfortunately, in André's enthusiastic attempt to drive the car off the platform, the studded tires gouged the polished wood! Shamefaced, the trio hurriedly bid many thanks and farewells to Mr. Pruden and his staff and quickly drove away.

They then fell victim to the complexities of international import/export regulations. They had filled the trunk of the 1800 with a fully itemized set of components, collections of which they planned to leave in each country through which they would recce, starting in Argentina. Therefore, provided they made it to South America, they would have a ready stash of parts at various points along the way. However, customs documentation clearly stated that everything—car and contents—must enter and depart each country intact. They were therefore forced to carry everything all through the recce, which at least meant that, should they get to Lima, they would have a full stock of replacement parts awaiting them.

Wouldn't they?

The route southwest from Buenos Aires gave the three men the opportunity to get to know one another within the confines of a car, each settling into his role as part of the team. Tubby was designated driver, while André took navigation and administrative duties. Rob was left to film and photograph the journey, and, in this fashion, they quickly formed a cohesive unit, enjoying one another's company. Rob recalled that André was much more relaxed now, especially compared with the evening of

The recce begins: André Welinski (*sunglasses, goatee beard*) among the excited crowd (courtesy Campbell McAuley).

the defection, and Rob was hugely impressed at the slick organization on display as they journeyed onwards across Argentina. Hotels had all been pre-booked, and meals were provided without any need for Rob to pay. Paperwork was meticulously handled, and, all the while, André's linguistic skills were in constant use. Rob also recalled 55-year-old Tubby, an experienced rally driver with many years of competition behind him, as hugely relaxed behind the wheel, deftly able to motor the 1800 along mile after mile without any drama. Rob assumed Tubby knew his way around an engine, just had Bob Holden did all those months earlier. It was only later that Rob would realize that, like himself, neither Tubby nor André had any particular mechanical skills at all!

They made steady, comfortable progress, not having to contend with driving against the clock, and passed from Argentina to Chile over the Andean foothills and then headed north along the Pan American Highway to Santiago, André steadily making notes as they travelled. Being an extremely easygoing and gregarious man, Rob had the gift of forming friendships wherever he went, and as his recent visit to Chile had brought him to Bariloche, he had struck up friendships with a few folks, so he was thrilled to see them again, this time waiting for the 1800 on the side of the road to give them an impromptu reception! The same welcome awaited them in Santiago, friends Peter and Shelley Steel making sure they had everything they needed, including a mechanical check over for the car. Later, André and Rob would sponsor the Steels when they migrated to Australia.

After Santiago, the team knew they would now encounter the rock-strewn, mountain roads that wound through the foothills of the Andes between Chile and Argentina, and as these would constitute some of the very long-distance *primes* John

Sprinzel and his team had devised, the sooner they had a taste of how it would be to actually drive them, the better. Rob recounted: "And boy, were these rock-strewn, bush tracks clinging precariously to edge of the mountain slopes, bad. That's an understatement. They were shockers!" They bade farewell to the Steels and set off, following the rally route and taking copious notes. At the border between Chile and Argentina, they encountered their first real logistical challenge. The frontier crossing was as remote as could be imagined, just a tin hut next to a boom gate blocking travel onwards. The sound of the 1800's approach brought from the hut a thunder-faced border guard, who stalked towards the car. Ever the diplomat, André climbed out of the car, all allegedly required paperwork in hand, and, in a mixture of Spanish and English, explained the reason for their appearance. The guard was singularly unimpressed, and matters quickly deteriorated. "The mood changed," Rob recalled, "and not for the best. André got serious about our need to get through the barrier. Document followed document; all three passports, with visas indicating we had been in Buenos Aires only a few days before, were ignored. Then André produced a very special document, signed by his old mate Leo Port, Lord Mayor of Sydney, requesting the help of 'to whom it may concern' for these three VIPs from Australia. It was a colorful document, large and impressive, complete with a very large official red seal. It made not a jot of difference to this sleepy, disheveled border guard. There was nothing he had seen that justified his requirement to lift that boom-gate and let us through." They were, it seemed, at an impasse. His mind whirring, André had an idea—money! Quickly, he whipped out his American Express card and waved it in the guard's face. In moments, the guard raced back to the hut, re-emerged and lifted the gate. They were on their way again!

They had been warned about altitude and its effect on both person and internal combustion engine, a danger not to be dismissed. In Potosí, which would be the finish of a 270-mile speed section, they were aware that this city, famous for its silver mines, stood at 13,400 feet above sea level. They were therefore pleased to discover that the oxygen-poor atmosphere did not seem to be unduly impacting either their performance or the 1800's. They knew the oxygen cylinders they carried were essential but still noted that driving at this altitude was possible, a happy reassurance for when they would return under competitive conditions.

On they drove, eventually reaching Lake Titicaca, where they stopped to admire the enormous stretch of water, knowing that on their return, there would be absolutely no time for sightseeing. Rob was intrigued by the fabled reed boats that worked the lake, filming the spectacle for later inclusion in the movie of the rally itself. They then proceeded to Cusco, where they stopped overnight in a hotel that offered an enclosed yard in which the 1800 could be securely parked. Late at night, Rob needed to retrieve something from the car. Stumbling around in the dark, he felt along the 1800's length. Heavy breathing and then a plop of something wet on the back of his neck scared him out of his wits. The hotel had failed to disclose that the secure yard was also the home of their "guard" llama! Needless to say, Tubby and André dined out on this horror story for days to come.

Knowing all attention would be on the rally when next they were in the area, they took time out to board a train and travel to see the extraordinary ruins of Machu

Overlooking La Paz (courtesy Campbell McAuley).

Picchu, Rob again filming the sights for insertion in his movie. On their return to Cusco, they had the opportunity to watch the time-honored Easter tradition of bearing the ancient crucifixion statue *Señor de los Temblores* in procession to the cathedral, the dramatic imagery still remaining in Rob's memory some 50 years later.

They were now close to the end of their recce, however, so motored on, eventually arriving at Lima, via La Paz, where they deposited the hugely dependable 1800 at the city's BLMC distributor, complete with its trunk-load of undisturbed, unneeded parts, safe in the knowledge that these would be awaiting them in the ever-hoped-for event that they would still be in competition when they returned to the Peruvian capital. Pleased and satisfied with their leisurely team-building journey, they boarded a London-bound plane and set off on the next chapter of their adventure—the rally itself.

On arrival, Tubby and André wasted no time in heading for the BLMC Special Tuning department in Abingdon to check on their recently arrived rally 1800 and see whether Special Tuning mechanics could give it a once-over and generally oversee any final preparations for the event. Meanwhile, Rob was reunited with Anne in England and whisked away to her family's farm not far from England's capital, from where he set about organizing all the visual and audio equipment that he would need to film the rally. Besides constructing a well padded, soft case for his movie camera—he could sleep against it in the confines of the 1800's rear cabin—he approached PAG Films Limited, a company that specialized in supplying chargers and power sources for filming equipment. They were able to develop a bespoke solution that would allow Rob to charge his sun-gun light, a necessity if he was to film at night, via the car's

A church in Cusco (courtesy Mike Wood).

alternator. He also made sure he had plenty of film, batteries for his camera, and a small cassette recorder. Finally, he specified a grab handle to be fitted onto the 1800's roof, which would enable him to hold on while hanging precariously out of the window to film at high speed!

At last, the reason for all their preparations—André's wheeling and dealing to secure sponsorship, the procuring of not one but two ex–Marathon rally cars, and the carefully orchestrated survey of part of the rally route itself—was upon them. On Saturday, April 18, 1970, they convened at Wembley Stadium for scrutineering and had the opportunity to meet up with various old friends and compatriots. Rob had gotten to know Andrew Cowan during the London–Sydney Marathon, first meeting him during his run from Bombay to London with Bob Holden. Cowan had gone on to win the Marathon. There was also a fair amount of ribbing by the all-Australian team towards their fellow countrymen Evan Green and "Gelignite" Jack, seeing as they would be driving for the British BLMC competitions team. Anne Grundon was on hand to witness all of this, never imagining she would be spending her birthday among rally drivers getting ready to drive to Mexico City!

The following day, No. 32, the sole Australian entry in the London to Mexico World Cup Rally, followed the heavily laden Trident Venturer sports car onto the starting ramp and was flagged away, Rob hanging out of the 1800's rear window to capture the spectacle on film. All three marveled at the crowds along the roadside through London and then south towards the Dover ferry port, where they arrived safely and, for the first time, met royal competitor Prince Michael of Kent. "The poor guy was doing his best to be 'one of the boys,' and doing a great job of it, whilst at the same time, desperately trying to avoid the TV and press cameras," Rob recalled. "That

No. 32 at Wembley, April 19, 1970 (courtesy Guido Devreker).

meeting was the first of many … with the prince and his Army officer crew members. They were driving an Austin Maxi—about the same speed as ours. As fate would have it, we were destined to see a lot that car and its crew along the way."

In France the rains came, persisting all across Europe as the field made its way towards the first major time control at Sofia in Bulgaria. At the various passage controls in Germany, Austria, Hungary, and Yugoslavia, Rob happily found that his many rally rivals were only too willing to be included in filming and, among the throngs of drivers, navigators, and mechanics, he struck up an easy friendship with celebrity competitor Jimmy Greaves, the British soccer player. The Australians were also able to get to know the five-car Soviet Moskvič team, André able to converse easily in their native Russian and, when needed, help sort any administrative issues on their behalf. "It was all pretty exciting stuff," Rob remembered, "and at times, I couldn't believe my luck in being right there in the middle of it all, and playing my small part of this extraordinary event."

As this long transport stage stretched on, inevitably, Rob was required take his turn behind the wheel. This would be his first test, his first experience of actually driving the 1800 in the rally. Yes, he had an international competitions driving license, but obtaining that had hardly involved any assessment of his driving skills! Now, sliding into the driver's seat, he was nervous but determined to show that he had what it took to be a rally driver. Motoring into the mountains, his confidence increased until, into a corner, he overcooked it, braked, and departed the bend too slowly. Tubby offered sage words of advice, telling him to "think driving" at all times and to go slower into the corner without brakes and then accelerate out. He also warned Rob not to ride the clutch if they were to get to Lisbon, let alone South America. Rob learnt quickly!

It was on the first *prime*, the Montenegro, that Rob finally saw why Tubby was their driver. As they sped away from the control, Rob recalled, Tubby "had a look about him that I had not seen before. This was my first glimpse of a master craftsman practicing his trade, learnt through years of competition driving over some of the roughest terrain in the world. Tense, but relaxed—serious but sheer joy, excitement and utter concentration written all over his face as he peered into the night, the powerful beam of the quartz halogen headlights showing the way. It was mesmerizing, exhilarating to watch." André and Tubby seemed to establish a high-volume, high-velocity rhythm, the navigator barking constant commands, the driver completely focused on the instructions and the road ahead. With mountain walls on one side and forest-covered valleys below on the other, the momentum of it all actually sent Rob to sleep; he woke only when the 1800 screamed to a halt at the finish control. Rob couldn't believe he had slept through almost the entire speed section!

The Australian driver-navigator combination brought them into Kotor just 13 minutes down on the target time and, with roadbook stamped and signed, they headed off to the next *prime*, the Serbian, starting at Glamoč, all the while teasing Rob for his sterling performance during their first trial!

Thus began a pattern for the team, André or Rob taking driving duties on transport stages and Tubby deftly speeding the car thought the *primes*. In this fashion, they made their way north and west, although the Serbian proved much more challenging, as it did for many of the other teams. Obstacles on offer included looming trucks on single-track roads and a bridge in varying states of disrepair, forcing many competitors to divert to whatever alternative route the map indicated. Despite best efforts, No. 32 lost 79 minutes on this speed stage.

The next stop was at the *Autodromo Nazionale di Monza*, the famous Italian racetrack in Monza, where competitors had the opportunity for a restorative rest and cars could be tended to, whether by the works teams of mechanics or by competitors themselves, before being deposited into *parc fermé*, in readiness for departure the following morning. An industrial dispute at the main hotel booked for the teams, however, meant that, the following morning, there were a few tired faces as cars lined up to get going and head for the next *prime*, the San Remo, high above the Riviera Ligure di Ponente, the West Ligurian Riviera. Near Imperia on the coast, cars turned right and climbed up to Ville San Pietro, where they waited in turn to head out onto the Italian speed section, which, despite the police-enforced, lowered average speed, still promised loose asphalt, rocks, the odd wandering farm animal, and even parked cars! Tubby hurtled into Camporosso 10 minutes down, although many of the faster cars avoided penalty altogether.

On now to France and the penultimate *prime*, the Alpine, a route very familiar to many of the European professionals but not to competitors from further afield, Tubby and André included. Both access to, and traversing of, this twisting speed section required expert navigation, not least because its start, after a passage control high in the Alps, was little more than a junction of four roads in the French countryside. On this *prime*, Rob switched on his cassette recorder and was able to capture probably the only time Tubby and André got into a heated, high-speed argument, disagreeing on the direction of a turn. Almost 50 years later, Rob couldn't recall who was right but, suffice to say, there were no lingering ill-feelings and the Australian team made it to the finish, albeit with 47 minutes lost.

There followed the extremely long transport stage out of France, across Spain, and into Portugal, Rob again taking his turn at the wheel to give Tubby, and then André, a well-earned rest. Endless miles crept by without incident, the 1800 not missing a beat, something Rob reflected on as being extraordinary, given the assorted mechanical mishaps that had befallen a number of the other rally cars thus far. They were therefore able to safely arrive at the start of the final European *prime*, the Arganil, running through Portuguese forestland to Pampilhosa. For the last time before Lisbon, Tubby accelerated away, bouncing and weaving the 1800 through the trees and finishing the *prime* with 26 penalty points. The 1800 wasn't the fastest car in competition, but it was definitely proving one of the most reliable.

At Lisbon, No. 32 was lying in 37th place out of 71 survivors. Safe in the knowledge that they had booked their passage to Brazil, and with the car checked and prepared for loading onto the ship that would carry vehicles to Rio de Janeiro, it was time to kick back. Rob also got the chance to get to know Prince Michael of Kent as, during the days spent in the Portuguese capital before competitors flew off to Rio,

At the bullfight in Lisbon: (*top row, left to right*) Wylton Dickson (*striped t-shirt*), André Welinski, Evan Green, Ken "Tubby" Tubman, unknown, and "Gelignite" Jack Murray (courtesy Campbell McAuley).

they spent much time together, Prince Michael taking a shine to this open, gregarious and very good-humored Australian. "For some reason we clicked," Rob recalled. "We became good friends in the rally along the way. … Michael came to us one day and said, 'I've been invited out by the British Leyland rep' or something, who had the franchise in Lisbon, 'and he's got a motor launch. I've been invited and I'd like you to come, can you make it?'" Thus, together with Evan Green and "Gelignite" Jack, Rob went down to the marina and looked around for any sign of a launch fit for a prince. Sitting on a harbor bench, Jack noticed activity aboard a rather dilapidated craft and wagered that this would be their boat. True enough, crates of beer and cases of ice were being loaded, so the men watched in fascination as the boat's diesel engine rattled to life, belching great plumes of black exhaust fumes into the air! Once aboard and chugging away from the dock, Jack turned to Prince Michael and said, "Michael, this bloody boat hasn't got enough bloody power in it to pull the skin off your auntie's rice pudding!" "That," Rob remembered, "really broke us up." How the Prince's security personnel viewed this excursion is unknown. "It was only when we were in Rio that we did have detectives there," recalled Kent's teammate Gavin Thompson. "We called him 'Odd Job,' or something like that! He used to hover around."

The royal friendship would continue on the other side of the Atlantic, as would further encounters with Evan and Jack, albeit of a rather less genial kind!

30

Rio to Montevideo

The official program of the 1970 *Daily Mirror* World Cup Rally described the 520-mile stretch from Rio de Janeiro to Ventania and the start of the first South American *prime* as "the only easy section"[1] of the entire event route to Mexico, and, indeed, most of the section was fast highway via the city of São Paulo, through which there was no fast route. The suggested straightforward nature of this section didn't prevent incident, however, although given that some cars leaving Rio still remained in various states of disrepair following the European leg, perhaps this was not completely surprising.

BLMC works driver Andrew Cowan went straight from the Rio control start to the mechanics and lost three hours as a consequence. Having qualified for shipping to Rio in 58th position, the team of Tony Walker, Dennis Leonard, and James Burdon had to retire after the Piedade passage control when their blue Vauxhall Victor FD station wagon skidded off the road. Fortunately, no one was injured. As previously described, the British London Metropolitan Police team of Penfold, McInally, and Jones had to give up when their 1800 broke down. The 17th/21st Lancer's 1800 blew its head gasket somewhere in the jungle not far from the Brazilian VW factory near São Paulo. Rugge-Price and his co-drivers Charles Morley-Fletcher and Philip Beaver hitched a ride to the VW plant and, using French as the means of communication, managed to arrange for the car to be recovered and then transported back to São Paulo, but not before the entire village congregated to have their photographs taken with the car and team! In São Paulo, Rugge-Price was struck down with dysentery and laid low for some time before medical intervention was eventually brokered. With arrangements made for the 1800 to be shipped home with some of the other retired rally vehicles, Jeremy, Charles, and Philip took a plane back to England. About halfway home, with alarm, Beaver suddenly recalled that he had stashed a revolver in the roof of the car. With ammunition! With his name attached!! It was therefore an anxious wait for the car to arrive back and be processed through customs, but, fortunately for all, especially serving officer Beaver, the offending weapon wasn't discovered.

Busy and congested São Paulo also saw Brian Englefield, Keith Baker, and Adrian Lloyd-Hirst get lost. "Suddenly we found a superb bit of dual-carriageway [two-lane highway], with no traffic on," Brian recalled, "so we went bowling down this, I'm trying to make up some time, and Keith suddenly says 'Stop!' …I hammered the brakes because we were just about to go under a bridge and the other side … was a humungous pile of earth. They'd run out of money and stopped building!" So bad was the traffic that, sitting in a queue, Brian actually got out of the car, went and had some breakfast in a café, and then only had to walk 400 yards farther along the road to get back into the car again! Unfortunately, a combination of this delay plus the continuing problems caused by the quill shaft meant they were too late into the Piedade passage control and were out.

One hour was the target time for the Parana *prime*, the entrance for which was positioned at a school some eight miles southeast of the town of Ventania itself. Staffed by Peter Harper, it would be open from 05:00 until noon on May 9 and allowed 90 minutes to cover the 125 miles to Bateias. Unofficial results issued from Montevideo on May 10 show that 59 cars received finishing times, having grappled with, among other things, "felled trees and a telegraph pole and an unnatural pile of rocks."[2]

The first taste of a South American *prime*, as devised by John Sprinzel and John Brown so many months before, proved exceedingly sour for quite a few competitors. Wire coat-hanger hero Tony Petts went out on the Parana, as did the SAFRAR Argentina Peugeot 404 of Lareta and Migliore. The Martin family's Silver Cloud arrived too late to start and was out, but not before suspension, damaged from a crash, had led to a local garage working tirelessly to effect repairs, if only so they could advertise that they repaired Rolls-Royces! As well as the misfortunes that befell the Englefield Triumph 2.5PI, No. 78, the Argentinian Peugeot 504 of Señores Ipar, Esteguy, and Esteguy suffered collision damage and expired. Unofficial results published a few days later did not list the Thai Toyota Corolla KE 10-B of Dutch tennis player Jan Leenders and Thai Olympic cyclist Preeda Chullamonthol, although they were recorded as having finished the next *prime*. Assorted other entries feeling battered and bruised by their run from Rio to the end of the *prime* were the Dutch Datsun 1600SSS, which ran out of gas, and the Lydden racetrack Escort GT, which sustained rear axle damage. Such were the conditions of the stage that not a single car cleaned it. Fastest to Bateias were Mäkinen and Aaltonen, picking up 15 penalty points each, followed by Mikkola with 16, Tony Fall with 17, and Paddy Hopkirk with 18. Fastest privateers were the Hunter/Mabbs team in their pale blue Porsche 911. Having excelled across Europe, the Citroëns struggled to find similar pace here, with Neyret and Trautmann having to settle for 10th and 11th places, respectively. Was this a sign or too soon to tell?

From Bateias, the route stretched 300-plus miles south to Ituporanga and the start of the Rio Grande *prime*. Checking what was originally planned as a 240-mile run to Canela, advance parties quickly ascertained that torrential rain had either submerged or completely taken out the various rickety wooden bridges beyond São Joachim. Faced with no alternative, the *prime* was halved, Ituporanga to São Joachim only, with a revised time allowance of one hour and 40 minutes. Competitors were made aware and hastily scribbled the revised instructions, finish control opening and closing times, and time allowance into their roadbooks.

While it was perhaps too early to come to any real conclusion after the Parana, the Rio Grande, truncated though it was, underlined Ford's move towards domination of the event. The European stages had obviously suited the Citroëns, both cars and drivers, an opportunity that had been seized by Trautmann, with Guy Verrier and Patrick Vanson not far behind. Now, perhaps because the first two South American *primes* were faster, perhaps because Trautmann's self-belief had been affected by his car's troubles coming off the boat, or perhaps because these *primes* just suited the nimble and very fast Escorts more, Ford took full advantage and delivered the five fastest finishers on the Rio Grande with Aaltonen losing 35 minutes, Clark 37, and Mikkola, Fall, and Mäkinen with 38 minutes apiece. Terry Hunter's Porsche now appeared to be on a mission to make up for lost European time, and, in a works 2.5PI, Brian Culcheth was showing that the Triumphs were definitely a force to be reckoned with. Trautmann had to settle for seventh place at São Joachim with Verrier a minute slower in eighth. The man who had led the event coming off the ship at Rio would live to regret his attempts to claw things back.

Unofficial results published a few days later recorded 56 cars as finishing the Rio Grande *prime*, and the war of attrition continued lower down the field. Missing in action now were the British Army Motoring Association Peugeot 504 of John Rhodes and Joseph Minto and, disappointingly, if only for press and PR purposes, the Royal Maxi of HRH Prince Michael and Captains Gavin Thompson and Nigel Clarkson. Also gone was No. 87, the Peugeot 504 of Derek Currell, his son Bob, and friend Frank Bryan. "Their car went perfectly through Europe—not a scratch, no punctures, just a change of plugs at Monza. Then, on the tough Rio Grande prime in southern Brazil, a small plastic tube punctured and the clutch fluid disappeared."[3] This section also saw the demise of the Yellow Buffalo, the big Jeep Wagoneer of the sole U.S. team Brian Chuchua, Bill Kirkland, and Richard Gould, when its axle broke. It was "an assembly line problem," Chuchua recalled. "They didn't put any grease in axle bearings when they assembled the cars and the fix came out afterwards. You had to drill a hole in the axle assembly and put in a Zerk fitting and then lube it with a grease gun. They forgot to tell us about it but they were having failures all over the country! We had the spare axle but we, at that time … we hand packed it and we put it together, it would do that, but the other axle, we never pulled the assembly apart." Although they were eventually able to get the Yellow Buffalo fit to roam again, they were out of time and out of the rally.

Having endured initial ambivalence from the prestige manufacturer, mechanical problems, herculean fixes—which involved improvised repairs and a borrowed part from a private version of the rally car—during the European section, and being towed into Lisbon, and despite a refit in Rio, the Bill Bengry Silver Shadow's sub-frame broke, thus ending the hope of a Rolls-Royce finish in Mexico City. Out but not down, however, the Rolls would be making a surprise appearance farther along the trail!

The run south and west from São Joachim to the Uruguayan frontier at Santana do Livramento, via Porto Alegre at the top of the Lagoa dos Patos or "Lagoon of Ducks," was described in the official rally program as easy. Veteran competitors Jean-Claude Ogier, Claude Laurent, Roger Clark, and Alec Poole all begged to differ as first the Argentinian works Peugeot 404 hit an oxcart in the dark and then, five minutes out of Porto Alegre, with Poole at the wheel, catastrophe struck. Whether distracted or unable to react to a sudden change in direction of the other car, Poole collided with a VW. "I was leaning backwards in my seat getting some food out of the

The Yellow Buffalo: No. 44, the Jeep Wagoneer of sole U.S. team Brian Chuchua, Bill Kirkland (*front passenger seat*), and Richard Gould (courtesy Guido Devreker).

back," Clark explained in David Campbell's book. "I ended up hard against the dashboard. I twisted my ankle, and I think that's the only time I've ever injured myself in a car."[4] Poole was uninjured, but the Escort was a wreck and much-favored Roger Clark was out of the London to Mexico World Cup Rally. He would soon be joined by another serious contender.

Over the border into Uruguay, competitors headed south to Tacuarembó and the start of the third South American *prime*, named for the country within which it would run. Likened in terrain to the Scottish Highlands, it would take cars 125 miles west to the city of Salto on the banks of the Uruguay River. The time allowance was 90 minutes, and the control would be open from 03:30 to 15:00 on May 10. By the time the last team had its roadbook stamped at Salto, the rally would be missing one of its major celebrities.

Fifty-one cars were listed as starting and completing the Uruguay *prime*, the fastest losing just 14 minutes, the slowest 129. First-time frontrunner was Andrew Cowan in a works 2.5PI, with BLMC teammate Brian Culcheth just a minute slower. A good showing then for the Triumphs, but it was Ford that celebrated, with Hannu Mikkola and Gunnar Palm now in first place overall. The Hunter/Mabbs Porsche continued to impress with a joint fourth fastest *prime* position at Salto but, sadly, taking the headlines on May 10, 1970, were René Trautmann and Jean-Pierre Hanrioud. Perhaps because they were over-extending in an attempt to regain their lead, perhaps because there was a slight error in the route notes prepared from survey work earlier in the year, or perhaps just because of a momentary loss of concentration,

The Ford GB team Escort of Roger Clark and Alec Poole (courtesy Guido Devreker).

but approximately six miles into the 125-mile section, approaching a bridge, the Citroën DS21 left the road and rolled three times before coming to a stop. Escaping with just minor abrasions and contusions, the hugely impressive French pair got the car towed back to the start, where mechanics spent hours trying to repair it. Trautmann tried again but the DS21's steering was useless, and they were out. As Brian Robins wrote, "'I was just going too fast into the bend,' René said afterwards, a bitter and broken-hearted man."[5] Adding insult to injury, after their glorious run in Europe, Mmes. Trautmann and Perrier had now been overtaken by the Smith/De Rolland/Watson team as leading women in their orange-and-white striped Austin Maxi.

Another entry in trouble here was the British RAF Red Arrows team. Having emerged from the exit control, driver Terry Kingsley was making for the service point when he lost control. "On dusty tarmac, I overcooked it a little, buoyed by the last section," he wrote. "We slid along the edge of the corner, knocking over a few parked bicycles and a motorbike."[6] As Kingsley tried to control the skid, a very old Ford appeared coming in the opposite direction and promptly stopped in the middle of the road. The Red Arrows' Austin Maxi struck the Ford, incurring serious damage to the driver-side front wheel. Further investigation revealed that "the steering rack was broken, the battery leaking…. The stub axle was seriously damaged … after beating back the wheel area about eight inches, the replacement wheel would turn, but at a ridiculous angle."[7] Seriously impeded, the team continued gingerly all the way to Montevideo but were only able to get everything repaired at the service point before the start of the Pampas *prime*. Elsewhere, entries failing to have a finish recorded at Salto were No. 21, the Astafiev/Stafonov/Garkusha Moskvič 412 and the

Thai Toyota Corolla (again!). Rumors of the Russian team's demise were, however, unfounded!

Ahead now was a transport section of approximately 350 miles to the country's capital, Montevideo, an arrival control, a short hop to special *parc fermé*, and a rest stop. Somewhere near San Jose de Mayo, on the way to the Uruguayan capital, No. 55, the British Royal Navy 1800, braked suddenly, causing the BMW 2002Ti of Ken Bass and Graham Waring to rear-end them. The 1800 escaped relatively unscathed, but the BMW suffered a broken radiator and the destruction of most of its lights. Both were able to continue and check in, ready for the following morning when cars would board a ferry bound for Buenos Aires, Argentina, and a 28-hour stage that would include two *primes*, one of 200 miles, the other of 380, that would take surviving competitors up into the mountains.

31

Driver, Navigator, Filmmaker, Spy (Part Two)

The men and women competing in the 1970 London to Mexico World Cup Rally had yet more time to embrace tourism once they checked into Rio's grand Hotel Glória, overlooking beach and sea. Therefore, with the exception of some of the professionals, who headed off to recce sections of the route that lay ahead, competitors entertained themselves with sightseeing, shopping, lounging by the hotel pool, or taking taxis to the famous Ipanema Beach. Breakfast became a social event in itself, and Rob was frequently joined by Prince Michael. "He'd say to me over breakfast, 'What are you doing today Rob?'" Rob recalled. "I'd say, 'Oh, I'm not doing much, I'm probably going down the beach to have a swim.' 'Do you mind if I come with you?' 'No, no, that'd be fine.' Of course, Michael never carried any money! Not that it mattered but I'd go and pay the taxi driver and all that and then we'd have a Coke and stuff. But it was all good and we became good friends." This burgeoning friendship would eventually lead to an extremely surprising social situation for Anne Grundon some months later!

Departure time finally arrived, not a moment too soon for some of the bored and apprehensive competitors. With cars unloaded, processed, and collected at the Rio docks, after a brief period in *parc fermé* adjacent to the hotel, teams checked and rechecked personal and mechanical items and made their way to the ceremonial start, where they would now leave in order of their position at Lisbon. At last, after 35 other rally cars edged into the crowds of excited onlookers—the René Trautmann car didn't actually start first as it was still being worked on after issues arose once the Citroën was dockside—the Australian 1800 was away, headed for the competitive start a few miles away. From there, competitors headed to Piedade and then Ventania and the first South American *prime* of the rally, the Parana. Once again, the 1800 showed no signs of the ravages of either the 4,500 miles across Europe or the long ocean crossing, and all was well as they approached the *prime*'s start control. Never destined to break any records for speed, No. 32 nevertheless completed the section in Tubby's capable hands, accruing an additional 43 points by the finish at Bateias.

Two more *primes* faced them before their planned rest stop at Montevideo, and while this section from Rio to the Uruguayan capital saw the demise of 19 cars, No. 32 escaped encounters with cattle, trucks, and perilous narrow wooden bridges to complete the shortened Rio Grande *prime*, picking up another 68 points, and the Uruguay *prime*, adding a further 39. They arrived tired but relieved into Montevideo, where they learnt that Prince Michael had crashed out of the rally. Ten miles into the Rio Grande, Royal Maxi crewmember Captain Nigel Clarkson took a descent too fast and didn't leave enough time for a bend at the bottom. The Austin went straight on, slammed into a bank, and broke the front driveshafts. When the team extricated themselves from the mangled Maxi, they could see the front wheels were splayed, way beyond in situ repair. "I could see that there was no way we were going to repair the car," Thompson recalled. "It was really sad, I was really upset… some of the papers blamed Michael but it wasn't Michael driving the car at all, it wasn't his fault… It was just so unnecessary because we were doing so well." They had to wait for a tow as other competitors hurtled by, bitterly disappointed after their respectable 39th position in Lisbon.

In Montevideo, Rob suggested to Prince Michael that, if he was interested, he could fly on to Lima, collect their recce car, backtrack, meet them, and then follow as their service car. Rob recalled that Prince Michael jumped at the chance, the story even being picked up by the press, but Royal officials quashed the idea, advising that it could pose a serious security threat. Instead, while Clarkson accompanied the Maxi back to England, this time within thresholds of diplomatic security, Prince Michael and fellow teammate Captain Gavin Thompson took up marshaling duties for the remainder of the rally. As it would turn out, it was probably fortunate that the royal rally man didn't attempt to retrieve the other 1800 from the Peruvian capital!

A ferry chugged surviving rally cars across the expanse of the River Plate from Montevideo to Buenos Aires, Rob laughing when he recalled Jimmy Greaves' comment as the Argentinian capital came into view: "Looks just like bloody Grimsby!" (Once home to the world's largest fishing fleet, by 1970, the eastern English coastal town of Grimsby was suffering somewhat of an image problem!) At the docks, as they drove off the ferry, competitors were greeted with a throng of excited onlookers and a brass band to serenade them on their way before they were then directed to join a police motorcycle-led convoy, which would lead them from the port, through the city, and out towards Saladillo.

The Australians were now in familiar territory, retracing their recce route from only a few weeks before, so Rob was given driving duties, pointing the car in the direction of other competitors, just a straightforward transport stage before the Pampas *prime* was reached. André and Tubby were dozing as they reached the outer suburbs of the city. "All of a sudden," Rob recalled, "the car stops. Nothing. Bloody hell! Immediately they wake up. 'What have you done? What have you done?' 'Christ, I haven't bloody done anything, the car has just stopped.' Tubby jumps out and, at that precise moment, he knew about as much about mechanics as I did! He opened the bonnet, and he had a look in and he said, 'I can't see any problems!'" A crowd began to gather as they tried in vain to get the 1800 running again, André using his Spanish to try to drum up some assistance from the rubbernecking onlookers. Then, out of the crowd came a little man. "I can see him now," Rob said, "a little fat bloke, and he had a grey dust jacket on, and he made his way through. He came and André said something to him, and he said, 'I might be able to help, I'm a mechanic or engineer' or something. He went over and he looked in the engine." In no time at all, he diagnosed a damaged distributor—the shaft was spinning but the rotor wasn't. This

"I think it's that way!" André Welinski, South America, May 1970 (courtesy Campbell McAuley).

wasn't something anyone had planned for, so there was no replacement part aboard the 1800. Undaunted, their sudden savior told André to wait, and he promptly disappeared, reappearing minutes later with the very part they needed! Where he got it, they never knew for certain, but they suspected he had found a civilian 1800 parked in a side road and quite simply pilfered the item!

No. 32 progressed without further drama, completing the Pampas before the rains came and slogging through the 380-mile Trans-Argentine *prime* to Bariloche, where they ran over a skunk and were stricken by the stink all the way up the Pan-American Highway to Santiago, by which time they had added a further 73 penalty points to their total. As this was a night stop, and the 1800 needed no serious repairs, they were again met and entertained by the Steels before getting some hard-earned rest in readiness for the following day's departure. Ahead lay three *primes*, a total of 871 grueling, spirit- and car-destroying miles of against-the-clock rallying, which, together with the endless transport sections, would take them up to oxygen-starved altitude before their next stop at La Paz. At least they knew what to expect, although this time there would be no chance to pause and admire the scenery.

More meteorological and environmental challenges meant that the first *prime* after Santiago was another that had to be hastily but cleverly rerouted, so, after a drive north, No. 32 bumped and hustled its way along disused rail tracks from Putaendo to Illapel, Tubby bringing them home 80 minutes beyond the 90-minute target time. Then, the route also remapped, they headed south, then east, rising up to the Argentinian frontier and arriving at the border at 11,600 feet via a carefully planned journey through an operational rail tunnel. Beyond that, an undulating drive took them to the start of the second longest *prime* of the rally, the 480-mile Gran Premio, a long, twisting adventure offering dust, sheer drops, high altitude … and more dust.

The location for the start control was changed at a late stage, with competitors being instructed to head for San José de Jáchal, although at least one team managed to miss this particular piece of information and had to make haste to correct the error. The control was open between 20:00 on May 14 and 07:00 the following morning, and, as with all *prime* starts, allowing for arrival time, a driver could decide when they would set off during the hours of operation. Depending on the time of day, some competitors might decide to wait until daylight, while others might decide to get going as soon as possible to reduce the amount of trailing dust clouds from preceding cars. At San José de Jáchal, No. 91, the BLMC 1800 driven by Jean Denton, departed at 20:17 on May 14 and headed off for the longest *prime* thus far. As with all the 1800s, theirs wasn't the quickest car in the rally, but this women's team was making steady progress. Other faster cars caught and passed them as they pushed on through the night and into the dawn, the sun coming up bright and strong. One of the faster cars was, of course, the works-prepared Triumph 2.5PI of London–Sydney Marathon winners Andrew Cowan and Brian Coyle, teamed with Peruvian Uldarico "Larco" Ossio. Having calculated an optimum departure time, they left a while after Denton, but a combination of speed and expert driving saw them close in on the women approximately 30 miles from the finish control at La Viña, having successfully passed Tubby, André, and Rob a short while before. Rally etiquette required a slower car to allow a faster car to get past, but on this narrow, dusty mountain road lined with empty air down to the rocks and gullies below, finding a suitable opportunity was tricky. So it was that, blinded by dust and dazzling sunlight, Cowan failed to see Denton follow a sharp bend around, and the Triumph plunged over the edge.

A combination of memory and film footage allowed Rob to recall the events in stark detail. "Tubby was driving and it was a dirt road and there were plumes of dust coming up ahead of us," Rob explained. "We went around this corner and Andrew was standing there, a lone figure on the side of the road. Buggar me, we'd only been talking a couple of hours earlier. He's bleeding from the head and I jumped out with my camera. Instinct. He came over and he put his arm around my neck and he said, 'Rob, please don't film, put the camera down and help the boys.' At that spot, our heads must have touched because, in the BBC film, I'm covered in blood. It's Andrew's blood from that first encounter." While Tubby stayed with the car, Andrew led Rob and André down the side of a ravine to where the Triumph had come to rest. The scene was shocking, the car a mangled wreck. Brian Coyle and Larco Ossio appeared to be extremely badly injured, and the group realized they had to get them back up to the road. Rob and André were able to remove the car's hood and used it as a makeshift stretcher to carry the injured men up the side of the ravine, now getting help from a BBC TV crew, which had also arrived at the scene. Tubby drove off to get help, returning pursued by a station wagon, so the rear seats were folded and Brian Coyle was carefully placed in the back, his head injury looking very bad. Rob accompanied him as the wagon sped away, while Larco and Andrew followed in other vehicles.

"We went into this hospital and went right into the operating theatre with Brian and Andrew was still walking around in a daze," Rob recalled. "They were checking him out, the doctors, and when we found there was nothing more we could do, we resumed, went off and I don't think we got the allowance for the time we'd stopped in our timing but there was no argument, we never bitched about it but I don't think we were given any allowance and we were late for the next *prime* or whatever it was." It was only later that Rob realized he had forgotten to pick up his camera, which he had left on a rock by the roadside. However, the BBC crew picked it up and returned it to him at the first opportunity, confirming that they had caught the entire rescue and recovery scene on film. The Australians were also very relieved to hear that Brian and Larco were not as badly injured as they first appeared and were responding to the treatment and care they were receiving. However, it would be a few days before Andrew discovered that the pain in his neck was actually the consequence of a fracture! All three eventually made a full recovery.

On the rally went, 33 cars clocking in at La Viña, the quickest losing just 45 minutes against the target time of eight hours, while the slowest lost five hours and 35 minutes. For André, Tubby, and Rob, stopping to assist the injured crew of No. 43 added 271 penalty points to their total. There would be no allowance, not even for helping out during a disaster.

Next up was the 270-mile Bolivian Coffee *prime*, which started just past the border at Villazón, some 310 miles to the north. Another tricky speed section, not least because there would be no rest until La Paz and competitors would therefore be suffering from fatigue after the arduous efforts to La Viña. The route again took cars along mountain roads with yet more yawning chasms below. While the two quickest cars—Polish driver Zasada in a works Escort and British Brian Culcheth in his works Triumph 2.5PI—dropped just 47 minutes here, the Australians brought the 1800 home two hours and 27 minutes beyond the target time. At the finish at Potosí, renowned for its silver mines and for being one of the highest cities in the world at over 13,000 feet, they were somewhat alarmed to realize that, among the large crowds gathered to watch the cars arrive, instead of firecrackers, excited spectators were actually pitching sticks of gelignite! Jack Murray would have been proud.

After Potosí, the route stretched over 330 miles northwest to the Bolivian capital, La Paz. Remaining at high altitude, a combination of tiredness and depleted oxygen levels posed an ever-present threat to competitors, especially as any repair requirement, even a puncture, could prove exhausting. Attitudes towards using oxygen from cylinders most of the teams carried varied. Rob recalled his team's reaction when given a small tank by a retired crew. "We said, 'Well, we probably don't need it but … we may as well.' So, we put it in and old Tubby … at one stage we were getting up high and he said, 'I wouldn't mind trying a bit of oxygen.' Righto. 'Holy Christ,' he said, 'this is good! I'm away!' He liked it so much that occasionally, and there was a tap that you turn on from the bottle … he would slip it on and turn the tap on. 'How's that?' 'That's better.' In the end we ran out. We ran out of oxygen before we got to where we would have needed it!" However, Rob believed that the gradual ascension to these heights acclimatized them, which was why they never really experienced any problems.

Other than the reception from a crowd of 60,000 cheering Bolivians, and the chance to sleep after their long and emotionally draining trek from Santiago, La Paz proved uneventful for the Australian team. Recharged, they set off on the next leg of the rally, the transport stage to Cusco, and the start of the longest test section, the 560-mile Route of the Incas *prime*, opening at 22:00 on May 17. Into the night sped 39 surviving cars, making for Lake Titicaca, only this time there would be no leisurely stop to admire the waterborne traffic. Again, the 1800 pulled along quite happily, further reinforcing Tubby's mantra that, if it isn't broken, don't try and fix it—countless times, as the car was performing well, they had shunned the helpful advances of BLMC service mechanics, determined that they would only seek assistance if something was wrong. The 1800 was never going to break any speed records, but, with smart driving and careful navigation, André, Tubby, and Rob were unwavering in their plan to be in at the finish.

Rob recalled that the *prime* was a "seemingly endless drive around winding mountain roads, eventually ending on a huge flat plain at the bottom of a valley. Bloody hot as well." Into Huancayo, at an altitude of 10,500 feet above sea level, they were placed 14th out of 32 logged finishers in the overall rally positions, still able to stick to their plan to get to Mexico City. Tired but relieved, they initially thought they were suffering from oxygen deprivation when they saw a mirror image of their car coming towards them! It took a few moments to realize that this was their recce car, the 1800 they had left in Lima, laden with the components they might need if anything needing replacing or repairing after the thousands of miles their car had suffered. But why? How? "It was Evan and Jack," Rob recalled. "So, we got the shock of our lives, and I remember this vividly because it was a stinking hot day and when I saw Jack Murray … he jumped out of the car and I said, 'Christ, Jack, bloody hell, it's hot!' We'd been at it for 500 miles or something. He said, 'Wait, I'll fix that,' and he went and got a bucket of water and he chased me with this bucket of cold water and threw it all over me. He said, 'That'll cool you down!'" André, however, was extremely unamused at their appearance and antics. Green and Murray had taken it upon themselves to retrieve the recce car in Lima and meet the field with the intention of offering whatever support they could. After this brief and soggy reunion, No. 32 continued on its way to Lima, the trio unaware of the more significant implications of what their fellow countrymen had actually done.

The Peruvian capital offered teams another opportunity to rest and recharge after their herculean endeavors through the mountains, and also a chance to find a little entertainment. With much amusement, Rob recalled how he and three or four competitors, including Timo Mäkinen, went off to "a brothel." "Well, when I say it was a brothel," he explained, "out of Lima there was a bit of a bordello … and I remember…. Timo Mäkinen was a big bloke and probably the best known and the fastest of anyone and it was a big Dodge or one of those fifties, sixties cars, about 300 miles long! It had big soft springs and the driver was going to show rally drivers how to rally and we were sitting in the back pooping ourselves. We had a few beers … on the way back, Timo made sure we didn't get the same bloke again! Timo was a lovely bloke." Of course, what happened in Lima stayed in Lima, and all too soon, survivors were lining up to clock in at the departure control and head for the last *prime* before the Colombian port of Buenaventura and the ship voyage to Panama.

The road north took cars on a 710-mile stretch along the South Pacific coast to Macará, just over the border into Ecuador. "We'd heard about the condors, these giant birds, and we could see them up there," Rob recalled. "Again, I think Tubby and André were sleeping or resting and I'm doing the transport section and a bird headed for me. I could see him way ahead and he dived on me and he smashed into the windscreen and got the pillar, the driver's hard pillar and split the glass. Bloody hell! Here we are, we're there and what? We're going to get put out by a condor, this big bird?" Recovering their wits, and noting that the windshield would hold, they carried on, now suspicious of these huge birds' seemingly malevolent intentions!

They completed the 250-mile Ecuador *prime* without problems and, in doing so, maintained their 14th position overall by the finish at Cuenca. Ahead lay 730-plus miles to Cali in Colombia and being classified as finishers of the rally. However, not far from their destination, with Tubby behind the wheel, the ever-reliable 1800 blotted its copybook. The front suspension bar broke, and they had no spare in the car. Deciding that Green and Murray would undoubtedly be at their destination with all the replacement components they had stocked in the recce car, they limped on, ensuring they were among the finishers at Cali. Despite their mechanical hitch, they were even able to improve on their overall position—whatever happened now, they were secure in the knowledge that they had officially finished in 12th place.

Feelings of relief and not a little pride were snuffed out, however, when they discovered what Green and Murray had done. In their enthusiastic haste to offer support to the professional BLMC teams, they had unloaded every last 1800 component in Lima and restocked the recce car with Triumph 2.5PI parts! André was furious, knowing the spacer bar they needed had been among the stash they had stored in the survey car. Little they could do but jury-rig a repair and nurse the slightly swaying rally 1800 along the truck-infested route to Buenaventura and onto the ship.

For the most part, the voyage to Panama was generally a time of eating, drinking, and merry-making, but not for André, who had carried his grievances onboard. A heated argument raged, made worse because, back in Sydney, Tubby had requested that Green adjust the 1800's gearing ratio to allow improved lowdown acceleration and speed, which Green had overlooked. "Gelignite" Jack's explosive nature was so diminished, in fact, that, as Rob explained, "When we got off the ship, where we had to backtrack to Panama City, Jack was waiting. He had buggered off and had set up a workshop and we had instructions to go straight to that workshop and there was Jack … waiting with the welding gear and Jack welded up our rod. It was a sense of what can I do to help these blokes? Now, I don't want to make a big issue about either of those things but it was just the one bad taste in the mouth on the whole rally."

With both car and spirits restored, the Australian team set off on the last, long section before Mexico City, a trip that would cross six international borders and include two more *primes*, the 220-mile Costa Rica Coffee and the 106-mile Aztec. From Paso Canoas to Cartago, Tubby finished the speed section 87 minutes down on the target time. Then, on the final *prime* of the rally, perhaps the hardest test, given tiredness, the route's conditions, and the pressure to keep it together, he applied caution, arriving at the Mexican finish control at Tuxtepec to collect 96 penalty points.

At long last, the official finish of the rally loomed at Fortín de las Flores. André Welinski, Ken "Tubby" Tubman, and Rob McAuley had done it. They had stuck to their plan and, despite a relatively slow car, had met everything thrown at them, from helping rescue an injured team to having their stock of replacement parts go walkabout to getting into battle with a big bird. Out of 96 cars that set off from London all those weeks ago, they were 11th overall, a huge achievement given the tales of woe, collapse, and catastrophe that littered the 16,000-mile route. All that remained was a drive to Aztec Stadium in Mexico City.

At the awards ceremony in Mexico City, compatriot Wylton Dickson presented André, Tubby, and Rob with a special prize for "Unselfish Sportsmanship," including a check for $240, with acknowledgment that they had selflessly paused their competitive effort to come to the aid of Andrew Cowan, Brian Coyle, and Uldarico Ossio. It was, of course, a time for celebration. "One of the highlights was going to a nightclub in Mexico City with [Prince] Michael," Rob recalled, "and we were at a table with Graham Hill and another famous racing driver, and people in the nightclub were going mad because Graham Hill and that mob were there and Michael and I were left on the fringe because we were nobodies! He said, 'Isn't it terrific?' He was a delightful bloke."

Months later, in England, Rob went on to stitch together all the film footage he had taken during the rally, even being allowed to insert the stock taken by the BBC TV crew during the Cowan crash. He employed the services of Australian actor Charles "Bud" Tingwell, a familiar face to British film and television audiences in the 1950s and 1960s, but a film editor friend listened to the results and gently pointed out that, with all respect to Tingwell, the commentary just didn't work. It needed the urgency, the depth of someone who had actually been there. Thus, anyone watching the movie today will hear Rob's own voice as narrator, all of his wry humor and recollection front and center. Also, during this period, as Prince Michael had given him his private number there in London, Rob decided to give him a call. "'Why don't you come over to my place for a drink tonight and bring your lovely lady with you?'" Rob recalled his royal friend saying. "So, I said, 'All right, give us the address.' ... I got off the phone and said, 'Annie, we're not doing anything tonight, are we?' She said, 'No, why?' I said, 'Well, I've just been talking to Prince Michael and we're invited to go to his place for drinks tonight.' 'You've done what?!' She couldn't believe it! Beyond belief that I would have the temerity to ring Michael up. I said, 'Look.... He's a mate that I met on the rally. Forget anything else. He's invited us for a drink.' Holy Christ, I've never seen anyone so het up in all my life! ...We parked that out there and she was still fuming, 'We shouldn't be here!' We went up and knocked on the door and there was Michael, he answered the door. He said, 'Do come up,' and I introduced him to Anne. Anne immediately relaxed, and the only person that was nervous was Michael, because he's given his man the night off because he was having a drink with a friend from the rally. So, he tried to be the host, and I remember Anne wanted a gin and tonic and she ended up with a scotch and soda or something. He completely ballsed it up trying to be one of the boys!"

After the World Cup Rally, Ken "Tubby" Tubman continued his involvement in rally motorsports, both in his native Australia and abroad. Together with André Welinski and Jim Reddiex, he won the 1974 Munich-Sahara-Munich World Cup Rally and also surveyed the Australian section of the 1977 London–Sydney Marathon. He died in 1993.

In addition to his 1974 World Cup Rally victory, André Welinski went on to successfully pursue a very wide range of business and commercial ventures across the world. He died suddenly in 2002, aged 70.

Rob McAuley went on to produce many other documentaries and was also a prolific writer. Ever a supporter of other writers and journalists, his generous and enthusiastic contributions to this book have been invaluable. Rob passed away in January 2020. He was 86 years old.

32

Trans-Argentina

The 52 cars still in competition by Montevideo were met by huge crowds as they arrived at the special *parc fermé* alongside the city's Colombia Palace Hotel on the banks of the Rio de la Plata or River Plate. As previously reported, a few were also met by armed police!

In accordance with the rally regulations, only competitors were allowed to work on bruised and battered cars in *parc fermé*, and, as darkness fell, with a large, voluble, and appreciative audience on the other side of the fence, crews tended to repairs by torchlight. Among the busy folks fixing or replacing damaged or expired components, the British team of Reg Redgrave, Bob Freeborough, and Phil Cooper needed to sort a suspension problem with No. 54, their BLMC Special Tuning–prepared 1800. A wheel was seriously out of alignment, and they had covered over 400 miles without recourse to repair after a roadside gully momentarily got the better of them. Freeborough and Cooper were seasoned and competitive Mini drivers, but Redgrave, a plastics recycling professional from Essex, had never rallied before and was no doubt having the time of his life, even if he wasn't exactly having much sleep! The Jopp/Cave/Kahn 1800 needed urgent attention to its cylinder head, and the Cortina Savage V6 of London–Sydney Marathon veterans Peter Graham and Leslie Morrish continued to suffer with the same overdrive problems it had had all across Europe. A common modification for European cars of the 1960s and 1970s, and a precursor to the commonplace fifth gear on manual boxes today, overdrive reduced engine stress and fuel consumption at high speed over long distances.

The watching crowd no doubt released the loudest cheer for the Moskvič team when, in lieu of a crane and winch or rotation cradle, a 10-strong team of Russians, ably abetted by any other willing competitor, picked up a 412 and put it on its side so welding repairs could take place underneath. Mark Kahn wrote of attempts to maintain strict regulations in special *parc fermé*: "John Sprinzel wearing an armband that said *Secretary of the Meeting* dashed up crying 'No assistance! No assistance!' But no further assistance was required."[1]

After 48 hours of driving, navigating, getting lost, avoiding obstacles, searching for gasoline, changing tires, jury-rigging repairs on dark and muddy trails, and, in the confines of more than one car, biting tongues and suffering in silence in the face of arrogance, ignorance, and/or incompetence, the crews of 52 cars fell into their beds and slept. Unfortunately for them, on May 11, 1970, it would be an early start.

Spirits were dampened as cars drove onto the Buenos Aires-bound ferry that morning as news came through that a Brazilian rally official had been killed in an automobile accident after helping close a control before Montevideo. José Crespo was travelling with two other rally officials when their car overturned near the city of Florianópolis. Few distractions were on offer during the three-hour crossing of the River Plate, although there was discussion about the German warship, the *Graf Spee*, that became involved in battle with British naval vessels after it had embarked on a campaign of destruction of allied cargo vessels in the South Atlantic during World War II. The *Graf Spee* eventually retreated up the estuary of the River Plate and docked at Montevideo, with British ships watching for signs that the German ship might make a dash for it back out into the Atlantic. Realizing the ship was trapped, its captain gave the order to scuttle the *Graf Spee* in the River Plate, and the wreckage was still there, just 36 feet down, as the Buenos Aires-bound ferry bore cars and crews across the expanse of water.

The dockside at Argentina's capital city was thronged with eager onlookers, and a military band heralded the competitors' arrival. Some crews signed autographs while others gathered themselves up for what lay ahead, a 120-mile neutralized section to the first Argentinian *prime*, the Pampas, a 200-mile slog across flat grasslands, which would offer either dust or mud, depending on weather conditions. If wet, the risk of flash flooding could not be ruled out, as the Citroën recce team had discovered a few months earlier. After that, there would be an even longer *prime*, the Trans-Argentine, 380 miles of mostly straight, unsealed roads, ideal for fast cars. Hazards would be more dust plus horses and herds of beef cattle. Then up and over the pass into Chile before heading northwards to Santiago, the entire section's time allowance being 28 hours.

Thus, with a police motorcycle escort alongside, and cheered on by roadside crowds, 52 rally cars departed Buenos Aires in order of standing and headed for Cañuelas where the police would depart and competitors would head on independently to the start of the Pampas at Saladillo.

Jim Gavin opened the *prime* control at one minute past nine in the evening on May 11, having quickly moved it across the road as previously described. Early arrivals took advantage of the service point, topping up fluids and replacing tires, courtesy of Dunlop. Then, with books stamped and start times recorded, they were off into the plains and the dash to Espartillar. For the frontrunners, it was fast, dry, and very dusty, making the passing of slower cars ahead extremely difficult. Nevertheless, 19 cars arrived at the finish control without penalty and the top-five leader board remained unchanged. Late starters on the *prime*, however, were faced with sudden and persistent rainfall, and the dust quickly turned to mud—this was where the Marshall Maxi ran out of puff. Also out with mechanical problems were the little SAAB 96 sedan of moviemaker Colin Taylor and Bert Jennings and the Cortina Savage V6 of Morrish and Graham.

The steward at the Espartillar control was Gerry Ryan, one of event organizer John Sprinzel's former co-drivers, and by the time he closed things up, 48 cars had headed off for the next *prime*, the Trans-Argentine, starting at the deep-water port of San Antonio Oeste on the Gulf of San Matias some 380 miles away. The route took competitors first south to Viedma on the northeastern edge of the Patagonian region and then due west to start the *prime* and drive. And drive. And drive! Mile after mile of extremely bumpy wide-open tracks with little or no traffic, finally beginning to rise up towards the Alpine-style architecture and chocolate shops of Argentinian ski resort Bariloche and the foothills of the Andes, Hillman GT competitor Rob Lyall recalling that route-finding was sometimes problematic across Argentina where there appeared many roads but only one on the map! Having selected what they thought was the correct road, they could only hope they hadn't made an error as it stretched on for 200 miles—they had, in fact, made the correct decision.

Somewhere between Espartillar and San Antonio Oeste, after an against-all-odds run through Italy, France, Spain, and Portugal, and then managing to get to Rio and keep going, the Anglo-Australian team of Evan Green, "Gelignite" Jack Murray, and journalist Hamish Cardno went out. Their repeated attempts to obtain the major repairs required had been thwarted, and the Triumph finally gave up the ghost out on the pampas when a piston went through the cylinder head. The British RAF Team of Flight Officer Donald Soames-Waring, Flight Lieutenant Andrew Thwaite, and Chief Technical Officer George Crichton had a lucky escape when their Cortina GT hit poorly lit road works near Bahía Blanca, necessitating three hours of repair work. They made it to Bariloche with 20 minutes to spare.

Forty-seven cars made it to the finish of the Trans-Argentine, although once again the Red Arrows Maxi was in trouble, driving without brakes for 60 miles, while the 1800 of Peter Jopp, Willy Cave, and journalist Mark Kahn was experiencing a constant lack of power and the Maxi of Smith/De Rolland/Watson, now the leading women's team, was increasingly in need of replacement shock absorbers. Not so lucky, the sole Spanish entry of Carlos del Val, Jaime Lazcano, and Victor Ochoa failed to reach the finish control and was out. Once again, the top-five leader board remained the same, and a total of 13 cars arrived at Bariloche without incurring penalty.

Surviving teams had no time to stop and admire the winter resort, however, so pressed onwards and upwards to the Puyehue Pass at an elevation of 4,000 feet, over the border into Chile and then down again, along the shore of Puyehue Lake before turning right at Osorno for the fast, 575-mile run north along the Pan-American Highway to Santiago de Chile. The Chilean capital meant surviving teams would have travelled a total of 8,300 miles since leaving London, effectively the halfway mark, where "drivers enjoy a rest before the roughest rallying tests ever."[2] Sadly, the RAF Cortina GT was late to Santiago and therefore disqualified. Also falling by the wayside here was No. 5, the Yugoslavia diesel-motor Peugeot 404 of Ivica Vukoja, Streton Đorđević, and Nestor Milanov, which "hit a bullock square on, punching the engine back into the cabin. The animal was still whole, but minus its head as an indication of its crash worthiness."[3] No. 9, the British Cortina Lotus of Ian Harwood, Frank Pierson, and London–Sydney Marathon veteran Barry Hughes, and No. 75, the Mercedes-Benz 220D of Canadian police officers Malcolm "Jock" Wilson and James Walker, were also out. Making it to Santiago but only after being arrested when their Hillman hit a 14-year-old boy as they drove through Los Angeles, south of the capital city, were British pair Rod Badham and Rob Lyall. Rob explained that, as they negotiated the crowds of spectators spilling onto the road, a traffic police officer had waved them forward at a junction. Apparently not looking where he was going, the young

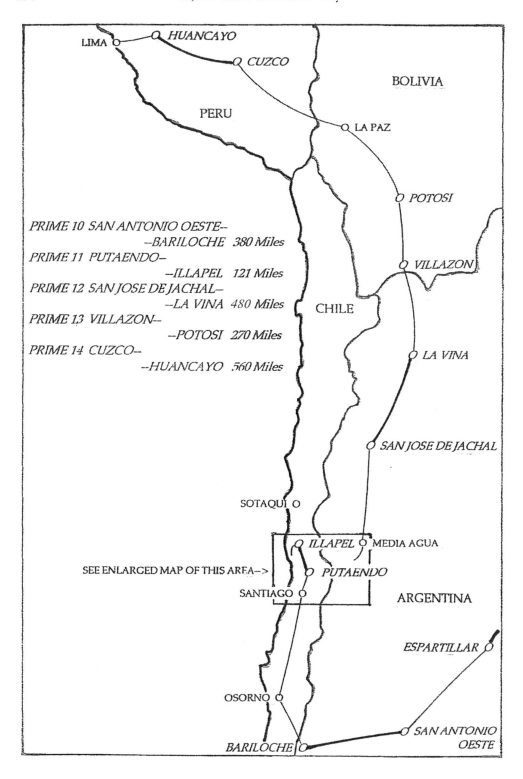

The route from Espartillar to Lima (map by Martin Proudlock).

No. 62, the SEAT 1430 of Spanish team Carlos Del Val, Jaime Lazcano, and Victor Ochoa (courtesy Guido Devreker).

boy cyclist made a dash for it, collided with the Hillman, and came through the windshield. The British *Daily Telegraph* initially reported that the boy suffered leg injuries. A police officer had witnessed the incident and confirmed that they were not at fault, so the Hillman duo was eventually released, the delay costing them eight hours and 11 places on the leader board. Tragically, subsequent reports claimed that the boy had succumbed to his injuries.

At the time of writing, it could be argued that female competitors in motorsports are still perceived as unusual. The fact that in 2020, two women, Jade Edwards and Jess Hawkins, were scheduled to compete in the British Touring Car Championships for the first time since Fiona Leggate in 2007 suggests that motorsport still fails to attract or encourage participation by women. In September 2020, the international motorsports governing body, the *Federation Internationale de L'Automobile* or FIA, reported that, for the first time since the 1970s, there would be two all-women teams competing in the 24 Hours of Le Mans endurance race. In April 1970, among the many male crews lining up to start the London to Mexico Rally at London's Wembley Stadium, there were just four all-women teams, two of which included veterans of the London–Sydney Marathon completed just 18 months previously. Much had been expected of hugely successful Irish rally driver Rosemary Smith on the way to Sydney, and now much was expected again, not least because French women's rally champion Claudine Trautmann would be Rosemary's key competition for the "Ladies' Prize" at Mexico City. Another female team, that of Jean Denton, Liz Crellin, and Pat Wright, however, was determined not to let Smith or Trautmann have it all their own way!

33

The Beauty Box
(Part One)

In her notes, carefully prepared for the many presentations and talks she has given about her life in rally motorsport, Pat Smith makes some fascinating observations about the state of play in 1970, from both British and international perspectives. Ecology and the environment were hardly day-to-day concepts, for one thing. "We were not green," Pat observes. "Fast cars were desirable. Motoring was a pleasure. Speed limits outside towns had only been introduced five years before. There were many fewer cars on the road, and we thought North Sea oil would never run out. Global warming was a thing of the distant future." She also highlights the popularity of long-distance road rallies across Europe and notes that these were increasingly including special stages—time-specific, multi-terrain sections that posed additional challenges to the many international competitors pushing their cars to the finish.

Pat's grandfather Bill established Allison's Garage in Brough, east of England's renowned Lake District, in 1921. The business prospered, and, eventually, Bill's son took over the management. It was into this setting that Patricia Allison was born. "It was cars, cars, cars, all the time—talking about them, servicing them in the garage and so on—and my dad was very encouraging," Pat explains. "He encouraged me tremendously. Cliff [Pat's brother], he started to race in 1952, I was only … 14 and I had a pair of smart, white overalls and acted as a mechanic and went all over the countryside to motor races. … I passed my driving test about two months after I was 17 and never looked back."

With her father's blessing, Pat had the chance to be trackside and watch her brother's progress as a racing driver: Cliff Allison went on to compete in many high-profile international racing events, including the Le Mans 24 Hours, the 12 Hours of Sebring, four Formula One Grand Prix races, and the Targa Florio, driving for Lotus and Ferrari. Perhaps inevitably, therefore, Pat grew tired of watching and helping where she could, and decided she wanted in on the action. So, in 1958, she borrowed her brother's Speedwell-tuned Austin A35 and entered her first local event, the Keswick Rally, persuading her boyfriend to serve as co-driver/navigator. "Well, he wasn't very good at the maps and we were lost within 10 miles … of the start," Pat recalls. "So, I'm tearing around these lanes, trying to get back on track and trying to catch up with things, and I overdid it on a corner, went up a bank on the right-hand side, turned the car onto its … side on the road. I managed to get out and we got it righted and we continued, and we did eventually get to Keswick, but we were out of the event by this time." Although not the most auspicious start to her life in rallying, the experience not only showed her that this was something she wanted to do again but also underlined the importance of navigational skill, a talent that would become hugely significant in the years to come.

Next up, she was presented with the opportunity to co-drive on an event, which introduced her to map-reading in a speeding car, during daylight and at night. More local rallies followed with Pat in the co-driver's seat until, at the 1959 London Motor Show, her father introduced her to Marcus Chambers, the British Motor Corporation's competitions manager. "We were at a dinner. I don't even know which dinner it was," she explained, "but I used to go to the Motor Show. My father used to go every year, because he had a motor business, and my brother, who was racing at that time … was quite famous … We saw them at another table and my dad said, 'Come on, let's go and talk to them.' So, we did, and we chatted about this and that and Marcus said, 'I'm looking for a co-driver for Nancy Mitchell, for the Portuguese Rally in December.' … and Marcus rather liked the idea that he had Pat Moss, whose brother was Stirling, and he would have Pat Allison, whose brother was Cliff. It would give them a bit of publicity." Nancy Mitchell had been racing since 1947 and competed in several European rallies throughout the 1950s, including the Monte Carlo, the Alpine, the Liège-Rome-Liège, and the Lisbon, in which she won the coveted women's prize, the *Coupe des Dames*, in 1953. BMC signed her in 1956, and she rewarded them with the European Ladies' Rally title two years in a row.

Marcus Chambers "sent me down to High Wycombe to meet Nancy Mitchell, who was a formidable woman," Pat explained. "Some people called her Mitch the Bitch, but she was charming when she wanted to be. She was charming, very sophisticated…. Nancy took me out in her own car, her Riley … and she gave me some fancy clocks to put on my knee and some maps and things and said, 'Right, take me from there to there in this exact amount of time' and so on. So she put me through a few navigational paces and that was it: we went and had tea and she put me back on the train to London. She'd given me the impression that she thought I was okay because I can remember sitting in the train back to London thinking cor, this is going to be exciting! Sure enough, Marcus asked me to do the Portuguese event with her." Nancy and Pat were one of the first teams to rally a Mini, the ubiquitous and hugely successful small car that went on to dominate the European rally circuit during the 1960s. Finishing the event, Pat was then offered the opportunity to help with surveying the forthcoming Monte Carlo event, during which she met Pat Moss and Tish Ozanne. As Nancy Mitchell was now considering retirement, Chambers decided to pair Tish and Pat, which would lead to a very happy working relationship for the next 14 years.

Pat's season with BMC came to an end in May 1960, but she continued to find herself being asked to co-drive on rallies throughout the 1960s, this time for private entrants. In 1969, she and Margaret Lowrey were the highest placed British entry on the Polish Rally, driving a Ford Escort and finishing 11th overall, and it was this achievement that brought them to the attention of the British *Woman* magazine—launched in 1937, the magazine remains in publication to this day. Towards the end of 1969, the magazine's motoring editor, Jean Barrett, was looking for ways to promote her column and the magazine itself. Learning about the planned 16,000-mile endurance rally from London to Mexico City, she approached the publishers with a proposal: how would it be if she entered the event as part of an all-women team, sponsored by the magazine? With images of a car emblazoned with the *Woman* magazine logo hurtling across two continents, they gave Barrett the go-ahead, so she began scouring for suitable team members. With their Polish Rally success, Margaret and Pat fitted the bill perfectly, so they were approached and quickly signed up. However, learning she was pregnant with her daughter, Corinne, Lowrey withdrew, leaving a rally driver-sized gap in the line-up, which was swiftly filled by circuit racing driver and 1968 London–Sydney Marathon veteran Jean Denton.

Denton had begun racing in 1963, first in a Mini and then in a Formula Three Cooper. Through her then husband, she met Tom Boyce, a gifted Canadian combustion kinetics specialist, and together they began rallying a Mini on club events in England. Boyce also persuaded her to replace the Mini with an MGB, which he spent time tuning to improve its speed and performance, and it was this car that they eventually entered in the 10,000-mile Marathon, finishing in 42nd place out of 56 finishers. With her mix of road rally, endurance rally, and circuit racing experience, plus her background in PR, she was an ideal replacement for Lowrey, and so it was that Pat and Jean Denton found themselves with Jean Barrett in a BLMC 1800 on a survey drive to Yugoslavia during winter 1969–70, partly to get an idea of what was to come and partly to introduce Barrett to the potential realities of non-stop endurance rallying. "We spent most of the time changing wheels from studded to un-studded tyres and putting on snow chains, according to the depth of the snow," Pat reported. "We did some all-night driving over high and twisty tracks and went for long periods without sleep or sustenance…. All this was enough to put off Jean Barrett." Now in need of another team substitute, Elizabeth "Liz" Crellin was recruited as Barratt's replacement. Crellin had won the British Trials and Rally Drivers Association Silver Star driver's championship two years in a row and had competed in the 1969 RAC Rally with her husband, rally driver Ron Crellin, who would go on to assist on the World Cup Rally.

With the team in place, attention turned to a car suitable to take on the 16,000-mile rally. With its Marathon pedigree and reputation for strength and reliability, BLMC's Special Tuning department took delivery of an 1800, one of several it was commissioned to prepare. The car was reduced to its bare shell before having its seams rewelded and strengthened. An increased capacity gas tank was fitted, and its standard hydrolastic suspension system was upgraded. Underneath, a strengthened oil pan guard was installed, and further protection was added to the car's transmission, exhaust, and drive shaft. The 1800's standard 108 cubic-inch motor was bored out to 115 cubic inches and uprated with an MGB camshaft. Special Tuning also added adjustable altitude breathers to regulate the fuel mixture during the rally's lofty, oxygen-depleted sections. The 1800's interior was cleverly redesigned to allow for both comfort and practicality and, to reduce overall weight, fiberglass doors, hood, and trunk lid were added. As a finishing touch, the car's royal blue bodywork was detailed with a white roof and, with a contemporary nod to the fact that the car was to be crewed by women, its headlamp cowls were adorned with pink flashes.

DAILY MIRROR WORLD CUP RALLY   PASAPORTE DE PARTICIPANTES

	PILOTO 1 CREW MEMBER 1	PILOTO 2 CREW MEMBER 2	PILOTO 3 CREW MEMBER 3	PILOTO 4 CREW MEMBER 4	DETALLES DEL VEHICULO
NO. **91**				FOTOGRAFIA DEL PASAPORTE PASSPORT PHOTOGRAPH	
NOMBRE / NAME	JEAN DENTON	PATRICIA MARGARET WRIGHT	ELIZABETH CRELLIN		MARCA / MAKE: MORRIS
FECHA DE NACIMIENTO / DATE OF BIRTH	29·12·35	6·4·38	3·5·45		REGISTRO / REGISTRATION NO: NOB 254 F
LUGAR DE NACIMIENTO / PLACE OF BIRTH	WAKEFIELD	BROUGH	SUTTON COLDFIELD		MODELO / MODEL: 1800 MK II
NACIONALIDAD / NATIONALITY	BRITISH	BRITISH	BRITISH		AÑO / YEAR:
SEXO / SEX	FEMALE	FEMALE	FEMALE		COLOR / COLOUR: BLUE + WHITE
OCUPACION / OCCUPATION	RACING DRIVER	HOUSEWIFE	HOUSEWIFE		VALOR TOTAL (DOLARES AMERICANOS): $2500
ESTADO CIVIL / MARITAL STATUS	MARRIED	DIVORCED	MARRIED		CILINDRADA / CAPACITY: 1798 CC
DOMICILIO / ADDRESS	13 LADBROKE WALK, LONDON, W.11.	13 FOXTHORN PADDOCK, BADGERHILL YORK	CLEMATIS COTTAGE EXCHANGE ROAD, ALREWAS NR. BURTON ON TRENT		NO. DE ASIENTOS / NO. OF SEATS: 4
					MARCA DEL RADIO / MAKE OF RADIO:
NOMBRE DEL PADRE / FATHER'S NAME	MOSS	ALLISON	GILLESPIE		CANTIDAD DE NEUMATICOS DE REPUESTO / NO. OF SPARE WHEELS:
NOMBRE DE LA MADRE / MOTHER'S NAME	TUKE	WILSON			PAIS / COUNTRY: ENGLAND
PASAPORTE NO. / PASSPORT NO.	159607	728987	P350435		MOTOR NO. / ENGINE NO: 18H/127/H/135
EMITIDO EN / ISSUED IN	LONDON	LONDON	PETERBOROUGH		CHASIS NO. / CHASSIS NO: M/H58D/107A
FECHA DE EMISION / DATE ISSUED	10·2·1970	20.4.1961	13·1·1970		CARNET NO. / CARNET NO:
LICENCIA DE MANEJO EMITIDA POR / DRIVING PERMIT ISSUED BY	A.A.	A.A.	A.A.		EMITIDO POR / ISSUED BY: R.A.C.
FIRMA / SIGNATURE	J. Denton	P.M. Wright	E. Crellin		FECHA DE EMISION / DATE OF ISSUE: SELLO DEL RAC

The Beauty Box crew: Jean Denton, Patricia "Pat" Wright, and Elizabeth "Liz" Crellin (courtesy Ted Taylor).

To assist with routine maintenance, the mechanical team even color-coded nuts, bolts, and spanners. Somewhere along the line, the car was nicknamed "The Beauty Box."

While Special Tuning toiled over this and other cars in readiness for the rally, the women made their own preparations for the unprecedented motorsports journey. Trips to the gym, medical advice, inoculations, and a visit to a decompression chamber were the order of the day, as were Spanish classes and, for Pat, the complicated machinations of arranging childcare for her three young children during her absence. With her PR skills, Jean took responsibility for communications with the magazine and for organizing all the paperwork and currency necessary for crossing countless borders between England and Mexico. Pat's father also helped, dumping a wreck into a ditch and having them use their Tirfor winch to drag it back out again, which they did with aplomb.

Woman magazine offered several fashionable but impractical items for the team to take on the rally, including cosmetics and even modish wigs, and tried to persuade them to wear up-to-the-minute white jumpsuits, which they rejected out of hand as hardly practicable for the messy grind of an endurance rally. They did, however, take the proffered disposable paper underwear, which came in handy on the rally whenever they needed to wipe the car's oil reservoir dipstick!

Departure day arrived, and, having been drawn as No. 91, Jean, Liz, and Pat had a fair wait before they were finally flagged away by England soccer team manager Sir Alf Ramsey at 12:21 on April 19, 1970. Crowds cheered and waved as the rally cars headed south out of London and towards the Dover seaport, before a short ferry voyage to France and the very long transport section across Europe to the time control in Bulgaria's capital, Sofia. Roles within the team had been agreed upon: Jean would be lead driver on the speed sections, Liz would provide relief driving duties, and, with her experience and meticulous eye for detail, Pat would be in the navigator's seat. "The drive was uneventful," Pat recalled of the section to Sofia. "I drove much of this; it is the navigator's lot to drive the easy sections."

Thirty-seven hours after leaving the French ferry port at Boulogne, they arrived in Sofia, the congregation of international rally cars coinciding with celebrations in honor of the 100th anniversary of Lenin's birthday. Crowds jostled and heaved to see the multi-colored automobiles motor in, collect their stamped and signed-for arrival times, and, depending on time available, grab some rest. Regulations stipulated arrival times per car based on their departure time from each previous time control. Therefore, as No. 91 left Boulogne at 20:31 on April 19, the allowable time of 37 hours to Sofia meant they needed to clock in before 09:31 on April 21, which they did with a few hours to spare, so they quickly found the hotel they had booked and grabbed a couple hours of precious sleep.

When the time came, Jean, Pat, and Liz were clocked away from the Sofia departure control, and they headed back the way they had come before turning left and heading cross-country to Titograd. "On the way, we were stopped by police for speeding, but a Russian competitor, who spoke the language, intervened and charmed the man," Pat reported. Others weren't quite so lucky, being forced to hand over on-the-spot fines, regardless of whether they had actually broken speed limits or not! No further interruptions impeded progress, so the women arrived at the start control for the Montenegro *prime* in good time. The team donned their crash hats, one advantage of which was "that the intercom enabled a co-driver to communicate with the driver (and listen to her swearing) while the third person tried to sleep." With Jean at the wheel, No. 91 sped away, the team trying to keep to the instruction from *Woman* magazine to just get to Mexico City. Thus, with a target of time of 65 minutes to complete the section, and with gravel, rocks, and a series of extremely scenic but precipice-lined hairpin bends to contend with, Jean got them to Kotor in 86 minutes from start to finish.

An extremely challenging drive to the next *prime*, the Serbian, took them along the Adriatic before turning north to Glamoč, a very difficult climb, which required fastidious map work from Pat. Off into the speed stage, on a corner, the women encountered two boys on a bicycle. With no time to react, the bicycle struck the 1800, sending the boys flying. Fortunately, there were no human injuries, but the bicycle fared worse, prompting the women to raid their cash box and give the boys money for repairs. Dodging other vehicular transport that lumbered alarmingly towards oncoming rally traffic, Jean arrived at the Bosanska Krupa finish control 48 minutes down on the target completion time.

The route now took cars out of Yugoslavia and over into Italy, headed for Monza and an overnight stop, a drive that gave Jean and Pat the chance to take turns in napping as Liz steered the 1800 to the time control. All was well as they entered the famous racetrack and delivered the car to the BLMC service crew before depositing it into *parc fermé*, and checking into their hotel to sleep in readiness for their early start

Crossing the Austro-Hungarian border in the Beauty Box behind No. 51, the SAAB 96 of Bert Jennings and Colin Taylor (courtesy Pat Smith).

the following morning, with a scheduled departure at 08:08. At this stage, they were thrilled to learn they were the leading women's team in the rally.

Now, cars headed for the Ligurian coast and then a scenic drive along the Italian Riviera before turning inland and up to Ville San Pietro and the start of the San Remo *prime*, a stretch familiar to any competitor who had driven the San Remo Rally. Pat reported that they had notes for this speed stage, put together from a previous visit, and these helped Jean bring them into the finish at Camporosso just 10 minutes beyond the two-hour target time through more tight hairpins and sheer drops. The team was working extremely well together as they set off for the penultimate European *prime*, the Alpine, another familiar section for seasoned Monte Carlo Rally competitors that included a passage control at the stunning, snaking Col de Turini mountain pass on the way to the start control at the rural, four-way junction, Les Quatre Chemins. The team hugely enjoyed this challenge through the French mountains, taking the 1800 to the finish at Rouaine with 24 penalty points, even though professional rivals Rosemary Smith and Claudine Trautmann were quicker, which meant Trautmann and co-driver Colette Perrier were now the leading female crew.

After Rouaine, the transport stage that followed was long and tiring, taking cars out of France, across Spain, and into Portugal. Driving duties were taken up by Liz and Pat, not least because Jean had started to feel unwell and was therefore banished to the back of the car so she could sleep. They needed her to be on form for the last European *prime*, the Arganil, a 45-mile sprint through pine forests to Pampilhosa, not least because it would be a speed section in darkness. Arriving in good time, they were able to have the 1800 serviced before heading out into the stage at three o'clock

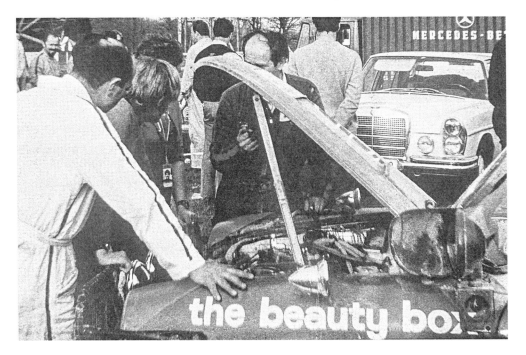

The BLMC service crew attends to No. 91, Monza, April 22 (courtesy Pat Smith).

At the bullfight in Lisbon: (*top row, left to right*) André Welinski, Evan Green, unknown, Ken "Tubby" Tubman, BLMC competitions boss Peter Browning, Pat Wright (in her *Woman* magazine wig!), Brian Culcheth, "Gelignite" Jack Murray, and Uldarico "Larco" Ossio; (*bottom row, left to right*) BLMC mechanics Michael "Mick" Hogan, Dudley Pike, Martin Reade, Ron Elkins, unknown (courtesy Pat Smith).

in the morning, where they battled with the narrow, dusty track while managing to avoid the complicated recovery effort of another competitor's car, the Argentinian Peugeot 404 of Gastón Perkins and Jack Forrest Greene, which had left the road and needed winching out of a gully. Collecting another 26 penalty points at the finish, the exhausted team pointed the car towards Lisbon and the end of the European section of the rally, arriving to discover they were in 26th place overall, out of 71 survivors. They were welcomed with bouquets of flowers and, ever mindful of their official sponsor, even sported the fashion wigs *Woman* had provided for the many photo opportunities at the Portuguese capital's harbor, even though pictures prove that a wig doesn't travel well on an endurance rally! No matter—they had booked their passage to Rio de Janeiro.

34

Triumph and Tragedy

Alongside the Carozzi pasta and cereal factory, the Santiago arrival control opened at one minute past midnight on May 13. Once clocked in, competitors were required to drive a short, neutralized section to the *Escuela Militar de Suboficiales*, or Military School of Deputy Officers, adjacent to which was a special *parc fermé* and the opportunity for competitors to work on their cars, again as long as they received no assistance from elsewhere. Thus, under the watchful eye of huge crowds, professional and amateur crews alike labored on their vehicles as the rain began to fall. Contemporary film footage shows works team mechanics, and even Ford boss Stuart Turner, shouting instructions to their drivers and navigators.

Entertainments on offer in Santiago were either an organized cocktail party at the city's Carrera Sheraton Hotel or a long shower and straight to bed. No doubt age and energy levels dictated which was selected as competitors braced themselves for the next day, the next week, the next 8,000-plus miles, and, most of all, the drive up into and over the Andes mountain range, an elevation of 15–16,000 feet. How would engines perform at those oxygen-poor altitudes? Would the much-discussed oxygen supplies be needed? Given the scary stories of oxygen-starvation symptoms of wild euphoria and/or severe despondency, how would the teams manage, all the while trying to keep cars going, keep performance up, keep delays to a minimum? The 4,900-mile stretch from Santiago to Cali and then Buenaventura in Colombia would involve the aforementioned altitude driving plus five *primes*, including the rally's longest at 560 miles. All this in an allowable time of 117 hours to reach Cali before a neutralized run down to Buenaventura and a ship crossing on May 22. None but the brave or reckless would have opted for cocktails!

As cars began to reach Santiago, rally organizers were busy getting marshals to the correct locations further along the route while also problem solving. Two marshals were flight-delayed, and there was all likelihood they wouldn't get to their control sites. Another reported that his car had broken down, also jeopardizing the control set up. "The next call was from the guys checking out the Aqua Negra Pass over the Andes," John Sprinzel recounts. "There was thick snow blocking the route and no sign of the promised bulldozer."[1] Finally, a report was received that a small earthquake had sealed off a section of the route in Argentina. Thus, as previously reported, there followed a mad scramble to redesign the route, get it printed and out to competitors, and send Speedy up to establish a new control.

Armed with revised instructions, 43 cars departed the control at Huechuraba,

Ice creams in Santiago! Ford GB mechanic Mick Jones (*left*) and Ford GB competitions boss Stuart Turner outside *parc fermé* (courtesy Pat Smith).

just north of Santiago's city center, and then drove directly northwards, again on the Pan-American Highway, to the city of Putaendo and the start of the severely truncated Chilean *prime*. Reduced from 200 miles to 121, competitors would be allowed 90 minutes to get to Illapel, taking in a passage control at the small town of Chincolco. Teams would need to be fast, accurate, and thorough on this *prime*, averaging 70 miles per hour on a narrow track over rocks, gravel, and deep ruts. According to Brian Robins, "the target time … was impossible; the organisers were out to net penalties and thin the field."[2]

Sent on their way by Valerie Morley, marshal at the Putaendo control, the teams found that the scramble over the *prime* bore out part of Robins's assertion. As cars careened into the hastily established control at Illapel to have their books stamped by Speedy, while there were no major surprises, all cars lost time with event leaders Mikkola and Palm picking up 51 penalty points. Of special note was the performance of the privately entered Datsun 1600 SSS of Dutchmen Jaap Dik and Rob Janssen. They'd had more than their fair share of mechanical and circumstantial difficulties all along the way and were, of course, responsible for their own repairs and servicing, so achieving 10th fastest on the Chilean was indeed an admirable feat. In fact, any suggestion that organizers were looking to reduce the number of competitors, founded or otherwise, could not be given weight as 42 cars made it to Illapel, leaving just the British Army Motoring Association Peugeot 504 of Moorat and Shaw behind, defeated by differential trouble. Having performed so well in South America thus far,

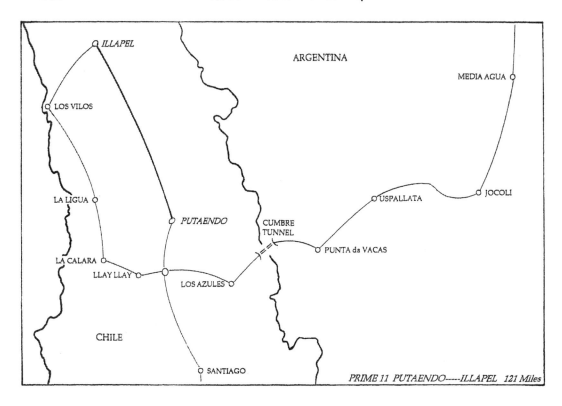

The route from Santiago to Media Agua (map by Martin Proudlock).

the Hunter/Mabbs Porsche was delayed over three hours on this *prime*, the low-slung sports car's exhaust system not coping well with the terrain.

Now, the new route all but doubled back on itself, taking competitors south along the coast to Los Vilos, La Ligua, and La Calara before turning left and heading for Los Azules and the Argentine frontier, to be crossed at an elevation of 10,500 feet via the Cumbre Tunnel at Las Cuevas, a two-mile railroad tunnel serving the Transandine Railway and apparently operating one-way traffic on alternate days. "It was supposedly closed for the Rally," Red Arrows driver Terry Kingsley wrote, "but we felt very confined and expected to see the 'light at the end of the tunnel' and hope that it was not that of an oncoming train."[3]

Forty-two cars rattled and jolted through the tunnel and thus over the border into Argentina, the Argentine Auto Club generously picking up the cost of entering the country. Then it was northwards towards Rodeo via small towns and villages, descending from Punta da Vacas to Uspallata and Media Agua before arriving at the hastily replanned start of the Gran Premio *prime* at San José de Jáchal, 480 miles that would climb to 15,000 feet and offer up gravel, bridges, straights, and hairpins with "don't look down" drops. "Just as well for the fast boys that it is dark here," the rally's official program stated. "They can't see over the edge!"[4] Originally recorded as 510 miles, the start control's location change shortened the stage by 30 miles.

All 42 cars made it to the control without incident. Open for 11 hours from 20:00 on May 14 to 07:00 on May 15, the times and distance offered competitors the

The Cumbre Tunnel, near Las Cuevas, Argentina (courtesy Brian Culcheth).

opportunity to tackle the Gran Premio in darkness or by daylight. Dubbed "owls" and "skylarks," the leading works teams opted for two different approaches here with the BLMC Triumphs and the lead Citroëns setting off as soon as the control was open, while all but one of the Ford works crews deciding to hang back and wait until dawn. Depending on arrival times from the border, other competitors also had the option to leave in darkness or at dawn. Thus, at exactly 17 minutes past eight on the evening of May 14, with Pat Wright navigating and Liz Crellin on hand to take the wheel as required, Jean Denton steered the Beauty Box 1800 into the *prime* and was away on the 480-mile slog to La Viña. Sometime later, London–Sydney Marathon winner Andrew Cowan also headed off in the works Triumph 2.5PI. Part of another three-up team, Cowan's brother-in-law Brian Coyle was navigating and Uldarico "Larco" Ossie on relief driving duty as and when required.

Red Arrows team leader Terry Kingsley described the trail as "like a giant dried riverbed, almost devoid of vegetation … incredibly dusty and cars way ahead could be tracked by the dust clouds separating them."[5] Opportunities for faster cars to overtake slower ones were scarce, either because the track offered few passing places or because swirling, impenetrable dust clouds blinded pursuing drivers. To add to the mix, the trail skirted drop-offs and there were enormous boulders strewn about.

There is an unwritten but accepted etiquette in rally sport that if you are caught by a faster car and that car flashes its headlights, as soon as it's safe to do so, you move to the side and let it pass. Rauno Aaltonen was definitely an advocate of this tenet, going so far as to make all attempts to push a slower car out of the way if they weren't prepared to pull over. Of course, in a huge cloud of trailing dust, a pursuing car would need to make all efforts to ensure the slower car before them was aware of their presence.

So it was that slowly, inexorably, Andrew Cowan caught and passed slower cars along the hazardous track, mile after mile, pure concentration for both driver and navigator, especially during hours of darkness. Cowan was in 10th place at Santiago and was undoubtedly determined to improve his position on this, the second longest *prime* in the rally. With the skill and dexterity that, after 10,000 miles of competition, took him to victory in Sydney, Australia in December 1968, Cowan maneuvered the Triumph sedan across this barren, deserted landscape where oxygen was less than plentiful. The long straights that this *prime* offered were really bringing the fuel-injected 2.5PIs, faster by design than the nimble Escorts, into their own, and Cowan was taking full advantage. With just 30 miles to go before the finish control in the village of La Viña, Cowan spotted another car ahead, another car trailing dust. With Coyle on point and Ossio asleep in the back, Cowan quickly bore down on the slower car. It was the Beauty Box, the British *Woman* magazine-sponsored blue and white BLMC 1800, sticking to the goal of just getting to Mexico City. Cowan now had them in his sights, ready to pass as soon as the opportunity presented itself. It didn't. Denton suddenly followed the track hard right, but, with visibility at a dust-shrouded minimum, Cowan was wrong-footed, and, as he braked in vain, the Triumph left the road, flipped, and landed on its roof some 20 feet below. The immediate aftermath and its consequences, all captured on film, are previously described, but, needless to say, Coyle and Ossio were injured and hospitalized and all three were out of the rally.

Three cars had real struggles to get to the finish control at La Viña. As previously described, Patrick Vanson's Citroën was delayed two-and-a-half-hours, having been in equal eight position with teammate Bob Neyret at Santiago, and calamity upon calamity befell Tony Fall's works Escort, including the need for co-driver (and soccer ace) Jimmy Greaves to be on constant puncture duty, plus suspension and half shaft damage, which ultimately saw a wheel completely disengage, and Fall having to push the stricken Escort into control on just three wheels and hub with Greaves steering. Ever with an eye toward newspaper sales, the British press continued to play up Greaves's part in all of it with a headline "Soccer ace Jimmy limps in with a push."[6] One can only assume rally ace Tony Fall was either oblivious to all the attention his co-driver was receiving or simply gritting his teeth and getting on with matters at hand. In another works Escort, Mäkinen and Staepelaere also slipped down the rankings after suffering brake problems.

For the frontrunners, a few changes resulted from the Gran Premio. Yes, Mikkola and Palm remained top dogs, fastest to the finish control losing just 45 minutes, but now Aaltonen and Liddon had moved up and were running second overall, after a second fastest run to La Viña. Zasada and Wachowski were third fastest, and Culcheth and Syer fourth in their 2.5PI, which placed them third overall. Battle was now joined for the top three places after this *prime*, although Hopkirk, Verrier, Zasada, Mäkinen, and Neyret were definitely not about to give up!

After the epic and extremely eventful *prime*, survivors would now make for the next, the Bolivian Coffee, some 300 miles north and, with the clue in the name, over the frontier from Argentina to Bolivia at La Quiaca, more than 11,000 feet above sea level, and on to the start control at Villazón, just across the La Quiaca River. With Cowan's retirement, 41 cars were now on their way north, just under half the number that had departed London almost a month before. Two more casualties would be added to the list by the time the field arrived at La Paz, the Bolivian capital.

Having incrementally improved their standing amid the ranks of the privately and commercially sponsored entries, highly experienced rally competitors Terry Hunter and Geoff Mabbs were now forced to bid farewell to their hope of reaching Mexico City. In Huacalera, about 110 miles from the Bolivian frontier, their blue, Bio-Strath–sponsored Porsche 911 would go no further when the car's air filter disengaged, allowing dust and grit to get sucked into the engine. Fortunately for them, they were rescued and looked after by a local German expat landowner.

Somewhere before the Bolivian frontier, the Ken Bass/Graham Waring BMW 2002Ti encountered a wayward truck, which took out the car's radiator, their second. The first had been destroyed when they ran into the back of the British Royal Navy 1800 before Montevideo. Without another replacement, they somehow managed to get the truck driver to tow them back to his home, where his repair of the damaged item enabled them to continue.

Forty cars arrived at the start control at Villazón, and after the journey through Argentinian wine country, it was now time to start climbing again as the Bolivian Coffee *prime* would take them upwards to the finish at Potosí, one of the world's highest cities at 13,400 feet. With their roadbooks attended to by Gerry Ryan, cars set off on the 270-mile trail with five hours allowed before penalties would be incurred. They had now been travelling for two days without rest, other than catnaps here and there, so all but the fittest were experiencing fatigue as they encountered a "pounding tortuous mountain run, with more dizzying drops, at night."[7] These dizzying drops would curtail another entrant's London to Mexico City adventure.

Fastest into Potosí were two cars, the Escort of Zasada and Wachowski and the Triumph 2.5PI of Culcheth and Syer, both losing 47 minutes, with the Verrier/Murac Citroën close behind. Among the private entrants, first-time rallyist Reg Redgrave's 1800 shared 10th fastest time with Peter Brown's Hillman GT, Patrick Vanson's Citroën, and Gastón Perkin's Peugeot 404. However, missing at the Potosí control was No. 21, the Moskvič of Ivan Astafiev, Alexander Safonov, and the last-minute replacement for listed competitor Stassis Broundza, Gennadi Garkusha.

Never destined to win prizes for speed, the Soviet Moskvič fleet nevertheless was making steady, relatively trouble-free progress, first across Europe and then through Brazil, Uruguay, Argentina, Chile, back into Argentina, and now in Bolivia. Other than a crash involving one of the Moskvič service wagons, all had been fine. Now, however, pressing on through the mountains, No. 21 left the road and plunged 60 feet down. Safonov and Garkusha escaped without injury, but Astafiev sustained a rib fracture and needed hospitalization. Despite the apparent seriousness of the accident, "to the amazement of all … [the car] managed to reach the control at La Paz."[8] Sadly, irrespective of this example of Soviet stamina and derring-do, they were out of time.

No. 21, the Moskvič of Ivan Astafiev, Alexander Safonov, and Gennadi Garkusha (courtesy Guido Devreker).

British pair Ken Bass and Graham Waring ran out of gas on the way to Potosí and, in the absence of any gas stations in evidence, were compelled to knock on doors in the hope they could beg, borrow, or buy fuel to enable their BMW 2002Ti to continue. A response in the affirmative came on the condition that Bass and Waring be guests of honor at a wedding party. Two hours later, replete with cake, celebration wine, and, at last, some gasoline, the confetti-covered pair were able to carry on, last into Potosí before it closed. Back in England, Bass's wife was bemused to read a press headline that announced her husband had married a mayor's daughter in exchange for gas!

Once competitors had managed to get their books stamped and signed by the somewhat indisposed Jim Gavin at Potosí, they embarked on a 330-plus-mile stretch, skimming first Lake Poopó and then Lake Uru Uru, both at 12,000 feet. Onwards via the silver-mining town of Oruro, the trail led competitors to La Paz and, if they were making good time, potentially up to 30 hours of rest. Somewhere along this desolate section, the Red Arrows Maxi required a replacement alternator. Placing a reflective red warning triangle in good sight for other cars approaching the Austin, team member Michael Scarlett set about removing the faulty component, which was dumped behind the car. Once the new alternator was fitted, a mysterious disappearance took the team aback. "When we thought better of discarding the old unit and also collecting the emergency triangle," Terry Kingsley explained, "both were missing. Even using the car's lights to cover the area, it was obvious that they had been taken. Scary stuff."[9] Less alarming, but still extremely challenging, the Bass/Waring BMW suffered a broken damper. Not able to disengage the spring, Waring hitched a ride to the nearest town to see if he could get the spring compressed while Bass set about changing the carburetor jets. With a small group of fascinated rural Bolivians gathering and gasoline dripping, Bass's spanner slipped and created a spark. A small fire started! Quickly retrieving their water tank, he tried to extinguish the flames but without success. Suddenly, some of his spectators stepped forward and threw handfuls of sand onto the fire, which of course did the job but left Bass the task of cleaning the exposed carburetors! They were eventually able to continue to La Paz, where crowds lined the route, saving the biggest cheer for another 2002Ti, that of Bolivian team of William Bendeck, Dieter Hübner, and Jorge Burgoa.

The orange and white striped Austin Maxi of Rosemary Smith and co-drivers Ginette De Rolland and Alice Watson had been making steady progress all across Europe and South America. With the Marshall's Maxi stuck in the Pampas mud, there were now only three all-female teams in contention for the women's prize at Mexico City, and while the Trautmann/Perrier team had taken Europe, Smith was not letting the French women have it all their own way. Each *prime* thus far in South America had first the Citroën, then the Maxi, then the Citroën headed for the women's prize. Back at Wembley, with the typical contemporary misogyny of the time, Lord Stokes, chairman and managing director of British Leyland, had looked at the Maxi team and said, "'Girls, if you get as far as Dover, I will be happy.' It was just as if he was patting a little girl on the head with this patronizing remark."[10] Now, on the way to La Paz, the Maxi's fan belt went. Smith popped the hood and climbed out to inspect things while Watson took the opportunity to stretch her legs. With a little help from

No. 54 team leader Reg Redgrave (*left*, with an unknown individual), happy to have reached La Paz (courtesy Teresa Jensen-Redgrave).

Tony Fall, who stopped to make sure all was okay—a common and constant gesture so many competitors made to others, especially in these desolate places—the Maxi was ready to get back on the road. But where was Watson? "When we found her," Smith recalled, "she … was covered in cactus flies … and they were sucking her arms, face and any bit of skin that was exposed."[11] Judicious use of the car's compulsory fire extinguisher saw the biting flies off, and the women resumed their rally. However, Watson developed a severe allergic reaction to the bites, forcing Smith to hustle the Austin down to La Paz, in the dark and in the face of oncoming trucks, to get Watson medical attention, allowing them to continue, even though it took a day or two for Watson's medication to really work.

This section was also where the works Triumph of Paddy Hopkirk, Tony Nash, and Neville Johnson suffered driveshaft damage and where Bill Bengry's Rolls-Royce Silver Shadow made its surprise, and most welcome, reappearance. With a little help from No. 3 thrown into the mix, Hopkirk made it to La Paz and took sixth place overall, but he was now 112 minutes down on continuing leaders Mikkola and Palm—a lot of time to make up before Mexico City. In fact, barring disaster, the prospect of catching the Finnish pair seemed increasingly unlikely with second-placed Aaltonen and Liddon 62 minutes down and third-placed Culcheth and Syer 65. Rounding out the top five were French pair Verrier and Murac and Polish duo Zasada and Wachowski. Worth reflecting then that by La Paz, Hannu Mikkola and Gunnar Palm had somehow contrived to lose just three hours and 52 minutes from the target time, while the slowest car, the Donner brothers' Ford Capri, was down 44 hours and a minute. That said, given the fact that 57 cars had now retired since London, no doubt Paul and Martin Donner were just happy to still be in competition!

Some three miles above sea level, the Bolivian capital was a hive of activity as increasingly fatigued cars were serviced and repaired, and increasingly fatigued men and women seized the chance to rest. They needed to: next would be the longest *prime* of all, the 560-mile Route of the Incas, and then the highest point of the rally, the Ticlio Pass at almost 16,000 feet. At that rarified altitude, even the practiced task of changing a wheel could render a competitor exhausted. Perhaps that decompression chamber training might come in useful after all!

35

The Beauty Box
(Part Two)

There were thousands of miles yet to go before they hit the Gran Premio *prime*, so, with the Beauty Box safely loaded onto the SS *Derwent*, Jean Denton, Pat Wright, and Liz Crellin happily joined other Rio-bound competitors aboard a VARIG Airlines jet on May 1, 1970. Spirits were high as the plane hurtled across the Atlantic, many rally passengers about to visit Brazil and South America for the very first time. For at least one team member, it was a very first plane journey!

Competitors disembarked into the evening heat and humidity at Rio's Antonio Carlos Jobim International Airport and, customs and immigration formalities done with, loaded onto a bus that carried them to the Hotel Glória with its roof-top swimming pool. "We were very well looked after," Pat reported, "with invitations from the British ambassador, Sir David Hunt, the Golf Club, local motor dealers, automobile clubs and friends." Ahead lay six full days before the rally restarted, and Pat, Jean, and Liz joined other competitors to visit Sugar Loaf, the Corcovado with its 98-foot Christ the Redeemer statue, and Rio's famous beaches. Competitor, author, and motoring journalist Mark Kahn recounts the tale, for many endurance rally enthusiasts now legendary, of the Russian competitor seeing the Redeemer for the first time: "He asked a Ford mechanic: 'Who is that?' 'Stuart Turner.' 'Who put it up?' 'Stuart Turner.' 'What is he saying with his arms outstretched?' 'Where are the spares?'"[1]

May 8 finally arrived, however, as had the *Derwent*, so competitors travelled to the city's docks to process all necessary paperwork before retrieving their cars. Now against the clock for getting vehicles to *parc fermé*, and then to the ceremonial start later that evening, rally teams and individuals carried out hasty checks of their rally cars and, where possible, performed any last-minute maintenance or, in some cases, rudimentary repairs—as a Special Tuning–prepared car, when necessary, No. 91 was able to take advantage of the slick servicing setup BLMC had organized for its professional teams, time allowing.

Pat reported that, at the rally's departure that evening, "the crowds of spectators were enormous—quite frightening—and there were scuffles and lots of police and general chaos." The women had to endure this as they waited for their turn to be flagged away, cars now leaving in order of position at Lisbon, and while they were no longer towards the back of the field, as No. 91, there were still 25 other rally cars that would set off before it was their turn.

At last, at 20:52 on May 8, No. 91 was away and headed for the actual start on the edge of the city, a drive classified as neutralized and with an allowable time of one hour. Unimpeded, they were then signed and stamped out of the start control and were on their way to Montevideo in Uruguay, via hundreds of miles of asphalt and dirt roads and three *primes*, all with an allowable time of 41 hours in total. "Population seemed sparse," Pat observed of the road to Ventania, "signposts rare, maps inadequate, and our British Leyland roadbook was invaluable."

For competitors, the South American "war of attrition" began early, and the field was already reduced by the time the Parana *prime* start control was reached. The Parana presented 125 miles of dirt road, to be completed in 90 minutes if points were to be avoided. Although this section claimed a few more casualties, Jean, Pat, and Liz logged a respectable time of 125 minutes at Bateias, actually one minute quicker than Rosemary Smith in the *Evening Standard* Maxi. The next *prime*, the 120-mile Rio Grande, proved much trickier as, even though it had been shortened in the face of heavy rain and flooding further along the original route, the women had to contend with a fire from dumped fuel at the start and generally much tougher terrain and conditions before reaching the finish at São Joachim, receiving an additional 86 penalty points. They were, however, still in the mix, unlike 15 other teams who had seen their South American adventure come to an end all too soon.

On the transport stage to the next *prime*, the Uruguay, general road conditions did not lend themselves to restful sleep, and, on a rest break in the back of the 1800, poor Pat found herself wondering whether wearing a crash-hat might be a good idea between speed sections, her head at one point making contact with the car's ceiling! However, Pat recalled that Uruguay met them with sunshine, and they successfully negotiated the 125-mile *prime* from Tacuarembó to Salto, 41 minutes beyond the target time and 26th fastest, shared with another Special Tuning–prepared 1800, that of Willy Cave, Peter Jopp, and Mark Kahn.

On the road to Montevideo, No. 91's starter motor gave out, which called for some careful thought when they needed to stop, making sure there was enough clearance to enable a push start from helpful volunteers, but they made it to the capital city and the arrival control on the banks of the Rio Santa Lucia, although they exceeded the 41 hours allowable time by two hours and eight minutes. Again, making sure there was room for pushing the car back out, they dropped the 1800 into *parc fermé* and collapsed into bed at the pre-booked Colombia Palace Hotel. Rest was essential since the next section, into Argentina and across to Chile in the west, would be arduous and very, very long.

Competitors were required to take their cars across the River Plate by ferry to Buenos Aires, a three-hour crossing, and, while they lined up for loading, Pat, Jean, and Liz again found themselves the center of press interest. "We were interviewed in Spanish—classes paid off. The Argentinians loved the women entries," Pat recalled. "They called us *Las Chicas* and wrote lots in their local papers." Civilian passengers were equally fascinated in the rally as the ferry chugged its way west across the wide estuary and, to add to the occasion, crowds and even a brass band were awaiting them on the Argentinian capital's dockside. Local authorities had decided to provide the rally with a police escort out of the city, which eventually became a race between

Jean Denton and No. 91, Montevideo, May 10, 1970 (courtesy Pat Smith).

leading cars and police motorcycles! At the first opportunity, the women sought out the BLMC service team and had their starter motor repaired.

Pat recalled that the first Argentinian *prime*, the Pampas, was uncomplicated, so she left it to Jean and Liz while she slept. "Brian Culcheth complained that it was too easy and the prize money spread out too thinly," she reported. That said, although a number of cars completed the stretch without penalty, this was where Pat's great friend and frequent rally partner, Tish Ozanne, came to a very muddy end! Escaping without incident, No. 91 continued on from the finish control at Espartillar and made for San Antonio Oeste, via Bahía Blanca, Pat driving the rain-slicked asphalt roads that eventually led to the windswept plains of Patagonia and the Trans-Argentine *prime*, a 380-mile trial that would take cars to Bariloche, the Andean foothills, and the Chilean frontier.

Once again, Jean and Liz were in the driver's and co-driver's seats as the miles sped by. The long distance meant the need to stop for gas, which was dispensed from drums at designated "fuel dumps," all provided by Castrol. At last, the popular Argentinian ski resort loomed, Pat noting that the landscape resembled Switzerland on a grander scale. Checking in 32 minutes beyond the target time, No. 91 then followed the route along the edge of Lake Nahuel Huapi before climbing up to the Puyehue Pass and across into Chile, stopping at the service point where the 1800's external blower horns were made secure in readiness for the descent to Osorno—with snow on the ground, the rally was definitely offering up every season! Pat reported that they took the black dirt road down the other side of the mountain, "keeping out of the way of trucks with no lights and buses, to the junction with the Pan-American

Highway, which would have taken us all the way to Mexico City, but the organizers had other ideas."

Driving from Osorno to the Chilean capital was a straightforward but very, very long journey of almost 580 miles. Organizers had specified a time allowance of 28 hours for competitors to complete the section from Saladillo in the east to Santiago in the west of the continent, and while a few other competitors faced a challenge or two heading north on the Pan-American Highway, Pat, Jean, and Liz drew into the control by Santiago's Carozzi factory unhindered, although they were clocked in 80 minutes down on their scheduled arrival time of 01:46 on May 13. At this point, after the thousands of miles travelled thus far, the careful negotiation of tricky speed sections, seemingly errant trucks, and other commercial vehicles and encountering rain, sun, snow, mud, and dust, they were still only halfway to Mexico City! Tired and relieved, the women were happy to discover that they were in 24th position overall out of 43 surviving teams and welcomed the chance for a 24-hour pause before tackling the oxygen-starved heights of the Andes and the long haul through Central America to the finish.

It was a very early start from Santiago on May 14; No. 91 was scheduled to depart *parc fermé* at 05:48 and then the rally restart control at Huechuraba in the city's northern limits at 06:28. All competitors had been advised that the next *prime*, the Chilean, had been rerouted as a consequence of poor weather conditions, which also rendered the original crossing point from Chile back into Argentina impassable. Deft

Santiago service stop: (*left to right*) No. 90, BMW 2002Ti without wheel; the Beauty Box, with cardboard box on hood; No. 33, Peugeot 504 worked on by two unidentified men; and one of the BAMA Peugeots with an unknown man in black leaning over (courtesy Pat Smith).

reorganization now routed cars on a shortened speed trial and then a new frontier crossing above the Paso de la Cumbre, the Cumbre Pass, to Las Cuevas, via an operational railroad tunnel, another feat of logistical dexterity. Keeping railroad tracks as a theme, the new *prime* route took cars along a disused line between Putaendo to Illapel, north of Santiago. Pat reflected that they were not sorry that the route had been shortened as even in its truncated state, it still offered up a twisting, hilly, and boulder-infested 121-mile test. Nevertheless, Jean successfully bounced and swerved the 1800 to the finish control, 24th fastest out of 42 survivors, all three women determined not to try to break speed records or risk damage to the car, not least because it was holding up so well thus far.

After looping back south towards Santiago again, the route then turned east and began the climb up into the Andes proper via, as Pat explained, "a pass known as the stairway to the stars" and through the railroad tunnel. Then they crossed the border into Argentina and drove north to the next *prime*, the start control having been moved from Rodeo to San José de Jáchal, Pat's handwritten notes showing the revised control address and reduction in target time for completion from nine hours to eight. The Gran Premio would be the second longest speed and time trial of the entire rally, an energy-sapping 480 miles. "It went through desert, gorges and passes and every car trailed a long plume of dust behind it so it was difficult to overtake," Pat explained. This was an exercise in stamina and concentration for Pat, Liz, and Jean, trying to juggle precision on the twists and turns with keeping one eye on the clock and another in the rearview mirror, should a faster car bear down on them.

One car that caught No. 91 in the dust cloud was its Special Tuning–prepared stablemate No. 3, the 1800 of Peter Jopp, Will Cave, and motoring journalist Mark Kahn, who highlighted the challenge in these extremely difficult conditions. "We picked up the tail lights of another car," he wrote. "It was Jean Denton's Beauty Box, which had started minutes before us. The dust thrown up by its rear wheels was impenetrable…. It was 90 kilometres (56 miles) … before Jean could pull over and we were able to pass."[2] Negotiating the obstacles thrown up in such conditions therefore also required an exhausting blend of focus and patience, and so it was that on the last 30-mile stretch to the finish control at La Viña, Andrew Cowan's powerful Triumph 2.5PI caught up with No. 91 and Cowan began looking for an opportunity to pass the slower 1800. Again, Jean was juggling giving her attention to the road and to Pat's precise navigation instructions, while also scanning for a passing place. "We could see Andrew Cowan's Triumph some way behind and suddenly his dust plume disappeared," Pat reported. "He had left the road and crashed…. We could see that others had stopped to assist so we kept going to advise the people at the next control." On reflection, Kahn believed that "it was the loss of Cowan that … was decisive in defeating British Leyland's hopes of winning the rally."[3]

No doubt a little shaken, Pat, Jean, and Liz clocked in at La Viña, the rigors of this grueling 480-mile endurance test evidenced by the time it took them from start to finish—over 12 hours, 258 minutes beyond the organizer's seemingly impossible target of eight hours. However, there would be no rest until La Paz, so, with gritty determination and a change of driver so Jean could at least relax a little, the women pressed on, beginning the ascent into Bolivia. "We didn't notice the altitude until we had a puncture at 12,000 feet and found we hadn't the energy we usually had to do the job of changing a wheel," Pat reported. So thin was the air, in fact, that, when the team stopped to eat at Villazón, the Bolivian border town and start of the next *prime*, the Bolivian Coffee, Pat sat down at a restaurant table and immediately passed out! When she came to, she found a medic administering a restorative remedy of coca leaves, which quickly had the desired effect, allowing the women to get going on the 270-mile speed trial to the silver-mining city of Potosí.

The Bolivian Coffee *prime* was "diabolical," Pat said, "all in darkness on a narrow, twisty road with no barriers. We changed drivers frequently." Taking absolutely no chances, they were checked in at the finish, Jim Gavin recording their time as 205 minutes beyond the five-hour target. Here in Potosí, BLMC had arranged for teams to eat with a local distributor, and the women were relieved to get to the enclosed location, such was the push-and-shove of eager Bolivian spectators all around. This repast was most welcome as ahead lay the 10,000-feet high Altiplano, the Andean plateau that would take competitors to La Paz.

On the journey, the 1800 began losing motor oil, forcing the women to make frequent stops to refill the reservoir, but they made it to La Paz, delivering the car to the BLMC mechanics for a thorough servicing. They could not, however, fix the problem, which meant that Liz, Jean, and Pat would need to carry on with replenished supplies of Castrol. First, however, the 24-hour pause offered them the delights of eating fish caught from Lake Titicaca, sleeping in real beds, and even browsing local shops and markets to buy a souvenir or two. Thus rejuvenated, they began the next leg of the rally from the Bolivian capital to Lima, capital of Peru, a 25-hour slog that would include continued altitude driving, the 16,000-foot Ticlio Pass, and the longest *prime* of all, the 560-mile Route of the Incas.

"We passed through the frontier post from Bolivia into Peru at Desaguadero without even stopping, handing out our printed passports to the enthusiastic border guards," Pat reported. "The organisers had done a wonderful job of smoothing our passage." The *prime* itself was tough, but as they were able to tackle it in daylight, they were treated to scenes of extraordinary landscape and vistas, the narrow track snaking back and forth up into the mountains with clear views down. Jean and Liz shared driving duties, studying the undulating road ahead while listening to Pat's instructions, until tiredness required Pat to drive the final 70 miles to Huancayo in northern Peru. Pat was full of admiration when she learned that Claudine Trautmann had not only driven the entire *prime* herself but reached the finish fifth fastest! A combination of caution and repeated stops to replenish engine oil saw Pat clock in at the control four hours and 43 minutes beyond the 11-hour target. The descent towards Lima offered yet more extraordinary views and, at the Peruvian capital, they were happy to learn that, out of 30 surviving teams, they were 20th overall. Less happy news came from the BLMC service crew, however, as the persistent oil leak was as a result of a cracked oil pan, not something they could repair. A stopgap sealant remedy was therefore administered, and, once the 1800 was delivered to *parc fermé*, again they luxuriated in the simple pleasures of sleep, food, a trip to a hair stylist, and some souvenir shopping. There was even the special treat of receiving letters from home, a joy for Pat as these came from her three young daughters.

La Paz market during the rally rest stop (courtesy Pat Smith).

Loaded with yet more supplies of motor oil, No. 91 headed off from Lima on the 35-hours-allowable section to Cali in Colombia. Before that, however, lay Ecuador and its namesake 250-mile *prime*, a mountainous stretch from Macará to Cuenca, with views overlooking jungle that would take competitors across the equator. Unfortunately, the temporary make-do fix applied by the BLMC mechanics at Lima just couldn't withstand the punishment inflicted on the 1800, and they were soon leaking oil and stopping for top-ups, which contributed to their 187-point penalty at the finish control. Undaunted, they forged onwards, arriving at Cali and therefore safe in the knowledge that, whatever happened next, they had achieved the official rally classification of "finisher," 19th out of 26 survivors.

After Cali, a perilous drive to Buenaventura brought them to the impending ship crossing to Panama, via a brief conflagration at a local hotel where, Pat explained, local officials posted an armed guard to safeguard teams from the ever-present threat of local bandits! Happy to finally escape the humidity and dubious comforts of the hotel, competitors joined their cars, civilian passengers, and a few retired rally teams aboard the MS *Verdi*, on which teams were afforded the opportunity to kick back after their heroic efforts thus far.

Docking at Cristóbal at the northern end of the Panama Canal brought heavy rain and a potential danger for Pat, Liz, and Jean. Their 1800 had emptied its entire reservoir of engine oil onto the ship's deck, and any attempts to start the car would be ruinous. "A shrewd travelling controller guessed our problem and removed the rotor arm so that the car had to be pushed off," Pat reported. "We were eternally grateful for his kindness." However, even with an oil refill and fresh supplies, another 51 hours lay

Sailing into a storm: aboard the SS *Verdi* bound for Panama (courtesy Pat Smith).

between them and Mexico City, so there was no certainty that the Beauty Box would hang together, especially as there were still two more difficult *primes* to come.

West out of Panama City and the roads began to deteriorate as they headed for the Costa Rican frontier and its namesake *prime*, 220 miles from Paso Canoas to Cartago. The women nursed and coaxed the ailing 1800 along the rough route through coffee plantations, again pausing frequently for more top-ups of oil, and eventually received their finish control stamp and signature from Valerie Morley, picking up 104 penalty points for their efforts. Of greater priority now, however, was simply meeting the challenge of driving the car the remaining distance, and surviving one last *prime*, to get to Fortín de las Flores, the official finish of the rally.

With that familiar feeling many drivers have when they know they have a problem but need to continue on the journey, fingers crossed that the destination will be reached, Pat, Jean, and Liz carried on, enduring the seemingly endless transport section out of Costa Rica and through Nicaragua, Honduras, and San Salvador, encountering many a boisterous crowd determined to wrest a trinket or two from each passing rally car and even rolls of thunder mistaken for artillery shells as they traversed Guatemala!

Somehow, they successfully parlayed the final *prime*, the Aztec, and its unexpected dangers, including a landslip over which a band of local road workers practically man-handled the car, and it was therefore with great emotional relief that Pat Wright, Liz Crellin, and Jean Denton drew into the hotel at Fortín, received a raucous musical welcome, and promptly threw themselves into the hotel pool, fully clothed! The blue and white (and pink!) BLMC 1800 had done it. Thanks to the careful

The Beauty Box at the border between Costa Rica and Nicaragua (courtesy Pat Smith).

stewardship of these three women—their stamina, prudent driving, and expert navigation skills—it had held out, even if it had left a small oil slick across Central America. The three were delighted to learn that, out of the final 23 cars that would drive the neutralized section from Fortín to Mexico City's Aztec Stadium the following day, they were 18th overall and, as a result of the Trautmann/Perrier Citroën's desperate retirement so close to the finish, runner-up for the women's prize behind Rosemary Smith, Ginette De Rolland, and Alice Watson.

Jean Denton continued her involvement with automobiles, taking senior managerial roles with a number of commercial garage companies before becoming head of PR for the Austin-Rover Group. She was awarded a life-peerage, becoming Baroness Denton of Wakefield in 1992 and went on to serve British Prime Minister John Major's government in the Northern Ireland Office. She died in 2001.

Elizabeth "Liz" Crellin carried on rallying during the 1970s, frequently co-driving for Pat Moss, before turning her attention to competitive equestrian events. She died in 2013.

Pat's superior navigational skills saw her continue competing throughout the 1970s, regularly co-driving for Tish Ozanne and Margaret Lowrey and reuniting with Liz for the 1970 RAC Rally and the 1971 Welsh Rally. Today, Pat remains a hugely respected and very welcome presence at occasional rally and endurance motorsports reunions and anniversary events. Her contribution to this book has been invaluable.

36

Driving on Top of the World

After the brief respite—including drinks with the British ambassador—in La Paz, it was time to move on, and so, with rally organizers John Brown and Dean Delamont doing the honors at the airport's departure control, 39 teams began their journey to the Peruvian frontier at Desaguadero. Time allowed to cover the 1,150-mile section to Lima, the Peruvian capital, was 25 hours. British RAF Red Arrows team driver Terry Kingsley described it as "a nightmare." "The road wandered and reversed itself time after time," he remembered, "making you consider driving straight down the hillside in the hope of intercepting the track lower down."[1]

Across the border competitors found themselves driving along the shores of Lake Titicaca, the vast saline body of water that lends itself to the mythology surrounding the Incas, the ancient peoples of the Peruvian Andes, whose empire stretched beyond contemporary borders into Argentina, Bolivia, Ecuador, Chile, and Colombia. From the incongruously warm waters of the lake to the snow-capped peaks of Janq'u Uma, Qalsata, Huayna Potosí, and Mich'ini, to name but a few, this was a place like no other. Sadly, for many competitors, their departure from La Paz was in darkness, and, to exacerbate things further, a nighttime storm made conditions difficult.

The road took cars at a maintained elevation of 12,500 feet through the cities of Puno and Juliaca before descending slightly to the Incan Empire's capital, Cusco, from where the twisting, icy, mountainous switchback trail of the Route of the Incas *prime* would begin. If John Sprinzel, John Brown, Tony Ambrose, and other event organizers had ever feared that the London to Mexico World Cup Rally would prove embarrassingly easier than intended, as was suggested when 39 surviving cars arrived at La Paz, they need not have worried. By the time competitors crawled, collapsed, or cruised into Lima, so very many miles away, the field would be substantially thinned.

With the dawn creating fire-like dazzle off the snowy peaks, Donald Morley stamped and initialed roadbooks, and the 560-mile *prime* was on. And up! Following some of the *GP Nacional de Carreteras Caminos del Inca*, or Rally of the Incas route, it snaked back and forth, sometimes above the clouds, other times through mist, always demanding concentration. The sensorial impact was relentless, with rocks and gravel drumming cars' undersides and dust encroaching on anywhere to which it had access, including the human body. Add to the mix the fact that oxygen was in short supply while tire rubber was at perpetual risk, and this odyssey into the Andes was, at times, beyond tolerance for many. Punctures were an epidemic. Ford works driver Tony Fall and co-driver Jimmy Greaves incurred and endured 11, all told! While Paddy Hopkirk sang the praises of BLMC engineers' ingenuity in developing for the works Triumphs the gasoline metering system that addressed the threatened assault on internal combustion engine principles, others suffered the consequences. The Red Arrows' Maxi suffered the twin enemy of no power and poor fuel as the team nursed the car up and up. Aaltonen's Escort suffered oil pan guard damage. Mäkinen's engine mountings gave away, although he ingeniously got them rewelded courtesy of a village en route. The Jopp/Cave/Kahn 1800 struggled with rear suspension problems, and the works Escort of Zasada and Wachowski suffered damage not long into the *prime*. Although they somehow obtained parts from an ordinary road-going car, they lost time at a service point while the rally-prepared suspension was restored.

Onwards and upwards the cars went, and still the war of attrition continued. Before Cusco, as previously reported, the Neyret/Terramorsi car broke its timing chain and could go no further. Then, into the *prime*, the Verrier and Murac car expired with suspension trouble, meaning the DS21 that had left Rio in third place, and the team that had repeatedly placed themselves in the top 10 for each *prime*, was out. Also failing to make it to the end of the *prime* were No. 84, the Moskvič of Emmanuil Lifshits and Victor Schavelev, and two Argentinians entries: No. 42, the Volvo 142S of Jose Araujo and John Batley, and No. 33, the Peugeot 504 of Carlos Zicavo, Aleides Specos, and Alfredo Verna. The automotive carnage was summed up by Datsun 1600 SSS driver Rob Janssen: "'It's like a graveyard out there…. I saw five cars damaged or broken along the road.' Tony Fall called it 'a bloody disaster. I've never known such a bad day in eight years' rallying.'"[2]

Any car that made it to the Huancayo finish control, the 75,000-strong crowd, and the familiar (not least because he was Donald Morley's twin brother!) face of Erle Morley would find no respite on the way to Lima as first the trail took them on to La Oroya, still at over 12,000 feet, before descending the 115 miles to the Peruvian capital on the south Pacific coast. As described before, this was where the British Army Motoring Association Peugeot 504 of Majors Preston and Bailey yielded to fuel injection troubles. In addition, although the Donner brothers finished the *prime* (with just 19 minutes to spare), altitude sickness had really taken its toll on them and they opted not to continue in competition to Lima in their Capri.

Despite heroic efforts, a run-in with the law, and completing the Route of the Incas, the Badham/Lyall Hillman GT was also too late to Lima and was therefore out of the rally. Through Bolivia they had had an encounter with an errant donkey pulling an elderly woman along by a rope. Rob Lyall recalled that Rod Badham hit the donkey to avoid the woman, later wondering if this had been the right choice, given the damage done to the car! Water was pooling on the ground at the Hillman's front end, but they were unable to lift the hood to inspect the extent of the problem. What to do? Presently, an army truck rumbled along, so Rob hitched a lift to its destination, the army base itself. Struggling to overcome the language barrier, he eventually managed to persuade those present to have the truck tow them to the next settlement, about 20 miles farther on. The car and its crew were deposited beside a collection of mud huts, one of which astonishingly revealed itself to be a workshop, complete

No. 79, the Datsun 1600 SSS of Rob Janssen and Jaap Dik (courtesy Guido Devreker).

with a large number of tools. However, before they could begin attempts to explain what they needed, the army base commander arrived, angry that Rob had somehow entered his secret camp! An international incident was only avoided when a young American appeared, working there to assist local farmers to rear sheep, and with his proficiency in Spanish, explained the plight of these two rally men. Thus, with the army truck pulling one way and the American's jeep pulling the other, the GT was straightened enough to get the hood open, revealing that the fan had holed the radiator and the header tank. When Rob slyly explained that the British Army could easily fix the damage if they were present, the Bolivian commander snatched the offending item, returning two hours later with the part completely repaired! This allowed Rob and Rod to continue; they made the next control just in time and carried out further repairs.

On they went, encountering the perilous dust clouds preceding cars threw up and having an extremely frustrating tussle with one of the Soviet Moskvičs that, as Rob recalled, resolutely refused to allow the faster GT to get past. Sometime later, they noticed the water temperature was increasing and discovered that the earlier collision damage had loosened the engine mountings, which in turn had damaged the bottom radiator hose. Again, providence intervened in the form of another truck, which towed them to the next settlement where weld-repairs were carried out. Unfortunately, 500 miles further on, the welding failed, Rob wryly recalling that Rod instructed him to go find a block of wood to wedge into the motor's bosses, no mean feat given that they hadn't passed a tree in a while! Eventually deciding to use their bottle jack, they carried on, more cautiously as they were now down to their last replacement bottom hose. They just needed to get to Lima, where Hunters were assembled under license, and all would be well. Tin-mining truck travel had been paused for the rally, but Rob and Rod were so late coming down from the mountains towards Lima that the mining traffic had resumed, which added to their lateness. And even though marshal John Brown knew that they were on their way, and therefore held the Lima control open for longer than scheduled, the GT appeared just five minutes after closure.

Frontrunners at Huancayo were Mäkinen and Palm, losing just 81 minutes, followed by Aaltonen and Liddon with 92, and Culcheth and Syer losing 99 minutes. Other relative flyers here were the French women, Trautmann and Perrier, consolidating their lead in the women's category, and the privateers Reg Redgrave, Bob Freeborough, and Phil Cooper, who moved to ninth place overall at Huancayo and seventh by the time they arrived at Lima for a rest stop of 18 hours.

Therefore, of the 32 teams that not only endured the mammoth, high-altitude grind that was the Route of the Incas, did their level best to achieve and maintain the average speed of 51 miles per hour needed to avoid penalty, but also got to the end before Morley closed the control, 30 cars were destined to move on to the Ecuador *prime*, the Colombian city of Cali, where they would be classified as finishers, and then down to Buenaventura and a ship-crossing to Panama. First, however, competitors needed to get their cars from the Lima arrival control at the General Motors factory to *parc fermé* at the Peruvian Automobile Club's headquarters, open from 21:30 on May 18 to 06:40 the following morning. After which, they could eat, soak in the bathtub, and/or crawl into a hotel bed, safe in the knowledge that, unlike 66 other teams, they were still in the game!

Having been advised of the possibility of landslide blockages on the Ecuador *prime* route, John Sprinzel was on hand to see cars off the following evening, saying, as Mark Kahn wrote, "something about cutting down time allowances because conditions had improved. Willy (Cave) said: 'Yes, but there's fog and ice and mud if it rains…' 'Well, that's why you joined,' said Sprinzel."[3] Not difficult to get the feeling rally organizer Mr. Sprinzel was enjoying being ever so slightly Machiavellian! Thus, with roadbooks stamped and signed, and with 35 hours allowed to reach Cali without penalty, 30 rally cars, in various states of disrepair, eased into the heavy city center traffic. For some, it was an immediate stop at a service point for required repairs. The Dutch Datsun needed welding, the Hopkirk 2.5PI had all new driveshafts fitted, the Beauty Box needed a leaking oil pan investigated, and the sole remaining British Army Motoring Association Peugeot 504 of Hemsley and Easton needed shock absorbers. For Willy Cave, Peter Jopp, and Mark Kahn, their departure from *parc fermé* and the start control towards the service point was halted by a collapsed clutch, which required a galvanization of effort to procure a suitable vehicle and driver to tow them to the BLMC mechanics. A beat-up VW van did the honors, albeit nail-bitingly slowly. Service team stalwart Douggie Watts examined the 1800 and diagnosed a disintegrating thrust race, which could not be repaired in the time the team had to get to the next control. Instead, they adjusted the clutch, replaced a suspension arm, fitted new brake discs, and welded a hole in the trunk caused by a leaking battery. Three hours later, they were on their way again, now faced with the challenge of

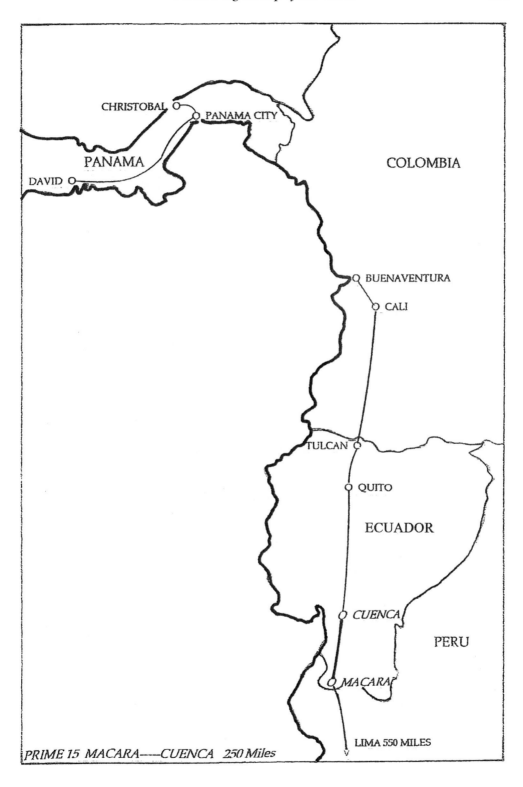

The route from Lima to David (map by Martin Proudlock).

"JOPIE": the BLMC 1800 of Peter Jopp (*driving*), Willy Cave (*front passenger*), and Mark Kahn (courtesy Guido Devreker).

getting to Macará and the next *prime*, the Ecuador Coffee, just over the Ecuadorian frontier.

Along the Pan-American Highway, all was well for the team until, ominously, a noise from the trunk caused them to pull over, anxious that the battery had come loose again. All was well, so they got back into the 1800, but it wouldn't start. The starter motor had failed! Now they needed a push start, which was helpfully provided by a truck driver, who towed them a short distance to get them going. They pressed on for another 70 miles or so, but the noise from the rear had returned, worse this time. Again, they stopped to inspect the cause, this time noticing that the rear suspension was sagging. It was dark now, and they were stuck for ideas when lights loomed on the road they had travelled thus far. It was Evan Green and "Gelignite" Jack! As previously reported, they had retired from the rally many miles before but were now acting as a service car wherever they were needed. Surveying the situation, Jack suggested unloading as much as possible from the sickly 1800 and putting it into their car, which they did. Next, they removed the spare wheels from the roof and loaded them into the rear of the car. All set, they once more readied to push start the car, but now the clutch had begun to fail again, Jopp frantically pumping it until the motor fired. With that, they were again on their way, lasting another 40 miles or so before the struggling suspension forced yet another stop. Now they discovered a leak from the 1800's hydrolastic system, so they retrieved the plug provided by BLMC for such an event; it effectively cut off the suspension fluid, allowing it to maintain effectiveness over three of the four wheels. They were off again, mile after mile, driver Cave becoming increasingly fatigued. They made it to Chiclayo, some 230 miles south of Macará, and stopped for refueling, the clutch deteriorating rapidly from another push start that the gas stop necessitated. They continued on for a short while until the motor finally quit. After 14,000 miles, No. 3 was done, and even a reappearance by Green and Murray couldn't make things better.

The run from Lima to Macará proved uneventful for remaining survivors, so it was now 29 cars that clocked in with Tiny Lewis for the start of the *prime* on May 20. Competitors were notified that Mr. Sprinzel was getting his way and the allowable time had been reduced from four hours to three! The *prime* ran 250 miles to Cuenca, through the mountains and valleys of the sierra region of the country, and all competitors made it through with Aaltonen and Liddon fastest, losing 51 minutes, the Escort of Mikkola and Palm and the 2.5PI of Hopkirk, Nash, and Johnson second (down 57 minutes), Mäkinen fourth (down 58 minutes), and Culcheth and Syer fifth (down 59 minutes).

From Cuenca, the field headed north, again rising and falling through valleys and over mountain ridges, a transport section of 440 miles to the Colombian frontier at Tulcán via the Ecuadorian capital, Quito, and taking in the spectacular view of Chimborazo. From Tulcán, cars would press on along roads lined with jungle to Cali via the whitewashed colonial buildings of Popayán. For the most part, progress was straightforward and uneventful, although somewhere between Quito and Cali, the yellow, JCB construction company-backed Hillman GT of John Bloxham, Peter Brown, and Robert McBurney broke its driveshaft. After such a compelling run from London, always in the mix among the private and commercially sponsored cars,

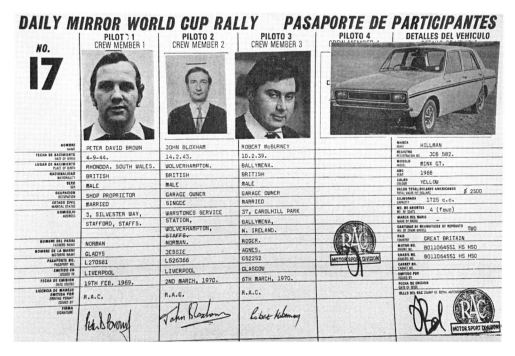

The crew of No. 17, the JCB engineering company-sponsored Hillman GT (courtesy Ted Taylor).

always showing that an endurance rally Hillman victory in Sydney 18 months ear-lier was no one-off, it seemed extremely unfair that this experienced amateur team should go out so close to classification as finishers. Another private entry that had kept going despite all sorts of mishaps, including some front-end damage on the Trans-Argentine, was the orange BMW 2002Ti of Bass and Waring. Now, sadly, its suspension gave way somewhere on the road through Ecuador, and the run was over. Joining them were Peter Kube and Lothar Ranft in the Peruvian 2002Ti, which also didn't reach Cali because of suspension issues and a broken rear axle. Bass and War-ing did manage to get the car transported to Buenaventura and loaded aboard the ship bound for Panama, where the BMW was repaired and saw them, out of competi-tion, make it to Mexico City. BMW asked whether they could examine the 2002Ti at the German factory, which they did, cataloguing all damaged or worn parts and then delivering replacements and the car itself back to Bass in England. Furthermore, Bass was invited to the BMW London distributor's Christmas party, where he was pre-sented with the key to BMW's premier model, a 2.8!

On the final run to the Cali control, a certain works 2.5PI had a lucky escape when a momentary lack of concentration saw Paddy Hopkirk crash off the road on a downhill stretch, losing them an hour. "It was a stupid accident," he explained. "The radiator and oil cooler were damaged but Neville (Johnson) did a wonderful job and managed to get us going."[4]

Timo Mäkinen and Gilbert Staepelaere stopped for gas in Popayán and were immediately mobbed by excited spectators, so much so that local police had to deploy tear gas and fire hoses to drive the fans back. This theme continued at Cali, where competitors were greeted by enormous crowds and baton-wielding policemen.

So, on May 21, just over a month after they had driven off the ramp in London, a steady stream of 26 rally cars made their way to the control at the Olympic stadium. Competitors got their roadbooks stamped and signed by Valerie and Donald Morley, delivered their cars to *parc fermé*, and took the chance to get some rest.

Tales were swapped as police guarded the closed off cars in Cali. French duo Coltelloni and Marang no doubt bemoaned the complete breakdown of their Cit-roën's front suspension and steering, which required a three-hours repair before they could set off on the road to Buenaventura, while Dutch pair Rob Janssen and Jaap Dik recounted how their Datsun's radiator had sprung a serious leak. With no recourse to proper repair and, as a self-servicing, and self-serving, entry, they were carrying welding gear, so Janssen stripped plastic interior trim from the 1600 SSS, melted it with the welding torch and used the goo to seal the radiator! The guys then needed to find a source of water. What to do? Upon discovering a creek somewhat below road level, the ever-ingenious Janssen rigged up their tow rope to lower daredevil Dik down to collect water. Lacking the strength to pull his co-driver back up the ravine, he used the car to tow Dik up and out, no doubt with poor Jaap rappelling in reverse, trying not to spill a drop! As competitors drifted off to sleep that night, they could most definitively say that they had been confirmed as finishers of the London to Mex-ico World Cup Rally. However, there was still a long way to go before Mexico City, and anything could happen along the way.

By 1970, Brian Culcheth had achieved eight class wins in international rallies and was second overall in the 1963 *Coupe des Alpes*. Later in 1970, he would go on to win the Scottish Rally outright and another class win in the RAC Rally. First, however, together with co-driver Johnstone Syer, he had the task of driving a BLMC competitions team-entered Triumph 2.5PI the 16,000 miles from London to Mexico City.

For Culcheth it would be the event of a lifetime.

37

So Close

Ironically, as a 17-year-old, Brian Culcheth learnt to drive while working as an errand boy, or gofer, for the *Daily Mirror* newspaper in London, England. He was also buying *Autocar* magazine at this time and noticed reports and news items about car rallies, which piqued his curiosity. By 1959, he was working for a North London car dealer and noticed a piece in the local newspaper about the car club for his area. He made contact and was invited along to their next meeting. The first person he met and got talking to was Peter Browning, who became a life-long friend. Browning would eventually go on to become head of the British Motor Corporation's Competitions Department, which in turn became BLMC's.

The opportunity to compete in a local motor rally quickly presented itself to Brian, but he didn't have a car. Or did he? Why not? So, off he set on his first Harrow Car Club treasure hunt in the family Austin A50, his parents in the back, a friend reading maps—badly—and all he did to prepare the family sedan was remove the car's hubcaps!

Brian was also a keen cyclist at this time and knew his way around map reading, which in turn led him to offering his services as a rally navigator within the club. However, while wrangling maps and offering directions to club drivers, he quickly concluded that he could drive a damn sight better than many of those he was assisting, so, deciding to regroup, he took a breather, saved every available penny he had, and bought a Sebring Sprite. Repeated success on club rallies and auto tests in the Sprite eventually got Brian noticed by Peter Browning's predecessor at BMC, Stuart Turner, which led to a co-drive in the 1963 Monte Carlo Rally. Turner continued to be supportive, even if he didn't formalize a professional working relationship between Brian and BMC, and when Brian decided to enter a borrowed Mini Cooper into the four-day Gallaher Circuit of Ireland Rally, it was Turner who suggested a suitable co-driver. Thus began a very happy, very productive relationship between Brian and Scotsman Johnstone Syer.

Turner continued to play a part on Brian's rally career, paying his expenses to enter rallies during the first half of 1966 while also asserting certain Machiavellian tendencies. Of the 1966 *Rajd Polski*, or Polish Rally, Brian recalled: "Turner had paid my expenses … yet in the middle of a long tight road section he told mechanics not to let me have any petrol. We lost time…. I was absolutely livid but was too timid to have ago at Turner…. Perhaps I would have earned his respect if I had spoken up."[1] Culcheth felt increasingly despondent during the second half of 1966, but things looked up when his old friend Peter Browning took over from Turner at BMC. "I got a call from Peter Browning," Brian remembered. "He … was now running the BMC team and offered me an Austin 1800 for the 1967 *Coupes des Alpes*."[2] Brian and Johnstone took 11th place overall and first in the 1800's engine size class. Only a month or so later, Brian and Johnstone were entered to run the 1800 in the British RAC Rally, but this was cancelled at last minute while the country struggled with an outbreak of foot-and-mouth disease, the extremely infectious viral disease that affects cloven-hoofed animals. This disappointment was tempered, however, when Brian was placed on retainer by BMC. So it was that Brian Culcheth became a works driver for the British Motor Corporation Competitions Department.

The 1968 Monte Carlo Rally was next on the calendar for Brian, followed by the Greek Acropolis Rally, both in 1800s. Then it was the unique, 10,000-mile London–Sydney Marathon, for which Brian undertook survey work from London to Bombay with Henry Liddon before competing in the event with Mike Wood and Tony Fall. Their adventures are documented elsewhere, but, suffice to say, they finished 24th overall, hampered by an altercation with a gully in the Iranian desert!

The first half of 1969 saw Brian become involved in the relatively new motorsport of rallycross, a mixed-surface circuit event, usually involving much mud, hills and troughs, and rough track, at British venues such as Lydden Hill in Kent and the Croft Circuit in Yorkshire. This also marked Brian's introduction to Triumph as a motorsports brand; he drove a heavily modified four-wheel-drive Triumph 1300. For the competitions department, 1969 also saw the first real consequences of British Leyland's takeover of BMC. Under the stewardship of Lord Stokes, who wasn't exactly enamored by the cost of BMC's motorsports department, "the big names— Timo Mäkinen, Rauno Aaltonen and Tony Fall—didn't have their contracts renewed for '69," Culcheth explained. "From memory, it was just Paddy Hopkirk and me that were retained."[3]

Next up in the rally calendar was the Scottish International Rally, which reunited Brian with Johnstone Syer and gave them their first taste of a Triumph 2.5PI in first-generation form. Although their finish was an inauspicious 23rd place, Brian liked the car, which certainly boded well for the future, not least because just one month later, in July 1969, BLMC announced to the press their three key drivers for the recently publicized 16,000-mile London to Mexico World Cup Rally—Paddy Hopkirk, newly recruited Andrew Cowan, and Brian Culcheth.

Following the *Tour de France* rally and more rallycross, in which Brian drove Mini Coopers, the BLMC Competitions Department quickly commenced a program of testing and then developing the cars they intended to enter in the World Cup Rally. Dismissing the soon-to-be launched Range Rover and the tough but slow 1800, BLMC competitions chief Peter Browning chose the Triumph 2.5PI for its primary assault on the road to Mexico City. And what better chance to test the car than to enter three of them in November's RAC Rally, to be driven by Hopkirk, Cowan, and Culcheth? The event proved challenging but extremely useful for BLMC, not least because Brian experienced gasoline feed problems, which led to the conclusion that the cars would need mechanisms to restrain and regulate the flow of fuel.

With the RAC out of the way, Brian was on a plane for the Argentinian capital,

Brian Culcheth testing a Triumph 2.5PI (courtesy Brian Culcheth).

Buenos Aires, to undertake survey work of the route all the way up to Mexico City. "We knew nothing about South America," he remembered. "Nobody had ever rallied there before. The only experience that we knew of was the original great Argentina road races, which Mercedes were dominant in, and an irony of that was that on the '62 RAC, I was due to co-drive a chap called Hermann Kühne, and Mercedes entered two cars, one for Eugen Böhringer, who was the European champion, and one with Hermann Kühne. Well, Kühne was killed in the Argentina road races on the very stages we were going to do in the World Cup Rally."

No doubt with this in mind, Brian set off south and west in a standard Triumph 2000, on loan from the Peruvian division of BLMC, with Peruvian racing driver Uldarico "Larco" Ossio. "We didn't make notes because he wouldn't have understood what to write," Brian explained. "It was only on the second recce that we started to make notes and … they were more safety notes." It was the first opportunity to test conditions, which Brian could then feed back to the competitions department. "We soon realised that this was going to be the toughest rally that any of us had ever thought about. To have three stages of over 500 miles was just phenomenal, you know, and then we had this section that was from Santiago to La Paz, this was 57 hours, non-stop, and it had three of these special stages, which were called 'primes' on the rally, and the first one was 200 miles and then there was the 500-miler and then there was a 270-miler, plus 1,000 road miles, and that was all to be done in 57 hours!"

Brian concluded that the stretch from Buenos Aires to Santiago, via the Puyehue Pass at 4,000 feet, was fast and would suit the Triumphs. At Santiago, Brian and Larco collected Paddy Hopkirk's co-driver Tony Nash from the airport and then sought mechanical attention for the Triumph, which was suffering from the relentless battering the route had thus far inflicted. Suspension, shocks, exhaust, and parking brake cable all needed attention, information that was communicated back to BLMC as it continued to develop the Triumph rally cars.

Brian described the next section, the 1,950-mile slog from Santiago in Chile to La Paz in Bolivia, as "the toughest and most demanding section ever in a rally. This statement still holds good today—it is a section that is unlikely to ever be surpassed."[4] So difficult in fact that, for Andrew Cowan and Paddy Hopkirk, the question of whether to be two-up or three-up for the rally answered itself—three! Nevertheless, Brian elected for two-up, himself and Johnstone Syer. It would be a shrewd choice.

The proposed rally route took them up to 16,000 feet and down again, during which punctures brought them to a halt for 14 hours before assistance arrived. Moving onwards, they encountered every kind of terrain, including seemingly impromptu and extremely hazardous plank bridges. During what was to be the 510-mile Gran Premio *prime*, their 2000's odometer packed up, and only the skill of a local welder got them going again. All in all, recceing this *prime* stage took Brian, Larco, and Tony two days. In competition, organizers expected cars to achieve it in eight hours!

As they continued onwards towards La Paz, the team further noted that the octane rating for altitude driving didn't suit the Triumph's standard-spec motor. This, together with the fact that the car's regular gas tank would be too small for the distances proposed, was also fed back to BLMC.

Continuing the survey from La Paz to Cusco and from there through the longest special stage of the rally, 560 miles, Brian recounts that "the road was indeed scary, so narrow in places with precipitous drops of hundreds of feet."[5] After this challenge, the team followed the remainder of the route, flying from Colombia to Panama and then using a rental car up to Mexico itself. From there, Brian flew home on Christmas Eve, 1969, and it wasn't long before he was meeting with the Word Cup Rally teams and other personnel to share his thoughts and comments about the route and the standard Triumph's shortcomings. Then it was off to test the second-generation Triumph 2.5PI, only recently launched, which included investigating different tire specs, ever determined to reduce the chance of punctures.

After undertaking recce work on the World Cup Rally's European leg, Brian and Tony Nash returned to South America, this time accompanied by the entire team for further survey work from Rio de Janeiro, during which they managed to all but destroy three Hertz rental VW Bugs. Their adventures included the deployment of a certain famous Argentinian racing driver to help rescue the RAC Rally Triumphs from customs in Buenos Aires.

Finally, after all the work, the miles covered, and the automotive stress testing, April 19, 1970, dawned. Brian and Johnstone had been drawn No. 88, so, having been called to the ramp, at 12:17 precisely, Brian eased the Triumph away, out of London's Wembley Stadium and into the northwest London streets all lined with cheering crowds that didn't seem to dissipate even as the car left London and headed south towards the port of Dover on the Kent coast and the ferry that would take competitors over to France.

Brian and Johnstone shared driving duties across Europe, and the journey proved uneventful all the way to the first European *prime*, the Montenegro, at the end of which Brian lost just one point. Then it was on to the Serbian *prime* in the Yugoslavian mountains. With tires changed to suit conditions, Brian roared away into the stage, but his efforts to "clean" it, or arrive at the finish control without penalty points, were foxed when, like so many other competitors, he encountered a wooden bridge missing its essential central section, thus forcing him to seek a detour and thus lose 15 essential minutes. "The bridge was a major topic at the next rest halt," Brian wrote. "Seemingly Ford and Citroën knew about it, but all the works Triumphs lost 15 minutes."[6]

On to the third *prime*, the San Remo in Italy, Brian felt that the time allowance of two hours for 72 miles was far too kind as a total of 23 cars arrived at the finish control at Camporosso without penalty. The fourth, the French Alpine, 67 miles in 90 minutes, with a couple of passage controls thrown in for good measure, was perhaps more realistic as it was fast on asphalt. Perhaps a little frustratingly, although five cars cleaned this stage, Brian lost another two minutes here, even if he was the fastest BLMC team Triumph at the finish control at Rouaine.

Johnstone did most of the heavy lifting for the transport section from France, through Spain, and up to the small Portuguese town of Arganil for the start of the final European *prime*, the Portuguese, while Brian slept. All went well until a few miles from the finish control when the Triumph had a puncture. They continued but lost three minutes, although again Brian was the fastest Triumph.

Thus, as the surviving rally cars lined up to be loaded for shipping to Rio de Janeiro, Brian and Johnstone were in sixth position overall, having amassed 32 penalty points, seven ahead of teammate Paddy Hopkirk and 23 ahead of Andrew Cowan. Brian was "fairly pleased" with their performance to Lisbon. "But we had had that bit of a drama in Yugoslavia," he observed. "On one of the stages, we arrived at a bridge that was closed … so we had to retrace our steps … in the overall picture it didn't make any difference but it did mean I was sixth at Lisbon instead of fourth."

While other competitors enjoyed the sights and sounds of Portugal's capital before jetting over to Rio, the entire BLMC team climbed aboard a specially chartered Bristol Britannia aircraft and flew from Lisbon to Rio via Recife. BLMC then told Brian and Johnston to rent a car and revisit the first two South American *primes*, the 125-mile Parana and the 240-mile Rio Grande. It was a fortuitous move as unrelenting rain had rendered substantial parts of the Rio Grande impassable, mud providing testimony as Brian was forced to turn the rental around with a little help from local folks. Thus, the Rio Grande was truncated to half its original length for the rally itself.

Brian reflected on the mindset going into the rally restart: "We had driven at eight tenths in Europe, and we planned to keep that pace up in South America because the 11,000 miles to Mexico, which now lay ahead, contained some of the most challenging roads ever encountered in rallying."[7] However, two *primes* later, Brian and Johnstone were forced to review this decision as the Ford GB Escort teams were driving extremely fast and had taken the top five places in both special stages while No. 88 managed only ninth fastest on the Parana and seventh on the Rio Grande. Thus, with a new game plan, the duo headed onwards for the third South American *prime*, the Uruguay, but not before a navigation error put them 50 miles off track and resulted in loss of time. It also put them behind slower cars, the dust trails from which greatly hindered the duo's attempts to overtake. It was these kinds of mistakes that could come with such a high price.

Having already recced the 125-mile Uruguay *prime*, Brian knew it would be fast, the fastest of the entire rally—"the most exhilarating drive of my career" he called it. "Holding 130 mph for mile after mile and drifting through the long curves at that speed was just fantastic."[8] Even when a clutch slave cylinder failed, it didn't dampen spirits as they were going too fast to need it, but a puncture six miles from the finish did. It was also a costly flat as the cash prize for fastest finisher on this *prime* went instead to teammate Andrew Cowan who eventually collected it by just four minutes. Frustration aside, however, after the nimble Escorts had been victorious on the two previous stages, there was much to be learnt in witnessing the Triumphs take charge on this extremely fast *prime*.

No doubt this was far from Brian's mind as he wrangled the wounded Triumph onwards to the Uruguayan capital, Montevideo, ever watchful of the clock, ever conscious of the damaged clutch. They made it with just eight minutes to spare before the control closed and thus denied themselves the chance to have the clutch slave cylinder replaced before *parc fermé*. Fortunately, repairs were carried out the following day, and as No. 88 drove onto the ferry bound for Buenos Aires across the River Plate, Brian and Johnstone knew they were in fourth place overall.

Together with Larco Ossio, who was now serving as backup driver for Andrew Cowan and Brian Coyle in the rally, Culcheth had recced the next section the previous November and December, and therefore felt the Triumphs were ideally placed to continue challenging the Escorts. It was therefore not a little galling to discover that well-meaning local authorities, anxious that they might be in the international spotlight, had decided to improve some of the previously unsurfaced roads. This, in Brian's view, rendered the target completion times for the Pampas and Trans-Argentine *primes* easily achievable for the professional teams, borne out by the fact that 19 cars finished the former without penalty and 16 cleaned the latter. The modernization of transportation infrastructure doesn't always benefit the endurance rally driver!

Surviving cars moved on west over the 4,000-foot high Puyehue Pass and then north towards Santiago de Chile and an enforced rest stop, at which works cars at least benefited from thorough repairs and maintenance—what Brian calls "a thorough spanner [wrench] check all round."[9] All this in readiness for the next, most challenging, most rigorous section of the entire rally, the 1,950-mile run from Santiago to La Paz in Bolivia, encompassing a crossing from Chile into Argentina at 12,000 feet and continued driving at an elevation of up to 15,000 feet, all the way to the Bolivian capital.

A perfect storm of snow and landslides closed off the original route of the sixth South American *prime,* the Chilean, so a hastily arranged reroute took cars north, then back down south, and finally east and upwards. Brian and Johnstone were sixth fastest on the revised *prime*, while the Escorts took the top four spots, fourth fastest shared with Paddy Hopkirk.

Onwards and upwards to the next, the Gran Premio, the almost unimaginable 480-mile challenge, to be completed in eight hours if penalties were to be dodged. In other words, competitors were to maintain an average speed of approximately 64 miles per hour up and over the oxygen-diminished mountain trail with constant twists and turns, sheer drops to left and right, nighttime driving, and dust, dust, dust!

From the hastily rearranged start control at San José de Jáchal, Brian was fourth away into the section behind the Escort of Poles Zasada and Wachowski and two of the French Citroën teams. "After 50 miles, I caught the Citroëns," he explained, "but I couldn't pass them because of the dust. And it was night and you can imagine how tiring—it was like driving in fog! Then, one of the Citroëns got a puncture so, luckily, I got past him, but then I was in the dust of the other one and it was another 150 miles in the dust before we came to the refueling." The race was on to see who could refuel the quickest, a battle won by the BLMC team, so they were back on the road first, which meant no dust and therefore a chance to pick up the speed. The relentless pace, mile after mile, required both driver and navigator to maintain steely concentration as they sped on, but one puncture, then another some 50 miles later began to take their toll. "That's when we started to feel it, you know, and Johnstone, he started seeing elephants in telephone wires and boxes in the road, so I said to him, 'Okay, you just rest and I'll just drive it.'" A mix of fatigue and oxygen deprivation can do that!

Johnstone was able to resume duties with 60 miles to go before the finish control, and they were at last home, fourth fastest with 85 penalty points. Astonishingly, Mikkola and Palm made it with just 45 points, followed by Aaltonen and Liddon with 61 and Zasada and Wachowski with 73. A little further from the control point at La Viña was a very much needed service point, and Brian doesn't know how he made those last four or five miles. "The mechanic carried me out of the car and I got three hours sleep before we moved on to La Paz," he recalled. Brian's experience on this *prime* brings into sharp relief just how arduous the drive was. Days of driving at altitudes between 5,000 and 14,000 feet, combined with dust, concentration, lack of sleep, expending energy to change tires, a badly cracked windshield—all the while trying to maintain the required speed to avoid penalty. Given this was 480 miles in eight hours, in those kinds of conditions, it's a testimony to the four frontrunners that they did it in between eight hours and 45 minutes and nine hours and 15, even if Brian stressed just how costly the punctures were!

The next *prime*, the 270-mile Bolivian Coffee, saw an intense tussle between Brian and the Zasada/Wachowski Escort. He caught the Polish pair, but dust and maybe just a wee bit of gamesmanship prevailed and at the finish control at Potosí, they shared the fastest time. The Zasada Escort would also prove an issue on the next section.

At La Paz, Brian seized the opportunity to have the 2.5PI's windshield replaced. However, when the mechanics came to unpack the part, although the box in which it was delivered specified Triumph 2000, the actual glass was for a Triumph 1300, a much smaller car! It was impossible now to put the damaged glass back in, so it was lucky that, in an instance of professional camaraderie, Ford boss Stuart Turner donated an Escort windshield. The correct height, it required much tape to secure it as it was a few inches too narrow. Better than nothing, however, not least because, as Brian observed, "the next section from La Paz to Lima was the most exciting of the rally."[10]

The 560-mile Route of the Incas *prime* would take cars along twisting mountain roads, undulating between 10 and 14,000 feet and all the while throwing up tight hairpins and sheer drops of a thousand feet or more. As if that wasn't enough, if you were going to escape penalty, you would need to average 50-plus miles per hour as the time allowed, initially given as 12 hours, was actually reduced to 11 by the time competitors reached the start control at Cusco. Brian and Johnstone were fifth away into the *prime* behind four of the works Escorts, including Zasada and Wachowski. "Zasada was a man in his world, you know, he hardly spoke much English," Brian recalled. "In fact, I was bloody annoyed with him … because soon after the start of the longest stage, the Cusco stage, he crashed. I came around the corner and he was blocking the whole road and I went up the bank and down and missed him, but I could have ended my rally…. I could have hit something." Undaunted, they continued, suddenly encountering the works Escort of Timo Mäkinen and Gilbert Staepelaere receiving some hasty repairs. Now it was just the Escorts of Mikkola and Aaltonen to catch, which Brian did, passing Aaltonen when the Finn suffered a puncture (but having to relinquish the lead when he too picked up a flat tire). As the road twisted forwards and back, the two Escorts were always in Brian's sights, but in the end, the 2.5PI was third fastest to Huancayo, losing just 99 minutes compared to Mikkola's 81 and Aaltonen's 92.

It was now becoming clear that Brian was engaged in a battle royal for second place with Aaltonen and Liddon; mere minutes separated them. Into the next *prime*, the Ecuador, Brian knew the trail was fast and would benefit the powerful Triumph, but a puncture allowed the Finn to finish fastest with Brian in fourth place. Thus, as the teams prepared for the ship crossing to Panama, Brian was in third place overall, 85 minutes behind Mikkola but only 18 behind Aaltonen.

After the two-day voyage, ending with a cruise up the Panama Canal, the restart at Panama City offered up two more *primes* and thousands of miles of transport stage. Brian knew that the first *prime*, the Costa Rica Coffee, required an impeccable performance, and, to begin with, that's what they were doing, passing Mikkola, who was undoubtedly responding to co-driver Gunnar Palm's encouragement to consolidate rather than give his usual 110 percent! Two punctures and a loosening windshield, however, robbed Brian of a fastest place, and he eventually finished with 51 penalty points, compared to Paddy Hopkirk's 40 and Mikkola's 46. They were disappointed, of course, but in the world of any sport, someone else's misfortune can often bring benefits for others, and so it was that Brian and Johnstone learnt how punctures and mechanical problems lost Aaltonen and Liddon 93 minutes at Cartago. As a consequence, the Culcheth/Syer partnership moved to second place overall.

The last *prime*, the Aztec, saw cars attempt the only Mexican stage on the rally and allowed Brian to use a few tactics. Fast to begin with, Brian saw Aaltonen in his rearview and let him pass. "We had 24 minutes over him, so I just sat outside his dust cloud to the finish."[11]

All that was left was a transport section to Fortín de las Flores, where the rally formally concluded. There Brian Culcheth and Johnstone Syer would receive confirmation of their second place, having picked up 625 penalty points, meaning 10 hours and 25 minutes over the expected completion time, between London and the end point compared to the 547 points, or nine hours and seven minutes, incurred by the winning pair of Hannu Mikkola and Gunnar Palm. First to congratulate them? Third-placed Aaltonen and Liddon!

When asked how he felt at the end, Brian replied: "It was thrilling but it was also a bit of a disappointment, really. I genuinely thought we were going to win it. We'd recced harder than anybody else, I'd done more reconnaissance than anybody, and I knew where to go fast and where not to go fast and I thought we would win it."

Despite British Leyland supremo Lord Stokes pulling the plug on the competitions department shortly after the World Cup Rally ended, Brian carried on competing nationally and internationally, usually with Johnstone, until he decided to retire in 1979. "I could have been more successful if I'd had more competitive cars, but I don't think I did badly," Brian reflected, looking back on his career. "I wouldn't swap places with the current rally stars, though. They complain about having to do stages that last only a few minutes. Heaven knows how they'd cope with having to do special stages of hundreds of miles."[12]

Brian Culcheth and Johnstone Syer rallied together for 12 years and their friendship spanned almost six decades.

Johnstone Syer passed away in 2021.

38

The Show Must Go On

Returning to their cars at Cali in Colombia in the early hours of May 22, some competitors were faced with the fact that local police had been unable to completely secure their vehicles. Some competitors reported possessions lost and stolen. Added to this, the Escort of leading pair Mikkola and Palm had somehow lost all of its oil! Sabotage? Conclusions could not be reached but, regardless, the vital lubrication was hastily replenished.

The surviving teams were also faced with a four-hour, neutralized drive through Colombian jungle and coffee plantations to the coastal city of Buenaventura, from where a ship crossing would take them across the Golfo Tortugas, or Gulf of Turtles, up into the Gulf of Panama, and then along the Panama Canal to Cristóbal on the Atlantic. Organizers had negotiated space for 35 cars on the Italia Line ship the MS *Verdi*, and provision had been made whereby if more than the allotted number reached Cali, anyone outside the top 35 would be invited to fly on to Mexico City at the rally's expense and assured they would be classified as finishers. Sprinzel, Brown and Co. were no doubt relieved that only 26 spaces would be required. Eventually, however, in addition to the finishers, the ship had room for another 12 cars, a mix of rally retirements and civilian vehicles, plus, as journalist embedded in the British RAF Red Arrows Maxi, Michael Scarlett, wrote, "an AMC Hornet engaged on a record attempt of World Cup Rally proportions—driving from Newfoundland, (down) the east coast of North America, round South America and back up the west side to Fairbanks Alaska, in less than 33 days, piloted by Mr. Louis Halasz, a lone American."[1] In fact, 44-year-old Cleveland, Ohio mechanic Halasz did complete his trans-America odyssey in 145 days, covering 38,477 miles and causing "an international incident, involving the State Dept. Colombia and Venezuela … out of Halasz's request for landing documents for Colombia. Venezuela, miffed, felt he should visit their country first, saying they wouldn't let him enter Venezuela from Colombia. 'Why not?' asked Colombia."[2]

Travelling marshal Mike Broad described the route from Cali to Buenaventura as "breath-taking. Starting from Cali … the road winds down to the coast in just over 100 km (62 miles). The road is gravel and mud, extremely narrow and dangerous." Bearing this out, and as previously described, this was where Hemsley and Easton almost lost both their car and their lives when their Peugeot 504 was all but flattened by one rogue truck among so many on this stretch. The Citroën of Vanson, Turcat, and Leprince also experienced bus-related damage here, but all others

The docks at Buenaventura, Colombia (courtesy Pat Smith).

made it without serious incident to the docks and checked into the designated hotel, although neither the lodging nor Buenaventura itself was to everybody's liking. "Jim (Gavin) had been delegated to travel overland to the port … to supervise the shipping arrangements to Panama," rally organizer Tony Ambrose wrote. "He phoned me to warn that the port was some kind of hell-hole. We anticipated some complaints from the competitors."[3] BLMC works driver Paddy Hopkirk was equally nonplussed. "The hotel in Buenaventura was disgusting," he wrote. "I went out round the back and saw the swimming pool, which had about a foot of filthy water in it and a dead dog lying in the bottom."[4] Competitors were generally advised not to leave the hotel for their own safety!

Thus, with not a little relief, cars and crews boarded the *Verdi* and set sail, all impressed with the pleasant vessel and its facilities. The voyage afforded both surviving and retired competitors some much-needed R&R, and they quickly took to the pool, clay shooting and other deck games, or just sunbathing. As Rob McAuley points out in his London to Mexico Rally movie, as it was so close to Hannu Mikkola's birthday, there was a real party atmosphere with music and dancing and, of course, copious amounts of alcohol for those who wanted it! After all that had gone before, much steam was let off by many rally men and women as they cruised north to start the last stretch, through five countries, enduring two more *primes* and 2,800 miles until the goal, the target, the endpoint, was reached, the Aztec Stadium in Mexico City.

Because the docks at Panama City were not equipped to wrangle the disembarkation of assorted rally and civilian vehicles, the *Verdi* entered the canal at Panama's capital and then, via the three locks, Miraflores, Pedro Miguel, and Gatun, traversed the canal northwards and, in terms of elevation, downwards by over 170 feet before being released into the Bahía Limón, or Lemon Bay, and the port of Cristóbal. Many a rally competitor stood on deck to observe this marvel of science and engineering, fascinated by the locomotives that kept the ship on track through the narrow locks.

At Cristóbal, during the lengthy process of unloading cars, competitors and other passengers onboard were serenaded by No. 82 team member—and national *Eisteddfod* winner—Welsh tenor Washington James singing *La donna è mobile* and BLMC rally supremo Peter Browning, who offered up a tune or three at the piano! Then, finally, enduring torrential rain, cars set off on a two-hour neutralized section to Panama City and the official restart on May 24, a drive that threatened to take a very long time when local police slowed competitors to procession-like speeds! Departure control was scheduled to be open between 20:00 and 23:00 and was overseen by ever-smiling John Sprinzel. Tragedy, however, was about to strike.

While the Trautmanns, Guy Verrier, and Francis Murac had been grabbing all the headlines for Citroën, another French team had stoically progressed across Europe and South America. Lying 14th when the rally restarted in Rio, old friends Paul Coltelloni and Henri "Ido" Marang had suffered much misfortune, breaking down four times. They had slipped to 32nd place by Montevideo, and, by Lima, only the British BMW of Bass and Waring had accumulated more penalty points. If not the oldest, Coltelloni and Marang were certainly two of the more senior competitors in the rally, and, between them, they had racked up many international events on the European circuit. Marang was a regular competitor on the Monte Carlo, Liège-Rome-Liège, *Coupe des Alpes*, and Liège-Sofia-Liège rallies throughout the 1950s and '60s, while Coltelloni had won the Monte Carlo Rally in 1959 and, in December 1968, with British co-driver John Tallis, had been controversially awarded the prize for highest placed private entry at Bombay during the London–Sydney Marathon, organizers initially dismissing Mercedes-Benz driver Innes Ireland's appeal that his team should have won! Ironically, a similar situation was now simmering about the Citroëns' standing in the London to Mexico event.

Cars left the Panama City control in the humid heat of the night and set off on the fast 300-mile transport stage to the Costa Rican frontier at Paso Canoas and the start of the rally's penultimate *prime*, the Costa Rica Coffee. Having previously been in attendance to help the Jopp/Cave/Kahn 1800 and the Australian 1800 team, Evan Green and "Gelignite" Jack now raced after the departing cars when the Red Arrows Maxi left its toolkit behind. Then, about 90 miles southwest of Panama City, at Penonomé, the inexplicable occurred when, without warning, a private car slammed into the speeding Coltelloni/Marang DS21. The crash was devastating; reports stated that the Citroën was cut completely in half. Both men were pulled from the wreckage moments before the car caught fire, but, although Paul Coltelloni recovered, Ido Marang sustained fatal head injuries and died on the way to the hospital. An appalling and deeply distressing incident after so many thousands of miles travelled.

The rally continued, however, the direction gradually shifting northwest. Allowable times for both the entire section to the endpoint at Fortín de las Flores in Mexico and the two remaining *primes* were adjusted downwards. Competitors needed to finish within 51 hours and 30 minutes to avoid a last set of penalty points, and organizers now required them to complete the 220-mile Costa Rica in two hours and 30 minutes, reduced from the previous three-hour target, an almost impossible feat.

The Costa Rica Coffee was a night stage and offered another opportunity for Brian Culcheth and Johnstone Syer to battle it out with Rauno Aaltonen and Henry Liddon for second place, so close were they on points. Ultimately, taking full advantage of having practiced here before the Rio restart, it was Paddy Hopkirk who was fastest to the finish control at Cartego, losing just 40 minutes, with Mikkola finishing six minutes slower. Culcheth was third fastest, now taking second place overall as previously stated, the Aaltonen Escort developing fuel supply problems on the coffee plantation-lined trail, which required over an hour to sort before they were able to get going again. Perhaps most remarkable, however, was the performance put in by Rob Janssen and co-driver Jaap Dik. The Dutch team had had more than their fair share of problems, repeatedly enduring cracked pistons in their Datsun all along the route, and even though they entered the *prime* with just six minutes left before the start control closed, having once again had to replace a piston, they drilled the car through the section to take the fifth fastest spot, beating Ford works drivers Tony Fall, Timo Mäkinen, and Rauno Aaltonen into the bargain! Here, however, was where the Hemsley/Easton Peugeot 504 succumbed to the damage it had incurred on the road from Cali to Panama City, leaving 24 cars to carry on to the *prime*. It was also where the Trautmann/Perrier assault on the women's prize began to falter.

From Cartago, competitors headed off for the last big transport stage of the rally, a 1,400-mile slog out of Costa Rica and across Nicaragua, Honduras, El Salvador, and Guatemala before crossing the Mexican frontier at La Mesilla, in the shadow of the Montañas Peña Blanca, and on to the last *prime* of the rally, the Aztec, with the start control at Oaxaca. The stretch was long and uneventful for all except Trautmann and Perrier, and the Soviet team of Gunnar Holm, Vladimir Bubnov, and Kastytis Girdauskas. The British *Daily Mirror* reported that an angry mob attacked the Soviet team, smashing their Moskvič's windshield, when they stopped for gas at the village of Santa Ana in El Salvador. With the help of armed police, the Soviets managed to escape the altercation but had to progress to Guatemala City, 75 miles distant, before their windshield could be replaced. As the *Mirror* reported, "police diverted other rally cars away from the trouble spot to a border crossing at San Cristóbal instead of the planned crossing at Valle Neuvo."[5]

Now, calamity struck Claudine and Colette when, with approximately 500 miles to go before the start of the Aztec, their Citroën permanently stopped. A miserable end for the women who, with more than a few serious challenges by the Smith/De Rolland/Watson team, had stamped their authority on women's participation in the very male world of endurance rallying.

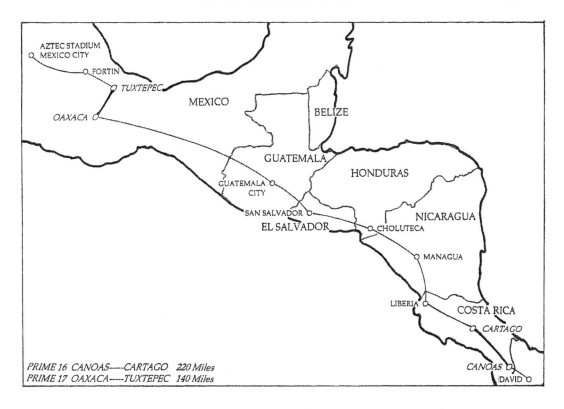

PRIME 16 CANOAS-----CARTAGO 220 Miles
PRIME 17 OAXACA-----TUXTEPEC 140 Miles

The route from David to Mexico City (map by Martin Proudlock).

So it was that, after some confusion for a few of the BLMC cars at the Mexican border, when it appeared that they had arrived at a crossing that wasn't fully prepared for them, 23 teams made it to Oaxaca. With some competitors arriving as much as 11 hours early, there was time to eat, work on cars, and sleep before the final speed test, the Aztec *prime*: 106 miles across asphalt, cobblestones, and rock-strewn mud in the foothills of the Sierra Madre mountain range down to Tuxtepec. This was to be the only *prime* to be held on Mexican soil. "John Brown was driving the advance car through … when he was stopped by bulldozers and workers, clearly ready to dynamite another bit of the mountain across his path," John Sprinzel wrote. "It was our luck that John arrived with his fluent Spanish, and was able to halt the explosive road works until our few survivors had cleared the section."[6]

When the control opened, Dean Delamont was on hand to wave cars away, one last effort for 23 tired teams and their ravaged rally cars. Always the voice of reason for his driver, Gunnar Palm again persuaded his rally partner Hannu Mikkola not to take any chances as they tore off into the *prime* and just focus on maintaining their 90-minute lead over Culcheth. This was, however, the last chance for Culcheth, who needed to try to reduce that time difference, so he went full pelt, as did Hopkirk. Fastest time to Tuxtepec? Brian Culcheth and Johnstone Syer, followed by Hopkirk, Nash, and Johnson in second and Aaltonen and Liddon in third. However, despite Culcheth clawing back 12 minutes of Mikkola's lead, it wasn't enough, and as the cars departed for the last transport stage before the finish, barring disaster, Mikkola and Palm were assured of victory, 78 minutes quicker than Culcheth and Syer, who in turn were 21 minutes up on Aaltonen and Liddon.

The organizing committee of John Sprinzel, John Brown, Dean Delamont, and Tony Ambrose had decided that the finish, the endpoint to this extraordinary endurance motorsport event, should occur at Fortín de las Flores, with the finish control located at the Hotel Ruiz and presided over by Sprinzel himself. From there, a neutralized victory procession would take cars to Aztec Stadium to arrive on the evening of May 27. The hotel and grounds were packed with people there to cheer the cars home, throw garlands of flowers around competitors' necks, and place enormous, highly decorated sombreros on competitors' heads. Flashbulbs exploded as photographers caught the money shots of Mikkola and Palm, Culcheth and Syer, and winning women's team Rosemary Smith, Ginette De Rolland, and Alice Watson, all laughing at the spectacle, poor Bryan Culcheth casting his eyes upwards at his impromptu and oversized head gear! Even as both organizers and enthusiasts waited on late-finishing cars such as the Dutch Datsun, now sporting collision damage to add to its catalogue of mishaps, and the Ford Escort GT of Doug Harris and Mike Butler, the party got underway and, of course, it wasn't long before assorted fully clothed competitors were taking an impromptu swim. "Tony (Fall) and I celebrated our achievement by jumping fully clothed into a swimming pool," sixth placed overall Ford works co-driver (and soccer star) Jimmy Greaves wrote. "There was a chair in the pool and for the next couple of hours…. I took up residence in that chair and bobbed about in the pool and drank bottle after bottle of Mexican lager."[7]

On May 27, 1970, as the minute hand ticked towards noon, all that was left was for Hannu Mikkola and Gunnar Palm, winners of the London to Mexico World Cup Rally, to climb into their works Ford Escort one last time and begin the 185-mile drive west to Mexico City and its *Estadio Azteca*, Aztec Stadium. Behind Palm and Mikkola came Culcheth and Syer in their 2.5PI, denying Ford a one-two-three hat trick, with Aaltonen and Liddon following on against all the odds after their Escort's mechanical marathon just to keep going. Fourth in line were Hopkirk, Nash, and Johnson in their 2.5PI for BLMC, and in fifth came Mäkinen and Staepelaere in their Escort. Leading private entry was French team Patrick Vanson, Olivier Turcat, and Alain Leprince, their Citroën DS21 in seventh position, although perhaps the real story of the privateers was British trio Reg Redgrave, Bob Freeborough, and Phil Cooper, who had brought their BLMC Special Tuning–prepared 1800 all the way from London, without organized servicing support, without authorized access to spare parts, at one point without a windshield and indeed with only two of the three-man crew having had any competitive rally experience, to finish in ninth place out of 96 starters. Asked why he entered the rally, 47-year-old Redgrave replied: "Simply because I am getting on and I feel I should do something worthwhile other than work."[8] Together with his teammates, Redgrave's performance and result was an enormous cause for celebration.

Motoring journalist and member of the 22nd place team in the British RAF Red Arrows Maxi, Michael Scarlett, reported that competitors found the three-hour drive a somewhat dull anticlimax to the monumental journey they had all just completed, and hijinks were the order of the day. Renowned joker Paddy Hopkirk gently

Film crew on the way to Aztec Stadium, Mexico City, May 27, 1970 (courtesy Pat Smith).

bumped the car in front, which set them all off and culminated with setting off a fire extinguisher, its contents sprayed between cars! The convoy jostled and swerved its way along, chaperoned briskly by Mexican police and enthusiastically by local drivers, press cars, and service crews.

As the cars entered the city, they were met by more civilian motorists, police cars, and motorcycles, all competing to escort the victorious Escort. On Harley Davidsons, the police outriders ensured "the rally cars were then taken on a whirlwind and considerably frightening tour of the city, in which they were encouraged to shoot red lights, to drive at speeds up to 70 mph or even more."[9] One press photographer even fell out of a moving car, so determined was he to get the perfect shot. Regardless, as the rain began to fall, winners Hannu Mikkola and Gunnar Palm were guided through the entrance of Aztec Stadium and came to a halt among the cheering crowds. Both climbed up onto the roof of the valiant Ford and raised their arms in victory, affording an excellent photo opportunity for the awaiting press photographers. On hand to congratulate the winners and welcome all finishers were 1968 Formula One World Champion Graham Hill, British Ambassador to Mexico Peter Hope, and Sir Stanley Rous, Secretary of the International Football (Soccer) Federation. As planned, Jimmy Greaves, sixth place finisher with Tony Fall, was on hand to present the somewhat desiccated chunk of Wembley Stadium soccer pitch turf to Mexico national soccer team captain Gustavo Peña Velasco. He was also on hand to visit England soccer team captain Bobby Moore, who had flown into Mexico City the day before. Moore was in hiding from the press after he had been accused of stealing a bracelet from a jewelry store in Bogotá, which had caused quite a stir in national and international print and broadcast media circles. "I'd had my fill of driving so I persuaded Tony Fall, the football writer Norman Giller and old pal, Lou Wade, to join me in a taxi for the 'safe house' where Bobby was staying," Greaves explained.[10] Employing assorted distractions and subterfuge, Greaves managed to avoid the scrutiny of assembled press people and embassy officials and sneaked around the to the rear of the building. Helped over a high wall by Fall and Giller, Greaves ran across a lawn and spied Moore through a set of French doors. "I carefully turned the handle … and, to my great delight, they opened and I walked into the room where Bobby was sitting," he wrote. "'Come on then, Moore, what have you done with that bracelet?' Bobby was so startled he nearly dropped his beer."[11] The Colombian authorities eventually concluded Moore was innocent, although the case itself wasn't officially closed until 1972.

The official London to Mexico World Cup Rally roadbooks included provision for time recording, stamps, and signatures at the final arrival control at Aztec Stadium. Whether this was merely symbolic or a realistic expectation, competitors were lucky to get their trusty vehicles into the stadium area at all, such were the crowds, and as the awards ceremony and formal celebrations weren't scheduled until the following day, most teams were able to depart after speeches given by the abovementioned luminaries and others, although it's anyone's guess as to how many interviews and photo calls Mikkola and Palm endured before they were allowed to withdraw.

The following evening, competitors, service crews, organizers, and other assorted VIPs gathered at the *Hacienda de los Morales*, the city's historic events venue and restaurant, for prize-giving and partying. Entertained with mariachi music and hosted by Mexico's President of Tourism Miguel Aleman, the gathered throng watched as "nearly 50 awards and over £40,000 ($96,200) in prize money were handed out."[12] Along with the *Daily Mirror* trophy, a silver globe atlas suspended on its axis within a crescent, the rally route etched across and between the continents, Hannu Mikkola and Gunnar Palm received first prize of $24,000. Brian Culcheth and Johnstone Syer received the runner-up prize of $7,200, and third-placed Rauno Aaltonen and Henry Liddon pocketed prize money of $4,800, as did first-placed private entrants Patrick Vanson, Olivier Turcat, and Alain Leprince. Women's prize winners Rosemary Smith, Ginette De Rolland, and Alice Watson were presented with $2,400 for their effort, Ford GB won the Manufacturer's Team Award, and the National Award went to Finland. Other prizes included Class Awards (for engine size categories), Lowest Classified Finisher, various individual *prime* awards, and two special prizes: "Rob Janssen took one for the sheer guts and determination he showed in getting the battered and much repaired Datsun to Mexico, and Ken Tubman took the other one for the way in which he jeopardized his chances by staying at the scene of the Cowan accident."[13] Despite assorted protocol hiccups—the event host allegedly forgot to acknowledge and thank the rally organizers and failed to memorize any of the prizewinners' first names—the party went on into the night. Only when revelers woke blearily on May 29 did thoughts finally turn towards home and/or whatever might happen next. For now, however, the unprecedented 16,000-mile-long, 16,000-foot-high London to Mexico World Cup endurance rally was done.

After his trials and tribulations during the rally, motoring journalist Mark Kahn, competitor in No. 3, the Special Tuning–prepared 1800, returned to earth with a bump, arriving home and confronting his mundane surroundings. "It was hard to believe that only a few days ago I had seen the dawn rise in the savage Andes," he wrote. "I looked at the map that my wife had put up in the hall with pins that she had stuck in it to mark our progress…. Mexico, where there was no pin. I … handed Barbara (Mrs. Kahn) a bracelet of beautiful Peruvian Indian workmanship.

… 'It's the stuff that dreams are made of.'"[14]

Epilogue:
None Tougher, None Rougher

On his journey home from Mexico City to London, via New York City, organizer Tony Ambrose suddenly began crying, tears dripping into his well-deserved large gin and tonic. "Looking back, I must have been extremely tired," he said. "The relief of a job well done that had tipped me over the edge."[1] John Sprinzel, John Brown, Ambrose, and all those who worked to seize Wylton Dickson's idea and turn it into a rally so exquisitely planned and executed had quite simply pulled it off! The logistics, the necessary personnel deployed across Europe and South and Central America, the much-needed cooperation of a host of national automobile clubs and organizations, the galvanization of international border crossing authorities, and the careful orchestration of land, sea, and air travel had all come together to deliver an endurance rally like no other, not least because so many lessons had been learnt from the London–Sydney Marathon 18 months previously. Too easy? Make the London to Mexico Rally tougher. Too accessible? Make the London to Mexico Rally more like a war of attrition, giving competitors almost impossible target times and average speeds over incredible distances and extraordinary landscapes and terrains. Too many last-minute, unforeseen natural obstacles? Use a well-oiled system to overcome the problems, deploying skilled people to review and reroute sections and make sure competitors are kept aware of any alterations along the road to Mexico City. All this plus the challenge of driving a car at altitudes of up to 16,000 feet through desolate areas and with potential peril at every turn! No wonder Ambrose shed a tear or two of relief.

To achieve this undertaking, there really needed to be a leader, someone who was able to seize an opportunity and use a network of contacts, whether influential or just committed to the cause of motorsports and motor rallying, to implement the vision. That man was John Sprinzel. He looked at the "first draft" of the organizing committee and realized it was made up of men who, while skilled and influential in their own right, were, with a few notable exceptions, not really savvy to the intricacies of executing a complex endurance rally. Yes, Dickson had piqued the interest of the *Daily Mirror* newspaper and had quite simply taken an idea at a drinks party and turned it into something tangible, using his persuasive PR skills, but it needed someone with experience on the front line of motorsport, someone who knew what was involved in competing in a rally, winning a rally, organizing a rally. Sprinzel was runner-up in the extremely challenging Liège-Rome-Liège Rally in 1960, competed in

The ideas man: Wylton Dickson, Lisbon, 1970 (courtesy Campbell McAuley).

the 1968 London–Sydney Marathon in an MG Midget, and won the 1959 British Rally Championship. Working alongside John Brown and Tony Ambrose was also a crucial part of the success formula. With Erik Carlsson, Brown had won the RAC International Rally of Great Britain and, by 1970, had taken podium positions on many UK rallies. Not only was Ambrose a hugely successful rally co-driver, but he had also been part of the London–Sydney Marathon's organizing committee. Sprinzel's eye for detail meant the hugely comprehensive set of rules and regulations for the London to Mexico World Cup Rally left no room for interpretation; all the rumblings about whether the Citroëns entered in the event should really have been classified as private or not were, in the end, interpretative and Sprinzel was clear about this. They qualified as private because they met the definition in the agreed-upon rules and regulations. The fact that Sprinzel obviously also had a devilish sense of humor, apparent at Wembley Stadium as cars were flagged away, and through his mischievous comments to competitors all along the route, only served to add some spice to proceedings. No doubt any number of competing teams cursed him as they learnt that target times for some stages and *primes* were reduced almost "in situ," and he undoubtedly constantly had an eye on performance throughout, repeatedly trying to balance the fine line between having too many cars surviving and not enough! "The majority of entrants had a ball—in spite of all the difficulties and challenges," he wrote in the third volume of his autobiography. "When I meet up with them nowadays, there is still a wonderful expression that appears on their faces when the talk turns to the London to Mexico World Cup Rally."[2]

Another leader, both strategic and operational, who had a profound effect on the rally and its outcome was Stuart Turner. Under the stewardship of Bill Barnett, Ford GB's performance during the 1968 London–Sydney Marathon had been extremely disappointing both for the company and for its rally drivers, so Turner's achievement in convincing Ford to invest in another off-calendar endurance rally was an achievement in itself. His steely determination, combined with his obvious willingness to learn from the Marathon and his knowledge of contemporary rally drivers' skills and experience, meant that Ford GB's assault on the prizes on offer at Mexico City was a meticulously managed and well-oiled machine, even if perhaps one or two eyebrows were raised at some of Ford's tactics for keeping their cars in play during the 16,000-mile competition, a subject still up for much discussion at the many reunion and commemoration events happening today! Turner was very able to gauge the climate across the European rally scene in the late 1960s and was acutely aware of other automobile manufacturers' evolving relationship with competitive motorsports. The takeover of Rootes by the American Chrysler Corporation effectively ended their involvement in rally, and the winds of change were also blowing chilly on the recently formed British Leyland Motor Corporation, which had brought together a confusing array of once-independent brands. Its chief Lord Stokes was clearly unconvinced that motorsport, and rallying in particular, had any impact on the cold, hard bottom line. Turner was therefore able to recruit a number of highly talented former BMC and Rootes works drivers and co-drivers from the United Kingdom and mainland Europe, including "Flying Finns" Rauno Aaltonen, Timo Mäkinen, and ultimately victorious Hannu Mikkola. He also made the far-reaching decision to utilize the emerging Ford Escort as the car to succeed in Mexico, while also dismissing Ford's fast but fragile Lotus-engineered eight-valve twin overhead camshaft engine in favor of the more reliable Ford Kent "crossflow" 1600 cubic-centimeter (98 cubic-inch) motor as the building block for mechanical enhancement by supremely talented Ford mechanical engineers. Furthermore, after discussion with survey teams and his cohort of rally drivers, he agreed that all of the Ford GB entries would field two-person teams, allowing himself to be convinced that the payload disadvantage of an extra team member, plus their kit, outweighed any benefit offered by having a relief driver on the long sections in South and Central America. Finally, having a carefully organized cohort of skilled mechanics dispatched along the route to meet the requirements of his cars and competitors meant that each time an Escort team arrived seeking urgent repair or simple servicing, needs could be met, often racing against the clock. This element was essential and allowed many a car to be restored to rally fitness after the pounding it had received in the hands of its driver, not least because each had a different rallying style, a different approach to speed and tactics. The service teams were keenly aware of the rules relating to what could and could not be replaced on a car and were therefore undoubtedly aware of the gray areas, where the boundary of those rules might be blurred or stretched a little! Turner also knew the importance of learning fast "on the job," evidenced by his instruction that Ford personnel return to England during the downtime in Lisbon to study and remedy the problems at least two of his teams had experienced with the Escort's axle setup.

Sympathy needs to be afforded to Peter Browning, competitions department head at BLMC. He had also needed to present a solid business case for the cost and effort required to field entries in the rally, especially because his boss, Lord Stokes, recently appointed as head of the newly formed British Leyland Motor Corporation, was more than a little ambivalent in his attitude towards his company's presence, and associated investment requirement, in motorsports. Kudos then to Browning for securing the resources necessary to secure a place in the lineup at Wembley, and such a broad challenge as well. He had successfully navigated the internal politics raging within the newly formed company, which had brought together personnel who had previously been working for competing automobile brand manufacturers, and had turned the *fait accompli* that Triumph should be the company's sporting marque into a formidable force for the event. Shrewdly, he had also seized the opportunity to offer up brand and marketing inclusivity by including two Austin Maxis in the arsenal, a product that had had a troubled advent, by motoring press receptions standards at least, at launch in the spring of 1969. Never a threat to break speed records on the rally, the Maxi actually proved itself an extremely reliable rally car on the way to Mexico, proved by the results at Mexico City. Adding another recently introduced product, the Mini 1275 GT, into the mix was an obvious nod to BLMC's marketing efforts, the fact that the rally-prepared 2.5PIs, Maxis, and Mini bore little comparison to products on display in showrooms around the world of little consequence! The actual performance of the Triumphs and Austins on the rally was also a testimony to the skills and experience of the many mechanical engineers who worked on the cars, even if some were ultimately frustrated by the challenge presented by the Triumph's innovative but complex fuel-injected engine. Again, as with Ford, Browning's skill in organizing servicing and mechanical support throughout the rally were exemplary, as borne out by the testimonies of both professional and independently entered teams running BLMC models. Finally, the exceptional tussle that emerged between Culcheth and Syer in their 2.5PI and Aaltonen and Liddon in their Escort, both fighting with every last breath of effort for second place, showcased both driving and navigating skill and the rally-toughness of the cars. Yet second place is not first, and Stokes had only really been interested in the top prize as a return for his investment, which meant that, despite the heroic and dedicated efforts of all concerned, the business-minded peer thought nothing of pulling the plug on the company's motorsports division, leaving bitterness and rancor in his wake.

"I don't know quite what the Mirror got out of this all," John Sprinzel wrote, "as I have no idea what their circulation was in Latin America."[3] Their circulation in the UK, at least, reached an all-time high in 1967, "with a record average daily sale of 5,282,137 copies."[4] However, according to Claire Cozens, writing in the British *Guardian* newspaper in 2003, the newspaper's "decline began when the Mirror's Hugh Cudlipp sold the Sun to Rupert Murdoch in 1969. Within nine years the Sun—under the towering leadership of Mr Murdoch and a succession of editors, including the legendary Kelvin MacKenzie—had overtaken its one-time stablemate."[5] It was during this period of uncertainty, therefore, that Wylton Dickson made overtures to the newspaper about sponsoring the London to Mexico Rally. No doubt reflecting on the extensive coverage and resultant publicity the British *Daily Express* newspaper had achieved in backing the 1968 London–Sydney Marathon, plus the potential opportunity for exploiting the link with soccer—the British nation's favorite sport—generally and the forthcoming soccer World Cup Championship in particular, the *Mirror*'s proprietors green-lighted the venture and proceeded to drip-feed publication of news stories and editorials about the rally throughout 1969 before ramping up to fever-pitch in the lead-up to April 19 and then producing extensive copy about the progress and adventures of cars and competitors all through April and May 1970. As for the *Mirror*'s budget, and its impact on rally motorsport, *Cars and Car Conversions* journalist and unlucky World Cup Rally competitor Richard Hudson-Evans wrote that, "in retrospect, the Mirror's £250,000 ($600,000) rumoured expenditure, in terms of international motoring co-operation, above all monetary and nebulous circulation consideration, can therefore be applauded."[6] Certainly, as with the London–Sydney Marathon in 1968, the World Cup Rally caught the public's imagination—assisted of course by an early example of celebrity cross-over or endorsement, demonstrated by the participation of a famous soccer player and a member of the British Royal Family—and brought this brand of motorsport on to the breakfast table of many a household across the country, perhaps to a level that would never be replicated. However, in terms of cold hard cash, whether the *Mirror*'s bottom line was improved is unlikely, given that the newspaper slowly declined in sales and popularity thereafter, passing from one owning group to another through the 1970s and 1980s.

One business that was able to emphatically reap the benefits of the rally was Ford, which artfully avoided the unhappy aftermath that befell Chrysler when a Hillman Hunter was victorious on the 10,000-mile endurance rally from London to Sydney, Australia, in 1968. Not for Ford the unplanned for scramble to capitalize on one of their products achieving international recognition; instead the company's mighty marketing machine seized the opportunity to mark the Escort's win in Mexico City. In November 1970, just six months after Hannu Mikkola and Gunnar Palm used their rally Escort as a podium to show off their first-place prize at Mexico City's Aztec Stadium, Ford launched the special edition Ford Escort Mexico and unleashed more than 10,300 cars on the automobile-buying public. Kudos to Ford for not just adding go-faster stripes and decals to a standard Escort: they instead deployed their Advanced Vehicle Operations department to engineer the car, fitting a contemporarily swift 1599 cubic-centimeter (97.5 cubic-inch) pushrod motor, which developed 86 brake horsepower and offered a top speed of a whisker under 100 miles per hour. With an eye on amateur racers, they even added panel strengthening in high-stress areas. So successful and desirable was the Escort Mexico that when Ford came to replace the car in 1975, they carried over the "Mexico" brand for its Mk. II model. Today, the legacy of the Escort Mk. I's sporting pedigree can even be seen in the sixth installment of the *Fast & Furious* movie franchise.

For competitors and those involved behind the scenes of the London to Mexico World Cup Rally, Sprinzel is quite correct in his assertion that memories are happy, that recollections are enthusiastically shared, even by those whose actual experiences were not perhaps as successful as had been hoped. Notwithstanding the keenness with which people have recounted stories for this book, the sense of camaraderie among those who took their places in the multitude of multi-colored rally cars for the

16,000-mile endurance motorsport competition from London to Mexico City, or who leap-frogged from city to city in assorted aircraft to make sure all mechanical needs were met, all rally controls were covered, all route obstacles overcome or addressed, endures to this day. Attend any event organized to celebrate the history of endurance rally or, if you're lucky, one of the reunion dinners that bring together these veterans of transcontinental motorsport, and the commonality, the shared history, is rich and tangible. For some, the World Cup Rally was the only time they competed in a rally. Others went on to take up other challenges, other events, whether local, national or international. Read down the list of entrants in the 1974 Munich-Sahara-Munich World Cup Rally or the second London–Sydney Marathon in 1977 and a host of familiar names appear, and not just the professionals! A fitting and emotional epitaph to the World Cup Rally adventure was written by Frenchman Paul Coltelloni in a note to Sprinzel after the event in which his co-driver Ido Marang was killed. "You know the price I have just paid for my old friend," he wrote in the letter. "But I want you to know that you have given to rally men everywhere an event which will be *magnifique* forever…. I must let you know that it was good."[7]

And what of the winners themselves? It's probably fair to suggest that, by 1970, Finnish rally driver Hannu Mikkola had developed a reputation for speed, which often meant taking risks in the heat of battle and sometimes failing to complete events as a result. That said, although the best of his career was yet to come, he had already won a number of titles by the time he was chosen to be part of Ford's attempt on Mexico City, emerging as yet another of the "Flying Finns," as Rauno Aaltonen, Timo Mäkinen, and Simo Lampinen were often called. And Mikkola's treatment of the broken bridge on the rally's Serbian *prime* emphatically confirmed this description! Swedish co-driver Gunnar Palm had an impressive track record as a co-driver to the likes of Erik Carlsson (with whom he won the 1963 Monte Carlo Rally), Bengt Söderström (sharing the honors for the 1967 European Rally Championship), as well as Aaltonen, Ove Andersson, and Tony Fall. Reputedly a voice of reason in a rally car, he is credited with encouraging Mikkola to apply a measured approach at key moments during the London to Mexico Rally, not least during the final *prime* in Mexico itself, when their points lead was unassailable and the prudent course was to maintain a solid pace, not take risks, and get all the way to the finish.

Which they did.

"I would sum up the event as an absolute copy book rally, which was very tough indeed," Mikkola wrote about the World Cup Rally shortly afterwards. "We were very proud to have beaten … 24 makes of car from 22 countries and to come home first among only 23 survivors."[8] When he was interviewed in 1988, Gunnar Palm reflected: "I liked the World Cup rally, it was a pity it was just a one-off event. The problem is that nobody will remember it in motorsports history because it was not part of a championship…. I entered the previous marathon, the London–Sydney, but for me that London-Mexico was the greatest."[9]

At time of writing, more than 30 years later, the burgeoning interest in the history of endurance rally motorsports is thankfully and happily proving him wrong!

Appendix 1:
The Entrants

No.	Entrant	Car	Team	Country
1	R. Buchanan-Michaelson	Triumph 2.5PI	Robert "Bobby" Buchanan-Michaelson Roy Fidler Jeremy Bullough	Great Britain
2	Bio-Strath	Porsche 911	Terry Hunter Geoff Mabbs	Great Britain
3	Peter Jopp	BLMC 1800	Peter Jopp Willy Cave Mark Kahn	Great Britain
4	Berry Magicoal	Hillman GT	Rodney Badham Rob Lyall	Great Britain
5	Ivica Vukoja	Peugeot 404 D	Ivica Vukoja Streton Đorđević Nestor Milanov	Yugoslavia
6	British Army Motoring Association	Peugeot 504	Maj. John Hemsley Sgt. Walter "Wally" Easton	Great Britain
7	Peter Garratt	Vauxhall Viva GT	Peter Garratt Chris Coburn Robert Grainger	Great Britain
8	British Army Motoring Association	Peugeot 504	John Rhodes Joseph Minto	Great Britain
9	Ford Sports Club—J.C. Withers Ltd	Ford Cortina Lotus	Ian Harwood Frank Pierson Barry Hughes	Great Britain
10	Cecil Woodley	Vauxhall Ventora	Cecil Woodley Robert Locke Philip Waller	Great Britain
11	Paul Donner	Ford Capri 1600	Paul Donner Martin Donner	Great Britain
12	Robert Neyret	Citroën DS21	Robert Neyret Jacques Terramorsi	France
13	D. Martin	Rolls-Royce Silver Cloud	David Martin William Martin Julian "Terry" Martin	Great Britain

No.	Entrant	Car	Team	Country
14	Sobiesław Zasada	Ford Escort 1850	Sobiesław Zasada Marek Wachowski	Poland
15	Temple Mead Motors	Ford Cortina GT	Ron Channon Rod Cooper	Great Britain
16	Wilsons Motor Caravans	Ford Escort Elba Motor Caravan	James Gardner Laurie Ritchie	Great Britain
17	J.C. Bamford	Hillman GT	Peter Brown John Bloxham Robert McBurney	Great Britain
18	Daily Telegraph	Ford Escort 1850	Hannu Mikkola Gunnar Palm	Great Britain
19	J.M. Perez Vega	VW Bug	José Manuel Pérez Vega Gabriel Maria Hinojosa Rivero José Antoñio Bárcena Compean	Mexico
20	Marshall Cambridge	Austin Maxi	Patricia Ozanne Bronwyn Burrell Katrina Kerridge	Great Britain
21	Avtoexport	Moskvič 412	Ivan Astafiev Alexander Safonov Gennadi Garkusha	USSR
22	Bob de Jong	Alfa Romeo 1600 Guilia Super	Bob de Jong Christiaan Emile Tuerlinx	Holland
23	H. Mead	Ford Zodiac	Humphrey Mead Winston Percy John King	Great Britain
24	Rallyegemeinschaft Ulm	Mercedes-Benz 280SE	Edgar Herrmann Dieter Benz Horst Walter	West Germany
25	Claudine Trautmann	Citroën DS21	Claudine Trautmann Colette Perrier	France
26	Springfield Boys Club	Ford Escort 1850	Jimmy Greaves Tony Fall	Great Britain
27	Alfonso Mondini	Porsche 911S	Alfonso Mondini Giuseppe Bottaro	Italy
28	Avtoexport	Moskvič 412	Leonti Potapchik Eduard Bazhenov Yuri Lesovski	USSR
29	Bolivian National Team	BMW 2002Ti	William Bendeck Dieter Hübner Jorge Burgoa	Bolivia
30	17th/21st Lancers	Trident Venturer V6	Capt. Christopher Marriott Capt. John Dill	Great Britain
31	F.W. Hill	NSU120 CS	F.W. Hill Tony Coote Mike Donnelly	Great Britain

No.	Entrant	Car	Team	Country
32	Ken Tubman	BLMC 1800	Ken Tubman André Welinski Rob McAuley	Great Britain
33	C.R. Zicavo	Peugeot 504	Carlos Zicavo Aleides Specos Alfredo Verna	Argentina
34	H.C. Penfold	BLMC 1800	Hugh Penfold Peter Jones Eric McInally	Great Britain
35	R. Sanchez Noya	Not Notified	Carlos Fabre Lestrade Rodolfo Sanchez Noya	Mexico
36	P. Kube	BMW 2002Ti	Peter Kube Lothar Ranft	Peru
37	T.W. Walker	Vauxhall Victor FD station wagon	Tony Walker Dennis Leonard James Burdon	Great Britain
38	Fixo-Flex Sport Team	Mercedes-Benz 280SE	Alfred Katz Alfred Kling Albert Pfuhl	West Germany
39	Adrian Lloyd-Hirst	Triumph 2.5PI	Adrian Lloyd-Hirst Brian Englefield Keith Baker	Great Britain
40	Avtoexport	Moskvič 412	Sergei Tenishev Valentin Kislykh Valeri Shirochenkov	USSR
41	17th/21st Lancers	BLMC 1800	Jeremy Rugge-Price Charles Morley-Fletcher Philip Beaver	Great Britain
42	José Araujo	Volvo 142S	José Araujo John Batley	Argentina
43	British Leyland/Football Association	Triumph 2.5PI	Andrew Cowan Brian Coyle Uldarico "Larco" Ossio	Great Britain
44	Brian Chuchua	Jeep Wagoneer	Brian Chuchua William Kirkland Richard Gould	USA
45	Doug Harris	Ford Escort 1300 GT	Douglas Harris Michael Butler	Great Britain
46	Daily Express	Ford Escort 1850	Rauno Aaltonen Henry Liddon	Great Britain
47	Paul Coltelloni	Citroën DS21	Paul Coltelloni Henri "Ido" Marang	France
48	Midland Bank	Ford Cortina Lotus	Richard Skeels John Alsop	Great Britain
49	Annabel's	Mercedes-Benz 280SE	Michael Taylor Innes Ireland Mark Birley	Great Britain

No.	Entrant	Car	Team	Country
50	John Caulcutt	VW Beach Buggy	John Caulcutt David Stewart Noel Hutchinson	Great Britain
51	Power Gardening	SAAB 96 V4	Bert Jennings Colin Taylor	Great Britain
52	R.K. Richards	Rolls-Royce Silver Shadow	Ray Richards Bill Bengry David Skeffington	Great Britain
53	D.E. Young	Ford Cortina GT	Doreen Whitman D. E. Young	Great Britain
54	R. Redgrave	BLMC 1800	Reg Redgrave Phil Cooper Bob Freeborough	Great Britain
55	British Royal Navy	BLMC 1800	Lt. Cmdr. Julian J. Mitchell Lt. A.S.G. Evans RPO R. Taylor	Great Britain
56	E. Celerier	Porsche 911S	Eric Celerier Michael Gauvain	France
57	N. Gabor	Citroën	Nicholas Gabor	France
58	Col. J.W. Weld	Volvo 132	R.J.G. Anderson E.A.T. Willcocks Tim Bosence	Great Britain
59	British Grandstand	Mini 1275GT	John Handley Paul Easter	Great Britain
60	Not Notified	Rover 3500 V8	Rapio Wik Bob Woods Robert Rath	Great Britain
61	Team Thailand	BLMC 1800	Viscount Errington Bill Heinecke	Thailand
62	Carlos Del Val	SEAT 1430	Carlos Del Val Jaime Lazcano Victor Ochoa	Spain
63	Safrar/Peugeot	Peugeot 404	E.R. Lareta José Migliore	Argentina
64	Gianpiero Mondini	Porsche 911S	Gianpiero Mondini Mario Contini	Italy
65	Shoot Football Weekly	Ford Escort 1850	Roger Clark Alec Poole	Great Britain
66	Safrar/Peugeot	Peugeot 404	Gastón Perkins Jack Forrest Greene	Argentina
67	Royal Fusiliers	Peugeot 504	Maj. Edward Moorat Lt. John Shaw	Great Britain
68	J. Walker	Ford Cortina	J. Walker J. Wheeler T. Turner	Great Britain
69	Team Dunton	Ford Capri 2300	Brian Peacock David Skittrall	Great Britain

No.	Entrant	Car	Team	Country
70	Royal Hussars & 17th/21st Lancers	Austin Maxi	Capt. HRH Prince Michael of Kent Capt. Gavin Thompson Capt. Nigel Clarkson	Great Britain
71	Avtoexport	Moskvič 412	Gunnar Holm Vladimir Bubnov Kastytis Girdauskas	USSR
72	British Army/Paris Match-Kerridge	Peugeot 504	Maj. Freddie Preston Maj. Mike Bailey	Great Britain
73	Grants of Croydon	BLMC 1800	Anthony Petts David Franks Robert Robertson	Great Britain
74	Evening Standard	Austin Maxi	Rosemary Smith Alice Watson Ginette De Rolland	Great Britain
75	J.M. Wilson	Mercedes-Benz 220D	Malcolm "Jock" Wilson James Walker	Great Britain
76	Safrar/Peugeot	Peugeot 404	Jean-Claude Ogier Claude Laurent	Argentina
77	Jan Leenders	Toyota Corolla KE 10-B	Jan Leenders Preeda Chullamonthol	Thailand
78	J.P. Esteguy	Peugeot 504	Emil Ipar Enrique Esteguy Juan Esteguy	Argentina
79	Rob Janssen	Datsun 1600 SSS	Rob Janssen Jaap Dik	Holland
80	Joseph Sherger	FIAT 2300 station wagon	Joseph Sherger James Sherger	Kuwait
81	Mike Tyrell	Hillman GT	Mike Tyrell James Fuller Bernard Unett	Antigua
82	J.M. Avilla	Not Notified	J.M. Avilla	Mexico
83	W.G. James	Hillman Hunter	Alun Rees Hywel Thomas Washington James	Great Britain
84	Avtoexport	Moskvič 412	Emmanuil Lifshits Victor Schavelev	USSR
85	Sunday Express	Ford Escort 1850	Colin Malkin Richard Hudson-Evans	Great Britain
86	Lavinia Roberts	Ford Mustang	Lavinia Roberts David Jones Lt. Arthur "Pat" Hazlerigg	Great Britain
87	Derek Currell	Peugeot 504	Derek Currell Robert Currell Frank Bryan	Great Britain
88	British Leyland/Football Association	Triumph 2.5PI	Brian Culcheth Johnstone Syer	Great Britain

No.	Entrant	Car	Team	Country
89	Conroy Motors	Mini Cooper S	Allan Keefe James Conroy	Great Britain
90	Ken Bass	BMW 2002Ti	Ken Bass Graham Waring	Great Britain
91	Woman Magazine	BLMC 1800	Jean Denton Pat Wright Liz Crellin	Great Britain
92	Leyland/Motor	Triumph 2.5PI	Evan Green "Gelignite" Jack Murray Hamish Cardno	Great Britain
93	René Trautmann	Citroën DS21	René Trautmann Jean-Pierre Hanrioud	France
94	British RAF	Ford Cortina GT	F.O.D. Donald Soames- Waring Fl.Lt. Andrew Thwaite George Crichton	Great Britain
95	W.D. Cresdee	BLMC 1800S	Robert Eves W. Dennis Cresdee Franklin Bainbridge	Great Britain
96	British Leyland/Autocar	Austin Maxi	Terry Kingsley Peter Evans Michael Scarlett	Great Britain
97	Ken Haskell	Peugeot 404	Ken Haskell David Paull Douglas Larson	Great Britain
98	British Leyland/Football Association	Triumph 2.5PI	Paddy Hopkirk Tony Nash Neville Johnson	Great Britain
99	Kim Brassington	Ford Cortina Savage V6	Kim Brassington Donald Carslaw	Great Britain
100	Societe d'Encourage- ment Automobile France	Citroën DS21	Patrick Vanson Olivier Turcat Alain Leprince	France
101	Guy Verrier	Citroën DS21	Guy Verrier Francis Murac	France
102	R. Pontier	Simca 1501S	Raymond Pontier Roger Lamoral	France
103	Daily Telegraph	Ford Escort 1850	Timo Mäkinen Gilbert Staepelaere	Great Britain
104	Peter Graham	Ford Cortina Savage V6	Peter Graham Leslie Morrish	Great Britain
105	Lydden Circuit	Ford Escort 1600 GT	Bill Chesson Robert East	Great Britain
106	José A.R. Artasanchez	FIAT 124 Coupe	Enrique Lamas-Fortes José Rodoreda- Artasanchez Adolfo Perez-Janiero	Mexico

Appendix 2:
The Scoreboard

No.	Entrants	Car	Position at Lisbon	Position at Mexico City
1	Robert "Bobby" Buchanan- Michaelson Roy Fidler Jeremy Bullough	Triumph 2.5PI	DNF	
2	Terry Hunter Geoff Mabbs	Porsche 911	19th	DNF
3	Peter Jopp Willy Cave Mark Kahn	BLMC 1800	20th	DNF
4	Rodney Badham Rob Lyall	Hillman GT	22nd	DNF
5	Ivica Vukoja Streton Đorđević Nestor Milanov	Peugeot 404 D	66th	DNF
6	Maj. John Hemsley Sgt. Walter "Wally" Easton	Peugeot 504	35th	25th
7	Peter Garratt Chris Coburn Robert Grainger	Vauxhall Viva GT	DNF	
8	John Rhodes Joseph Minto	Peugeot 504	49th	DNF
9	Ian Harwood Frank Pierson Barry Hughes	Ford Cortina Lotus	26th	DNF
10	Cecil Woodley Robert Locke Philip Waller	Vauxhall Ventora	DNF	
11	Paul Donner Martin Donner	Ford Capri 1600	62nd	DNF
12	Robert Neyret Jacques Terramorsi	Citroën DS21	7th	

No.	Entrants	Car	Position at Lisbon	Position at Mexico City
13	David Martin William Martin Julian "Terry" Martin	Rolls-Royce Silver Cloud	71st	DNF
14	Sobiesław Zasada Marek Wachowski	Ford Escort 1850	12th	8th
15	Ron Channon Rod Cooper	Ford Cortina GT	18th	14th
16	James Gardner Laurie Ritchie	Ford Escort Elba Motor Caravan	DNF	
17	Peter Brown John Bloxham Robert McBurney	Hillman GT	13th	DNF
18	Hannu Mikkola Gunnar Palm	Ford Escort 1850	2nd	1st
19	José Manuel Pérez Vega Gabriel Maria Hinojosa Rivero José Antoñio Bárcena Compean	VW Bug	51st	DNF
20	Patricia Ozanne Bronwyn Burrell Katrina Kerridge	Austin Maxi	35th	DNF
21	Ivan Astafiev Alexander Safonov Gennadi Garkusha	Moskvič 412	31st	DNF
22	Bob de Jong Christiaan Emile Tuerlinx	Alfa Romeo 1600 Guilia Super	DNF	
23	Humphrey Mead Winston Percy John King	Ford Zodiac	DNS	
24	Edgar Herrmann Dieter Benz Horst Walter	Mercedes-Benz 280SE	DNF	
25	Claudine Trautmann Colette Perrier	Citroën DS21	21st	24th
26	Jimmy Greaves Tony Fall	Ford Escort 1850	10th	6th
27	Alfonso Mondini Giuseppe Bottaro	Porsche 911S	DNF	
28	Leonti Potapchik Eduard Bazhenov Yuri Lesovski	Moskvič 412	42nd	12th
29	William Bendeck Dieter Hübner Jorge Burgoa	BMW 2002Ti	43rd	13th
30	Capt. Christopher Marriott Capt. John Dill	Trident Venturer V6	DNF	

No.	Entrants	Car	Position at Lisbon	Position at Mexico City
31	F.W. Hill Tony Coote Mike Donnelly	NSU120 CS	DNS	
32	Ken Tubman André Welinski Rob McAuley	BLMC 1800	32nd	11th
33	Carlos Zicavo Aleides Specos Alfredo Verna	Peugeot 504	45th	DNF
34	Hugh Penfold Peter Jones Eric McInally	BLMC 1800	48th	DNF
35	Carlos Fabre Lestrade Rodolfo Sanchez Noya	Not Notified	DNS	
36	Peter Kube Lothar Ranft	BMW 2002Ti	56th	DNF
37	Tony Walker Dennis Leonard James Burdon	Vauxhall Victor FD station wagon	58th	DNF
38	Alfred Katz Alfred Kling Albert Pfuhl	Mercedes-Benz 280SE	15th	16th
39	Adrian Lloyd-Hirst Brian Englefield Keith Baker	Triumph 2.5PI	67th	DNF
40	Sergei Tenishev Valentin Kislykh Valeri Shirochenkov	Moskvič 412	47th	20th
41	Jeremy Rugge-Price Charles Morley-Fletcher Philip Beaver	BLMC 1800	68th	DNF
42	José Araujo John Batley	Volvo 142S	54th	DNF
43	Andrew Cowan Brian Coyle Uldarico "Larco" Ossio	Triumph 2.5PI	11th	DNF
44	Brian Chuchua William Kirkland Richard Gould	Jeep Wagoneer	61st	DNF
45	Douglas Harris Michael Butler	Ford Escort 1300 GT	52nd	23rd
46	Rauno Aaltonen Henry Liddon	Ford Escort 1850	9th	3rd
47	Paul Coltelloni Henri "Ido" Marang	Citroën DS21	14th	26th

No.	Entrants	Car	Position at Lisbon	Position at Mexico City
48	Richard Skeels John Alsop	Ford Cortina Lotus	DNF	
49	Michael Taylor Innes Ireland Mark Birley	Mercedes-Benz 280SE	DNF	
50	John Caulcutt David Stewart Noel Hutchinson	VW Beach Buggy	DNF	
51	Bert Jennings Colin Taylor	SAAB 96 V4	41st	DNF
52	Ray Richards Bill Bengry David Skeffington	Rolls-Royce Silver Shadow	63rd	DNF
53	Doreen Whitman D. E. Young	Ford Cortina GT	DNS	
54	Reg Redgrave Phil Cooper Bob Freeborough	BLMC 1800	23rd	9th
55	Lt. Cmdr. Julian J. Mitchell Lt. A.S.G. Evans RPO R. Taylor	BLMC 1800	53rd	DNF
56	Eric Celerier Michael Gauvain	Porsche 911S	DNF	
57	Nicholas Gabor	Citroën	DNS	
58	R.J.G. Anderson E.A.T. Willcocks Tim Bosence	Volvo 132	DNF	
59	John Handley Paul Easter	Mini 1275GT	DNF	
60	Rapio Wik Bob Woods Robert Rath	Rover 3500 V8	DNS	
61	Viscount Errington Bill Heinecke	BLMC 1800	DNS	
62	Carlos Del Val Jaime Lazcano Victor Ochoa	SEAT 1430	60th	DNF
63	E.R. Lareta José Migliore	Peugeot 404	DNF	
64	Gianpiero Mondini Mario Contini	Porsche 911S	DNF	
65	Roger Clark Alec Poole	Ford Escort 1850	16th	DNF
66	Gastón Perkins Jack Forrest Greene	Peugeot 404	64th	16th

No.	Entrants	Car	Position at Lisbon	Position at Mexico City
67	Maj. Edward Moorat Lt. John Shaw	Peugeot 504	29th	DNF
68	J. Walker J. Wheeler T. Turner	Ford Cortina	DNS	
69	Brian Peacock David Skittrall	Ford Capri 2300	DNF	
70	Capt. HRH Prince Michael of Kent Capt. Gavin Thompson Capt. Nigel Clarkson	Austin Maxi	39th	DNF
71	Gunnar Holm Vladimir Bubnov Kastytis Girdauskas	Moskvič 412	33rd	17th
72	Maj. Freddie Preston Maj. Mike Bailey	Peugeot 504	46th	DNF
73	Anthony Petts David Franks Robert Robertson	BLMC 1800	38th	DNF
74	Rosemary Smith Alice Watson Ginette De Rolland	Austin Maxi	24th	10th
75	Malcolm "Jock" Wilson James Walker	Mercedes-Benz 220D	57th	DNF
76	Jean-Claude Ogier Claude Laurent	Peugeot 404	17th	DNF
77	Jan Leenders Preeda Chullamonthol	Toyota Corolla KE 10-B	50th	DNF
78	Emil Ipar Enrique Esteguy Juan Esteguy	Peugeot 504	44th	DNF
79	Rob Janssen Jaap Dik	Datsun 1600 SSS	55th	21st
80	Joseph Sherger James Sherger	FIAT 2300 station wagon	DNF	
81	Mike Tyrell James Fuller Bernard Unett	Hillman GT	DNF	
82	J.M. Avilla	Not Notified	DNS	
83	Alun Rees Hywel Thomas Washington James	Hillman Hunter	28th	15th
84	Emmanuil Lifshits Victor Schavelev	Moskvič 412	34th	DNF
85	Colin Malkin Richard Hudson-Evans	Ford Escort 1850	DNF	

No.	Entrants	Car	Position at Lisbon	Position at Mexico City
86	Lavinia Roberts David Jones Lt. Arthur "Pat" Hazlerigg	Ford Mustang	DNF	
87	Derek Currell Robert Currell Frank Bryan	Peugeot 504	59th	DNF
88	Brian Culcheth Johnstone Syer	Triumph 2.5PI	6th	2nd
89	Allan Keefe James Conroy	Mini Cooper S	DNF	
90	Ken Bass Graham Waring	BMW 2002Ti	39th	DNF
91	Jean Denton Pat Wright Liz Crellin	BLMC 1800	26th	18th
92	Evan Green "Gelignite" Jack Murray Hamish Cardno	Triumph 2.5PI	69th	DNF
93	René Trautmann Jean-Pierre Hanrioud	Citroën DS21	1st	DNF
94	F.O.D. Donald Soames-Waring Fl.Lt. Andrew Thwaite George Crichton	Ford Cortina GT	70th	DNF
95	Robert Eves W. Dennis Cresdee Franklin Bainbridge	BLMC 1800S	DNF	
96	Terry Kingsley Peter Evans Michael Scarlett	Austin Maxi	29th	22nd
97	Ken Haskell David Paull Douglas Larson	Peugeot 404	DNF	
98	Paddy Hopkirk Tony Nash Neville Johnson	Triumph 2.5PI	8th	4th
99	Kim Brassington Donald Carslaw	Ford Cortina Savage V6	DNF	
100	Patrick Vanson Olivier Turcat Alain Leprince	Citroën DS21	5th	7th
101	Guy Verrier Francis Murac	Citroën DS21	3rd	DNF
102	Raymond Pontier Roger Lamoral	Simca 1501S	DNS	
103	Timo Mäkinen Gilbert Staepelaere	Ford Escort 1850	4th	5th

No.	Entrants	Car	Position at Lisbon	Position at Mexico City
104	Peter Graham Leslie Morrish	Ford Cortina Savage V6	32nd	DNF
105	Bill Chesson Robert East	Ford Escort 1600 GT	66th	DNF
106	Enrique Lamas-Fortes José Rodoreda-Artasanchez Adolfo Perez-Janiero	FIAT 124 Coupe	DNF	

Interviews

Interviewee	Interview Date
Bailey, Mike	May 18, 2018 and April 20, 2019
Beaver, Philip	September 17, 2016
Besanceney, Claudine	June 17, 2017
Black, Lavinia	October 23, 2016
Broad, Mike	May 26, 2020
Burrell, Bronwyn	August 20, 2016
Cardno, Hamish	October 7, 2017
Chuchua, Brian	October 3, 2016
Culcheth, Brian	August 8, 2016
Easter, Paul	November 5, 2016
Englefield, Brian	October 11, 2016 and October 17, 2016
Gavin, Jim	July 16, 2019
Hazlerigg, Patrick	January 9, 2017
Hemsley, John	May 18, 2018 and April 20, 2019
Hinojosa Rivero, Gabriel	June 8, 2020
Hutchinson, Noel	August 25, 2016
Kerridge-Reynolds, Katrina	February 26, 2017
Lees, Andrew	May 9, 2020
Marriott, Chris	July 5, 2019
McAuley, Rob	October 7, 2017
Price, Bill	July 31, 2019
Smith, Pat	August 17, 2016
Stewart, David	June 19, 2020
Thompson, Gavin	November 16, 2016
Vanson, Patrick	October 29, 2016

Chapter Notes

Preface

1. Innes Ireland, *Marathon in the Dust* (London: William Kimber, 1970), 142.

Introduction

1. "Neymar: Paris St-Germain sign Barcelona forward for world record 222m euros," BBC, August 3, 2017, www.bbc.co.uk/sport/football/40762417.
2. Evan Green, *A Boot Full of Right Arms* (Stanmore, NSW: Cassell Australia, 1975), 10.
3. Bill Price and Paddy Hopkirk, *The Paddy Hopkirk Story* (Yeovil: Haynes, 2005), 146.
4. "Mirror to the World," *Motor Sport*, August 2010.
5. *Ibid.*
6. Richard Hudson-Evans and Graham Robson, *The Big Drive* (London: Speed and Sports, 1970), 5.

Chapter 1

1. Tony Ambrose, *Ever the Bridesmaid* (Philip Ambrose, 2019), 137.
2. "The Mirror stages the greatest Car Rally," *The Daily Mirror*, June 6, 1969.
3. "A Russian car is No 1 entry in Mirror World Cup Rally," *The Daily Mirror*, June 10, 1969.

Chapter 3

1. *Daily Mirror World Cup Rally 1970 Wembley–Mexico City Official Regulations.*
2. *Ibid.*

Chapter 7

1. "Ford of America May Race in the World Cup Rally," *The Daily Mirror*, September 23, 1969.
2. "World Cup Rally Drivers Warned," *The Daily Mirror*, November 6, 1969.
3. "U.S. Rough Riders Join World Cup Rally," *The Daily Mirror*, November 22, 1969.
4. "RAF Men Will Go the Hard Way to Mexico City," *The Daily Mirror*, December 1, 1969.
5. Ambrose, *Ever the Bridesmaid*, 138.

Chapter 8

1. *Daily Mirror World Cup Rally Wembley–Mexico City April 19–May 27 Official Program.*

Chapter 9

1. Chris Cowin, *British Leyland: Chronicle of a Car Crash 1968-1978* (self-published, 2012, 2014), 8.
2. Marcus Chambers, Stuart Turner, and Peter Browning, *BMC Competitions Department Secrets* (Poundbury: Veloce, 2005), 146.
3. *Ibid.*
4. *Ibid.*, 147.
5. Price and Hopkirk, *The Paddy Hopkirk Story*, 152.
6. "Route, Runners and Risks," *Motor*, April 18, 1970.
7. Cowin, *British Leyland*, 47.
8. Mike Carver, Nick Seale, and Anne Youngson, *British Leyland Motor Corporation 1968–2005* (Stroud: The History Press, 2015), 12.
9. Brian Moylan, *Works Rally Mechanic* (Poundbury: Veloce, 1998), 107.
10. "Route, Runners and Risks."

Chapter 13

1. Robert Connor, *The 1968 London to Sydney Marathon* (Jefferson, NC: McFarland, 2016), 23.
2. British Leyland, *Uldarico Ossio* [press release], October 1969.
3. Rosemary Smith, *Driven* (London: Harper-Collins, 2018), 108.
4. *Ibid.*
5. Green, *A Boot Full of Right Arms*, 7.
6. Brian Robins, *The Great Race* (London: IPC Newspapers, 1970), 9.
7. Stuart Turner, *Twice Lucky* (Yeovil: Haynes, 1999), 96.
8. Jimmy Greaves, *Greavsie: The Autobiography* (London: Time Warner, 2003), 398.
9. David Campbell, *Roger Clark: Portrait of a Great Rally Driver* (London: ghk, 1990), 48.
10. Turner, *Twice Lucky*, 96.
11. Campbell, *Roger Clark*, 51.
12. "Guide to the Daily Mirror World Cup Rally," *Autocar*, April 16, 1970.

Chapter 15

1. "Forget the Marathon—this one is for real," *Autosport*, April 16, 1970.
2. "World Cup—To Sofia," *Motoring News*, April 23, 1970.
3. "Forget the Marathon—this one is for real."

Chapter 16

1. TenTenths Motorsport Forum, "Ozanne Patricia 'Tish,'" www.tentenths.com/forum/showthread.php?t=123582.
2. Ross Bentley, *Ultimate Speed Secrets* (Minneapolis: MBI, 2011), 51.

Chapter 17

1. www.collinsdictionary.com/dictionary/english/recce.
2. *Ibid.*
3. Roger Clark with Graham Robson, *Sideways … to Victory* (Croydon: Motor Racing, 1976), 118.
4. Turner, *Twice Lucky*, 96.
5. *Ibid.*
6. Bill Price, *The BMC/BL Competitions Department* (Yeovil: Haynes, 1989), 240.
7. Price and Hopkirk, *The Paddy Hopkirk Story*, 153–154.
8. Price, *The BMC/BL Competitions Department*, 249.

Chapter 18

1. *Daily Mirror World Cup Rally Wembley–Mexico City April 19–May 27 Official Program*.

Chapter 19

1. Hudson-Evans and Robson, *The Big Drive*, 17.
2. Mark Kahn, *Mexico or Bust!* (London: George G. Harrap, 1970), 40.
3. *Ibid.*, 41.
4. Hudson-Evans and Robson, *The Big Drive*, 17.
5. Kahn, *Mexico or Bust!*, 13.

Chapter 20

1. "Daily Mirror World Cup Rally," *Motor*, May 9, 1970.

Chapter 21

1. Hudson-Evans and Robson, *The Big Drive*, 20.
2. "World Cup Rally: Wembley to Lisbon," *Autocar*, April 30, 1970.
3. Chris Sclater with Jonathan Pulleyn, *Memories of a Rally Champion* (self-published, 2017), 43.
4. *Ibid.*, 44.
5. *Ibid.*, 45.
6. *Ibid.*, 44.
7. "World Cup Rally—To Lisbon," *Motoring News*, April 30, 1970.

Chapter 22

1. "Wembley-Mexico," *Champion*, June 15–July 15, 1970.

Chapter 23

1. Hudson-Evans and Robson, *The Big Drive*, 26.
2. Kahn, *Mexico or Bust!*, 58.
3. *Daily Mirror World Cup Rally 1970 Wembley–Mexico City Official Regulations*.
4. "World Cup Rally—To Lisbon."
5. "Rally sweeps over the Alps," *The Daily Mirror*, April 24, 1970.

Chapter 25

1. Robins, *The Great Rally*, 20.
2. "Quick repair—by coat-hanger," *The Daily Mirror*, April 25, 1970.
3. "Millionaire Aid for Rolls," *Sunday Mirror*, April 26, 1970.
4. "Portugal salutes hero of the rally," *The Daily Mirror*, April 28, 1970.
5. Robins, *The Great Rally*, 22.

Chapter 26

1. "1970 World Cup Rally Triumph or Disaster?" *Wheels*, May 1982.
2. *Ibid.*
3. *Ibid.*
4. *Ibid.*
5. "Daily Mirror World Cup Rally," *Motor*, May 2, 1970.
6. "1970 World Cup Rally Triumph or Disaster?" *Wheels*, June 1982.
7. "Daily Mirror World Cup Rally."

Chapter 27

1. "Competitor's Diary," *Motor*, May 16, 1970.
2. *Ibid.*
3. Robins, *The Great Race*, 32.
4. Smith, *Driven*, 133.
5. Kahn, *Mexico or Bust!*, 77.
6. Robins, *The Great Race*, 32–33.

Chapter 28

1. "Competitor's Diary."
2. "1970 World Cup Rally Winning, Losing, Crashing," *Wheels*, July 1982.
3. *Ibid.*
4. *Ibid.*
5. *Ibid.*

Chapter 30

1. *Daily Mirror World Cup Rally Wembley–Mexico City April 19–May 27 Official Program*.
2. "Daily Mirror World Cup Rally," *Motor*, May 16, 1970.

3. "Robbery in Rio!" *The Daily Mirror*, May 15, 1970.

4. Campbell, *Roger Clark*, 51–53.

5. Robins, *The Great Race*, 35.

6. J.T. Kingsley, *Into the Red* (Durham: The Pentland Press, 2000), 267.

7. *Ibid.*

Chapter 32

1. Kahn, *Mexico or Bust!*, 96.

2. *Daily Mirror World Cup Rally 1970 Wembley–Mexico City Official Regulations.*

3. Kingsley, *Into the Red*, 269.

Chapter 34

1. John Sprinzel, *Lucky John* (Kingham: Coulthard Press, 2013), 259.

2. Robins, *The Great Race*, 39.

3. Kingsley, *Into the Red*, 269–270.

4. *Daily Mirror World Cup Rally Wembley–Mexico City April 19–May 27 Official Program.*

5. Kingsley, *Into the Red*, 270.

6. "Soccer ace Jimmy limps in with a push," *The Daily Mirror*, May 18, 1970.

7. *Daily Mirror World Cup Rally Wembley–Mexico City April 19–May 27 Official Program.*

8. "Daily Mirror World Cup Rally," *Motor*, May 23, 1970.

9. Kingsley, *Into the Red*, 271.

10. Smith, *Driven*, 129.

11. *Ibid.*, 137.

Chapter 35

1. Kahn, *Mexico or Bust!*, 75.

2. *Ibid.*, 116.

3. *Ibid.*, 117.

Chapter 36

1. Kingsley, *Into the Red*, 271.

2. Robins, *The Great Race*, 48.

3. Kahn, *Mexico or Bust!*, 148.

4. Price and Hopkirk, *The Paddy Hopkirk Story*, 157.

Chapter 37

1. Pablo Raybould with Brian Culcheth, *Brian Culcheth: Global Travels of a Rally Champion* (self-published, 2020), 53.

2. *Ibid.*, 56.

3. *Ibid.*, 83.

4. *Ibid.*, 102.

5. *Ibid.*, 104.

6. "Brian Culcheth 1970 WCR European Section," *Triumph World*, Summer 2016.

7. "Brian Culcheth 1970 WCR South America (Pt. 1)," *Triumph World*, August/September 2016.

8. *Ibid.*

9. *Ibid.*

10. "Brian Culcheth 1970 WCR South America (Pt. 3)," *Triumph World*, December 2016/January 2017.

11. Raybould with Culcheth, *Brian Culcheth: Global Travels of a Rally Champion*, 117.

12. *Ibid.*, 119.

Chapter 38

1. "World Cup Maxi No 96," *Autocar*, June 25, 1970.

2. "Hornet Takes Rugged Trip to Alaska … Via S. America," *Detroit Free Press*, June 25, 1970.

3. Ambrose, *Ever the Bridesmaid*, 141.

4. Price and Hopkirk, *The Paddy Hopkirk Story*, 157.

5. "Police Save the Russians from Angry Village Mob," *The Daily Mirror*, May 27, 1970.

6. Sprinzel, *Lucky John*, 262.

7. Greaves, *Greavsie*, 400.

8. "What a Rally!," *Daily Mirror*, May 28, 1970.

9. "Goal to Mikkola," *Motoring News*, June 4, 1970.

10. Greaves, *Greavsie*, 400.

11. *Ibid.*, 401.

12. Robins, *The Great Race*, 76.

13. "Goal to Mikkola."

14. Kahn, *Mexico or Bust!*, 173.

Epilogue

1. Ambrose, *Ever the Bridesmaid*, 142.

2. Sprinzel, *Lucky John*, 262.

3. *Ibid.*

4. Alanah Reid, "A History of the Daily Mirror," www.historic-newspapers.co.uk/blog/daily-mirror-history/.

5. Claire Cozens, "Daily Mirror sales fall below 2m," *The Guardian*, April 11, 2003, www.theguardian.com/media/2003/apr/11/pressandpublishing.mirror.

6. "It's All Happening," *Cars and Conversions*, July 1970.

7. Robins, *The Great Race*, 80.

8. "The World Cup Rally," *British Racing News*, July 1970.

9. "The Race of My Life," *Autosport*, May 19, 1988.

Bibliography

Ambrose, Tony. *Ever the Bridesmaid.* Self-published, Philip Ambrose, 2019.

Bentley, Ross. *Ultimate Speed Secrets.* Minneapolis: MBI, 2011.

"Brian Culcheth 1970 WCR European Section." *Triumph World*, Summer 2016.

"Brian Culcheth 1970 WCR South America (Pt. 1)." *Triumph World*, August/September 2016.

"Brian Culcheth 1970 WCR South America (Pt. 3)." *Triumph World*, December 2016/January 2017.

British Leyland. *Uldarico Ossio* [press release]. October 1969.

Campbell, David. *Roger Clark: Portrait of a Great Rally Driver.* London: ghk, 1990.

Carver, Mike, Nick Seale, and Anne Youngson. *British Leyland Motor Corporation 1968–2005.* Stroud: The History Press, 2015.

Chambers, Marcus, Stuart Turner, and Peter Browning. *BMC Competitions Department Secrets.* Poundbury: Veloce, 2005.

Clark, Roger, with Graham Robson. *Sideways … to Victory.* Croydon: Motor Racing, 1976.

"Competitor's Diary." *Motor*, May 16, 1970.

Connor, Robert. *The 1968 London to Sydney Marathon.* Jefferson, NC: McFarland, 2016.

Cowin, Chris. *British Leyland: Chronicle of a Car Crash 1968–1978.* Self-published, 2012, 2014.

Cozens, Claire. "Daily Mirror Sales Fall Below 2m." *The Guardian*, April 11, 2003. www.theguardian.com/media/2003/apr/11/pressandpublishing.mirror.

"Daily Mirror World Cup Rally." *Motor*, May 2, 1970.

"Daily Mirror World Cup Rally." *Motor*, May 9, 1970.

"Daily Mirror World Cup Rally." *Motor*, May 16, 1970.

"Daily Mirror World Cup Rally." *Motor*, May 23, 1970.

Daily Mirror World Cup Rally 1970 Wembley–Mexico City Official Regulations

Daily Mirror World Cup Rally Wembley–Mexico City April 19–May 27 Official Program

"Ford of America May Race in the World Cup Rally." *The Daily Mirror*, September 23, 1969.

"Forget the Marathon—This One Is for Real." *Autosport*, April 16, 1970.

"Goal to Mikkola." *Motoring News*, June 4, 1970.

Greaves, Jimmy. *Greavsie: The Autobiography.* London: Time Warner, 2003.

Green, Evan. *A Boot Full of Right Arms.* Stanmore, NSW: Cassell Australia, 1975.

"Hornet Takes Rugged Trip to Alaska … Via S. America." *Detroit Free Press*, June 25, 1970.

Hudson-Evans, Richard, and Graham Robson. *The Big Drive.* London: Speed and Sports, 1970.

Ireland, Innes. *Marathon in the Dust.* London: William Kimber, 1970.

"It's All Happening." *Cars and Conversions*, July 1970.

Kahn, Mark. *Mexico or Bust!* London: George G. Harrap, 1970.

Kingsley, J.T. *Into the Red.* Durham: The Pentland Press, 2000.

"Millionaire Aid for Rolls." *Sunday Mirror*, April 26, 1970.

"The Mirror Stages the Greatest Car Rally." *The Daily Mirror*, June 6, 1969.

"Mirror to the World." *Motor Sport*, August 2010.

Moylan, Brian. *Works Rally Mechanic.* Poundbury: Veloce, 1998.

"Neymar: Paris St-Germain sign Barcelona Forward for World Record 222m Euros." BBC, August 3, 2017. www.bbc.co.uk/sport/football/40762417.

"1970 World Cup Rally Triumph or Disaster?" *Wheels*, May 1982.

"1970 World Cup Rally Triumph or Disaster?" *Wheels*, June 1982.

"1970 World Cup Rally Winning, Losing, Crashing." *Wheels*, July 1982.

"Police Save the Russians from Angry Village Mob." *The Daily Mirror*, May 27, 1970.

"Portugal Salutes Hero of the Rally." *The Daily Mirror*, April 28, 1970.

Price, Bill. *The BMC/BL Competitions Department.* Yeovil: Haynes, 1989.

Price, Bill, and Paddy Hopkirk. *The Paddy Hopkirk Story.* Yeovil: Haynes, 2005.

"Quick Repair—by Coat-Hanger." *The Daily Mirror*, April 25, 1970.

"The Race of My Life." *Autosport*, May 19, 1988.

"RAF Men Will Go the Hard Way to Mexico City." *The Daily Mirror*, December 1, 1969.

"Rally Sweeps Over the Alps." *The Daily Mirror*, April 24, 1970.

Raybould, Pablo, with Brian Culcheth. *Brian Culcheth: Global Travels of a Rally Champion.* Self-published, 2020.

Reid, Alanah. "A History of the Daily Mirror." www.historic-newspapers.co.uk/blog/daily-mirror-history.

"Robbery in Rio!" *The Daily Mirror*, May 15, 1970.

Robins, Brian. *The Great Race*. London: IPC Newspapers, 1970.

"Route, Runners and Risks." *Motor*, April 18, 1970.

"A Russian Car Is No 1 Entry in Mirror World Cup Rally." *The Daily Mirror*, June 10, 1969.

Sclater, Chris, with Jonathan Pulleyn. *Memories of a Rally Champion*. Self-published, 2017.

"Soccer Ace Jimmy Limps in with a Push." *The Daily Mirror*, May 18, 1970.

Sprinzel, John. *Lucky John*. Kingham: Coulthard Press, 2013.

TenTenths Motorsport Forum. "Ozanne Patricia 'Tish.'" www.tentenths.com/forum/showthread.php?t=123582.

Turner, Stuart. *Twice Lucky*. Yeovil: Haynes, 1999.

"U.S. Rough Riders Join World Cup Rally." *The Daily Mirror*, November 22, 1969.

"Wembley-Mexico." *Champion*, June 15–July 15, 1970.

"What a Rally!" *The Daily Mirror*, May 28, 1970.

"World Cup Maxi No 96." *Autocar*, June 25, 1970.

"The World Cup Rally." *British Racing News*, July 1970.

"World Cup Rally Drivers Warned." *The Daily Mirror*, November 6, 1969.

"World Cup Rally: Wembley to Lisbon." *Autocar*, April 30, 1970.

"World Cup Rally—to Lisbon." *Motoring News*, April 30, 1970.

"World Cup—to Sofia." *Motoring News*, April 23, 1970.

Index

Numbers in **bold italics** indicate pages with illustrations